A TIME TO DIE

A TIME TO DIE

Tom Wicker

Haymarket Books
Chicago, Illinois

First published in 1975 by Quadrangle/The New York Times Book Co.
Published in 1994 by the University of Nebraska Press
This edition published in 2011 by Haymarket Books under license from the
University of Nebraska Press.

Haymarket Books
PO Box 180165
Chicago, IL 60618
773-583-7884
info@haymarketbooks.org
www.haymarketbooks.org

ISBN 978-1608462-15-5

Cover design by Eric Ruder
Cover photo shows inmates of Attica state prison raising their fists to show solidarity
in their demands during a negotiation session with state prisons Commissioner
Russell Oswald, September 10, 1971 (AP Photo/Bob Schutz).

Special discounts are available for bulk purchases by organizations and institutions.
Please contact Haymarket Books for more information.

This book was published with the generous support of Lannan Foundation and the
Wallace Global Fund.

Printed in the United States.

Library of Congress CIP data is available.

For the dead at Attica

There's always time to die. I don't know
what the rush was.

HERMAN BADILLO
September 13, 1971
Attica, New York

Contents

Afterwards   299

(Illustrations follow pages 56 and 280)

Preface

After twenty-two years of reflection on the massacre at the Attica Correctional Institute on September 13, 1971, I believe even more strongly than I did at the time that it need never have happened.

I'm still shocked at the callous procedures of the State of New York, which resulted on that day in the deaths of twenty-nine inmates and ten hostages, all killed in six minutes of indiscriminate gunfire by state policemen and "corrections officers"—prison guards.*

I find it as hard as ever to believe that, for the eighty-three inmates wounded in the same fusillade, *no* medical care had been planned and, for hours after the shooting stopped, little was provided.

It is no less sickening today that after the orgy of shooting was ended, another orgy was allowed to begin—the torturing and beating of inmates who had been recaptured, by guards whose conduct had helped precipitate the same inmates' revolt.

I am no more able than I was in 1971 to understand or explain why prison officials afterwards told the lie that the ten dead hostages had had their throats cut by inmates, when in fact they were victims of wild police gunfire—or why my colleagues in the press accepted and spread that lie, without rigorously questioning it.

But most of all, I am haunted by the belief—grown to near certainty—that none of this necessarily had to happen. A remark by Herman Badillo, one of the outside mediators who tried and failed to stop the slaughter, gave this book its title: *There's always time to die. I don't know what the rush was.*

---

*The death toll at Attica actually was forty-three. But four of these deaths are not attributable to the police attack on September 13. A prison guard was killed in the initial uprising on Sept. 9, and three inmates, including the prison bookie, were killed by persons unknown during the revolt.

That seems to me more pertinent today than when Badillo and I were huddled in a prison chamber with the other mediators—all in the awful awareness of the guns being fired a hundred yards away. What *was* the rush?

The inmates had rioted and barricaded themselves in D-yard—one of the prison's four recreational grounds—on Thursday. The lethal recapture of the yard was carried out early Monday, September 13. Over that long weekend, no hostages had been harmed. No violent breakout from the prison had been attempted, or was possible.

Nothing, in fact, was more certain than that the roughly fifteen hundred inmates holding out in D-yard were not going anywhere, and offered no threat to the good folk of New York or the nation. They were still surrounded by thirty-foot walls and a formidable array of state police and prison guards, all armed to the teeth. The inmates' demand for and some outside sympathizers' pledge of transportation to "a Third World country" were no more than hollow rhetoric, impossible of fulfillment.

Sanitary conditions in D-yard, where rudimentary latrines had been dug, were bad and getting worse. Food was scarce and unappetizing— dry sandwiches grudgingly delivered by prison officials. It was getting cold at night for men sleeping outdoors in northern New York in September, and the original sense of exhilaration—at being out of the deadening prison routine and the harsh rule of the "hacks"—was drizzling away for many of the inmates in the rains falling on D-yard.

The inmate leaders' discipline appeared unchallenged from within, and these leaders had been adamant in their resistance to the state's limited settlement offers. But who could tell when the mass of those in revolt might decide that a peaceful settlement was better than risking the violent recapture of the prison?

(I do not suggest that a shift of power among the inmates *would* have taken place. But none of those who planned the attack could have been sure on September 13 that it would *not* happen.)

Concern for the hostages, moreover, was real but in this context misplaced. Not only had they not been harmed in four days of captivity, but they had been reasonably well cared for; outside observers like me attested to that. More important, the hostages' safe release was the only real bargaining weapon the inmates had. If they began to hurt, much less kill, hostages, they would throw away their only hope of gaining any part of their goals, as well as assure an armed attack on their stronghold.

Actually, the inmates had not even *threatened* harm to the hostages unless such an attack took place. There was no reason save personal malice and official distrust to doubt that they would hold the hostages harmless as long as an attack was not launched. In a very real sense, then, to order that attack was effectively to sign death warrants for at least some of the hostages. And so it proved, although their deaths were not at the hands of the inmates, as the authorities had anticipated—and virtually accepted in advance.

Had state officials decided to wait out the revolt, their patience in all probability would have been rewarded with an eventual settlement, possibly even a surrender, the release of the hostages, and the return of the inmates to their cells. If such a peaceful end to the revolt had *not* come about in days or weeks, an armed attack still could have been considered—with more sensible and humane planning and tactics, one hopes, than were evident on September 13.

One week, two weeks—would it have mattered how long it took for D-yard to give in, if it ultimately did so? What would it have mattered, as against the thirty-nine lives lost, ten of them not "murderers, rapists and thieves" (as inmates were routinely termed) but prison employees, the husbands or fathers or brothers of respectable people living in Attica or Batavia and other towns nearby? The same question was asked twenty-two years later, when the Branch Davidians perished in flames at Waco: why wa it necessary to end that standoff on that day and in that way?

Arguments against the sensible policy of waiting were available, of course—though I am not at all sure that such a policy ever was seriously discussed at the level of official decision. It was necessary "to reopen the institution"—though only D-yard was closed. "Law 'n' order" (this was the age of Nixon, Agnew, and George Wallace) had to be restored—though why that could not have been done at less cost by waiting longer never has been explained.

The public was fearful—but no one save the families of the hostages was threatened, and they more by the planned attack than by waiting. The hostages had to be rescued at all costs—which was rather like burning that village in Vietnam in order to save it. The inmates had shown they would never yield, so officials insisted that "we can't wait any longer" and "we have no choice"—all of which were conclusions, not facts.

More persuasively, Governor Nelson Rockefeller—who gave the final order for the attack—argued that if he even appeared to be yielding to the inmates in D-yard, revolts would break out at other state prisons, with more hostages taken; and if he came personally to Attica, the inmates might demand the presence of President Nixon too. But a simple, strong, and pointed policy of waiting for D-yard to give up—not yielding—could hardly have had any of those effects.

The passage of two decades has only strengthened my belief that two other considerations actually motivated Rockefeller. One was political. The governor had entered a tenuous rapprochement with his old rival, Nixon, and had not entirely given up his own political hopes; and he believed that the president's emphasis on "law 'n' order" made it politically imperative that the supposedly liberal Nelson Rockefeller should crack down on the D-yard inmates, show strength, get tough with criminals. Merely waiting would not be sufficiently muscular.

But I doubt that political calculation alone would have moved Rockefeller to act so conclusively, had it not been for a more powerful personal compulsion. The inmates, any inmates, were the dregs of society; and the broadcast rhetoric of these particular inmates was loudly Marxist and revolutionary, condemning the very society of which Nelson Rockefeller was one of the wealthiest beneficiaries and most powerful defenders. I believe the D-yard inmates profoundly offended him ideologically; and he believed it his responsibility to society to silence them.

Three years after the attack on D-yard, Rockefeller was nominated for vice president of the United States by Gerald Ford, who had succeeded Nixon. Rockefeller then told a Senate committee "that if [the Attica revolt] would happen again I would think that . . . the proper way to proceed" would be "to go ahead . . . without weapons." No senator pointed out that this remarkable change of heart had come too late to save thirty-nine lives.

There may be, however, one useful, but not redeeming, consequence of the Attica massacre. Since then, in the innumerable prison conflicts that have arisen in various states, no governor or anyone else has turned armed forces loose in unrestricted attack on rebellious inmates. (The sanguinary prison riot in New Mexico was largely a struggle between groups of inmates.) On their side, inmates have seemed to realize what Attica survivors say was not widely believed in D-yard in 1971—that the state was willing to kill them in order to "reopen the institution" and would come in shooting.

Not until the revolt at the Lucasville prison in Ohio in early 1993 was there anything like "another Attica" uprising, in size or duration. That incident ended in a negotiated settlement, not armed attack—almost as if, on both sides, a lesson had been learned from the massacre in D-yard.

Readers coming upon *A Time to Die* for the first time, in this Bison Book edition, may well wonder why its author referred to himself throughout in the third person, as "Wicker" or "he" rather than "I." As I often explained after the original publication, I then had before me the recent examples of *The Armies of the Night* and *Miami and the Siege of Chi-*

cago, in which Norman Mailer had used this device with impressive success.

Mailer's work, whatever he intended, showed me a way to solve the problem of writing about myself, my background, my personal life, my efforts and failures at Attica, without sentimentality or pretentiousness on the one hand, without too much reserve on the other. It was easier to write fully and—I hoped—truthfully about an abstract personage called "Wicker" than about "I" or "me."

The closing word of *A Time to Die,* written in the near aftermath of the events of September 13, 1971, describe my feelings as I was leaving Attica on that terrible day: *He knew there would have to be a time for anger.*

That time came. For years, I seized every opportunity to speak and write about the need for changes in the squalid and inhumane U.S. prison system, for a measure of rationality in the treatment of offenders in America. How much good *that* did can best be told from the fact that in 1971, there were about 250,000 Americans in the prisons of the day; but on May 9, 1993, the Justice Department announced that 883,593 persons were warehoused in these fortresses of degradation (mostly the same as in 1971). The U.S. now has more prison inmates that any nation in the world, per capita and absolutely—a shameful first place.

I long ago concluded, therefore, that my small personal crusade was in vain—that prison reform, in fact, was the most hopeless social cause this side of gun control. The fear of crime was and remains so great in this country that people are not only willing but anxious to "lock'em up and throw away the key." That the dollar cost of this policy is insanely high, while its social purpose of reducing the incidence of crime has abjectly failed, seems to a fearful citizenry to be irrelevant.

Therefore, though I seldom speak or write about prisons nowadays, I am gratified that this account of a bloody inmates' uprising, and of the efforts of fallible human beings to end it peacefully, is once more seeing print and may perhaps find new readers. A child of failure, written in pain and travail, *A Time to Die* was dedicated to "the dead at Attica" in the hope that in its pages those unhonored dead might be seen at last as men, not numbers. Forlorn as it may be, and even after so many years, that hope seems to me worth clinging to.

Tom Wicker
June 7, 1993

September 8–10, 1971

CHAPTER

I

The Thing Jumps

The luncheon of the Bill Fay Club on Friday, September 10, 1971, was a gregarious affair as usual. The scene of the feast was the executive dining room of the National Geographic Society, in the Society's elegant building on Seventeenth Street Northwest, a few blocks from Lafayette Square and the White House. Members had sipped sherry in the office of Franc Shor, a Geographic editor, then moved into the dining room for lamb chops and an excellent wine. Shor's girth suggested his standing as one of Washington's ranking gourmets; among many other accomplishments, he was the mainspring of the Bill Fay Club—an ad hoc group named in memory of a former Irish Ambassador and conversationalist of renown. Members met at random for good food and what they assured themselves was "the best talk in Washington." Sometimes, it may have been.

Around Shor at the long table high above Seventeenth Street were Ambassador Frank Corner of New Zealand; Ambassador Egidio Ortona of Italy; A. Doak Barnett, the China specialist (a visitor that day); J. Carter Brown, the director of the National Gallery of Art; John Walker, Brown's immediate predecessor; William McChesney Martin, the former chairman of the Federal Reserve Board; Herman Wouk, the novelist; Richard Scammon, the political analyst and statistician; Edward P. Morgan, the radio and television commentator; and Tom Wicker, political columnist and associate editor of *The New York Times*. Former Secretary of Defense Clark Clifford and Herbert Block—the *Washington Post's* famous Herblock, as gentle in person as ascerbic in ink—were frequently at the club table, but were not present that day.

These were erudite men, in everything from art to politics, as Tom Wicker had come to know. He always studied Franc Shor's wine choices with care, and was perennially surprised to find himself able to hold up his end of the conversation, and even on occasion to bring the table to his own point of view. But much of his life had been a surprise to him; and it was not only in the executive dining room of the Geographic that he sometimes had a vivid sense of having come a long, long way.

By the time cigars were passed around that day—Wicker had rid himself of a heavy cigarette habit and rather sanctimoniously smoked nothing—he was in the lazy euphoria of splendid wine, just the right amount of excellent food, and the esteem of good company. Many people spend much of their lives vainly trying to arrange such moments, when it is possible to delude oneself that he or she is in tune with life. Even his pending divorce was something that Wicker, at the moment, felt he did not have to think about, although he knew soon enough it would have to be faced. His children did not know it was coming.

The phone rang discreetly, as befitted its place in the executive dining room of the National Geographic Society. The call was for Wicker.

"The most exciting thing," his secretary said breathlessly. "They want you to come to Attica."*

"Where?" He had had quite a lot of wine.

"You know, the prison where they're rioting."

That Friday morning, as Wicker had read *The New York Times* at breakfast in his big brick house on Cleveland Avenue, he had paid small attention to the story from Attica or to the front-page picture that showed smoke rising ominously above the walls of the prison. As it usually did with a good picture, *The Times* had buried this one below the fold. It was one of what Wicker called his "writing days." His articles appeared on a regular schedule, at that time Tuesday, Thursday, and Sunday; that made every Monday, Wednesday, and Friday a "writing day"—although he frequently delayed his Sunday article until Saturday morning, out of the newspaperman's immemorial reluctance to write until deadlines forced him to.

There had been no reason for Wicker to pay much attention to the news from Attica—upstate New York where the prison was located was far off his accustomed rounds; ordinarily, *The Times'* metropolitan desk needed no help from the Washington Bureau in covering such a remote part of New York territory. Wicker had written about

---

* Throughout this book, remarks printed as direct quotations are either foot-noted to a reliable source or are from conversations in which the author took part, and which he has reconstructed from memory or notes. Where memory, notes, and sources have proved insufficient, conversations have been paraphrased as closely as possible, without quotation marks.

prisons on occasion, but he was looking that morning for an event of more general interest as the subject of an easy Sunday column. He was in no mood for anything complex or requiring much work or thought. But he had not found his subject by the time he strolled along L Street to Shor's luncheon.

"They'll fly you in a helicopter," his secretary said.

"From here?"

"From Buffalo. I'm checking the flight schedules to Buffalo now. They want you as quickly as you can come."

Wicker thought of the late afternoon years before when the White House had received word of Joseph P. Kennedy's stroke in Palm Beach. President Kennedy had determined to go to his father's bedside at once.

"So which of you guys," Pierre Salinger had demanded of the quickly assembled White House press corps, "can catch a chopper for Andrews Air Base right this minute? We can get a pool aboard Air Force One, but it's got to be now."

"I'll go," Tom Wicker had said, immediately, automatically, with the honed instinct of the newspaperman to go where the action was, for a story—which in his calling was a chance—big enough to outweigh the difficulties of getting it, big enough to dwarf the conventional arrangements of life. He had thought instantly that the President would remember those who had been with him at such a time, who had dropped everything to go. And that would be useful later to an ambitious reporter.

But Attica? Wicker would not even have known it was near Buffalo, if Kathy Wellde had not said so. He was no longer as ambitious as he had been in his youth; no one could have been. And what was Attica or a prison riot to a political columnist? There was not much promise there for the Sunday column he still had to do. The trip would impossibly complicate his deadline problem. Besides . . .

"I suppose it might be dangerous," Mrs. Wellde said.

Wicker was not a daredevil—the opposite, if anything. Unlike many of his generation, he had not been in wartime combat. Once, in the swift water of the Potomac River, he had sensed death at his shoulder and fought to live; but he had never deliberately risked his life, for thrill or duty, nor did he pay much deference to those who did. These men were seldom, he thought, impressive in ordinary circumstances, which he regarded as the prime ordeal.

"Who called? The governor?" As a political reporter, Wicker knew Governor Nelson Rockefeller of New York fairly well.

"Some Assemblyman's office. They said the prisoners asked for you to come."

"How the hell could that be?" But he knew, because he knew his own work. It was possible—far more possible than that Nelson Rocke-feller might be seeking his help—that those unknown, faraway pris-oners *could* think of him in some way as sympathetic to their plight. He thought he might be the only daily newspaper writer of his time to whom such men would think they could appeal. And if that were so, going to Attica might turn out to be an opportunity—it might provide an experience and a story few other writers could have had. That might make him think better of his work, even of his life. Besides, he realized, he had nothing more useful to do.

"Well . . . get me on the first plane," Wicker said. He hung up and turned back to the table to make his excuses; but the other members of the Bill Fay Club already were up and moving to and fro, talking no doubt of Michelangelo.

Maybe "the thing was supposed to jump" on the Fourth of July. That was the only day of the year when the authorities normally let inmates roam more or less freely among the four walled exercise yards of the Attica State Correctional Facility in upstate New York.* But the way an inmate named Julio Carlos heard it, someone in the prison administration got word from a stool pigeon, and kept the yards closed and under tight security on Independence Day.[1]†

Carlos, a 31-year-old Puerto Rican reared in Brooklyn, had served 10 years for armed robbery; he was prison-wise and may have known something about July 4, but more likely he was aware of a general climate of revolt, not a specific plan for it. There were plenty of signs for experienced eyes to see, that hot summer of 1971, that Attica was ready to "jump" at any time.

New York's Commissioner of Correctional Services, Russell G. Oswald, in fact, had gone to Governor Rockefeller in May and "poured out" worries about a tight budget and "prison unrest." Oswald thought the unrest was "being fomented and exacerbated by internal and external revolutionary political activities, which were increasingly zeroing in on the criminal element in our society."[2]

In early July, as if to confirm Oswald's fears, he was sent a petition by the "Attica Liberation Faction." Twenty-seven changes were de-manded in the "brutal, dehumanized" conditions the inmate signers said they were suffering at the hands of the "vile and vicious slave-masters" in the prison administration. One of the signers, Herbert X. Blyden, had been a ringleader of the inmate uprising in the Tombs in New York City the year before.[3] A fruitless exchange of letters between Oswald and the Liberation Faction followed this opening.

---

* See endpapers for a plan of the prison buildings and grounds.
† Notes for each chapter begin on page 323.

Attica's cells were overcrowded, too—about 2250 men in a facility that Superintendent Vincent R. Mancusi considered not really secure for more than 1600. Worse, Mancusi thought, was the fact that some of the overcrowding was due to the unwelcome presence of inmates like Blyden, shipped out of the city to state facilities after the Tombs rioting. The superintendent also was uneasy about 30 inmates who had taken part in an abortive riot at the Auburn Correctional Facility in 1970, and who had been transferred later to Attica.[4]

But perhaps the worst fears of all for veterans like Mancusi were caused by changes in the nature of the inmate himself. In 1971, 54 percent of Mancusi's charges were black; 9 percent were Puerto Rican. Forty percent of all inmates were under 30 years of age, 62 percent had been sent up for violent crimes, and nearly 70 percent had done time before, either in a state, federal, or local "joint." Almost 80 percent were from New York, Buffalo, Rochester, and Syracuse—urban street kids, virtual foreigners to the men of placid upstate villages like Attica or Batavia or Warsaw, where Mancusi's guards lived. The Attica Correctional Facility was filled with youthful, violent men of criminal experience, men whose political and social backgrounds and points of view were alien to those of their keepers.[5]

As for Mancusi himself, he was, so Julio Carlos believed, "the cause of all this [prisoner unrest] . . . with the little petty things he do." That was a widely held view behind the walls of Attica. Mancusi's guards, moreover, were all white, save for one Puerto Rican; so were the prison administrators and virtually all the civilian employees.

But Attica had the reputation of a relatively trouble-free prison—a mess-hall demonstration had to be tear-gassed in 1957, a sit-down strike had lasted only two hours the same year, and another not much longer in 1962. In 1970, there had been a peaceful two-day work stoppage in protest of commissary prices and metal shop wages.[6]

The situation was obviously more threatening in 1971. Once, racial and religious animosities had been strong within Attica's 30-foot walls; but that summer guards had seen distressing signs of unity among the Black Muslims, Black Panthers, and Young Lords (Puerto Ricans) who dominated the non-white prison population. Guards liked to see that population divided against itself, directing its energies into internal feuds and rivalries; unity could only direct those energies elsewhere. Everyone on the prison staff felt the tension building that summer.

"I can't tell you what a change has come over t[he] brothers in Attica," wrote Sam Melville, inmate No. 26124, in August to a former inmate. He continued in his semi-shorthand style: "So much more awareness & growing, consciousness of themselves as potential revolutionaries, reading, questioning, rapping all t time. Still bigotry & racism, black, white & brown, but one can feel it beginning to crumble in t knowledge so many are gaining that we must build solidarity against our common oppressor—t system of exploitation of each other & alienation from each other."⁷ Censoring such mail did nothing for the nerves and good humor of the prison staff.

"I haven't carried my billfold in there in six weeks," one corrections officer said that summer. A lawyer who went into Attica in the first days of September to interview a client told New York State Senator Thomas F. McGowan that there was "a strong feeling in there against the administration." An inmate, Wayne Trimmer, predicted to Richard Roth of the Buffalo *Courier-Express* in mid-summer that there would be trouble unless "palpable changes" were made in the hard and excruciatingly boring prison life. Mancusi was particularly nervous because Oswald had refused to transfer to another institution the five signers of the Liberation Faction's petition. Oswald thought it was "too simplistic" to keep transferring hard cases like the Auburn rebels, in the hope that if kept on the move they would be kept out of troublemaking. Mancusi strongly disagreed.⁸

On August 21, George Jackson was shot to death in what prison authorities said was an attempt to break out of San Quentin prison in California. Jackson had been a hero among non-white prisoners—as was "anyone that believed in freedom," according to Julio Carlos. Black people generally did not believe the official story of Jackson's death. Other inmates in other institutions regarded it as flagrantly and ludicrously unlikely that Jackson, as the authorities claimed, could have hidden a gun in his Afro haircut after talking with an attorney in the San Quentin visiting area. On August 22, over 800 Attica prisoners on the first breakfast shift appeared in the mess hall and sat quietly, ominously, without eating. Each wore black—if no more than a shoestring around his arm—somewhere on his clothing.⁹

"When things get that quiet," a guard said later, "you're scared, anybody's scared." Besides, an old hand like Mancusi, a 35-year veteran of New York's prison bureaucracy, knew such a demonstration took organization, and that organization took leadership. That was confirmed for him a few days later when, for no reason Mancusi could see, inmates reporting sick trebled from the normal 100.¹⁰ (Apparently they believed Oswald would be visiting Attica that day and would be present at sick call.¹¹) One prisoner, N.B.A. Red, actually complained directly to Mancusi about the mess-hall fare, during a chance, face-to-face encounter in a prison corridor. Mancusi disputed Red's complaints, and later had Red ordered to keep-lock for his temerity.¹²

Mancusi and his staff, nervous about conditions in their institution, cracked the whip a little. They instituted more frequent searches of cells. They infuriated inmates who subscribed to newspapers by cutting out any references to prison conditions and disturbances; and they cancelled prizes (usually paid for from the prison commissary profits) for the annual Labor Day athletic contests. Inmates generally brooded over these and other policies they considered harassing and vindictive.[13]

All in all, it was no wonder that on September 2, Russell Oswald hustled up to Attica to talk with Mancusi and a prisoner representative, Frank Lott, a black and one of the five signers of the July petition. Oswald assured Lott that changes were coming—he had already lightened censorship of inmate mail, he could claim, and instituted night training programs in the shops for limited groups of interested inmates.[14] Mrs. Oswald was sick, and the commissioner hurried away to be at her side. But in a tape-recorded message played three times for the inmates on the prison communications system, Oswald pledged: "I assure you that changes will be made." But he asked for time to accomplish such reforms as law libraries for the inmates, improved training for corrections officers, extended work-release programs, and better vocational training.[15]

Oswald's pledges were not good enough. Those who knew of the Liberation Faction's exchanges with Oswald reflected bitterly that a summer of "democratic" efforts to effect change had yielded them nothing. The Commissioner's speech was "a lot of words," thought Richard X. Clark, a Black Muslim imprisoned for armed robbery— "the same words people had been saying for years without anything ever happening."[16]

After the speech, some inmates hurled their earphones against the wall; many felt that Oswald's having used the prison communications system rather than talking to them in person confirmed official indifference to them as human beings. "He didn't so much as make one concession, such as giving a man soap or giving a man an extra shower," an inmate recalled. At Attica, one shower a week per inmate was the rule. "He didn't make any concessions whatsoever."[17]

A week after Oswald's visit, on September 8, Herbert X. Blyden wrote Senator John Dunne, the chairman of the New York Senate Committee on Crime and Correction, that "all we received were promises of change. . . ."[18] But most Attica inmates were skeptical about promises; and later that very day, "the thing jumped."

At about 3:45 P.M., Lieutenant Richard Maroney entered A-yard during the afternoon recreation hour.[19] Maroney had been mayor of Attica village for 10 years, but to the inmates of the Attica Correctional Facility he was known as a "hard-rock disciplinarian-type guard." For a moment he watched the men playing cards or checkers, loafing, watching the yard television set, walking about, or "rapping." He did not see, near one wall, Richard Clark conducting a quiet "mosque meeting" for eight or nine Black Muslims. If he had,

Maroney probably would have broken up the meeting as a violation of one of Attica's many rules against "inmates congregating in large groups."

Maroney did see a black inmate in what the officer thought was a scuffle with another black he recognized as Leroy Dewer. Dewer was one of the prisoners who had been sent to Attica after taking part in the Auburn uprising, which automatically made him an object of special concern to prison authorities like Maroney.

Many inmates insisted later that Dewer and his friend—still unidentified—were only in a friendly scuffle, at worst in a fairly hard game of "body punching," a rugged form of inmate horseplay that makes prison guards nervous. Maroney had an officer call out on a bullhorn for the two inmates to stop. They didn't, so he sent two officers to bring the scufflers to him. One of the offenders slipped away into the general throng of inmates, as the officers approached. But Dewer came along, understandably nervous because he had been in enough disciplinary troubles to have been warned that another count could send him to solitary confinement—what the administration called "segregation" and Attica inmates knew as "the box"—in Housing Block Z (HBZ).

From his place by the wall, inmate Richard Clark saw Maroney "motion" for Dewer to leave the yard; Maroney had ordered Dewer to his cell. Instead, Dewer—no doubt with visions of "the box" in his head—tried to melt back into the crowd. Maroney seized his arm; Dewer turned and struck the officer in the chest, not hard. Maroney kept coming, and Dewer struck him in the chest again. These were unheard-of acts of defiance from an inmate. A large crowd—many just curious, but many excited and angry—had gathered around the two struggling men and the two officers with Maroney. Undoubtedly, Dewer's resistance increased the excitement of the other inmates.

In the crowd was Ray Lamorie, a white prisoner who was one of Attica's best chess players and also a coach of one of the prison football teams—which included the D-block Messiahs and the B-block Brown Bombers. He had been showing his team members some rougher points of line play, but abandoned that to rush to Dewer's support. Reports differ on how vehement his defense was—some who were present say he tried to hit Maroney. In any case, the false impression later gained credence with prison authorities (although Maroney, at least, knew better) that Lamorie was the inmate who had been scuffling with Dewer in the first place, setting off the whole incident.

Another lieutenant, Robert Curtiss, joined the milling throng in A-yard, and tried to break it up. But by then the surrounding inmates were so angry and menacing that the officers decided to beat a retreat—another unprecedented event at Attica. Apparently, in the overcharged atmosphere of that summer of 1971, other inmates in A-yard had at first felt that Dewer was being unfairly punished for little or no offense. Then the unusual sight of him striking Maroney had obviously excited them further. They spontaneously helped Dewer resist being taken away. Maroney and Curtiss prudently let the matter drop—but only for the moment.

Superintendent Mancusi immediately decided that such defiance could not be tolerated. After the evening meal, Mancusi ordered, Dewer and Lamorie would have to go to segregation. But when guards went for him, the tough Dewer again put up a struggle, one that could be heard throughout Cell Block A; and he had to be carried off by four officers, one to each arm and leg. Lamorie—though he and most other inmates knew he was being wrongly accused of scuffling with Dewer —went more quietly. But his departure, too, caused an eruption in the rest of A-block.

One inmate hurled a full soup can from his cell. It hit Corrections Officer Tom Boyle in the face, giving him a cut that required several stitches. Other officers charged inmate William Ortiz with this feat of marksmanship. Like wildfire, the word spread that "the man" had hauled off Dewer and Lamorie to "the box" where "everybody knew" they would be beaten and mistreated (although there is no evidence that, in fact, they were). In A-block, the box was regarded as unnecessary punishment in this case and, by some, as a betrayal of what they had thought was a promise by Lieutenant Curtiss that no such action would be taken.

Leaving A-block with Lamorie, Curtiss heard a final shout behind him: "We'll get you in the morning, motherfuckers!"

Later, A-block fell strangely quiet. One inmate remembered the night as one that had made a deep, almost eerie impression—"the people were even afraid to think of what would occur . . . like a lot of guys wouldn't say anything the whole night. A lot of guys didn't sleep . . . and nobody would venture a word."

Despite what the world called good fortune, Tom Wicker was a disappointed man who believed he had fallen short. Having turned 45 three months before the Attica authorities hauled Leroy Dewer and Ray Lamorie off to the box, he was overweight, affluent beyond his sense of decency, a writer who feared he had written nothing that would last, a political commentator who believed he preached mostly to the converted. He secretly doubted his own character and openly questioned many of the values of the society in which he lived.

Wicker was the youngest child of Delancy David Wicker, a railroad conductor of forbidding rectitude, and Esta Cameron Wicker, a woman of powerful personality from a proud Scotch family. Both were of limited education and high intelligence. Out of obscure but lasting influences in their own lives, they had effectively set apart their two children—Tom and his sister Kathleen—from much of the world about them, in Hamlet, North Carolina, in the 1930s and '40s.

Hamlet was then, and is now, a place of just over 4000 inhabitants, where the main north–south tracks of the old Seaboard Air Line Railway (now merged into the Seaboard Coast Line) intersect the railroad's less important east–west line from Wilmington to Rutherfordton, North Carolina, and an even less important fifth spoke radiating southeast to the aristocratic city of Charleston, South Carolina.

There were those everywhere who knew Hamlet as an inevitable stop on the rail trip to Florida. From older generations a few still remembered that before the age of dining cars the old terminal restaurant in Hamlet had been a memorable eating place for weary travelers. Later, the terminal itself, with its magnificent mansard roof, was admitted to the National Register of Historic Places.

But that had been far in the future when Tom Wicker had grown up in Hamlet, watched the W.P.A. put down the first cement sidewalks, seen tanks rumble through the streets on maneuvers in the early days of World War II, and played barely competent football, basketball, and baseball at the old all-white Hamlet High School—still standing—on Hamlet Avenue hard by Jim Samuel's Gulf Service and catercornered across the intersection from where Ma Crofton's hot dog stand used to be.

Ma Crofton, who was sometimes suspected of bootlegging, also told fortunes and had visions. Once, when Esta Wicker's pocketbook, in which she had left her engagement ring, was stolen from the Wicker house, Ma Crofton had been consulted and was able to "see" the pocketbook hidden in the walls of the house of a black woman who had done some housework for the Wickers. Neither ring nor pocketbook was ever found ("Honey," Chief Miller said to Esta Wicker, "we'd have to tear that whole house down"), but nobody in the Wicker family ever doubted what had happened to them.

Aside from Ma Crofton's occult powers, this story did not seem strange to anyone in Hamlet. Virtually everyone knew that blacks—niggers, nigruhs, Negroes, or, more often, colored people (depending upon a white's sensibilities)—were at best irresponsible and at worst without much shame or scruple. Few were considered vicious. They were called Negroes or colored people in the Wicker family; D. D. Wicker once had washed out Tom's mouth with soap when he had used the word nigger. He had grown up with the prevailing impression that blacks were, if anything, objects of humor, to be enjoyed for their dialect, quaint ways, and indolent good nature, but not to be taken seriously either as threats or as fellow human beings.

That there were a lot of Negroes about was obvious. It was generally conceded that there was something to be said for them—who fried chicken better? Or killed hogs, or weeded gardens, or made such magnificent music at church during the August meetings? Esta Wicker believed no white knew as well as they how to make a compost pile. Whether anything was wrong with the blacks' situation was not much on any white mind. At "dinnertime"—the midday meal hour—black yard help was handed a generous plate at the back door and it was only natural that the plate later was scalded against whatever might be "catching."

Tom and D. D. Wicker wished desperately for a "white hope" to dethrone Joe Louis, to whose broadcast fights they listened with hopeless regularity. It never occurred to the boy and probably not to his father to wonder if Negroes minded sitting in the balcony at the old Hamlet Opera House, or not being admitted to the First Methodist Church, or why Dr. Mask, the principal of the Capital Highway (black) High School, was reported to be the only registered Negro voter in town. It fitted, somehow, with the town's humorous notion of the incompetent and inconsequential black that in the solidly Democratic South Dr. Mask should also be a Republican, even in the age of Franklin D. Roosevelt.

In young Tom Wicker's Hamlet, as in Conrad's exotic islands, "white men looked on [black] life as a mere play of shadows. A play of shadows the dominant race could walk through unaffected. . . ." He could hear black feet scuffling overhead at the movies, but it never entered his mind that the sound was ominous, that if he could hear the colored people, he might someday have to see them.

When morning came to Attica on Thursday, September 9, 1971, the men on William Ortiz's cell tier in A-block insisted he be allowed to go to breakfast with them, although he had been ordered kept in his cell ("Keep-lock") on the charge of hitting Corrections Officer Boyle with the soup can.[20] A relatively inexperienced guard, Gordon Kelsey, followed his orders and refused to let Ortiz out; but then Kelsey neglected to close the lockbox around the levers that operated the cell doors. Without Kelsey's knowledge, another inmate pulled the lever for cell 17. That released Ortiz, who joined the others as they marched off, with the tallest inmate in the lead—another of the annoying disciplines of Attica. Going by the same kind of rules, Kelsey also permitted no talking on the march to the mess hall, located behind C-block.

But breakfast passed without incident. Then Ortiz and the other men were marched through "Times Square"—the strategic point of intersection for four passageways connecting A, B, C, and D cellblocks—on the way to A-yard for the usual morning exercise period. During breakfast, however, the absence of Ortiz from his cell and his presence in the mess hall had been discovered. This was another defiance Mancusi decided not to accept. Mindful of the inmates' reaction to Dewer's resistance the day before, the superintendent ordered "Five Company"—of which Ortiz, Ray Lamorie, and Richard Clark were members—back to their cells. When all were in, Mancusi intended to return everyone but Ortiz to A-yard, thus avoiding the necessity of seizing Ortiz from the midst of Five Company.

Lieutenant Curtiss, thinking fast as to how to accomplish this maneuver, ordered the door through which Ortiz and the men of Five Company would have to pass into A-yard to be locked before they got there. That door opened from one side of the passageway that ran from Times Square to A-block. Curtiss knew that after Five Company passed through Times Square, its iron gate would be routinely locked behind them; so if the side door through which they subsequently would have to pass to get into A-yard was locked ahead of them, Kelsey would have no choice but to march Five Company on down the passageway to A-block and their cells, where Mancusi's order to keep-lock Ortiz could be carried out.

Curtiss hurried down to the Times Square–A-block passageway to take charge personally. He entered the passageway at about 8:55 A.M. to find Five Company and two other A-block companies standing about between the locked door to A-yard and the locked Times Square gate behind them. Apparently not realizing the extent to which A-block inmates had been upset by his handling of the Dewer–Lamorie incident the night before, or that by many of the men in the passageway he was now regarded as a betrayer, Curtiss strode along the passageway toward the long lines of men. They appeared calm enough and were not making undue noise as Curtiss came to the head of Five Company at the locked door to A-yard.

"You no good mother!" someone shouted.

Immediately, Curtiss was hit on the side of the head. He went down heavily. Kelsey and two other guards ran down the passageway to help him. A swarm of men set upon them. Badly beaten, the three officers nevertheless managed to escape and at least some of the A-block inmates helped them. Curtiss, momentarily ignored in the assault on the other officers, got up and ran along the passageway toward the A-block offices, trying to get to a telephone. Pursuers overtook him, ripped out the phone, took keys from another guard, and began opening all the A-block cells.

For a strange and unexplained ten minutes or more, the riot that exploded so suddenly did not spread out of the passageway and A-block; nor was there any quick or concerted reaction to the outburst by Mancusi and his staff. Both sides appear to have been too surprised by what had happened to have acted immediately. The prison authorities, moreover, were handicapped both by the lack of an adequate communications system within the institution and by their own failure to have developed a "riot plan" for coping with such an emergency. There had never been drills or training sessions for a general uprising in the institution and the only emergency planning was for fires and natural disasters.

So, almost fifteen minutes after Curtiss was knocked down, a group of uncontrolled inmates was able to surge in the other direction down the passage from A-block toward Times Square. There, William Quinn, an amiable young guard who had a reputation for overlooking minor rules violations, was in control of heavy metal gates to each passageway—gates the institution depended upon to seal off and isolate any trouble that might arise.

The gate to the passageway leading to A-block was locked with a heavy metal bolt. No one knew it that Thursday morning but the crucial bolt was defective—a crack was hidden deep under the many layers of prison paint it had received over 40 years or so. The cracked bolt quickly gave way under what a watching guard, Paul Rosecrans, said was "strictly body force. They just kept ramming themselves against those gates." The defective bolt was critical; had the gates held at Times Square, the rebels would have been confined to A-block and the passageway, and the rebellion could not have spread throughout the prison.

As inmates poured into Times Square, William Quinn was badly injured, his skull fractured in two places. The rioting inmates, moreover, were in command of the vital prison center of communications at Times Square. Quickly they opened the passageways to B, C, and D blocks, opening routes throughout the prison.

Violence flared everywhere, as the excitement spread, and the rioters swarmed through the prison buildings with pieces of pipe, lengths of chain, broomsticks, any weapon that came to hand. Some were wielding homemade "blades." Others seized sledge hammers and hatchets from prison stores. In the melee at Times Square, prisoners captured two tear-gas launchers stored there. They quickly invaded the commissary, captured the metal shop, seized stocks of football helmets and baseball bats from the storehouse, and soon were in command of most of the huge square formed by the cell blocks and their four enclosed exercise yards and four connecting passageways meeting at Times Square. They set fire to the schoolhouse, the chapel, and other buildings, and a thick cloud of smoke rose over the prison, joining its siren in alarming the town of Attica to the plight of its fathers and husbands.

The inmates were angry men suddenly free to turn on their jailers, and many did so with ferocity—particularly against the toughest among the guards. Violence was widespread and fearful. "Anybody wearing a blue [guard's] shirt in a thing like that, he got to go," Julio Carlos recalled 10 days later.

Numerous officers were beaten severely, forced to run a gauntlet of swinging clubs, stripped naked, abused and threatened. An inmate swinging a long-handled shovel broke Guard Phillip Watkins' arm. Other officers were hit over the head, or about the body, with pipes and chain. When the commissary fell, Officer Richard Fargo was beaten by a mob of inmates with bats, shovels, shovel handles, and a machinist's hammer. Oswald relates that Officer Albert Robbins, in charge of the garage, was felled "with a pipe blow in the gut"; that the rebels stormed the metal shop by using a forklift truck as a battering ram; that Officer Kenneth Jennings was struck by one inmate eight times with a weight-lifting bar; and that inmates attacked one group of officers with burning mattresses, long poles, tear gas, lye soap, and streams of water from fire hoses. But when William Quinn died two days later, he became the only person killed in the inmates' takeover at Attica.

Nor were all Attica inmates bent on taking physical revenge, or even on rioting. Richard Clark says he helped carry the injured Quinn to a gate to turn him over to prison authorities, and also claims to have participated in the release of six more guards from A-block, before he knew that a general insurrection was taking place and hostages were being held. An unknown prisoner stopped the man with the shovel from beating Phillip Watkins more severely. Many other such acts have been authenticated. For instance, Frank Strollo, a captured guard, was in a group "protected" by two prisoners he knew.

A good many inmates hid out in cells and elsewhere, trying to avoid participation in the uprising; some succeeded. Others were caught up in events not of their own making or desire, and simply went along as passively as possible. A few impassioned inmates wanted to kill some or all of their captives right away, but cooler heads prevailed. Black Muslims, in particular, stood determined watch to protect the hostages. Besides, the emerging leaders realized that hostages were their only real weapons, once the surge of violence was over. In all, the rebels took 40 hostages on Thursday, September 9, and two more guards were found hiding in the cell blocks the next day (but four who were in weak physical condition were later released, while the uprising continued).

After their initial paralysis, the prison authorities reacted quickly. Oswald was notified at his office in Albany. He sent word to Governor Rockefeller, who was attending a meeting of the Foreign Intelligence Advisory Board in Washington. State police were summoned and began arriving at Attica in force before noon. Earlier, a state police helicopter hovered over the prison—but not for long, because the defiant inmates shouted to guards that they would kill the hostages unless the "chopper" departed. Within hours, therefore, bargaining for the lives of the hostages—and indirectly for the lives of the rebelling inmates—had begun.

Corrections officers and troopers quickly and with minimum force—no loss of life or serious injury—recaptured A and C blocks, as well as E, a detached building, and C-yard. Soon thereafter, the rebels were confined mostly to D-yard, the farthest from the Administration building, and to A-yard, although there the troopers' guns overlooked the inmates. It was in D-yard that the uprising began to take social, political, and military shape; and its first leader was Roger Champen, a lean, tall black who was naturally called "Champ" by the other inmates.

Champ was 38 years old at the time, a New York City boy who had come from a good home, got his high school diploma, and found himself shipped off to combat in Korea. His ambition had been to be a policeman, but he came home from the army a drug user. A year later, he was in Elmira prison in New York for an armed robbery that ultimately cost him 40 months behind bars. Embittered and disillusioned, Champ often reflected during that stretch that he could have been killed in Korea but couldn't get a decent job in his own country.

In that mood, and that situation, he did not long stay out, once he got out. In November 1958, he went back to prison for 20 to 30 years for armed robbery. Thirteen years later, after such lonely struggles of self-discipline and self-analysis as others may only imagine, Roger Champen was free of his drug habit and a self-taught jailhouse lawyer. He had spent countless hours in his cell reading law and history, he had for years conducted prison law classes, and he was one of the best-known and most respected inmates at Attica, among whites as well as blacks—not least because he had been known to throw passes 40 to 50 yards during prison football games.

Champen took no part in the uprising. While it erupted around him, he remained in his D-block cell, "overwhelmed" and deep in thought as to what to do in such sudden and amazing circumstances. Other inmates, many of them students in the law classes he had for so long conducted in the prison yard, came to his cell asking what they should do—what *he* was going to do.

Finally, Champ went down to D-yard and took a quick look at the mob of inmates milling about, at the cigarettes and other captured supplies strewn on the ground. Then he went to a corner of the yard, sat down and thought some more—no doubt about the two felonies on his record, and how much tougher it would be when he finally got out if more were added as the result of a riot in Attica. But he could also see that the rioting inmates were beginning to fight among themselves; and Roger Champen was a natural leader.

"I was reluctant to get involved in what happened," he recalled. "The only reason I got involved was because I knew a lot of people and I knew I had a rapport with most people. I could talk and they would listen. . . . So then you see arguments—two guys arguing with another guy about something trivial and that's when I thought somebody better say something soon because if we don't it's going to become something in here that we can't handle."

Champen went to the center of the yard, took an officer's bullhorn from another inmate, and started talking. Someone made him get up on a table, and he kept talking—a huge and commanding figure.

"We got to pull ourselves together," he told the other inmates, and began issuing instructions. His reputation, his air of calm, the fact that he was nearly 40 years old in a predominantly youthful group, and the good sense in his orders to find blankets and bedding, strip the commissary, search out water cans and other necessities, began to turn the chaos of D-yard into rudimentary organization.

Entering D-yard at about that time "was as though we had stepped into another world," Richard Clark thought. "Suddenly the sun was shining and everyone was smiling. . . . I felt liberated; I had a sense of freedom."

CHAPTER

2

Inside the Walls

In a fierce dinner-table debate with James Baldwin, Tom Wicker had once declared a willingness to trade his white skin for Baldwin's literary talent. If obviously futile, this proposal reflected a genuine frustration and a searing ambition. He had always wanted to be a writer, and had become one, but not as he had anticipated.

In September 1971, he thought his best claim to accomplishment was that he had done a professionally competent job of covering the murder of John F. Kennedy in 1963, when Wicker had been *The New York Times'* White House correspondent and for hours its only reporter on the scene in Dallas. He thought the best writing he had ever done was in his coverage of Kennedy's funeral. These were substantial credentials, but not the stuff of immortality.

On the other hand Wicker was perhaps overconscious that, not least as the result of November 22, 1963, he had succeeded the legendary James Reston in 1964 as chief of *The Times'* Washington Bureau. In 1966, he also had replaced the legendary Arthur Krock as writer of *The Times'* thrice-weekly editorial-page column, "In the Nation." In that column, in 1970, he had written approvingly of a decision by Federal Judge Constance Baker Motley establishing a code of prisoners' rights in the case of one Martin Sostre;[1] and in August and September, just before the Attica uprising, he had written sympathetically about the death of George Jackson at San Quentin. Unknown to him, the Jackson articles[2] had been given wide circulation in the black press and on the prison grapevine.

Wicker prized such newspaper work, but it was by no means what he had set out to do. Encouraged to read by his mother—who once won a coal-fired heating stove in an essay contest sponsored by the Hamlet *News–Messenger*—Wicker turned early to fiction and while still in high school consumed innumerable novels, mostly historical romances, countless serials in the *Saturday Evening Post* (which as D. D. Wicker's secular bible arrived every Monday as inexorably as washday and school, with Tugboat Annie, Alexander Botts, and Crunch and Des), tall stacks of pulps later saved in the garage against what dire reading emergency he was never sure, and yards of detective novels, from the Hardy Boys to Ellery Queen. By the time he was graduated from high school, he was irrevocably resolved to be a famous author. Nothing else would do.

During four desultory years of uninspired study at the University of North Carolina, he improved his reading tastes somewhat, and tested his skills in Professor Phillips Russell's creative writing course, in which Wicker began his first novel and forever succumbed to the addiction of writing. For the next twelve years, while he worked full time as a journalist, he was constantly at work on subsequent pieces of fiction, long and short.

But it was not until he had been adrift in the great world for several years that a newspaper colleague, Bob Barnard,[3] influenced him to read—and, by implication, to write—seriously. Barnard had delivered Wicker an erudite cocktail-party lecture on the beauties and intricacies of *Ulysses*, then made Wicker read his own Williams College English-class copy, replete with underlinings, marginalia, and lecture notes. That opened Wicker's eyes to literature, more than had any college course, and he began to pursue books relentlessly. A few years later, a year at Harvard on a Nieman Fellowship had on him an additional intellectual impact that he compared to the religious unhorsing of Saul on the road to Damascus. By then, he lusted for nothing less than the achievements of a Faulkner or a Melville.

Emerging from Chapel Hill into the post-World War II years, however, he had found society consistently readier to value him as a newspaperman—if at that only slightly—than as any kind of a novelist. He had a certain facility, and unlimited energy; they enabled him between 1951 and 1961 to publish six novels (not counting one he had written in the name of a wealthy acquaintance who paid him well for the job). He knew this was more than many writers saw in print during their lifetimes. But none of his books found an audience (including the ghost-written opus) and none earned money worth his time and effort. More important, none pleased him; he had read too widely for that, and he was a harsh judge of his own work.

But with time out for a two-year Korean War hitch in the Navy (during which he wrote one of his novels), Wicker had moved in the same years from temporary editor of *The Sandhill Citizen* (circulation 1,800 a week) of Aberdeen, North Carolina, to a variety of positions on the afternoon daily *Robesonian* (circulation 7,000) of Lumberton, North Carolina, thence to a one-year stand as information director of the North Carolina State Board of Public Welfare, and from that bureaucratic mite gratefully back into journalism with the Winston-Salem *Journal* (circulation 75,000), for which he was at various times copy editor, telegraph editor, sports editor, Sunday features editor, city hall reporter, editorial writer, and Washington correspondent.

This copious education in the craft of newspapers was interrupted for his fellowship year at Harvard. After that, he moved westward to become an associate editor of the Nashville *Tennessean* (circulation 200,000). It was in Nashville, as 1959 became 1960 and a dark new decade slouched toward a nation taking leave of Eisenhower, that he was reached almost on successive days by a publisher's rejection of a novel he had just finished and by an offer to join the Washington Bureau of *The New York Times* (circulation 900,000). He was 33 years old, the father of two, and it seemed evident to him that his future was in journalism, not fiction (although the rejected novel eventually was published in 1961 by another house).

In Washington, he spent a year of invaluable learning as a *Times* reporter on Capitol Hill, then found himself White House correspondent and national political correspondent. These were hungry years of ambition and effort, and they were rewarded beyond Wicker's expectations when in 1964 he was made chief of the Washington Bureau, a position his great predecessors, Krock and Reston, had made the most prestigious in journalism.

But Wicker's years in this demanding office were not happy, for him or for *The Times*, and it was small consolation that old friends would write to point out how far he had come from Hamlet and *The Sandhill Citizen*. As with his novels, he soon knew he had fallen short of the great achievement he coveted. Again, ambition and effort had taken him far—but not far enough.

In 1968, he resigned as bureau chief and devoted himself to writing "In the Nation." It was a sensible decision, and colleagues envied him the freedom, notoriety, and lecture fees of a columnist; but in fact, he was settling for something like half the loaf he had so fiercely sought. Still, he traveled widely, lived well in the brick house on Cleveland Avenue, and sent his children to splendid schools. His articles acquired a following. He even found time to return to fiction, like a man discovering an old flame grown lovelier with age.

But in September 1971, his fiction seemed no more promising than it had been a decade earlier. Nor did he think his newspaper work had had enough value to sustain his passionate desire to signify as a writer. His personal life was breaking up and falling away, just as he had come to believe that he was fixed forever in its course. Of all his surprises and disappointments, that had been the most shaking.

Entering D-yard that Thursday morning might have given Richard Clark a "sense of freedom"; but neither he nor any of the other 1280 rebels savoring its liberation atmosphere was anywhere near real freedom. Beneath the cloud of smoke rising from the prison, the 30-foot walls of Attica still surrounded Clark and the other inmates. The helicopter was just off the scene; the police already had shown their power. Early in the afternoon, they recaptured B-block, which frowned down on D-yard.

What they might have done later in the day never will be known, because at about 2 P.M. Russell Oswald arrived to take charge of what he thought would be a quickly negotiated settlement, arranged with rational men who wanted to improve conditions at Attica, as he did. His earlier conversations with Frank Lott had convinced him that there need be no bloodshed, and he certainly wanted none. On the flight from Albany to Attica, he had decided that his "first responsibility . . . was to save as many lives as possible."[4]

At 63 years of age, Oswald was considered a liberal and a reformer in the corrections field. A graduate of the University of Wisconsin and of Marquette Law School, he had a master's degree in psychiatric social work from Loyola University and had worked in corrections in Wisconsin and Massachusetts. Governor Averell Harriman had brought him to New York to be chairman of the State Board of Parole, and Nelson Rockefeller had made him Commissioner of Correctional Services on January 1, 1971. In that post, Oswald had determined to improve a department that had been, by his own testimony, fiscally starved, a staff whose professional training and preparation had been neglected for years, and correctional policies that were outmoded and ineffective.

But Oswald overestimated his reputation as a reformer, at least among the inmates who were his sharpest critics. Most of them knew that, despite a pledge of no reprisals after the Auburn uprising, some of the inmate participants had been beaten. Oswald did not realize that many of the Attica inmates thought he was the man who had given the Auburn pledge (he had not even been Commissioner then). His visit to Attica on September 2 had seemed to many prisoners no more than a panicky response to their "George Jackson memorial" at breakfast on August 22. That he had spoken to them by tape recording rather than in person seemed typical of the way the prisoners felt themselves treated—as something less than persons.

Even in his optimism about negotiations, Oswald was not prepared, at first, to confront the prisoners, particularly in their D-yard stronghold. Instead, soon after his arrival, he authorized entry into the yard for Professor Herman Schwartz of the law faculty at the State University in Buffalo, and for Assemblyman Arthur O. Eve of Buffalo. Schwartz, an authority on wiretapping and other criminal justice matters, was a former aide to Senator Estes Kefauver of Tennessee, a veteran of the civil rights movement, a prison critic, reformer and legal counsel to a number of inmates. Eve was an articulate young black who had worked for prison reform in the New York State Assembly, and who had helped organize Project SEEK, a multimillion dollar community development program in Buffalo and upstate New York. Each had come to Attica of his own accord, on hearing of the uprising.

Oswald had every reason to regard these men as good emissaries; but, at least in Richard Clark's view, their credentials, too, were not as strong as Oswald thought. Eve had publicly promised "no reprisals" after Auburn; to Clark, he was therefore "just another politician." Schwartz had a reputation, according to Clark, for "talking down" to inmates and taking too long in handling their appeals.[5] Besides, some inmates had heard Schwartz quoted in a radio broadcast as having said that the uprising was due to "petty grievances," an unfortunate choice of words that offended them—and which Schwartz later could not recall having used.[6]

By midafternoon, the rebelling men had nominated numerous leaders, or members of a "negotiating team"—two from each cell block. They had organized a sort of police or security force to maintain order, and had appointed guards for the hostages, who had been located within a ring of wooden benches not far from the center of D-yard, and who were being guarded by the ever-alert Muslims. Cleanup details were sent out and homosexual couples were told to come out from under their blankets and make love later on. Rationing of captured food was imposed. Leaders also demanded—and got—the voluntary surrender of some drug stocks taken from the hospital in C-block.

A sick bay of sorts was set up, staffed by men with rudimentary medical experience in the armed services or in prison. Lookouts were posted, and tables were set up for the leadership group and its secretariat—a typewriter or two had been liberated, as well as a public-address system. When Schwartz and Eve arrived in D-yard about 3 P.M., they found a rough social and political order functioning, although six hours earlier all its inhabitants—alienated, angry men, many of them unschooled, violent, and admitted lawbreakers—had been prisoners of the state of New York, under constant surveillance, and reduced to little more than lockstep circumstances.[7] The rebels, moreover, were ready to do business—but not with Herman Schwartz and Arthur Eve.

Instead, they handed Oswald's emissaries a list of five demands (see Appendix One)—no reprisals by prison administrators for the uprising; transportation for those who wanted it to a "non-imperialist" country; a federal takeover and operation of the Attica prison; an observer committee to oversee future negotiations; and the reconstruction of the prison. The prisoners also produced a list of persons they wanted on the Observer Committee (see Appendix One). Thus enlightened, Eve and Schwartz returned to the administration building where Oswald's advisers and aides—particularly Mancusi and Walter Dunbar, Oswald's principal deputy—argued hotly against his going into the yard; he would become the inmates' most important hostage, they insisted with much logic.[8]

Oswald climbed to a second-floor walkway that overlooked Times Square and called out to inmates visible there that he would meet their leaders at any neutral spot, perhaps the walkway between where he stood and Times Square. They shouted back that he would have to meet with the inmates in their territory, "talking to them on a level man to man and not down." Oswald returned to his advisers. Schwartz thought he heard the commissioner tell Dunbar, "We'll have to go in," and got the impression that Oswald thought the matter had to be resolved quickly—which in view of the inmates' stand meant he had to order an attack. Dunbar and the police officials, Schwartz thought, were urging this course.

Schwartz recalls that "I somewhat heard them and said, 'What about the 35 lives [of the hostages]?' or something like that, I've forgotten the exact details. And I sort of huddled with Eve and pushed it again with Oswald. . . . He got very unhappy looking. He talked to Dunbar, as I recall, a few minutes and in his kind of paunchy, round-shouldered, small fat-man way, looked down and said, 'I've got to go in.' "[9] His staff argued that if the inmates took him hostage, Rockefeller could never order an attack and risk the commissioner's life.

An encounter earlier that day between inmates and the authorities had been a disaster. Before Oswald's arrival, Superintendent Mancusi had summoned Richard Clark and another inmate, an older man named Waldo, to the barred gate that opened from A-block to the corridor leading to Times Square—the corridor in which the revolt had flared that morning. The scene of many such conferences in ensuing days, the gate area became known as "No Man's Land," or sometimes as "The DMZ."

Clark and Waldo arrived there with a list of demands similar to those presented to Oswald in the July manifesto of the Attica Liberation Faction. But the demands were never presented to Mancusi. Here is Clark's account of the meeting:

Mancusi was at the gate. "Are you going to give me back this institution and return to your cells?" he demanded.

I said, "It's not ours to give back. You've got 1200 men in there. We're in no position to tell that to those men. And anyhow," I said, "I couldn't get back to my cell now if I wanted to. You got guards blocking all the entrances, and all the cell doors are locked."

He started sputtering. He got green. Suddenly a brother ran up to us. He's dead now and I can't remember his name. He started saying something to one of the guards, to put his gun down, and Mancusi shouted to him, "Shut up, boy!"

What? I said to myself. There's no point going through with this. We can't get any respect from him, so there's no point even talking to him.

"We want to see Commissioner Oswald," we said. "Here are our demands. And we want newsmen and reporters so we can make sure none of the promises the state makes are broken."

And we left.

Mancusi picked up the megaphone and shouted to us, "Come back here. I'm not finished with you."

I said, "Yeah, but we're finished with you."[10]

Clark's account may not be precise but it evokes the atmosphere between inmates and authorities. These first exchanges also suggested that if Russell Oswald's high hopes for a negotiated settlement were to bear fruit, he would have to enter D-yard, despite his original plan to talk to the inmates on neutral ground. On the spot he made what he later called a "battlefield decision." That, Herman Schwartz thought, took "guts of a very high order." But Oswald felt that he "had no choice. I could not live with myself if I did not walk down that tunnel to save the lives of the hostages."[11]

At about 4:45 P.M., Oswald, with Schwartz and Eve, entered D-yard, under the inmates' guarantee of safety. At the leadership table, the commissioner recognized several inmates—Clark, Blyden, Lott, Champ, Jerry Rosenberg (a white jailhouse lawyer in for life on conviction for the murder of two New York city policemen). Oswald, boldly enough, told the assembled negotiators that the July manifesto had seemed to him to be a mere copy of a set of demands originally made by inmates of Folsom prison in California.

He found the negotiators ready neither to trust him nor to make a deal. "We knew he wasn't gonna come through," Julio Carlos remembered later, "that he was gonna promise and promise and in a year's time he might come up with a little better food and books."

After much oratory, the negotiators demanded and Oswald agreed to several preconditions for substantive negotiations—removal of armed troopers from surrounding rooftops, a report on the condition of Lamorie and Dewer, who were still in "segregation," food, water, radios, and news reporters to watch and report on any further negotiations.

Oswald, Eve, and Schwartz left unharmed at 5:15. At 5:45 P.M. they returned with reporters from *The New York Times*, the *Buffalo Evening News*, as well as reporters and cameramen from the Buffalo radio and television stations.[12] Again, Oswald had rejected his associates' pleas that he not risk being taken hostage; and again he had decided against a forcible attack on D-yard. Major John Monahan, commander of Troop A, New York state police, had advised the commissioner on his first emergence from the inmate stronghold that more than 500 state troopers, 250 sheriff's deputies from nearby counties, and 250 correctional officers were at hand—"sufficient force," Monahan had said, "to regain control of the facility." So sure were the troopers that Oswald would order the attack that national television broadcasts were able to pick up Captain Henry F. Williams' battle instructions to state police:

> Your instructions are that your weapon is not to be taken, nor are you to be taken. You will be sent in in groups of five-man teams, and you'll operate as a five-man unit. You're to meet force with force. There have been some of the prison personnel severely injured here this morning, and we certainly don't want to see any of our people hurt. But just remember—no indiscriminate fire. However, you're not to be taken—nor is your weapon to be taken away from you. So you'll use whatever force is necessary to maintain your own security.[13]

But Oswald was not only "quite sure" by then that a negotiated settlement was possible; he also believed that "to regain control of the facility" would require a "furious hand-to-hand battle." Since as yet "no viable quantity of the CS disabling gas" was on hand, he knew firearms would have to be used. He also knew that would not rescue the hostages. Oswald had "sensed the mood of the rebels" for himself in D-yard—"I had felt the scarcely controlled fury almost breathing down my neck. Those men were capable of murdering the hostages." Talk, Russell Oswald was certain, was the only alternative to the violent deaths of the captured men.[14] And Herman Schwartz had become convinced, at close range, that Owald wanted "to avoid bloodshed at all costs."[15]

Elliot James Barkley was 21 years old, a tall black from Rochester, New York, with a history of drug use. Convicted at 18 for cashing a forged money order for $124.60, he had been sent to the Elmira Reformatory for four years. Paroled in January 1970, he rejoined his family, who were rated good people in the black community of Rochester; but then he was picked up for driving without a license, a violation of parole. For that, he was sent to the maximum security prison at Attica where—although he was in no real sense a leader—he became a well-known exercise-yard orator.[16] When D-yard was organized after the uprising, Barkley and Richard Clark were elected to represent A-block inmates.

Roger Champen recalled:

> Barkley was more close to me than any of those I've mentioned. Primarily because he's younger and the fact that I relate to younger people more readily than older ones, because of the fact that I figured if I had had someone to tell me the things that I know now, perhaps I would have looked at life differently earlier. So I tried primarily to reach out for the younger element.
>
> . . . Barkley and I used to read. I gave him law books. I tried to get him involved in law. He was an excellent reader. He would read, he would have an appetite for reading that was tremendous. He would come and get books from me to read and then we'd sit down and discuss it. . . . Being that he was young and inexperienced, books—I tried to explain to him—were just an outline of life. You had to actually live life, you couldn't live like out of a book. The book gives you the diagram for life, the outline, and you fill in the rest for yourself. . . .
>
> And he was *eager* to get back outside, to go in the community and work in the community. He felt that he could help younger children. . . .[17]

If Russell Oswald did not know L. D. Barkley—no one in Rochester or in Attica seems to know how Elliot James Barkley became known as "L.D."—when Oswald first entered the D-yard stronghold, he surely did when he emerged from it for the second time that Thursday night September 9. Barkley, with television cameras carrying his image and words to the world, again presented the inmates' "immediate demands." More than that, with his reedy voice, his youthful face and "granny glasses," his fiery manner and words, he conveyed the anger, the frustration, the determination that everyone who entered D-yard sensed in the inmates—at least among their active and articulate leaders.

> We have composed this declaration [L. D. began] to the people of America to let them know exactly how we feel and what it is

that they must do, and what we want, primarily, and not what we—what someone else wants for us. We's talking about what we want.

The entire incident began—it seems to be a little misunderstanding about why this incident developed here at Attica, and this declaration here will explain the reasons.

The entire incident that has erupted here at Attica is not a result of the dastardly bushwhacking of two prisoners September 8 of 1971, but of the unmitigated oppression wrought by the racist administrative network of this prison throughout the year. We are *men!* We are not beasts and we do not intend to be beaten or driven as such.

The entire prison populace—that means each and every one of us here—has set forth to change forever the ruthless brutalization and disregard for the lives of the prisoners here and throughout the United States. What has happened here is but the sound before the fury of those who are oppressed.

We will not compromise on any terms except those terms which are agreeable to us. We call upon all the conscientious citizens of America to assist us in putting an end to this situation that threatens the lives of not only us, but of each and every one of you as well.

We have set forth demands that will bring us closer to the reality.

We want complete amnesty, meaning freedom from all and any physical, mental and legal reprisals.

We want, now, speedy and safe transportation out of confinement to a non-imperialistic country.

We demand that the federal government intervene so that we will be under direct federal jurisdiction. We want the governor and the judiciary . . . to guarantee that there will be no reprisals, and we want all facets of the media to articulate this. . . .

Russell Oswald, hearing all this from a few feet away, decided L. D. Barkley was a "pure revolutionary."[18]

Herman Schwartz, also listening closely, realized that there was not going to be a rational negotiation "such as in the labor–management context or anything like that." Instead, he saw at once, there was going to be a confrontation "between two sovereign entities who had a deep hatred and distrust for one another." Nevertheless, he urged the inmates to get down to more "meaningful" matters than Barkley's "immediate demands," advice which did not please the rebel leaders.[19] Nor did they accept Oswald's pledge that there would be no physical or administrative reprisals. They told him to put it in writing. Then, just before the commissioner, Eve, and Schwartz left D-yard at 6:44 P.M., Jerry Rosenberg, the jailhouse lawyer, handed Oswald a typed list of fifteen "practical proposals." They did not bear much resemblance to L. D. Barkley's rhetoric, but included such demands as :

> Apply the New York State minimum wage law to all state institutions. STOP SLAVE LABOR. . . .
> End all censorship of newspapers, magazines, letters and other publications coming from the publisher. . . .
> Allow all inmates, at their own expense, to communicate with anyone they please. . . .
> Give us a healthy diet, stop feeding us so much pork, and give us some fresh fruit daily. . . . Give us a doctor that will examine and treat all inmates that request treatment. . . .
> Remove inside walls, making one open yard, and no more segregation or punishment.[20] [See Appendix Two for a complete text of the "practical proposals."]

While Oswald conferred with state police officers and by phone with aides of Governor Rockefeller and the governor himself, Eve and Schwartz returned to D-yard at 7:30 P.M. for a fourth session—this time accompanied by Assistant Commissioner Dunbar and Assemblyman James L. Emery of nearby Geneseo, New York. Dunbar engaged in acrimonious exchanges with inmates but Schwartz had what seemed to him a profitable conversation with some of the jailhouse lawyers. They wanted not just Oswald's pledge but a federal court injunction against administrative and physical reprisals, and Schwartz undertook to get it for them. Later, Roger Champen was invited out of D-yard, under safe conduct guarantees from Oswald, to confer with Schwartz and the commissioner on a draft of the injunction.

Champen noticed, but discounted, one of the major facts of the matter at Attica—the guns in the hands of the troopers.

> In all the years I've been in prison . . . I'd never seen guns in the yard. I'd never seen a gun fired from the tower because no one has ever gotten to the walls. So the gun is like part of the scenery. You never think of the guns as a thing that of itself could cause harm. The walls, the guns, the guards all was one. Now when I walked down the hall there . . . and was met by a state trooper carrying a magnum and a rifle, I saw all kinds of guns. But my mind was centered on what I came to do, so that I put aside for the moment the guns I saw as being necessary

evils. . . . Guards have guns like men wear pants. So although
it had some initial effect on me, when I started talking about the
legal aspects with Oswald, I never thought about it.[21]

Champen's conditioned indifference to the guns was unfortunate. At
the moment, however, it seemed unimportant, as he and Schwartz
agreed on the following consent order:

Upon the consent of defendants, it is hereby ORDERED that:

Defendants, their agents and employees, are enjoined from
taking any physical or other administrative reprisals against any
inmates participating in the disturbance at the Attica Correctional
Facility on September 9, 1971.[22]

With this draft in hand, by 11:30 P.M. Herman Schwartz was on his
way in a New York state aircraft from Batavia, New York, to Manchester, Vermont, where Federal Judge John T. Curtin of Buffalo was
attending a judicial conference.[23]

Oswald had informed Governor Rockefeller that he intended to
continue the negotiations, a course Major Monahan by then approved.
But Rockefeller was worried; he said he hoped Oswald would avoid
"any appearance of vacillation or indecision," although he also told the
commissioner that he was "fully supportive" of the course he was
pursuing. Rockefeller left full command of the situation to Oswald,
although by Thursday night two of the governor's closest associates
were at Attica as his "personal representatives"—Dr. T. Norman
Hurd, director of state operations, and retired General A. C. "Buzz"
O'Hara, formerly commander of the state's National Guard and, in
September 1971, its Commissioner of General Services.[24]

The beginning of negotiations, however hostile the atmosphere, and
the agreement on the injunction draft, had encouraged Russell Oswald
in his belief that he could yet save the situation.

"That is it, isn't it?" he had asked Herman Schwartz before the law
professor left for Vermont. "They should release the hostages now,
right?"[25]

But nobody could be sure, and there was at least one other tactic to
be tried. Among the "immediate demands" first presented to Schwartz
and Arthur Eve, later put to the nation in L. D. Barkley's fiery speech
for the television cameras, was the request that a group of outside
persons be permitted to enter the prison. It was not certain what they
were to do; Barkley had demanded "negotiations through" such a
group, but whether they were themselves to be negotiators, arbi-
trators, observers, go-betweens, or guarantors of an agreement was
clear to no one. The rebels nevertheless had been specific about *who*

they wanted (see Appendix One)—the civil rights attorney William Kunstler, Arthur Eve, and Minister Louis Farrakhan of the Black Muslims, for example. Another name on the list was that of Tom Wicker.

Wicker was not flown from Buffalo to Attica in a helicopter. He was met, instead, by John Anna, a New York state trooper in plain clothes, who drove him in a police car through the late afternoon sunshine to the prison. It was a warm fall day and the two-lane highway took them for an hour through the rolling landscape of western New York, looking drab and tired from the long hot summer. It was not wealthy country in any season; the farmhouses were gaunt and sad, and the few towns, such as Batavia, looked used up and worn out. There were "Watch for Deer" signs along the road, but the country seemed too somber for sports.

Wicker was often depressed to see country—the Appalachian hills, for instance—where so short a time before so many men and women had risked so much to make a new world of hope and plenty (he was an avid reader of American history), and where all that struggle had come to so little—to the hard, narrow existence he could sense in the ugly frame houses and from the fields long unploughed. For this the pioneers had gone to the wilderness?

Here—he felt it in his bones—the search for Arcadia had come to an early end, as in so much of his own home country. Life had moved on westward, or somewhere, and on those stranded in what was to have been the promised land suspicion had settled like age. Not many of the people of the countryside he was passing through, Wicker speculated, could believe any longer that life would get better and better, that the destiny of Americans was ever onward, ever upward. They would be determined now only to yield nothing of what they had. And who had the right to fault them for that?

Trooper Anna filled him in on what had happened at Attica, but he knew no more than Wicker about what the "observers" were supposed to do. An intelligent and articulate man, Anna had the public employee's ability to confine himself precisely to his own responsibility, which was to get Wicker to Attica and through the prison gates. He gave Wicker little, if any, idea of the tactical situation within the prison, much less what ought to be done.

But the prison was a tough place, he said. He was certain the inmates had plenty of grievances—although he was not sure what they all might be. He certainly hoped the hostages could be brought out safely, but nevertheless he had a good deal of sympathy for the defiant inmates. He was a policeman; he was proud of it; he had worked hard and gone to school to learn his profession. But he had come to believe the problem today was not just a police problem. Policemen could not do it all, no matter how professional they were. Something had to be done about the conditions in the cities that anyone could see were causing most of the crime. That was where most of the inmates of Attica came from—the cities.

The police car moved quickly through Attica village, past a sign announcing a population of 2975 and one of those municipal directories that listed nine churches and, among other organizations, an historical society, a garden club, Grange 1058, a rod-and-gun club, and a rodeo association. But the town did not seem much of a place in its isolation, and Wicker was surprised to learn later that it boasted—in addition to the prison, its major employer—a Westinghouse plant, lumber mills, a box factory, two banks, and two weekly newspapers. From Route 98, Anna turned on Main Street, crossed Tonawonda Creek in the middle of town and made a right turn on Exchange Street, up a hill. A few hundred feet further on, Anna braked the car for a roadblock.

"I'm taking Mr. Wicker in to meet with the commissioner," Anna said to the man in uniform who bent over to peer into the car; the uniform appeared to be that of a county sheriff's department. The man who wore it was carrying a rifle and had a heavy pistol in a holster at his hip; a long billy club hung from his belt, as did a heavy flashlight. There were three other deputies manning the roadblock. Each carried the same weapons, except that one had a shotgun instead of a rifle. There were a lot of weapons in that roadblock, Wicker thought, and no way to know how many more in the police car parked at the side of the road.

It was his first glimpse of the profuse weaponry available to the law officers on duty during the Attica uprising. But Wicker did not then understand that so many guns must sooner or later become a force in themselves, an imperative acting upon the men who supposedly control them. If the weapons are in hand, the question of those who have them ultimately becomes, "Why not use them?" The more weapons, the more insistent the question; and the burden of explaining why *not* to use them falls on those who have no guns. But those who have no guns have little credence with those who do.

Anna displayed his credentials and they were through the roadblock in seconds. To the left in a parklike setting of trees and lawn there was a substantial Georgian mansion—the home of the Attica Correctional Facility's superintendent Vincent Mancusi, and the most imposing dwelling in Attica village. Just beyond this house rose the prison wall—massive, sand-colored, ugly, frightening in the darkening afternoon. The first sight of Attica's walls often overwhelms visitors; and

for men who are going to be locked within those walls, the impact can
be much worse, as one has recalled:

> In 1969, they moved 44 of us to Attica from Sing Sing. . . .
> We were shackled, chained, handcuffed, the whole thing. . . . I
> first saw Attica from a distance as we came down from Batavia
> . . . and I can still remember the thought that went through my
> mind: "Oh my God, this is a concentration camp!" . . . I knew
> that at last I was going to the big house.[26]

No American institution, in fact, is so forbidding as the prison. This
may be because so few Americans know anything more about prisons
than what they may have gleaned from old Cagney and Bogart movies.
As men abhor the unknown, they shun the prison. It is, they tell
themselves, none of *their* business, no concern of the ordinary citizen,
who need never go there. As for the others, no one *had* to commit the
crime that put him or her in that dark place. To the extent the prison is
thought of at all by the law-abiding citizen, it is likely to evoke
vaguely shocking impressions of rape and violence, unspeakable acts.
Where a prison must unavoidably be seen, good men and women are
apt to hasten past as if it were a cemetery which in some ways it is.
More often, the prison is hidden from the general view.

Wherever it may be located, the great walls rise, typically, like those
of an ancient, turreted fortress. Like a fortress, too, the prison is
designed as much to keep outsiders out as to keep inmates in. The
American fortress prison conceals, in fact, a classically closed society.
No one not a part of its harsh life can really know what goes on behind
the walls. No one within, not the most alert warden, not the best-
informed inmate with his avid ear to the grapevine, can know with
exactitude everything that happens in its shadowed society. The great
world goes about its business, but the prison is a dark pocket of
mystery and silence—"the black flower of civilized society," Haw-
thorne called it.

In New York state, in particular, comfortable society had by 1971
made certain that the black flower flourished mostly out of sight—
hence mostly out of mind of the comfortable. Attica isolated in
Wyoming County far to the northwest, Dannemora on the Canadian
border, Great Meadow, Green Haven, Wallkill, Auburn, Clinton,
with their idyllic names—all were well-hidden from the great population centers where crime flourished. When criminals were banished
from society in New York state, most were as effectively removed
from their communities and families and jobs—if any—as if they had
been swallowed by the sea; which meant that law-abiding or at least

unapprehended citizens did not have to gaze upon these human ware-houses and thus be aware of the repressed or warped or mistreated or hopeless or malignant humanity within.

But the hiding of the prisons had other pernicious consequences. Families and friends had difficulty visiting during the limited hours when it was permitted; the round trip bus fare from New York City to Batavia (nine hours each way) was $33.35, and the round trip taxi fare from Batavia to the prison was $12.00. Medical and legal and social work agencies, abundant in the cities, could not easily extend their services to the far corners of the state. Small, prison-based communities like Attica, far from the clash and clangor of urban life, came to have exclusive jurisdiction over the city's offenders. Since in contemporary times those offenders were more and more often black or Spanish-speaking, the prison-based villages, white and rural, had less and less understanding or sympathy for their charges.

Tom Wicker had realized little of any of this on the late afternoon when he first saw the walls of Attica. He had no more real knowledge, if perhaps a deeper abstract concern, than any other American who never had been "sent up." Twenty years earlier, he had been the information director—or publicity man—for the State Board of Public Welfare in North Carolina, and each month had had to visit the state prison in Raleigh—begun in 1869, its main building completed in 1883—to "close" the Board's professional magazine at the prison print shop. But he remembered little more of that experience than the niggling fear he had felt while being led through the prison yard and while going about his business with the inmate printers. As a reporter and columnist in Washington, he had followed the emergence of the fear of crime as a major political issue. In studying it, he had become intellectually convinced that prisons were, in bureaucratic jargon, "counter-productive"—that they were, as Ramsey Clark had called them in a book to which Wicker had contributed an admiring foreword, "factories of crime."

From such conviction had sprung his articles on Martin Sostre and prisoners' rights; from a general engagement with the disadvantaged and maltreated, he had leaped to instinctive sympathy for George Jackson and to the realization that prison-wise blacks were not going to believe the strange official story of his death—as indeed few had believed it. But none of that came to any real experience of prisons or prisoners, and Wicker was painfully aware of his ignorance as John Anna drove slowly across the paved parking area in front of the massive wall, before which an olive drab helicopter waited ominously.

The wall seemed to stretch for miles. At the midpoint of the paved area it turned outward at a slight angle and came to a point; but the point was blunted by a six-sided turret rising higher than the walls and topped by an incongruous cupola. The official entrance to the prison was through this turret, and above the door—sharply arched, rather like that of a Gothic church—prominent letters announced "Attica Correctional Facility." Anna hurried Wicker into the turret and explained the visitor to an unimpressed guard in gray-blue prison uniform. When he had signed them in, they went out the other side of the turret and into an open area between the mighty wall and the main prison buildings.

Ordinarily, Wicker judged, this would have been a quiet and almost parklike area, save for the wall looming above it; green lawn stretched away on either side of a concrete walk. That afternoon, the area was full of activity. State troopers and sheriff's officers were there in force, some lounging about, some in formations, some eating at stands that had been hastily erected. The atmosphere was tense, military; many of the men wore heavy, polished boots; some were in crash or battle helmets. Wicker was self-conscious in his casual clothes, as if he had appeared without socks for a formal dinner. Again, he was struck by the overwhelming presence of weapons. Every officer seemed to have a pistol at his side, a heavy club; many carried rifles and shotguns; some had tear-gas launchers; others had gas masks swinging at their belts. There were military-looking trucks, stacks of boxes, extended fire hoses, commanding men moving about, shouted orders—every sign, Wicker thought, of an army preparing to move out. Faces grim and unsmiling peered at him, but no one spoke to him.

Perhaps 50 yards beyond the turret, the walkway led to the main lobby of the administration building. It was crowded with men, noisy with their talk, which echoed from the hard institutional walls, the concrete floor. Anna paused, looking around.

"I'm supposed to turn you over to Captain Williams," he told Wicker, who had read in *The Times* about Captain Henry F. Williams of Troop A, New York State Police. Captain Williams, who had been put in tactical command of all police forces at Attica, looked to Wicker like a man who would be quite willing to issue an order to attack—not that he was military in appearance. His short-sleeved white shirt was stretched tight across a sizeable paunch, he was wearing dark glasses, and—unlike most of the men in the lobby—was carrying no visible weapons. But to Tom Wicker, Captain Williams looked like a tough man indeed—there was a lot of muscle in that paunch and under the jowls a bull neck that appeared unyielding. His hair was cropped into an unfashionable crew-cut and his narrow black knit tie had an air about it of woe to the hippies.

"Glad to have you here," Williams said, shaking hands. "Sure hope you can help us out."

"I'll try, Captain. What do you want me to do?"

"Well, the other observers are meeting upstairs with the commissioner. You might as well go right on up."

"How's it looking?"

Williams shook his head, unsmiling. "Something's got to give. We can't wait much longer." He did not say why, but designated a trooper to show Wicker the way.

"I sure wish you all the luck in the world," John Anna said shaking hands. "You fellows sure are going to need it in there."

"What do you really think?" Wicker said, out of Captain Williams' hearing. "Can we do anything?"

"I sure hope so," Anna said. "I sure hope you can just get those boys out of there alive."

As he watched Anna walk away, Wicker suddenly realized he had thought almost not at all about the hostages. For the first time, as he watched Anna hurrying back toward the prison entrance, Wicker began to realize the possibilities of what he had been so precipitately pulled into. Men might die here. The summons from Arthur Eve had caught him unprepared and he had rushed off to Attica almost without thinking, dashing to the airport while drowsy with wine, without a suitcase or a toothbrush or a clean shirt, on the vague assumption that he would return to Washington that night or at the latest the next morning.

On the flight to Buffalo, while studying *The Times'* account of the inmates' rebellion, if he had had any coherent notion of what he was expected to do at Attica, it was that he and a few other persons trusted by the inmates would give a sort of guarantee by their presence—a good-faith endorsement—to whatever agreement was to be reached by inmate and prison negotiators. With no better sense of his mission than that, he had caught the first plane, in part because of his reporter's instinct to go where the action was, more because of a certain faint pride at having been asked for help by men who had so few to whom they could turn.

Now, in the military preparations all about him, in the clicking and gleaming of the omnipresent weapons, in Captain Williams' laconic *something's got to give*, John Anna's gravity, above all from the overwhelming sense of the great walls closing about him, isolating him from the ordinary world and its accepted restraints, Wicker sensed that he might have gone beyond his depth. Here amid the guns, within the secretive walls, there was not likely to be the orderly and due process to which he was accustomed, upon which his calling so heavily relied. The threat of violence was all about him, in the very atmosphere of Attica. Lives—even his own—might depend upon something he did or said or failed to do.

He looked with foreboding at the grim faces around him, at the military bustle. He did not know what to do or even where to start, and he sensed that he probably had no real business being there at all. For most of his life he had followed the advice of Heyst's father in *Victory*—"Look on, and make no sound." He had lived by the reporter's peculiar standard, the ethic of the press box rather than of the participant. At Attica, he might no longer be able to play his easy, familiar role of privileged onlooker.

But he followed his guide up the stairs with a curious kind of resolution. It was high time, he thought, that he held himself to a line. What was a life if it was never put to challenge, not just by foolhardy choice but as a logical and perhaps inevitable consequence of the way a person had lived and believed? However little he might actually belong there, his life and work had brought him to Attica, almost as if to demand of him that he validate the work by committing the life. As for *how* he met the challenge, that seemed for the moment less important than that he should recognize and accept it.

Besides, he thought irrelevantly, with sudden bravado, as if the wine had returned to his brain, he had had a good, long run for it; he had come a long way before they laid a glove on him.

3

Nobody Gets Killed

STEWARDS' ROOM, said the black lettering on the glass door at the end of a short corridor. Wicker's escort hesitated, then led him into the room and to a short, stout, jowly man in shirt sleeves—Russell Oswald.

"I sure do appreciate your coming," the commissioner said, shaking hands. He had a worried face, sad eyes, an air of sincerity. Rapidly, he filled Wicker in on what had happened, as he saw it.

"But I'm not going in there anymore," he said. Then, quickly, as if to banish misundertanding, "Not that I'm afraid. But this morning they tried to take me. I can't do anybody any good if I'm just another hostage." At his side, the pipe-smoking Assistant Commissioner of Correctional Services, Walter Dunbar, nodded sagely.

Oswald had returned to D-yard that Friday morning at 11:25 to find the inmates more truculent than on Thursday. The trouble had started over the Schwartz–Champen injunction, on which Oswald had placed such high hopes.

After a harrowing night of travel and worry, Herman Schwartz had returned to Attica at about 6:30 A.M. with the injunction signed by Judge Curtin—but not by Judge Constance Baker Motley, whose signature the prisoners also had demanded. She had been at the conference in Manchester, Vermont, but could not sign an order that did not affect her jurisdiction unless authorized by the Chief Judge of the Second Circuit, Henry Friendly, and he had refused to intervene.

The injunction was unsealed, since Judge Curtin had not taken his seal to Manchester. But Schwartz was unworried early on Friday morning when he summoned inmates to No Man's Land and gave them a copy of the signed injunction. At 8:30 A.M., he and Arthur Eve returned to No Man's Land and were startled to hear Richard Clark, a "tall, shaven headed, strong black man," declare that "this thing ain't worth shit." The injunction, Clark said, was worthless because it didn't have a seal. Schwartz knew the seal was meaningless, but sent off a copy of the injunction to Judge Curtin's Buffalo chambers to be sealed, just to quiet any further inmate doubts.[1]

But when Oswald, Schwartz, Eve, Emery, and three new "observers" or "negotiators"—two black ministers from Rochester, Raymond Scott and Marvin Chandler, and Lewis Steel, a white radical lawyer who had represented some Auburn inmates after the uprising there—went into D-yard just before noon, the atmosphere was tense and bitter.

To some extent, the inmates' rancor may have been staged, or false. Television cameras trailed Oswald again, and some of the men of D-yard probably realized—as Herman Schwartz did—that the cameras inevitably turned the moment into "political theater" as well as political negotiation.

Besides, as Roger Champen put it, "Everybody wants to be known. . . . You know the cameras in there? A lot of guys in there stood in front of them, they wanted people to see them. Like, 'oh, this is my time to be seen.' "[2]

Posturing for television is no less likely inside a prison than outside, and the presence of cameras in D-yard during most of the negotiations undoubtedly had its effect on them—just as the cameras have their effect at a political convention or outside a congressional committee's doors. Television cameras and the waiting press *outside* Attica's gates could never be far from the minds of Russell Oswald and his associates, either.

The meeting opened with sharp questions about the injunction. Why hadn't Governor Rockefeller signed it, if it was a "consent order"? Where was the seal? The order might prevent reprisals for participation in "the disturbance on September 9, 1971," but what about September 10 or any subsequent day? Schwartz tried to defend the document. Roger Champen, who had helped draft it, said nothing—an example of a phenomenon Wicker came to know as "protecting your constituency" and to which he watched participants at Attica fall victim one by one, until his own turn came.

Finally, Jerry Rosenberg—he and Champ were the inmates' most respected jailhouse lawyers—shouted to the crowd: "This injunction is garbage!" It did not guarantee criminal amnesty, he declared, it was limited to one day, and it didn't have a seal. Then he ripped the document into two pieces of paper. There was an enormous roar after his tirade, which the exhausted Schwartz thought was designed at least partially to gain Rosenberg acceptance among the black inmates. Schwartz, himself, numb from effort, travel, sleeplessness, decided there was no use replying further. He would not again enter the yard, he decided, because he obviously did not have the inmates' confidence.

Then it was Oswald's turn. The inmates screamed abuse at him, demanded to know why he hadn't carried out reforms, why there had been reprisals at Auburn. The Fifteen Practical Proposals (see Appendix Two) were read again, and there was discussion of an inmate proposal to hang a hostage in front of Oswald, "to show him we mean business." At one point, "a handsome, short, youngish man, with fiery black eyes just hurled out attacks on Oswald and the others did too, attack after attack. . . ."

Finally, an inmate grabbed the microphone and demanded: "Why don't we keep him in here?"—Oswald, he meant. This sent up another roar; suddenly Herbert Blyden stood up from the negotiating table and told the commissioner: "I can't run this any more." Schwartz, frightened by the threat to Oswald, reminded Richard Clark that he had promised the negotiators safe-keeping. Oswald reminded the inmate leaders that he had returned Champ, as agreed, the night before.

"You think you've got trouble?" Clark looked at Oswald and asked. "How would you like to be us? How would you like these troubles? How would you like to try and control this?"

Ultimately, however, the inmates in the yard—after what Schwartz considered "a rather nervous 10 minutes"—loudly shouted down the suggestion to take Oswald. The incident left the commissioner understandably shaken; and he did not return to D-yard while the inmates held it.[3]

But this threatening experience had not caused Oswald to give up hope for a negotiated settlement, since he had believed from the start that the alternative was bloodshed. Rather, it apparently caused him to place greater reliance on the outside observer group than on his own discussions with the inmates. That meant that he now considered the observers to *be* the negotiators. As he put it later, "I had a feeling that there were many effective people among those observers, people who could relate to a number of leaders in the yard, and I had a feeling we had to try because if we went in, there would be a loss of life and this was what I was trying to avoid."[4]

By the time Wicker arrived in the Stewards' Room late in the afternoon of Friday, September 10, the observer group was largely assembled, although not many of them—certainly not Tom Wicker—understood then or later the extent to which in Oswald's mind it now was *up to them* to arrange a settlement and prevent bloodshed. Whatever Oswald thought, his view of the observers as negotiators had not been made clear to most of them; in fact, what their role was to be was the subject of heated conversations in the Stewards' Room, as Oswald briefed Wicker on what had happened so far.

The room where the observers had gathered was long and narrow, crowded with four desks and chairs and other pieces of nondescript office furniture. There was a typewriter on one desk, a telephone on another; incongruously, in these sterile official surroundings, a cheap print of what looked like a Renoir blond at a piano clung to one wall, a still life to another. The only other art was a photo of a New York state prison camp, looking cheerfully woodsy in comparison to the walled fortress Wicker had just entered. Four windows looked out over prison scenery, two of them affording a splendid view along the inner side of the forbidding wall. The Stewards' Room, Wicker gathered, had been a sort of duty room for prison officials in calmer days; that afternoon it was crowded and noisy, blue with tobacco smoke, and it remained so for most of four days in which Wicker came to know its every corner.

There at his arrival was a varied group of officials, observers, legislators, some of whom did not return after their first day at Attica. Later, others joined the group. Some of them left, too. Some who left ultimately came back, and some of those departed again. It was never possible to predict, for that reason, who might turn up in the Stewards' Room at any time, or to be precisely sure who had been there at a particular moment.*

Wicker was met by Arthur Eve, a stocky, affable man who thanked him for coming. Lewis Steel, Ministers Scott and Chandler, and James Emery, all of whom had been in D-yard already, were there. Steel—young, a bit dour, with something independent, almost aloof, seeming to set him apart—made a strong, immediate impression on Wicker. Herman Schwartz, whom he knew by reputation, was meeting another invited observer, the radical lawyer William Kunstler, at the Buffalo airport.

With the help of the governor's office, Oswald had expanded the observers far beyond those originally invited by the inmates. Of that original group, Clarence Jones—a tall young man with a mustache, formerly an aide to Martin Luther King, now an affluent Harlem businessman and publisher of the *Amsterdam News*—was on hand, as were Richard Roth, a lanky Buffalo reporter, and David Anderson of the Rochester Urban League.

In an effort to find Minister Farrakhan—who never was located that weekend—the governor's office had sought the aid of another former aide to King, the Reverend Wyatt Tee Walker of Yonkers. Walker, by then an adviser to Rockefeller on urban affairs, had come to Attica himself. At Oswald's urging, the governor's office also had invited Representative Herman Badillo of the Bronx, a former New York City

---

* For a comprehensive list of men who at one time or another took part in the observers' deliberations, in and out of D-yard, see Appendix Three.

mayoral candidate who had helped settle the uprisings in the city's jails
in 1970. Badillo, readily enlisting, had brought along in the state plane
that flew him to Attica both Walker and Jones, as well as State Senator
Robert Garcia of the Bronx and Alfredo Mathew, a fiery and controversial Puerto Rican who was principal of Community School District
No. 3 in Manhattan.

All were in the Stewards' Room when Wicker arrived, as was State
Senator John Dunne of Garden City, the patrician-looking Republican
chairman of the Joint Legislative Committee on Crime and Correction,
and State Senator Thomas F. McGowan, a former Buffalo policeman
and prosecutor. Either then or later, Republican Assemblymen Frank
Walkley of Allegany and Wyoming (the county in which Attica is
located) and Clark Wemple of Schenectady were much with the
group.

Wicker spoke to Badillo, whom he knew, was introduced to Jones
and Garcia, and began listening to the talk. It struck him at once that
no one was really in charge. He had learned long since that it was not
for nothing that parliamentary procedure had been devised. And he
drew the immediate conclusion that the group was too large—although
it was to be larger. But surely, he thought, organization would evolve;
that was the law of life.

As near as Wicker could gather, Oswald had already gone through
the Fifteen Practical Proposals, responding as best he could. It was easy
enough to promise loose generalities like "religious freedom" and to
"modernize" the inmate education system; but the minimum wage
(then $1.60 per hour) for inmates who were ordinarily paid an average
of about 25 cents a day obviously was a matter the state legislature
would have to decide, with considerable help from the voters.

Even so, one of the men who was in and out of the Stewards' Room
that afternoon thought Oswald already was going much too far in
making concessions to the inmates. Superintendent Vincent R. Mancusi, with his thin, ascetic mouth and his grim face, was not amused, in
any case, by the fact that Oswald had mostly superseded him in overall
command at Attica; and he looked sourly upon the outside observers
being imported into an institution he tended to regard as "his"—or at
least as belonging to the corrections bureaucracy through which he
had laboriously inched his way upward. The outsiders did not seem to
Mancusi to be much concerned with the fate of his guards being held
hostage in D-yard, and he was irritated that the discussion was concentrated on inmate complaints about the things wrong with "his" institution.

"The various demands were read off," he grumbled later, "and
Commissioner Oswald was saying yes, yes, yes, and I was sitting there
wondering how I could run the institution after this with those

demands having been granted."[5] Mancusi, was not, however, without his sentimentalities; some of the observers were amazed to hear him declare that he could not understand why the inmates had gone on such a rampage. Why, he wondered out loud, would they try to tear up and burn down what was, after all, "their home"?

Clarence Jones, who struck Wicker as the most forceful of the observer group, argued vehemently that he would not enter D-yard as the bearer of mixed and inconclusive tidings resulting from Oswald's "yes, yes, yes" and an occasional "no." To do so, he and Eve agreed, would cast the observer group as messenger boys for the state authorities, in which role they could have little or no influence with the inmates.

Besides, someone else said, the injunction fiasco suggested a deeper problem than the Fifteen Proposals—criminal amnesty for the revolting inmates (not for their original crimes but for any that might have been committed in the uprising).

"That's right," Lewis Steel said. "Let's don't kid ourselves here." He had a somewhat scornful manner. As a lawyer who had represented many prison inmates and often visited them, he knew more of life within the walls than most of the group; as an assertive political radical, a "movement lawyer," he never had had much confidence in the good will or the integrity of state authorities, let alone the corrections bureaucracy or the Attica administration.

"The issue here is amnesty," Steel went on. "Those guys in there know what happened after Auburn. They know inmates were indicted that time for everything the prosecution could think of, even stealing a guard's keys. Lots of them are probably due out pretty soon. They've got jailhouse lawyers. They know there could be charges up to kidnapping, and if that guard dies [a reference to William Quinn, the keeper of the gates at Times Square who was then in serious condition in a hospital at Rochester] there's a murder rap for somebody. Maybe for a lot of them. Those guys have to get amnesty. If they can't get it, there won't be any negotiated settlement."

The discussion shifted to amnesty. What *were* the possibilites? Oswald was asked.

"I've already pledged no administrative reprisals," the commissioner said. "I consented to the injunction, you know that. That's all I can do. Criminal amnesty is up to the District Attorney of Wyoming County."

He did not know, he said, what the D.A.'s attitude was. Urged on by Badillo, Jones, and others, Oswald then went to the single phone in the Stewards' Room and asked the prison switchboard to put him through to Louis James, the Wyoming D.A., who lived half an hour away in the county-seat town of Warsaw. While the telephone conversation was going on, Badillo went over with Wicker the Fifteen Practical Proposals and Oswald's attitudes—basically generous—toward them. But it was quickly apparent to Wicker that most of the fifteen did not offer serious difficulties. They were, on the one hand, susceptible to quick action by the authorities; and, on the other, they were not the kinds of demands the inmates were likely to hold out for at all costs.

"We ought to be able to pull something together out of all that," he told Badillo. "But Steel makes sense. I think amnesty is going to be the real issue here."

"Maybe not," Badillo said. "We didn't have to promise amnesty to settle the Queens jail riot."

Just then, Oswald put down the phone. The room fell silent.

"District Attorney James says he doesn't have the authority to grant criminal amnesty," the commissioner said. "If he did, he wouldn't do it. So there's not going to be any amnesty, gentlemen. Absolutely not."

That seemed final enough—and to Tom Wicker, all too ominous. Steel's argument had made a profound impression on him. It had logic, it rang true. From that point, Wicker never wavered in his personal belief that amnesty was the central question. Unless an acceptable answer to that problem could be found, he believed, nothing else would make much difference.

But Wicker did not despair. Like most of the others then in the Stewards' Room, he was a middle-class product of a system he regarded as fundamentally rational. He took it for granted that no one wanted the irrationality of bloodshed and death, and that all concerned would accept that irrationality not even as a last resort—which implied some degree of acceptability—but only if it became literally unavoidable by anything men could do. Surely, he thought, starting from Louis James' "absolutely not," reasonable men could find a formula that would, for all practical purposes, mean something close to amnesty without men like James and Oswald having to admit that it *was* amnesty.

Wicker's supposition was the natural outgrowth of a life spent largely in the observance of public affairs, where the highest premium is always on the ability to "work something out," to "find a formula" for compromise. These things could always be done. Wicker knew that, if he knew nothing else—he had, in fact, first had that wisdom imparted to him by none other than Lyndon Baines Johnson when Wicker had been a young Southern reporter in Washington in 1957. He had caught Johnson's eye with his coverage of the first civil rights act, the compromise formulas for which were then being worked out by Majority Leader Johnson, who was not reluctant to tell an awed young reporter how it was done. But not fully understanding what was happening at Attica, Wicker was not allowing for the fact that difficult matters can be worked out, and compromise formulas found, *only* when all forces in a rational procedure work toward that end. He had not yet seen, as Herman Schwartz had, that the novel process in which they were involved could be scarcely rational at all, either on the part of the state or on the part of the inmates—rational, that is, in the sense that each side could pursue its interest coldly, rather than yielding to passions, prejudices, fear, and hatred.

By the time Russell Oswald announced the results of his call to Louis James, the sun was far down toward the low hills that rolled away from Attica. Many of the observer group were tired of waiting for late arrivals, of the aimless talk in the Stewards' Room; so even though there was no clear agreement on the role of the observers and no specific mission at that time for them to perform, a group decision was reached to enter the yard. (To say that this decision was "taken" or "voted" would be to attribute too much order to a basically shapeless group.) Newcomers were anxious to get a sense of the men and the situation they were dealing with. Eve and other early veterans of D-yard thought it was necessary to let the inmates know that the ob-server group was assembling and about ready for whatever it could do.

Wicker was of mixed feelings. He was intensely curious about D-yard and the men barricaded there. On the other hand, as the moment approached to go unguarded among them—as, for instance, a prison official went solemnly about the room collecting the wallets and wrist watches of those who were going in—his earlier bravado disappeared. He was not afraid so much as uneasy. People do not lightly go into the unknown or put themselves outside the accustomed avenues of appeal. So, as men will in such situations, Wicker began whistling past the graveyard; to Jones and Badillo he got off a few quips, and laughed a bit too loudly at theirs.

In the second floor lobby, they lined up two by two, so that a prison official, Captain Ernest Montanye,[6] could list the names of those going in; he explained jovially that the authorities wanted to make sure everyone came out. The procession moved down the stairs to the main lobby, where Captain Williams and the numerous other men standing around gazed at the observers impassively. It was a gaze with which Wicker became all too briefly familiar, for as the double line moved along the narrow corridor from the lobby of the administration build-ing past two barred gates opened for them into the No Man's Land area on the lower level of A-block, he saw it on the face of every guard and trooper he passed—a gaze not so much of hostility (that came later) as of rigid indifference.

These observers—black, Puerto Rican, probably liberal—these out-siders, city men in civilian clothes, without guns or clubs, seemed to excite no interest in the armed and helmeted forces of law and order. It was as if they took for granted that the observers could not make any difference—that they were only a formality to be gotten through, one more time-consuming nicety, like warning an arrested man of his rights, before the inevitable business at hand could be attended to by armed and empowered patriots, as it had to be, as it should have been at once.

At No Man's Land, there was a pause as inmate representatives were summoned to the iron-barred gates. Wicker looked around and once again was struck by the number of weapons on hand. Perhaps a dozen or so troopers and corrections officers were in the immediate vicinity, some on a catwalk above their heads. In the confined space of the corridor—another crossed it and led off right and left—with its con-crete floors, iron bars and steps, its pitiless overhead lights, the troopers in their jackboots and helmets seemed larger and more threatening than life. As had the deputies at the roadblock, each carried sidearms, club, heavy flashlight, a rifle or a shotgun. The echoes of their steps rang heavily through the corridor, and they looked with iron indiffer-ence at the observers. Wicker was in shirtsleeves, having shed jacket and tie in the Stewards' Room; but he felt that it would not have mattered had he been in black tie or Buddhist robes. Without guns or boots, he did not signify at No Man's Land.

Two inmates appeared on the other side of the A-block gate to take charge of the observers. Two by two, the group passed through the open gateway into the passageway where the uprising had started—out of the embrace of the state into the hands of the inmates who had revolted against the state. The observers, Herman Badillo later wrote, were "crossing a frontier like that between two foreign countries."[7] Wicker was acutely conscious, as he crossed No Man's Land and entered the passageway, that he was leaving behind the arrangements and instruments by which his civilization undertook to guarantee him order and safety—the law with its regulations, officers, and guns. At the moment he stepped from under their protection, he realized not only how much he ordinarily assumed their presence without ac-knowledging or even recognizing it, but also how much, even in a civilization, law seemed to assume, in the same unspoken manner, its dependence, at bottom, upon guns.

Broken glass crunched under the observers' feet. In the air, there was the smell of burned wood and what Wicker thought was a faint whiff of tear gas—a stinging odor he knew from Chicago in 1968 and from the "Martin Luther King riots" in Washington. Far down the corridor there was a makeshift barricade of mattresses, tables, chairs;

behind it were several inmates with their faces masked in various ways, all holding baseball bats or other kinds of clubs.

The observers' footsteps echoed loudly in the low-ceilinged passageway. On either side of it at intervals of a few feet, inmates stood in rank. Some were masked—there were towels with eyeholes, sweatshirts wrapped around heads, again with eyeholes, handkerchiefs and other cloths over the lower part of the face, even what appeared to be a woman's stocking pulled over one inmate's head. But some of the men's faces were unmasked, too, and Wicker thought they were strikingly different from the carefully expressionless faces of the lawmen. Almost all were black and Puerto Rican faces; most were smiling, or at least welcoming. "Right on, brothers!" someone said, and it was taken up as a refrain and echoed with the observers' footsteps in the long corridor: "Right on, brothers!"

The barricade forced the observer group to bear right through the door into A-yard—the very door that Lieutenant Robert Curtiss had ordered locked 35 hours earlier, to force Five Company back to A-block. Hard by that door, the first blow of the actual uprising had felled Curtiss; and, as the observers passed through it and down several steps to A-yard, the signs of the ensuing violence were all about. An observation point from which guards had once looked over the yard was to the right of the door and steps; it was burned out and on a counter under its window a plate of someone's uneaten breakfast remained.

More masked and unmasked inmates awaited the observers in A-yard—far across which, near the cell block beyond it, a handball backboard rose incongruously, a sign of other times. The observers were led at roughly a 45 degree angle across A-yard toward another passageway and door. There they were halted. A stocky and imposing inmate with a bull neck and massive features seemed to be in charge. He wore a wool cap and a blanket cut as a poncho. In the late September afternoon, it had grown a little chilly, although Wicker wondered if the blanket might not be more costume than necessity.

"Side by side," the bull-necked man called out in a voice of command. "Two by two." Then, in a softer voice, "Nobody gets hurt. We give our word on that." Wicker was glad to hear it. He took heart also from the elaborate system of "counting off" the inmates went through in order to establish exactly how many observers were going in. "Got to make sure you all come out," the bull-necked man said, and Wicker was glad to hear that, too.

Finally, the count was relayed to a group of inmates on the walkway that ran along the roof of one of the passageways that intersected at Times Square. On the walkway above the passageway through which the observers already had marched, another rough barricade had been built at about the same point as the one in the passageway itself. The sun had gone down but it was not yet dark. In the windows of A-block, rising massively behind them, no one was to be seen, although Wicker thought he caught a glimpse of troopers' helmets on its roof. He was moving farther all the time from the assurances of the society he had known.

As if to dramatize how far he and the others were being asked to venture into territory unknown to them, the inmates had arranged still another count-off point. In order to pass into D-yard from A-yard, the observers would have to pass across a passageway similar but running at a right angle to the one they had just left. On the walkway atop this second passageway inmates lounged against a railing and called down jovially to the observers:

"Y'all come on in here with us, brothers, this the place to be. . . ."

"Hey, white man! You in the right place now."

"Right on, brothers! Power to the people!"

"Look at dat one. . . . Man, he look like he been here before!"

The bull-necked man explained that "for security reasons" (already the inmate leaders had picked up bureaucratic jargon, Wicker noticed ruefully) the observers would pass across the passageway by twos. When the door opened into A-yard, the first pair would go through, the door would close behind them, and they would cross the passage-way, then be let out another door into D-yard. After that, another two would be let through. Wicker, whose partner was Clarence Jones, watched with apprehension as the first couple—Eve was one of them—disappeared behind the heavy door. Most of the rebels, it seemed to him, were black, and so he was unashamedly glad to be teamed with Jones. Even so, as their turn arrived and the door swung open, Wicker wondered fearfully whether they would be seized and bound, maybe knifed or beaten, the moment that ominous door swung behind them.

As he and Jones started up the steps, he thought to himself what he often thought, with resignation, during airplane takeoffs: *Well, there's nothing I can do about it now.* He could have balked, of course, turned back at the last minute; presumably in A-yard he was overlooked by enough state troopers to prevent his being held. But that was only theoretically possible. He knew he would walk into that passageway, even if it meant seizure and death, because if he broke and ran he would even more certainly be destroyed, not necessarily in other men's eyes, but in his own. So he went steadily up the steps, through the doorway. *There's nothing I can do about it now,* he thought.

It was almost completely dark in the passageway and Wicker had the fleeting impression of candlelight and of dark and shadowy forms packed on either side of him. There was no shouting but a few low voices repeating the familiar refrain *right on, brothers!* A few steps ahead, the door to D-yard was opening. At that moment, Wicker caught a glimpse—no more than that—of a white inmate, the first he had seen, who was manning the door. There was a tattoo on his arm. The man did not look directly at him, but in the weak, yellow light, like that in a medieval painting, there was something—so it seemed to Wicker in his nervousness—hard and desperate about the white face, the tattooed arm, the rigid intensity with which the man's body seemed to be charged, as if he were about to spring from the darkness and strike right through the mask of affluence and ease and order that shielded the faces of men like Tom Wicker from the hardest weathers of human existence.

That glimpsed face was white in the surrounding darkness; that sensed intensity knew no race, no color. It was the barely restrained force of the others, those on the underside of life. Here they had taken power; here he was in their power. Perhaps, he thought, that had always been possible, if he or they had known it.

He and Jones went down the steps into D-yard.

Wicker's first impression was of masses of men—silent, packed together, waiting. The front rank was the inmate "security team"—a long curving human chain whose members stood with locked arms, each man facing in the opposite direction from those on either side of him. Behind this effective barricade, the other inmates seemed to be pressed closely, to get a good look at these outsiders entering their territory. A high proportion of those in D-yard probably had little interest in the observers, but to Tom Wicker, that September evening, there seemed to be thousands pressing against the security chain, all staring at him.

The chain curved away to the right of the door in the passageway and guided the observers in a long swing toward the center of the high wall of what he came to know as D-block. As he walked, Wicker studied the faces of those in the chain and those he could see behind them as closely as he fancied they studied him. In the fading light, they did not seem to be unfriendly faces; some of them were smiling and the few shouts that came from the crowd sounded cheerful enough.

They were all around him—blacks, many obviously Puerto Rican, a good number of whites. He could have touched hundreds of them as he and Jones walked along the human chain. He felt himself in their power. Yet, they seemed far away, too, because they were on the underside and he was not. That made a long distance between them, a gap across which he wondered if he could ever reach—a gap not so much between losers and winners, fortunate and ill-starred, or even rich and poor as between native and foreigner. Across that gap, they eyed one another without hostility, but without much understanding, either. Perhaps it could go either way. But Wicker had no more time to think about that as he and Jones approached the brick facade of D-block, or to reflect upon who—he or they—was native and who, foreigner.

At the foot of the brick wall with its regular ranks of barred windows, a number of long tables had been pulled together. At the end nearest A-yard, a rooflike structure had been thrown up, and under this what appeared to be a secretariat was at work. Wicker noticed in particular a white youth with a thin, sensitive face, looking little more than of schoolboy age, who was pecking away at a typewriter—for what purpose, Wicker never learned. A group of inmates, nearly all black, stood and sat behind the tables. As the observers arrived, these inmates—obviously some kind of leadership group—offered their hands and generally friendly greetings. A tall, handsome black wearing spectacles, with bitter lines at his eyes, unsmiling, put out his hand to Wicker.

"Who're you?" he asked bluntly, not volunteering his own name.

"Tom Wicker."

"*The New York Times,*" the inmate said, still not smiling. "Imagine meeting you here."

Wicker retreated swiftly into cliché. "How's it going?"

"You tell me, man. This ain't shit in here."

He had not risen, nor had the bitter lines of his face changed. Despite the "ain't shit" his accent was not of the ghetto. Wicker sat down across from him, intensely self-conscious. He wanted to continue the conversation but he did not know how; and before he could think of anything to say, his and everyone's attention turned to a broad-shouldered inmate who seemed to be acting as master of ceremonies.

Holding a microphone that once had been used by the prison band— the amplification system seemed to carry easily through the yard—he was calling for attention. "Brothers!" he shouted in a strong, slightly husky, faintly accented voice. "The world is hearing us! The world is seeing our struggle! And here's the proof before your eyes!" He swept an arm grandly from under a blanket cut poncho-style and indicated the observers gathered at the table. "Look at these men from all over this country coming here at our call, brothers, coming here to witness firsthand the struggle against racist oppression and brutalization. We got to show them so they can tell the world what goes on behind these walls!"

"Right on, Brother Herb!" someone shouted from the crowd, and there was sudden cheering. Other voices called:

"You tell 'em, brother!"

"The truth, Brother Herb, the truth!"

"You know it, man, you tell it!"

Brother Herb was ready. "Now, brothers, dig where I'm comin' from." The inmates had to show the observers how well the hostages were being treated, Brother Herb declared, holding the yard in nearly absolute quiet. The brothers wanted the observers to see the difference between the way the pig ran the prison and the way the brothers took care of the pig. And they wanted the world to know that *they* would no longer submit to being treated like animals instead of men.

The inmates—"You, brothers!"—had been made the scapegoats of a rich white society, Brother Herb told them in crude but passionate phrases. They had never had a chance to rise in a racist and oppressive America, and when they had refused to yield to slavery and brutality or had reached out for what they rightfully considered their share, society had locked them up, the prison being no more than the actual representation of the life they were forced to lead even on the outside. But all over the world, Brother Herb assured his rapt audience, the downtrodden and the oppressed were listening to the words of Attica, taking heart from them, beginning to cast off their chains, lift up their heads.

"And we are the vanguard!" Brother Herb roared. Then he waited for the cheering to rise wildly and fall again. "We are standing here for all the oppressed peoples of the world, and we are not gonna give up or knuckle under, we gonna show the way! For we *have* the way!"

Wicker was a Southerner who responded to eloquence. He understood right away that Brother Herb was a great orator, and why. Herb was a man who could stir his audience—not just its black members, either, Wicker had noticed—as easily as if they had been children at a puppet show, because in his imperfect but passionate rhetoric, as in their hearts, there was the same bitterness and welling rage. In him, the stored emotions of the voiceless found a voice. Whatever his exaggeration, Brother Herb was a man who, being of them, spoke genuinely for the disadvantaged and the left-behind, the frustrated, the angry, and the alienated. He was a man who spoke with the cutting edge of an essential truth that his hearers knew from their lives to be a truth.

A Virgin Islander, Herbert Blyden had been reared under the loose care of an aunt among (as he later wrote) "thirteen cousins in one household where you either fish or cut bait. My upbringing was violent to say the least. . . . After reaching my teens I was ready for making it in any jungle, be it Harlem or Vietnam." Sent to a boys' training school at 13, he fathered a child at 15, and was sent away for four years while still a teenager for cashing forged money orders. He came out already proclaiming the injustice of prison life, but soon was sent back for five years after agreeing to plead guilty to an attempted minor robbery. After that, federal job training did not remove the familiar disability of even the well-intentioned ex-con; for some jobs he could not be hired by law, and most others were denied to him by employers who did not want to hire former inmates. In 1971, Blyden was serving time at Attica on a charge of armed robbery—he steadfastly denied being guilty—and was also awaiting trial for having participated in the Tombs riot in New York.

"I was violent at birth because the sign foretold the coming of a rebel lion—Leo," he wrote. "But Attica and the Tombs are situations which developed as a result of the lack of concern for people like me, not *when* we are incarcerated but before we are put away. . . . The time for change is now. . . . Study the history of the Lion and you will get the message!"[8]

After bringing the D-yard brothers to a cheering pitch, Brother Herb closed gently, "And now we gonna meet these brothers from the outside. . . . We gonna let these brothers that's here to help us introduce themselves."

One by one the observers stood up, gave their names and titles. The inmates cheered each one politely. By far the biggest ovation went to John Dunne. Republican suburbanite though he was, he made himself a favorite with many inmates by his repeated inspection trips to state prisons and by indefatigable legislative work on their behalf. Wicker drew moderate applause and was vaguely pleased. But he realized that, through Brother Herb's oratory and the obviously hopeful welcome the inmates were giving the observers, not only had his fears started to fade, but he was beginning to feel certain emotional links to men who had seemed so far removed. It was a puzzling, sobering thought— puzzling, because whatever the conditions in the prison and the world, and despite Brother Herb's talk of revolution, most of the men in the yard, by any recognized definition, were not political prisoners but hardened criminals; sobering, because the effectiveness of any role Wicker might play as an observer would be hindered if he became a partisan of one side or the other.

While the introductions were going on, Jones, Eve, and others had made it clear at the leadership table that the observers were in the yard mainly to make their presence known, to get a feel for the situation, and to check on the hostages—not to get down to the questions of inmate demands or the authorities' response. This did not please Roger Champen, Richard Clark, and others at the leadership table; but they accepted it and urged new efforts to bring in William Kunstler and Bobby Seale, in particular.

It was not then fully apparent to Wicker how much the inmate leaders had accomplished in bringing rudimentary order and discipline to D-yard. Rules had been established and enforced—for instance, that no inmate could go through the mess lines twice until everyone had been through once. The leaders had had latrines dug since water had been cut off from the few D-yard toilets. Mattresses and sheets had been distributed to most of those in the yard—and to all the hostages. Even a postal system of sorts had been set up to try to get out mail to the inmates' families. An effective, racially integrated security force, that at one time or another included more than 300 men, had been organized. Walter "Tiny" Swift, a life inmate who had been convicted of murder and who was a prison-hospital nurse, had set up a medical aid station that functioned throughout the revolt. At one point, Champen and Swift had even dealt with an inmate who went into catatonic shock. "He froze up as stiff as a board and we picked him up and it was like picking up a piece of carpentry." They provided a tent for the man in shock which became known as the "mental ward."[9]

The bull-necked inmate who had marshalled the observers into the yard had been redeploying the arm-linked men of the security chain. Now they curved away from the leadership table toward the far wall of D-yard, opening a guarded path from the leadership table to the area where the hostages were being held. Champ, perhaps the tallest man in the yard, had taken the microphone, and as Wicker and the other observers moved slowly along the security chain—they were going away from the leadership table and more deeply into the mass of inmates—Champ began to exhibit his own kind of oratorical skill.

Before the revolt, Champ and Herbert Blyden had never met— although Blyden once had been impressed when, after coming with a football team from another block to D-yard, he had listened from the rear to one of Champ's law lectures. When they found themselves on the leadership committee for the rebelling inmates, they recognized in each other "the ability to lead," although Blyden was more "political" and "aggressive" than Champen. The latter particularly admired Blyden's ability to "get across his position clearly."[10]

Champ was not at all an impassioned rabble-rouser like Brother Herb but was nevertheless a fluent speaker who seemed to keep the crowd's attention at difficult moments. As the observers approached the hostages, he kept up a low-pitched monologue about what great treatment they were receiving—"better'n we ever got from *them*. That right, brothers?"

Champ's voice had a curious, calming quality for which Wicker was grateful as he gazed into the faces—some smiling, some wary and suspicious, most impassive—of the inmates beyond the security chain. He was struck once again by the different world into which he had come. Out there, beyond the walls, everything seemed familiar, organized, its terrors and threats largely avoidable, or at least definable. In D-yard, despite the rudimentary order the inmates had imposed on themselves, all was strange, without dependable foundation; the *possibilities* of terror and pain and fear seemed infinite, unavoidable.

Not far from the center of D-yard—near a concrete handball backboard like the one they had seen in A-yard—the observers found the circle of hostages. A ring of wooden benches formed a perimeter around them, and on or by it stood a number of inmate guards, all with towels or blankets hiding their faces. They were black Muslims, but Wicker never learned whether their heavy masking had anything to do with their religion or whether the job of guarding the hostages was considered particularly vulnerable to legal reprisal. The Muslims had taken over the assignment to protect the hostages from less disciplined inmates; and even the hostages later agreed that they had done a good piece of work.

"They livin' better'n we do," Champ said of the hostages. "Got blankets, got cigarettes, got mattresses, candy bars, medical treatment. Never had it so good, I bet. Leastways, we never did. That right, Cap'n? That right, Lootent? You ever had it so good's you got it here? You ever give us the breaks we give you? Man, you ain't dead, you alive, you got a mattress to sleep on, but the way *you* treat *us*, we wa'n't shit. Jus' hardly livin' at all."

The hostages stared dully at Wicker and the other observers. His first thought was to count them, but some were moving about within the ring of benches and it was impossible. Then he realized that, anyway, he was only trying to avoid facing them and their predicament. If *he* felt alone, a stranger in a dark and unknown place, what must *they* feel, total captives as they were of men who were beyond the law? He realized, with a shock almost physical, making his knees give a little, that some or all of these men might die—tonight, tomorrow, the next day. And it did not lessen his horror to know that all men die "soon or late," because all men do not die by violence and decree. There would be no dignity or decency for these poor hulks huddled together against the gathering darkness, under the rough planking that had been erected to give them a partial shield from the sun. There would be nothing but terror and pain and the degradation of animals in a slaughter pen.

Wicker forced himself to look at the hostage nearest him. "You fellows . . . uh . . . all right?" he finally said. The hostage stared at him with blank eyes, an unmoving face. He had closely clipped hair, a two-day stubble of beard, a blanket cut like a poncho. He looked too fat to be a prisoner, Wicker thought irrelevantly.

"Anything we can do?" he said, ashamed of the banality of the words and thought. Around the circle, other observers were speaking to or staring at the hostages, who sat or stood, lumpish and silent in their gray prison garb. Some were answering monosyllabically. Several had bandaged heads, and Wicker saw one with an arm in a sling—mute testimony to Thursday's eruption of violence. But as nearly as he could tell, all seemed in reasonably good condition.

"We'll . . . uh . . . try to get you out of here. Soon as possible," Wicker said to the fat hostage. "I mean as soon as we can." The man's face did not change nor his eyes blink. It was a relief to walk away from the silent circle, the huddled men.

I know what our mission is, Wicker was thinking. *Now I know. . . .*

". . . Naw, man, you can't take no pictures of hostages," Champ was saying in his endless, amiable monologue. "Hostages don't want no pictures taken, we don't want no pictures taken, aint gonna be no pictures taken." Wicker could not see who wanted pictures, but it must have been one of the "pool" of reporters and photographers who had been allowed to follow the observers into D-yard. Then someone must have remonstrated further with Champ.

"Well, we'll take a vote," Champ said, his voice on the speaker system unchanged, calm, conversational. "We got a real democracy here, we'll take a vote on the pictures. Can't say that's not fair. Now everybody that thinks there ought to be pictures of the hostages, everybody thinks that . . . you lis'nin' to me, brothers, you hearin' me? Everybody thinks there ought to be pictures say 'Aye'." And the ayes came back strongly. "Now everybody don't want no hostage pictures taken, this here's the time to vote 'no'." There were a few scattered noes and Champ went right on. "So we gonna have pictures after all but anyone don't want his picture taken, just turn his back. Just turn his back, that's all he got to do. . . ."

Wicker took a quick look over his shoulder. A number of the hostages were turning to face into the circle, and he knew he would have, too. He would not have wished anyone who loved him or even knew him to have seen him in the death pen, able only to wait his turn.

As he returned to the vicinity of the leadership table, Wicker spotted the heavy-set Brother Herb standing alone—a little wistfully, Wicker thought, as if he wanted the microphone back.

After facing the silent ring of hostages, Wicker was eager to talk, touch someone, sense the quickness of life. Besides, he had not yet had much chance to talk to any of the inmates. He approached Herb, trying to look friendly.

"That was a hell of a speech you made, Brother Herb. Mind if I ask your full name?"

Brother Herb looked at him haughtily. "I am Attica," he said, and moved with dignity into the crowd.

The observer group left D-yard as it had arrived, marching two by two, amid much counting off and shouts of "Right on!" and "Tell it like it is, brothers!" They had been in the yard barely thirty minutes but as Wicker hastened across the dark passageway exit from D-yard, then crossed A-yard toward No Man's Land, it seemed to him that it had been hours.

When they passed through the iron gates that frowning guards held open for them, back into the civilized world, Wicker was at once conscious of the troopers and the guns. They were all about in the clanging steel and concrete, on which the heels of heavy boots rang out like shots in the night. He knew the troopers were on "his side," the representatives of society, clad and armed for society's work. He knew the guns were his protection, the symbol and instrument of that enforced order the absence of which had made D-yard a place of such uncertain terrors.

Yet, the troopers and the guns did not reassure him. He could sense (perhaps it was anticipation) the growing if controlled hostility of the troopers—as if it was dawning on them that it was unseemly, indecent for good Americans to deal as equals with thieves and rapists and addicts, blacks at that. So perhaps the men doing it were *not* good Americans. As for the guns—guns dealt in death, and death was not what Tom Wicker was at Attica to abet. He had realized that in the moment he turned away from the hostages. *Nobody gets killed.* That was his goal, but the troopers' guns dealt in death.

Wicker stopped before one of them, a tall man lounging against a wall, pistol and club at his belt, a rifle slanting downward across his body.

"Pretty rough in there," Wicker said.

"Huh," the trooper said, his face wrinkling. "I had my say, I'd make it rough."

"Let's move it along," somebody said. "Let's get these gates locked."

Wicker went down the ringing corridor, sensing the trooper watching his back, still aware of the overwhelming presence of the guns. Herman Badillo walked beside him.

"Funny thing," the congressman said. "I get the feeling they liked us better in there than they do out here."

Inmate security guards waiting in "D.M.Z." to meet with State officials.
(*Wide World*)

Foreground, "Times Square," the intersection of tunnels and catwalks; background, rebelling inmates in D-yard.

(*Wide World*)

Inmate negotiating committee with Commissioner Russell G. Oswald in D-yard, Thursday, September 9. Sitting (elbows on table, wristwatch) is Richard Clark. Half rising is Carl El Jones. Standing: (behind Jones) Herbert Blyden, Frank "Big Black" Smith, Roger Champen, L. D. Barkley, and unknown inmate who has broken into the negotiations.

(*Wide World*)

Commissioner Russell G. Oswald leaving D-Yard after hearing inmate demands, Thursday, September 9, led by Richard Clark, and followed by an unidentified man, Herman Schwartz, Arthur Eve (in striped shirt), and two inmate guards.   (UPI)

Hostages in D-yard.   (WGR-TV News, Buffalo, N.Y.)

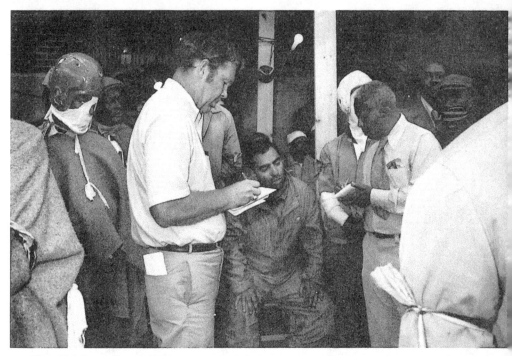

Tom Wicker, left, and Dick Edwards, right, interviewing hostage Frank Strollo, Sunday, September 12.

William Kunstler, Saturday, September 11, telling inmates he will represent them in negotiations with prison officials. Observers, seated in foreground, left to right, Tom Soto, Alfred Mathew, Robert Garcia, Herman Badillo, unidentified, Clarence Jones, Arthur Eve.

Inmates demonstrating their solidarity.
(Wide World)

Tom Wicker interviewing an inmate, Sunday, September 12. Between them is Richard Clark. Extreme left is Rudy Garcia, with Jose Paris in dark glasses and smiling behind him. Behind Paris, also smiling, is Tom Soto.

(Bill Whiting)

Capt. Henry Williams of the New York State
Police, at Attica, Friday, September 10.
(Robert M. Metz)

Jaybarr Kenyatta, outside main gate.
(NY Times / William E. Sauro)

Congressman Herman Badillo, right, and Tom Wicker, waiting for Bobby Seale, Saturday, September 11.

(NY Times / William E. Sauro)

Bobby Seale, left, and associate entering the prison, Saturday evening, September 11.
(NY Times / William E. Sauro)

State police troopers watching negotiations from cellblock roof.

The Mirrors of C-Block

Clarence Jones caught up to Badillo and Wicker in the ground floor lobby of the administration building. "Some of the brothers got the wind up about C-block," he said. He had already picked up the language of D-yard, Wicker noticed; it was another warning signal that all the observers were stepping into identification with the rebel inmates.

"They're getting rumors the guards are tear-gassing the inmates and beating them up, and they want some of us to check it out," Jones said. "You guys want to come?"

Russell Oswald denied the report but authorized the inspection, and Walter Dunbar showed the way. Arthur Eve, John Dunne, Wyatt Tee Walker, Lewis Steel, and Alfredo Mathew went along. In ordinary times, the party could have gone back the way they had come, turned left at Times Square and followed the passageway to C-block. But that route was blocked by the rebellion and Dunbar led them out the front of the administration building and around it to the right, with the great outer wall rising to the left.

It was dark by then but the entrance yard of the prison was garishly floodlit. There were not as many troopers and deputies on hand as there had been in the afternoon, but military preparations still seemed to be going forward, though on a much smaller scale. Near the main gate a hamburger stand put up by a local civic group was doing brisk business among the troopers and deputies. Armed and uniformed men lounged on the grass. The small group of observers went all the way to the outside of C-block, turning right past what Dunbar said was "HBZ" (Housing Block Z, where inmates like Dewar and Lamorie were kept in "the box").

Dunbar proved an amiable guide. A pipe-smoker with a friendly manner, he was, Wicker thought at the time, a more impressive man than the rumpled Oswald. Quick inquiry had disclosed that Dunbar was a professional who had been director of the California Department of Corrections and chairman of the Federal Board of Parole before becoming Oswald's executive deputy. He seemed knowledgeable but not pedantic or calloused, he was friendly and approachable without being effusive, and he seemed genuinely interested in the views of the observers trailing along with him. He immediately conveyed the impression that he was a forward-looking man who would be on the right side if tough questions of life or death had to be answered. Later, Wicker realized that in the bizarre circumstances into which he had stumbled, Dunbar's manner—more that of a college professor than of a lifelong bureaucrat or a former prison guard—had been reassuring but misleading.

As the group walked along the forbidding outer wall of C-block, inmates stood at its barred windows and shouted down at them:

"Get us out of here! Help!"

"We need water!"

"They're starving us. . . ."

"Death to the pig!"

"Need help, brothers . . . help. . . ."

". . . and beating us!"

Some of the inmates rattled metal—perhaps tin cups or forks—against the bars of the windows. That and the continuing shouts put up a furious din that continued until the observer group passed out of sight of the windows and entered C-block.

The entrance hall was a mess. For some reason, pools of water stood on the concrete floor. In one corner there was a box with a few crude sandwiches remaining in it. An open drum full of water stood nearby. Dunbar explained what the group wanted, and corrections officers—with the contained but visible hostility Badillo and Wicker had noticed in the troopers—grudgingly opened a first-floor cell tier. The huge metal door to the tier swung inward with a mighty groan and screech, as if its hinges had not been oiled in decades.

As the horrid sound of metal wrenching on metal echoed down the cell tier, Wicker—who happened to be the first of the observer group through the doorway—saw a small mirror pop out the square window of each of the perhaps twenty solid steel doors that lined either side of the long concrete and steel corridor before him. The sight puzzled him. It struck him first that mirrors, being of glass, were potentially dangerous weapons that ought not be allowed in inmates' hands. Then he saw that the men in the cells had no other way to see who was coming. The small apertures in each of the solid cell doors prevented any one in a cell from looking anywhere but straight across the corridor to the opposite cell with its identical small window. So when shrieking metal signalled the opening of the door to the tier, the only way the men in the cells could see who was approaching them was to look in the mirrors they could hold out through the small openings.

Wicker was literally stopped in his tracks by the spectacle of the mirrors. What he was seeing was not physical brutality, but worse— that a man could not know who was coming unless he had a mirror handy, that he was made to live his life, or a large part of it, behind a blank door with the smallest of openings. With the power of revealed truth, as if a blindfold had been torn from his eyes after years in darkness so that what he first saw would remain as indelibly graven on his brain as if scarred there by light itself, Wicker understood that these men were caged. And he saw in the same instant of blinding truth that to cage a human being was to place the person caged in the condition of a beast in the zoo.

Was there a more degrading and degenerative act one person could inflict upon another? One could kill, but death has more dignity than some kinds of life. One could mutilate, but only the ephemeral body, which could heal itself. A human being could withstand physical brutality, or try to. But to cage a person designated him as less than human, less than a part of mankind—as did the automatic assumption of someone like Tom Wicker that no prison inmate could even be trusted with a mirror, lest it be used as a weapon.

And what did it do to those who kept the cages, that their charges were placed in the condition of beasts? Ultimately, were they not bound to regard those charges as beasts? How could their own humanity withstand that unnatural regard? And all society was the keeper of the caged; the men with clubs were only its agents.

It did not diminish the power of this revelation when Wicker later learned that cells with solid steel doors were preferred by some inmates to the barred variety more familiar to moviegoers, for the good reason that solid doors offered more privacy. When Wicker did learn that, it only told him how desperately humans in cages will seek to retain some vestige of their kidnapped humanity, as the keepers go by outside, tapping their clubs against the imprisoning steel.

Caging men as a means of dealing with the problem of crime is a modern refinement of man's ancient and limitless inhumanity, as well as his vast capacity for self-delusion. Murderers and felons used to be hanged, beheaded, flogged, tortured, broken on the rack, blinded, ridden out of town on a rail, tarred and feathered, or arrayed in the stocks. Nobody pretended that such penalties were anything other than punishment and revenge. Before nineteenth-century American developments, dungeons were mostly for the convenient custody of political prisoners, debtors, and those awaiting trial. American progress, with many another gim "advance," gave the world the penitentiary.

In 1787, Dr. Benjamin Rush read to a small gathering in the Philadelphia home of Benjamin Franklin a paper in which he said that the right way to treat offenders was to cause them to repent of their crimes. Ironically taken up by gentle Quakers, Rush's notion was that offenders should be locked alone in cells, day and night, so that in such awful solitude they would have nothing to do but to ponder their acts, repent, and reform. To this day, the American liberal—progressive— idea persists that there is some way to make people repent and reform. Psychiatry, if not solitude, will provide perfectability.

Three years after Rush proposed it, a single-cellular penitentiary was established in the Walnut Street Jail in Philadelphia. By the 1830s, Pennsylvania had constructed two more state penitentiaries that followed the Philadelphia reform idea. Meanwhile, in New York, where such reforms as the lock-step had been devised, the "Auburn system" evolved from the Pennsylvania program. It provided for individual cells and total silence, but added congregate employment in shops, fields, or quarries during a long, hard working day. Repressive and undeviating routine, unremitting labor, harsh subsistence conditions, and frequent floggings complemented the monastic silence; so did striped uniforms and the great wall around the already secure fortress. The Auburn system became the model for American penitentiaries in most of the states, and the lofty notions of the Philadelphians soon were lost in the spirit expressed by Elam Lynds, the first warden of Sing Sing (built in 1825): "Reformation of the criminal could not possibly be effected until the spirit of the criminal was broken."[1]

The nineteenth-century penitentiary produced more mental breakdowns, suicides, and deaths than repentance. "I believe," wrote Charles Dickens, after visiting such an institution, "that very few men are capable of estimating the immense amount of torture and agony which this dreadful punishment, prolonged for years, inflicts upon the sufferers."[2] Yet, the idea persisted that men could be reformed (now we say "rehabilitated") in such hellholes—a grotesque derivation from the idea that man is not only perfectable but rational enough to determine his behavior through self-interest.

A later underpinning of the nineteenth-century prison was its profitability. The sale and intraprison use of prison-industry products fitted right into the productivity ethic of a growing nation. Convicts, moreover, could be and were in some states rented out like oxen to upright businessmen. Taxpayers were happy, cheap labor was available, and prison officials, busily developing their bureaucracies, saw their institutions entrenched. The American prison system—a design to reform criminals by caging humans—found a permanent place in American society and flourished largely unchanged into the twentieth century. In 1871, a Virginia court put the matter in perspective when it ruled that prisoners were "slaves of the state."

The rise of organized labor put an end to contract-labor, prison-profit practices. And in the twentieth century, prison's most obvious physical brutalities and hardships have been considerably diminished—although as late as 1969, investigators found the Arkansas State Prison a medieval pit of tortures, beatings, and murder. But some new inhumanities also were introduced, in the name of progress. Notable among them was the indeterminate sentence, intended to reward the "reformed" prisoner with a shortened sentence, but in practice posing a new and cruel uncertainty for the inmate, providing guards and administrators another means of harassing and intimidating offenders into being "good prisoners," and removing inmates a long step further from due process and equal application of the laws—concepts largely unknown inside prison walls.

Similarly, organized labor's victory over "slave labor" by prisoners has not been an unmixed blessing. Although inmates are no longer rented out at cheap rates to private employers, the reform movement that put an end to that practice also achieved federal laws that prevent the movement of prisonmade goods in interstate commerce, and state laws that forbid their commercial sale within individual states. Ridding itself of any possibility of cheap prison-labor competition, organized labor also effectively limited the possibilities of prison industry, thus making useful job training for prisoners or productive prison work careers all but impossible. This is a major factor in the idleness, boredom, and futility of prison life, and the inability of so many former inmates to find or keep decent jobs.

And if the Arkansas bestialities were the exception to the general rule of modern prisons, it still cannot be said that prisons today are much different in any other fundamental way from their predecessors of the last century. In fact, 20 prisons from 100 to 158 years old were still in use in 1967, as well as 41 more that were then at least 80 years old.[3] As late as 1961, the centennial year of the Civil War's beginning, James Bennett, then director of the Federal Bureau of Prisons, pointed out that more than a hundred prisons in operation at that time had been built before Grant took Richmond.

The longevity of these old fortresses is not only deplorable but important in itself. Their "durability and inflexibility . . . define and limit the programs that go on within them. The buildings create such barriers to meaningful reform that however correctional policies may evolve, the prisons are not crucibles for new programs or approaches."[4] The old buildings are too expensive to replace, in many instances, and the public and its politicians usually fight prison closings with the tenacity of a mother protecting her children; so the old prisons are only supplemented. And their design is not congenial to any purpose but secure custody of the inmates—if that. Even the total silence that once prevailed remains to some extent a part of prison life today.

Thus, the nineteenth century reaches nearly to the twenty-first in its long and baleful influence on the treatment of offenders in America and in its legacy of self-delusion—the ingrained American idea that society can make better men and women by sending them to prison, by putting them in cages. However idealistic its origins, that delusion has produced a protracted record of senselessness, futility, dishonor, and inhumanity. An observer not half as sharp as Dickens, after the most limited survey of "modern" conditions in these dismal fortresses of repression and fear, would not come to conclusions much more charitable than his of more than a century ago.

As soon as the C-block inmates saw civilian outsiders entering their tier, they all seemed to cry out at once. None had been out of their cells since the day before, none knew much of what was going on in D-yard, most were in a state of nervous excitement. As Wicker would talk to one inmate through the small opening of a door, others clamored for him to talk to them. In the echoing tier with its steel and concrete surfaces, the voices and the clatter were momentarily deafening. Gradually, however, the noise and excitement slackened, and the observers were able to talk to most of the men on the tier.

Wicker's nose and eyes had told him as soon as he entered that there had been no tear gas recently in that confined space. Nor was there evidence of anyone having been beaten, although Cell 23 complained bitterly of hay fever and the inmate next door showed a nasty gash in his shin which needed medical attention. When this cut was called to a guard's attention, he promised without enthusiasm to report it. Conditions were nevertheless far from good. Toilets were not working and some seemed to be clogged or overflowing. Some men complained they had not been fed, contrary to Walter Dunbar's assurances. Most of the cells were untidy and depressingly bare.

One white inmate approached his door furtively when Wicker looked into his cell. He was slight, sallow, shifty-looking.

"Hi," Wicker said, trying to be casual. "What'd they get you for?"

"Drunk driving."

"They put you in *here* for that? How long?"

"Four years." He would not look Wicker in the eyes.

"Four years! For drunk driving?"

"Well . . . repeated offense, see? Listen . . . tell 'em I ain't in this, hear?"

"I guess they can see that."

"They see what they want to see. But you tell 'em, you're a white man, too, you tell 'em Cell 15 got no part of this shit, I ain't lifted a finger and I ain't going to. You tell 'em that."

"I'll tell 'em," Wicker said, not knowing who to tell. He moved on, discomfitted by Cell 15.

He had not expected to find a Holiday Inn in C-block or anything like the comforts of home. Yet, more than the steel doors depressed him about the conditions in which C-block inmates lived. The cells were about six by nine feet—roughly bathroom size in an American house. Each contained a bed, stool, small table, toilet, cold-water sink, a two-drawer metal cabinet, and barely enough floor space for a man to take a step or two. Each cell was lit by one dim bulb suspended naked from the ceiling. The only amenity beyond bare necessity was a set of earphones for the prison radio. Even after the excitement had slackened, the noise level was little short of deafening—as it had to be in a tightly enclosed corridor where everything was concrete and metal. In C-block, even with a window in each cell, men were reduced to the lowest condition of existence, save perhaps only what some endured in "the box."

Not far from Cell 15, Wicker was speared by an impassioned speech demanding that those in C-block be allowed to join "the brothers in D." Wicker tried to explain that the prison authorities wanted to put an end to the revolt and were hardly likely to let more rebels into D-yard. This reasoning made no impression; he was face to face with one of the most peculiar aspects of the Attica uprising. Many of its participants and supporters regarded it less as a power play or an unexpected opportunity (or danger) or even a political act (whether in the cause of prison reform, black power, or social revolution) than as a *proper condition* in itself, of greater validity than the restoration of accustomed authority.

This was manifested, for example, by inmate outrage at the notion that the administration might attempt to "starve out" the men in D-yard. Many inmates seemed to think it was the administration's duty to sustain the revolt—by food, water, medical care, etc.—rather than to end it. And the C-block prisoner seemed to think he had a "right" to join men who also had a "right" to hold D-yard.

Wicker never quite adopted that attitude as some of the other observers did. He could see a possible *need* for the uprising as a protest against conditions, but that was only to say that the state should improve the conditions—which he wholeheartedly believed. Wicker's instinctive, conditioned, middle-class loyalty ran to the state and its institutions, even when his sympathy ran to their victims, because he had a strong belief in the good *intentions* of the state, which he tended to confuse with its people. Whatever the deficiencies of the state's institutions, Wicker brought to Attica a belief in the state's ultimate ability to serve its citizens, if properly and persistently prodded by the people.

In another cell, an overflowing toilet brought an unpleasant phrase out of Wicker's memory—some stricture he could not quite recall on a man who would "shit where he eats." To be forced to shit where he slept, at the head of his bed as it were, was an indignity Wicker resented for the meanest inmate—yet, even as he thought it, he knew that if the idea of prison was accepted *at all* it required such toilet arrangements. You could hardly have the inmates in and out of their cells, back and forth to the urinal, at will. He was seeing more specifically, as he had instinctively when the mirrors popped out from the cages, that the *idea* of prison was wrong.

"Man, this shit ain't had to happen," another white inmate, an intense, voluble young man, muttered conspiratorially through the opening in his cell door. "They listen to some of us, this ain't had to go this way at all."

"What happened?"

"Take Mancusi. We tried to get him the word but he don't listen to nobody. What I mean is, they could see the joint was gonna blow, they don't need nobody to tell 'em *that*, but if they'd listen to some of us, what we wanted was to have this group that'd meet with 'em, see? Tell 'em where the shit was at, what maybe they could do to help things along. I mean like things you got to be in here to *know*, that they can't see for themselves."

"You mean a sort of grievance committee?"

"Like that, yeah. Meet with Mancusi every week or so, clue him in a little, get some things straightened out. Get certain hacks off certain shifts, shit like that. But Mancusi, he don't listen. He don't give a shit for no guys in here. He just wants to run the joint the way he wants to run it."

"Sounds like a good idea you had," Wicker said. "Did you actually try to set it up?"

"Tried to get Mancusi the word. We sent him word. But he never did a thing."

"Maybe I'll get a chance to talk to him about it." Wicker moved on to a cell occupied by a jolly-looking black man, somewhat older than most of the prisoners seemed to be.

"How you doing in here?" Wicker said.

"Fine," the black man said. "I just takin' it easy havin' a ball."

"You weren't in the riot?"

"Man, ain't no shit like that for me." He laughed heartily.

"Okay, then," Wicker said. "What they got you in for?"

"Rape. Nine years."

"Jesus, man. That's a hard way to get it."

The black laughed again. He would have laughed at the Titanic going down. "Not if you like it good enough," he cackled. "Man do anything, he want that stuff bad enough."

"Listen," Clarence Jones said, clutching Wicker's arm. "I found a guy down here's been in this place twenty-seven years."

After a quick inspection of a second tier—again, the flashing mirrors, the overflowing toilets, the clamor and shouting, but still with no odor of gas and no sign of beatings or serious harassment—the small observer group and Dunbar returned to the administration building. From the barred windows of C-block, the inmates shouted and rattled their cups again, but in the open area between the high wall and the brick buildings everything was quiet, almost peaceful—except for the armed men still to be seen.

Wicker handed Jones a piece of paper. As they had trailed out of the first C-block cell tier, a black inmate had slipped it to him, whispering, "Take this to the brothers." The folded note was addressed to "Big Black."

"Look at this," Wicker said. "You see anything wrong with delivering it?" The note seemed ordinary to him, but it did evoke what he took to be the atmosphere of the prison and the attitudes of inmates. In a rather precise, spidery hand—the i's were dotted with small circles—it read:

Brothers:
The situation in C-block is thus: We are lock in, we have requested to be let out in the yard, but that's out. The water situation is very dim, they say a main is busted—I think not! but we have been getten water from the Brothers, from the windows and from the pig, when ever he feels like giving us some.

Brothers please don't give! *This is new for them and they don't know how to react!*

We are ok.

Hold on as long as you can
    Big Black
    Bro. Herb
    Bro. Richie
      Carlos
      and all of you
        Right On!
        Husey/ or Toby

(I've just heard the news on the phones, you are looking very good, keep it together)

Jones handed back the note. "They're a lot more optimistic than I am," he said. "You know, I've been around prisons before, and I guess I've always known it, but going in there just now really made me realize how much an institution like this is a microcosm of the outside society."

"How do you mean?"

"Well, did you see any blacks in there, or any Puerto Ricans? Guards, I mean?"

"None. But a lot of both behind bars."

"That's what I mean. Malcolm X used to tell blacks they were all in prison—that America means prison for blacks."

A civil rights recitation in reply would have been ludicrous. There was nothing Wicker could say about the gains some blacks had made that Jones would not know—gains that Wicker himself knew to be so long overdue, so grudgingly "given" by those who had set and maintained the conditions of American life as to be laughable when cited as reasons why black men ought to have faith in America. To suggest that the educated, well-dressed, obviously affluent Jones was himself a refutation of Malcolm X's bitter dictum was only to make the impolite point—of which Jones would be more sharply aware than any white— that a few prominent exceptions did not change the rule, that it was the white man's world that was the issue, not the few blacks who had pushed or pulled or insinuated themselves onto its periphery. Malcolm X also had pointed out that even in the days of slavery there had been "the field Negro" and "the house Negro"—and that if the latter ate and lived better, he was therefore the more closely dependent on the master's will and whim.

"Mister Dunbar," Wicker said, instead of answering Jones, "how many black guards in this place?"

Dunbar removed his pipe, cleared his throat, and looked interested. "I'll have to check that out. Not many, I'd say, but we've been working on it. These things take time, you know. There's no discrimination, of course. Everybody's eligible, regardless of race, but it's hard to find qualified people." Dunbar was friendly, serious, concerned. He was doing his best, the commissioner was doing his best, everyone was doing his best.

Wicker knew how to answer *that*. He had been hearing it for years and had even said it himself, before he had "integrated" the Washington Bureau of *The Times* by hiring a black copy boy—not, of course, a reporter, because in those days it was hard to find qualified people. But he did not trouble to puncture Dunbar's pretense. His question had been no more than his evasive Southern way of responding to Clarence Jones and Malcolm X—of conceding their point without knowing anything to do or say that would change or answer it.

When the group from C-block joined the other observers in the Stewards' Room, they found several new arrivals—notable among them the famous radical lawyer William Kunstler. Wicker had some reservations about Kunstler's revolutionary reputation, but he knew that reputation would give Kunstler more standing with the inmates in D-yard than any other white observer—even Dunne. Kunstler's name had headed the list of those the inmates had asked to come to Attica. More than the other lawyers on the committee—save perhaps Lew Steel—Kunstler had ample experience with black militants and was steeped in criminal law. He was the best-known national figure—although in a public relations sense, his particular reputation was a mixed blessing—to respond to the inmates' appeal. After his entry into the Stewards' Room, he combined all these qualities with eloquence, passion, and the force of his personality to become probably the most important member of the group.

Informed, for example, that no one had been able to contact any ranking member of the Black Panther Party, a representative of which had been specifically requested by the inmates, Kunstler said matter-of-factly, "I'll get Bobby."

He consulted a pocket address book, went to the phone at one end of the Stewards' Room, and placed his call. For a few minutes he held the phone to his ear but continued to take part in the animated talk among the observers; then he turned his back, spoke for a few moments in a low voice, and hung up.

"Bobby can't get here until late tomorrow," he said, "but he's coming." No one had to be told he meant Bobby Seale, the Black Panther chairman, whom Kunstler had represented when the Chicago Seven had been the Chicago Eight.

Wicker's moderate but not insensitive political antennae began to vibrate. The arrival of Kunstler and the coming of Seale would immediately "radicalize" the observer group, if not in fact, at least in the public eye. A group most prominently represented by a Puerto Rican member of Congress, a black publisher, and a white columnist for *The New York Times* was one thing—bad enough, perhaps, to the "silent majority" to which so many politicians lately had been addressing themselves, worse if it became known that the group's chairman was Eve, a black militant in the New York legislature—but the same group with the Black Panther leader and his famous radical lawyer superimposed . . . ! "All we need now is H. Rap Brown," Wicker muttered to someone.

His concern was at that time external. The makeup of the observer committee early Friday evening had not suggested to him the character the group ultimately would assume, and with most of those milling about in the Stewards' Room, he felt relatively comfortable politically. Already, however—although Oswald and the pipe-smoking Dunbar seemed hospitable enough—Wicker could see that the observers' welcome among the guards and troopers was thin, indeed. He guessed it was as thin with the corrections bureaucracy and perhaps in the Rockefeller administration itself. The more the observers resembled Black Panthers or the S.D.S., the less effective they could be on that side of the equation of agreement they would be trying to arrange, however much more "clout" they might have with the inmates. But the observers would need credibility with both sides, and Wicker was not sure on which side they might need it most.

The observers, he thought, might at some point wish tactically to speak over the heads of prison officials and inmates to the public—either to bring pressure at some critical moment or to inspire confidence in an agreement. Again depending on which public they wished to address—the constituency of the inmates or the constituency of "law and order"—a committee seemingly radicalized by the presence of Bill Kunstler and Bobby Seale might or might not be a good thing.

At a meaner level of calculation, Wicker wondered if his own association in the public mind with these radical figures might damage him. It was a normal if not uplifting thought, of a kind he had had frequently in his years of ascent. Sometimes he had responded with contempt for such hesitations; at other times he had acted upon them ignobly or timidly. In the Stewards' Room, he simply dismissed the thought. Since his personal goal had come to him in D-yard, while he stood before the hostages—*nobody gets killed*—he had not doubted that the stakes were too high for anyone to guard himself. Risks were necessary; it would be better to go home than to quail before them.

Herman Schwartz, who had returned to Buffalo for a night's rest after delivering Bill Kunstler to the Stewards' Room, had not been too tired to brief Kunstler on his view of the situation. Schwartz, after all his efforts, was understandably resentful of the treatment his hard-won injunction had received that morning in D-yard. But he had not failed to learn the lesson of the episode:

> [Oswald] felt that by getting the injunction, allowing observers in at the negotiations, and by agreeing to an ombudsmanlike overseer's group to make sure that there were no reprisals . . . that he had done all that he was supposed to, and I kind of agreed with him. He also had agreed in principle to most of the fifteen demands. We were very mistaken indeed. As [Lewis] Steel

realized the minute he arrived, the issue of criminal amnesty was central although the other demands were required as well.[5]

Steel, too, had had a chance to talk privately with Kunstler. Whether he and Schwartz had persuaded him, or whether Kunstler had perceived the reality for himself, Kunstler said in his first remarks in the Stewards' Room that criminal amnesty appeared to be the central issue.

By then, T. Norman Hurd, a mild-mannered, academic-looking man who was Rockefeller's "director of state operations," was on the scene as the governor's personal representative. Kunstler's statement surprised him; later, he repeated it by telephone to Robert Douglass, the governor's secretary. Douglass told Hurd "to impress on the observers that amnesty really wasn't a viable issue as we saw it."[6]

The on-the-scene judgement of Steel and Schwartz, both of whom knew inmates and prisons and had been in D-yard, was that criminal amnesty for the inmates was the central issue (Schwartz having come to that conclusion belatedly). Kunstler agreed with them. Yet, by early Friday evening, not only had District Attorney James, who had never been inside the prison, ruled out criminal amnesty, but so had Governor Rockefeller, through Douglass—neither of whom had been anywhere near Attica, let alone D-yard.

Wicker, agreeing with Steel, Schwartz, and Kunstler, and aware of James' stand though not of Douglass', saw the situation as discouraging but not hopeless. Not knowing inmates or the politics of black power, he supposed that at some point the inmates' self-interest in improving their hard lot and in ending the uprising before they were attacked might cause them to modify their demand for amnesty. Not knowing Rockefeller or the bureaucratic mentality of his own society as well as he thought he did, he believed that if 38 hostages' lives could be redeemed and order peacefully restored to the "institution" (as Oswald, Dunbar, and Mancusi reverently spoke of it), total rejection of amnesty could be softened by the sort of ingenious formula lawyers were paid high fees to devise in other clashes of interest.

Wicker argued that even if amnesty were the central issue, it still was necessary to push the inmates to an exact list of demands, to find out what priority they placed on each, and how they wished the observers to go about trying to arrange a settlement. Besides, others pointed out, the observers had been assembled at the inmates' request and had a simple duty to consult with them as much as they could. So it was decided to make another trip into the yard as soon as possible. One observer recalled that first the group "in a hurried but careful manner . . . decided that we must remain neutral intermediaries if we were to have any chance of preventing the loss of the hostages' lives."[7]

Wicker no longer had any serious notion of the observers as a sort of guarantor group, sealing with their good faith an agreement to be negotiated by the state and the inmates. No doubt Oswald's offer to talk with an inmate committee on neutral ground was still good. But as Wicker and the others again readied themselves to go into D-yard, the hard fact was that the observers, however they might have voted to describe themselves, were not mere "neutral intermediaries." If offers and demands were to be made into agreements, it would have to be arranged by this "strange, interracial, interfaith, ad hoc, semiofficial, semipolitical"[8] group of ill-matched men, not all of whom understood the group's position or admired all of its members.

The observers were by then a strange assortment indeed, larger and noisier than when Wicker had joined them a few hours before, now straining the capacity of the Stewards' Room and the nerves of anyone who tried either to hear everyone's words or to get in a few of his own. A trio of young public interest lawyers from Washington had prevailed on Oswald to let them join and had arrived that afternoon—Julian Tepper of the National Legal Aid and Defender Association; Tony Fitch, an expert on prison matters for NLADA; and Dan Skoler, who worked with an American Bar Association prison project. More "third world" was on hand, too—William Gaiter, a quiet black who had an air of authority and competence, and Domingo Rodriguez, a bearded Puerto Rican, both of BUILD, a Buffalo community organization. Arthur Eve had summoned them, too.

There was too much moving about in the crowded, smoky room to get a good count, and Eve kept passing sign-up sheets, probably never getting everyone's name on the same page. Wicker reckoned there were at least two dozen men in the Stewards' Room, not counting the prison officials who occasionally wandered in (all but Oswald and Dunbar looking pained at the scene).

The observers were to become even more ill-matched. When Oswald appeared in the Stewards' Room for a last word before the group went back to D-yard, Kunstler raised a new question.

"Commissioner," he said, "I'm told you don't like Tom Soto and I don't want to bug you, but he's outside the gates. I promised him I'd ask you if he could come in and join us."

"Nothing but a troublemaker," Oswald said, not decisively. At that time, the commissioner seemed to be losing his grasp on the situation. In a whispered conversation after the observers' first trip into D-yard, he had told Wicker of his concern for Mrs. Oswald, who was in the hospital; then he had confided that he was under heavy pressure "from all over the country to get it over with." His round face was mournful, his shoulders slumped, his belly sagged. Oswald's was not an imposing physical presence, but Wicker sensed in him an earnest decency, an intent to do the best he could as long as he could—without much confidence that he could for long withstand the forces against him. Wicker did not know Tom Soto, but he doubted the commissioner could prevail in such a matter against the vigorous advocate, Kunstler.

So it proved. Kunstler argued that, while Soto had not been specifically invited by the inmates, they had listed his organization, the Prisoners' Solidarity Committee, among those from whom they wanted representatives. Moreover, Kunstler continued with lawyerly skill, Soto was on the scene, right outside the main gate, giving radio and television interviews. The inmates were bound to learn of his presence. If they knew Oswald was keeping him out, might that not cause more trouble in D-yard, where Soto was well known, than anything Soto could do if admitted?

Oswald wavered, unwilling to concede or close the argument. Eve and others who knew Soto seemed reluctant, but Kunstler pressed his point. Then Eve proposed that Soto be allowed in, but only as one member of the observers' group, to make no independent statements or arrangements of his own. Oswald glumly allowed that issue to be voted upon and Soto was admitted—more, it seemed, by the unwillingness of those who did not know him to cast a veto than by any enthusiasm from those who did know him.

While they waited for Soto, Wicker learned that the newcomer was a young Puerto Rican radical who had won his political spurs in a building takeover at City College of New York and who lately had been organizing and working among prisoners for the Solidarity Committee, which had an affiliation with Youth Against War and Fascism.

Just that morning, as Herman Schwartz had returned from his overnight quest for a federal court injunction against reprisals, Soto had engaged him in colloquy outside the prison. Schwartz's injunction was no good, he said, because it could be appealed. Schwartz demanded to know if Soto was a lawyer or had consulted one. Since he was not and had not, Schwartz "yelled at him that he didn't know what he was talking about, that [the injunction] was by consent, and therefore not technically appealable." Schwartz felt Soto was trying to undermine the possibility of agreement for his own political organizing purposes, and feared that Soto's view of the injunction could infect the inmates' attitudes. Soto, foreshadowing the amnesty issue, had replied that morning that protection from official reprisals, which the injunction provided, was not good enough and that actually the inmates should be freed as they had only committed "crimes of survival."[9]

All in all, Tom Soto did not sound to Wicker like a man to cool things among the observers. When he appeared in the Stewards' Room, he seemed well cast for his own part—tall, lean, swart, with a clipped mustache, burning eyes, and a cold, challenging manner that announced his contempt for the sordid group of compromisers and manipulators he saw before him. Wicker put him down wearily as a zealous follower of some harsh political doctrine of revolution and the firing squad—a true believer, who might be troublesome and would surely be a bore. Besides, he thought, from his moderate's point of view, the more radicals and militants in the group, the more dogmatic and rigid argumentation it would likely hear. And that would make it all the harder for the group to come to any kind of rational decision, let alone work out compromises.

But Soto readily enough agreed to the restrictions on his activities that Arthur Eve spelled out. He and the other observers began lining up for the march into D-yard.

5

Into the River

Fires flicker from oil drums atop low, flat rooftops . . . and here and there flashlight beams pick out alert faces, many of them framed in football helmets painted white or orange. . . . Curving in a long line from the entrance toward the dark rise of D-block are the inmates—arms locked, shoulder to shoulder, each man facing in the opposite direction from the two to which he is linked. Beyond this solid human barrier are the faceless hundreds of others—and somewhere in the darkness, huddled on mattresses within a tight ring of wooden benches, their hostages.

This is another world—terrifying to the outsider, yet imposing in its strangeness—behind those massive walls, in this murmurous darkness, within the temporary but real power of desperate men. "Nobody gonna get hurt," the helmeted security men are saying soothingly, but it is not reassuring. It only reminds the observers that in this dark world, the powerless have taken power. . . .[1]

"We enter a different world, as if crossing through the looking glass into a scene which is even more awesome and forceful than that of the walled prison. The sky is cloudless tonight; the half-moon and numerous bonfires illuminate the courtyard. . . . Sporadic greetings and feelings of appreciation are voiced by inmates whom we pass."[2] So Julian Tepper, entering the yard for the first time, felt the moment. Somewhere in the throng of prisoners faceless beyond the linked arms of the security chain, Sam Melville watched the outside world coming to treat with those who so shortly before had been caged, and was moved to write:

Agincourt. Evening around the campfire. Power people! We are
strong. We are together. We are growing. We love you all.
Ho Ho Ho Chi Minh. Please inform our next of kin.[3]

To Tom Wicker, although he was now familiar with the inmates'
procedures, the second march into the yard was more unsettling than
the first. Under the moon and the bonfires on the walkway, his sense
of separation from the familiar flared again as the observers counted off
in A-yard and marched two by two across the corridor and into D-
yard. Once again, the tattooed man swung the last door and this time
his face in the dim light seemed even more desperate and piratical, as if
he both guarded and gave access to dread things. The faces in the
security chain seemed more darkly knowing in the moonlight. Wicker
did not want to show fear because he was too proud and because he
sensed that boldness and honesty were his best guarantees in that
company of hard and watchful men. But he did fear that he could not
protect himself physically, if that became necessary. He had relied too
long and too easily on what his world regarded as security—that
comforting substitute for self-sufficiency.

Worse, it was not really true that as he liked to tell himself with
spurious fatalism, he could do nothing about his situation. Wicker
knew something about real helplessness. Fifteen years earlier, in a
foolish accident in a rapid stretch of the Potomac River, he had come
up sputtering and coughing on the downstream side of a capsized
canoe that was wedged solidly against rocks.
"Get the paddle!" a companion had cried above the roar of the
water.
Wicker had let go of the slippery canoe and started after the
paddle. The water was not deep. He could walk along the rocky floor
of the river and larger rocks were on every side, promising safety. But
he knew instantly that this was delusion. The tide of the water was
irresistible, casting him before it as carelessly as if he were the paddle;
and he had no more power than the paddle to turn, swim against the
current, guide himself, or stop. The rocks at which he clutched were
worn smooth and slippery by time and the water. He clung to each as
he came to it. The relentless water tore him loose every time, and
pushed him on as effortlessly as if he were a leaf or an insect on the
surface. He was helpless, out of control, beyond the power of human
effort. As coldly as the water sucking at his ankles, as surely as it pounded
him from the deceptive rocks, Wicker knew there was nothing he
could do. That was the moment in which he had recognized, not his life
played back before his eyes, but the iron indifference of things, the
blind chance by which the world in its turning and life in its passing

struck down men and objects alike, and went on unchanged. In that moment of awful vision into the heart of the matter, Wicker had not been afraid, precisely because there was nothing he could do, no way he could fail, crack, escape, make things worse or better for himself or anyone. For once, he need not even try to be worthy, for no one could be worthy of a force so powerful and so uncaring and so flawlessly impartial that it merely swept before it what was there.

But I don't have to look, he had thought, and let his feet go out from under him so that he lay for a moment on his back, almost comfortable on the surging crest of the river, before it hurled him out and 76 feet down among the rocks and whirlpools and icy depths at the foot of the Great Falls of the Potomac.

Later—a long time later, it had seemed—the same impersonal force that had taken him down threw him up again and as carelessly, far downstream, against a ledge where he could grasp dry rock above the water. He had never known how he came to be the only man ever to plunge over the Great Falls and live; but that chance could be no different from—in fact, was a part of—the chance that could have killed him, in an indifference so perfect that it made no distinction between life and death.

But D-yard was not the river, although sooner or later, in the one as in the other, chance would be about its blind and aimless work. But in the yard it would matter a great deal what Tom Wicker and the other observers did. They could win the inmates' trust or destroy it. They might save lives or doom them, including some of their own. What each of them did at any moment might profoundly affect what all of them could do in whatever time they had. With fear wringing its soft hands in his stomach, Wicker resolved that it would not be his weakness that caused the observers to fail, if they did. It worried him that he knew so little of the other men upon whom he had to depend. He had more faith in his own will and self-discipline, if not much more, than he had in the ability of men to work and hold together—particularly strangers and adversaries, the comfortable and the concerned, gathered in so odd a company as the Attica observers.

The long curving security chain led them once again to the tables against the brick wall of D-block. High up that wall, the few weak lights that ordinarily would have lit the yard dimly had been supplemented by a few makeshift lamps rigged by the inmates. Far more light was provided by a pair of brilliant television lamps placed between the main body of inmates massed in the yard and the inmate leaders and the observers at the negotiating tables. Roland Barnes, a black cameraman for WGR-TV of Buffalo, had virtually moved in with the D-yard brothers and was filming as much of their activities as they would permit. Oswald seemed to make no serious effort to get him out. The night meeting was not being carried live, but much of Barnes' film would appear on various news programs the next day—a prospect of which neither inmates nor observers were ignorant and which undoubtedly fuelled some of their oratory. It was to be "political theater" again.

On the inmates' side of the table were many of the faces the earlier group of observers had seen that Friday afternoon—L. D. Barkley, Richard Clark, Champ, Jerry Rosenberg, Frank Lott, the white youth at the typewriter. Once again, Brother Herb was at the microphone, ranting and powerful. Wicker looked in vain for the handsome, bitter black who had recognized him earlier as from *The Times*.

The first order of business* was the introduction of the newly arrived observers. Soto was first and got the ceremony off to a rousing start. Standing straight, slim, militant, he gave his name and affiliation. Then he held his clenched fist above his head and shouted, "Power to the people!" bringing a predictable roar from the massed inmates. Soto, Wicker saw, was as advertised, and was already outside the spirit if not the letter of his agreement with the other observers.

The presentation of Bill Kunstler was a bigger moment. A recognizable figure with his long hair and sideburns, his glasses characteristically pushed up on his high forehead, Kunstler took the microphone confidently and waited for the welcoming ovation of the inmates to die away.

"Palante!"† he shouted, raising another roar. "*All* power to the people!"

Wicker did not suspect either Soto or Kunstler of insincerity; quite the opposite. He would have been more comfortable, in fact, dealing with poseurs, as he had found most people to be. Convinced men were likely to be unyielding men, and all too often unseeing as well. But, whatever moved Soto and Kunstler, Wicker questioned whether charging up the inmates' revolutionary juices was the best way to get a quick settlement. His own instinct was to get down to cases, begin working out compromises.

Wicker knew Kunstler well by reputation, slightly by acquaintance. From the nearly forgotten civil rights movement in the South, Kunstler had earned a reputation as a forceful advocate of school

---

* The sequence of speeches and events in D-yard on the night of September 10–11 is confused as between the accounts of McKay, Oswald, Badillo, Tepper, and the memories of other participants. The account in this and the next chapter is based primarily on the author's own notes, supplemented by these other sources. Unless otherwise cited, all direct quotations are from the author's notes. Indirect quotations are based mostly on these notes, supplemented by other reliable sources.
† A slang expression for "para adelante," meaning forward.

desegregation and other causes. Later, though Wicker had been generally sympathetic to the Chicago Seven, outraged by the charges on which they were tried, and shocked by Judge Julius J. Hoffman's conduct of their trial, he nevertheless thought Kunstler had allowed the defense too nearly to become part of the circus.

Wicker had wanted to see the seven acquitted, as they should have been, on the merits of their case, not ranting back at Judge Hoffman or engaging in their own antics and polemics. Wicker thought the defense had consistently wasted the asset of the judge's and prosecution's indefensible behavior by responding with behavior that, if not equally indefensible, was seen as such by millions of Americans who might otherwise have been taught the graphic lesson that their government could and did persecute instead of prosecute.

From the Chicago trial—in which he himself had been sentenced for what Judge Hoffman called contempt of court—Kunstler had emerged probably the best-known "movement" lawyer and one of the most active, eloquent, and bold spokesmen of radical political sentiment in America. Wicker had considerable admiration for him; Kunstler probably could have made a fortune in routine law practice but had spurned it for reasons that were bound to have included a passion for justice. Yet Wicker could not help but wonder whether Kunstler's fervor was not to some extent what he and his clients would call an "ego trip," and whether it served deserving clients any better than solid, nonpolitical legal counsel—not that for Kunstler's kind of clients it was all that easy to get "solid, nonpolitical" counsel.

This was essentially a political moderate's view of a man who had gone further in the political direction in which Wicker himself tended than Wicker ever had been willing to do. It was a view compounded of respect, envy, and suspicion—respect for the genuine beliefs he thought to be at the root of Kunstler's radicalism, envy of the willingness with which the lawyer put himself repeatedly on the line for those beliefs, suspicion that Kunstler's way was not entirely altruistic and, worse, not as effective as more restrained counsel might have been. Besides, the more "committed" a person was, Wicker believed, the more the "commitment" became acceptance of an ideological position, and therefore the less intellectually independent the committed person could be. Tom Wicker could submit to no intellectual discipline but his own—shaky and derivative as he feared it often was.

Herman Schwartz, who knew Kunstler better, expressed a more generous view:

. . . Kunstler, who has the same background [as I do] overcame this because he's probably a bigger man and because he's

personally committed. . . . Chicago radicalized [him] very
sharply. Before Chicago, I think [Kunstler] was very much like
me, as were most of us lawyers in the civil rights movement, all
of us wearing button-down shirts and striped ties. That's a
different world, a different ball game. And unless you've been
personally subjected to something which radicalizes you experi-
entially, then I think that it's just not likely you'll be able to mix
with . . . black militants . . . and that would be very difficult
for me. . . .[4]

Wicker believed something else, too, which he doubted that political
believers like William Kunstler really understood—that there was little
reason to have faith in *any* society that men and women might be able
to establish, if that faith demanded the elimination of injustice. If
society was a way in which people tried to live together, injustice was
inherent in the notion, since mankind was fallible and aggressive.
People could change any society, but no society could change people.
Therefore, as Wicker saw it, the aim of a society of men could be at
best to *limit* injustice; and its true measure was the value, if any, that it
placed on that goal. Thus, talk of revolution and overthrow made
Wicker uncomfortable intellectually. What he knew of history im-
pelled him to ask: Overthrow society and *replace it with what? With
what old injustice to what new victim?*

That night in D-yard, Kunstler immediately showed the largely
black crowd his impressive credentials. Speaking as a lawyer for the
Black Panthers, he said pointedly, he could assure the inmates that
either Huey Newton or Bobby Seale was on the way. Meanwhile, the
observers and he, Kunstler, were there to do what they could. He was
not as yet clear what that might be; he and the others were only
beginning to sort out the issues. But already Kunstler could see one
thing: "You have power, which means you can reach ears."

At this reference to the hostages—an unseen but constant presence
beyond the TV lights, in their guarded circle somewhere in the
murmuring crowd—Wicker thought, then forced himself to think no
more, of huddled and fearful men, listening to the howling enthusiasm
of their captors. Kunstler was right enough. The hostages gave the
inmates power, and men with power could make themselves heard—no
question of it. But beyond making themselves heard, did they have
power that could, in fact, be used as *political power*—as a means to an
end?

The power of life or death for the hostages was real enough and
could be wielded by any inmate with a homemade blade from the
metal shop. But the use of such power as that—however it might be

dubiously certified in revolutionary theory—was political weakness not political power, because to kill the hostages was to destroy the power. Power derived from custody of the hostages in their miserable ring could be *political power* only as long as they were alive to be threatened by the blades, and maybe not even that long. The power of the inmates actually was enough to gain them a hearing and maintain a stalemate only while the state held the lives of the hostages dearer than it held the control of its institution.

Most of the inmate leaders probably understood the limitations on power obtained through hostages; they were intelligent men. "We never concerned ourselves with killing the hostages," Roger Champen insisted. "The hostages were the only means of negotiation. . . . For years, whenever we had to bargain with the state in trying to get some programs instituted, we only had the administration's word. . . . It was never kept, *never* kept. And we felt that by having the hostages we would also have the ability to more or less force them to keep their word. So we wouldn't even consider harming the hostages."[5]

The trouble with that was that inmate rhetoric, including that of most of the leaders, constantly presented another picture—that of desperate men who were determined, if necessary, to bargain for their demands with the hostages' lives. Indeed, the captured guards' being in custody without the threat of death, implicit or explicit, would have generated considerably less "power" for the rebelling inmates. That was a dilemma never satisfactorily resolved: if they did not, as Champen insisted, intend to kill the hostages, they still had to convey the impression that the hostages' lives were at stake. The inmates were plagued by the ancient problem of credibility; the very threats needed to provide the "power" of which Kunstler spoke were bound to harden the state's attitude toward those who made or implied such threats.

"Many of us love you," Kunstler was saying, "and many of us understand what a shitty decrepit system we have here in New York and elsewhere." Kunstler wanted to convince the inmates that they could trust him, hence trust the observer group with which he was associated. "We are your brothers," he continued, "we hope." Which exactly stated the case—the observers hoped to be *considered* "brothers" by the inmates, so that any agreements the observers could work out might be accepted by them.

Kunstler emphasized that the inmates themselves had to set their own conditions for agreement. It was up to them to say what they wanted. These demands the observer group then could take directly to the state authorities. The observers had no power to commit the state; and they understood that they could not make an agreement *for* the inmates, either.

"You are the political people," Kunstler concluded, drawing another ovation before he sat down.

"Now that," said Brother Herb, reclaiming the microphone, "was rather well put." It was the tribute of one to another who knew how to make his case to a crowd. Then Herb paid a bigger tribute. "Brother Bill," he asked, "will you be our lawyer? Will you represent the brothers as only you can?"

Kunstler returned to the microphone, looking surprised. He hesitated a moment, then agreed—to another ovation. How being the brothers' attorney could square with being a neutral observer, Wicker was not sure, but Brother Herb was ready with instructions for the new counsel. As for what the brothers wanted, he said, there was no doubt whatever:

"All . . . all . . . ALL of the fifteen demands!"

The crowd of inmates roared their approval. As usual, Herb had them in the palm of his big hand. One by one, he read each of the fifteen Practical Proposals, dramatically, powerfully, pausing for the cheers that rose for each.

But in the Attica "negotiations," nothing could be quite so precisely defined as the phrase "Fifteen Practical Proposals" suggests. It seemed to be a studied technique of the inmates to keep their demands so confused and confusing that they could never be quite pinned down to what was central and what was not. Or perhaps there was no procedure by which all of D-yard could agree on a firm set of demands, then stand by them. At any rate, when Brother Herb had finished reading the fifteen, he immediately added two more.

"Mancusi must go!" he shouted. Though he had been unimpressed by the disapproving manner of the superintendent, Wicker flinched to hear this. It meant trouble, if seriously pressed, because hell hath no fury like a bureaucracy defending itself, and Wicker feared the one thing the corrections bureaucracy would never accede to was a demand—no matter how justified by evidence—for the removal of one of its own. That would be to concede that the man and the bureaucracy had been wrong in the first place.

"Doctor Williams must go!" Brother Herb also proclaimed, referring to the prison physician Dr. Selden T. Williams. This turned out to be quite reasonable. The 51-year-old Dr. Williams, who did no more than run a morning sick call for the prison as a sideline to his private practice, was interviewed after the uprising ended and did not even try to disguise his hostility to the inmates.

"The critics should try living with the inmates," Dr. Williams said. "These convicts aren't appreciative of anything. They're rapists, murderers. They're animals. And you want me to be sympathetic. I think they got what they deserved. . . . I do try to be impartial, but I find it hard."[6]

In the harsh world of Attica before the uprising, Dr. Williams in fact had spent most of his time with inmates separated from them by a wire screen. When they lined up for sick call, he and an associate prison doctor, Paul G. Sternberg, were on the other side of a waist-high counter; the screen ran from the counter to the ceiling. No examinations were given, except in rare cases. The patient described his problem. Through the screen the doctor gave him medication, often aspirin, sometimes a placebo, not infrequently a tranquilizer if the complaint was psychological. Sometimes one of the doctors would dismiss the complaining inmate since both believed they could tell by looking at a man whether he was malingering. Cases judged serious enough could be treated in the 26-bed infirmary. If necessary, men could be sent to outside hospitals, usually Meyer Memorial in Buffalo. In the prison, there were no special diet facilities, no rehabilitation or withdrawal programs for drug addicts, and psychiatric help was so limited in comparison to need as to have been virtually useless. Attempts at group therapy programs invariably foundered for lack of time, facilities, and personnel. Only dental care was anywhere near adequate at Attica in September 1971.[7]

The primitive delivery of medical care was only one of many dehumanizing, dangerous, and disspiriting conditions that existed there —and, in greater or lesser degree, in virtually every American prison. Overcrowded, underfinanced, overaged, designed for security and segregation, administered senselessly and often vindictively, most of these institutions mocked the notion of "correcting" their inmates.[8]

Of all prison conditions, the most damaging may be the stupefying monotony and boredom of prison life. Charles B. Lankford, an inmate for more than 20 years, who had done stretches at Attica and Sing Sing and who was a rehabilitation official in Fairfax County, Virginia, in 1971, has reconstructed a typical day in "the joint" as follows:

6:00 A.M.	Wake up, get ready for breakfast, clean cell, be counted.
6:30	Breakfast (march in column of twos, tallest in front, shortest in rear).
7:00	Back to your cell.
7:30	Sick call.
7:45	Work call.
8:00	Work.
Noon	Lunch.
12:30	Back to your cell and be counted.

1:00	Back to work.
3:00	Lights flash. Time to quit work, line up.
3:15	Back to your cell and/or to yard for recreation.
4:00	Line up for supper.
4:15	March to mess hall.
5:00	Lock up for rest of the night. Be counted again.
7:30	Bell rings. No more talking for the rest of the night.
10:00	Lights out.
11:00	Radio earphones off. Absolute quiet.[9]

At Attica, a similar schedule resulted in 14 to 16 hours of cell time *every day*—and more on weekends, when there was no work—including about 10 hours of silence.

Authoritative estimates are that 33 to 40 percent of all American prison inmates either have no work to do or none but maintenance duties; "hard labor" is a delusion. Not only are inmates learning nothing that will be useful beyond the walls, except in crime, but inside the walls, unless they are exceptional men and women, their lives are deteriorating in idleness, bitterness, stupefaction, and trouble making.

"I was lucky," a former Attica inmate recalls. "I went to work right away as an electrician—for 10 cents a day. I used to make $2.50 a month, and with that money I had to swing everything." Even though in that case the inmate had learned a useful trade, or the rudiments of it, "when I came home I had no family, and then when I tried to get into the electricians' union they would not accept me because I was an ex-addict and an ex-convict. . . . There was nothing I could do, so I went back to stealing and back to prison. . . ."[10]

At Attica in September 1971, about 60 percent of the inmates worked at prison maintenance jobs, heavily featherbedded; 20 percent worked in the metal and other industrial shops, also featherbedded for lack of real jobs; the rest were in overcrowded and not very effective school and vocational training programs. Only six men were on "work–release"—leaving the prison by day to work in outside jobs but returning at night. Prison wages by then ranged from 20 cents to $1.00 a day. The average monthly wage was $7.50. Most of the more desirable and better paid jobs, as in the outside world, were held by whites; with few exceptions, blacks and Puerto Ricans had to take what was left.[11]

Recreation in prison is little more abundant than work—mostly card games, dominoes, checkers. The Attica inmates could crowd around a single television set in each of the four yards, listen to radio and televison sound on earphones in their cells (three channels only), and had some organized team sports. Games like bridge and chess could be played, sometimes in tournaments, more often in difficult conditions between cells or in the crowded yards. When subzero weather made the yards unsuitable (from October to April), two movies were shown on weekends. The annual recreation budget, culled from commissary profits, amounted to about $1.00 per inmate.[12]

But in almost every prison drugs are available, there is much clandestine gambling, and no security rules ever devised have prevented men from making fierce alcoholic beverages. Attica was no exception. Lankford recalls that a riot almost began there long before 1971 when guards dealt harshly with an inmate who "had made some booze—it's done all the time in prison kitchens, using raisins and stuff and letting it just sit for about three days." But such "fun and games" are the exception; Lankford remembers the monotony at Attica when he was there, that "each cell block has its own yard, approximately 100 yards square, like a box. Each block has 450 to 500 inmates, and what they do during yard time is just to walk around and around and around and around."[13]

The folly and dangers of such idleness are compounded by the overcrowding that is the general rule in prisons. There were nearly 700 more inmates at Attica in 1971 than the 1600 it had been designed for. In 1970, there were 250 inmates in one open dormitory with insufficient toilet facilities in the maximum security prison at Rahway, New Jersey. At the same time, in one wing of the Trenton, New Jersey, "maxi"—built in 1798—four men were living in cells designed for one, all using a single toilet in the ill-ventilated cell.[14] As late as 1964, the federal prison system had single-cell capacity for less than 30 percent of its inmates. At McNeill Island, Washington, 10 inmates were quartered in "an area no more than 15 by 20 feet."[15]

In 1971, when David Hall became governor of Oklahoma, he found the McAlester prison had 2350 inmates in a facility built for 1500. Governor Hall reduced this explosive overcrowding to 1636 inmates, before an eight-day outbreak of rioting that caused $20 million in damages at the prison in the summer of 1973 (less than two years after the Attica uprising). A report on the dangerous conditions at McAlester had been made *in 1958* jointly by the National Council on Crime and Delinquency and by a legislative committee; but no action was taken until Hall took office 13 years later.[16]

One recent reason for overcrowding that is not generally recognized by the public has been cited by John O. Boone, then a District of Columbia corrections official, later a short-lived "reform" commissioner of corrections in Massachusetts. He said in 1971, of the District of Columbia's Lorton Prison:

Right now, we are badly overpopulated. We have a normal complement of fourteen hundred eighty-four. At this time, we're

moving pretty close to nineteen hundred. We are badly overcrowded as a result of about a thousand new police [in Washing-
ton], ten new judges, court reorganization, and in a great sense
no provision for the influx into correctional institutions.[17]

The new emphasis on "law and order," arising from the fear of crime
that became widespread in the 1960s, thus *worsened* prison conditions.
So if it is true, as most criminologists believe, that prison conditions
breed crime, the public and the politicians may have been deluding themselves that law and order actually were being served by putting more
people in prison.

Instances of overcrowding—inmates said later it was not the least of
the causes of discontent at Attica—could be multiplied, and such
conditions are to be found in institutions in virtually every state. The
most obvious consequences are high tension, inmate anger, rampant
violence, and homosexuality. What may not be so obvious, but is in
subtle ways more damaging, is every inmate's consequent loss of
dignity, privacy, and status as a separate and individual man or woman.

As for homosexuality, every inmate, guard, prison administrator, or
investigator can testify to its prevalence, at Attica and every prison;
much of it is accompanied, of necessity, by violence. Captain Presley
Middleton of the Bucks County, Pennsylvania, prison staff told
Leonard J. Berry, "Now if you put five men into a little small cubicle,
five men, five grown men in a cell, assumin' you're livin' together for
let's say three weeks, you can rest assured somethin' gonna take place
in that cell. . . . You can't stop it."

Talking to Berry, an inmate at the Indiana state prison expanded on
that: "Now, um, a lotta guys don't agree with me, but I think that
homosexuality causes 70 percent of all your violent acts in here. Maybe
higher. . . . They don't know what caused it. Ah, it's unheard of for
inmates in here to just walk in the room, say, 'Yeah, the guy was tryin'
to fuck me.' You don't do that. You've got to follow the rules of
convict society or you're an outcast. You can't afford to be an outcast
in here."

Homosexual rape is as common in prisons and jails as metal doors.
The first night of the D-yard society during the Attica revolt, two
young inmates were raped at knife point by several other inmates in a
washroom near Times Square.[18] A 26-month study of Philadelphia jails
documented 156 sexual assaults on prisoners and estimated that 2000
might have occurred in a two-year period. Another study concluded
that in a large women's prison about 50 percent of its inmates had some
form of overt sexual experience during their incarceration. After all,
only one prison in America—Parchman in Mississippi—permits conjugal visits (some others are beginning to experiment with weekend

leaves for conjugal purposes), and most have rules even against mastur-
bation although, as one authority observed, "Nobody—inmate, staff or
visitor—is in a prison very long before seeing an inmate masturbating
in a toilet, shower, or cell."[19]

So it is not surprising that men segregated from women, and women
from men, living lives of desperate boredom and despair in crowded
conditions, seek any kind of flesh for sexual solace—whether taken
forcibly or by mutual consent. "I remember the first time I forgot
what it was like to fuck a woman," a California inmate told Berry.
"That day, man, was a helluva day. I lay there all night tryin' to
remember. I couldn't remember how it was like. And that was a year
and a half ago. And that's a helluva experience, man—to forget."

"He comes in there, he's small, he's frail, he's cute, and after you're in
prison awhile, you know, boys start looking much cuter," a "daddy"
who had spent 20 of his 30 years behind the walls told Linda Charlton,
a reporter working on one of the countless stories about sex in prison.[20]

Homosexuality per se is not necessarily outrageous behavior. Even
rape may be injurious only to those who suffer and commit it. But
prison homosexuality, so much of which is a temporary expedient for
heterosexuals rather than a genuine choice of a way of life, helps make
prison life different and dehumanizing, degrading and demoralizing.
And prison rape contributes heavily to the ethic of force that domi-
nates every prison. The patterns of prison sex, in fact, raise sharply the
question whether what a former prison medical officer has called
"forced segregation of dangerous individuals within a small perimeter"
makes any sense at all. These sex patterns are one more assurance that
most inmates will leave prison more antisocial than they were when
they entered.

Violence and brutality, though perhaps not on the nineteenth-century scale, are as obvious as homosexuality in American prisons.
Lankford recalls, "I've seen blood ooze from the heads of Attica
inmates hit by guards with sticks. I've watched stomachs caved in by
the clubs of the 'hacks.' I've seen inmates fall, only to be kicked in the
ribs for no justifiable reason. . . . I've lain on the floor in 'segregation' . . . and I've listened to prisoners who had been tear-gassed 'just
for the fun of it.' "[21]

But not all the violence in prison is employed by guards against
inmates. Guards have been assaulted, beaten, wounded, kidnapped,
killed by inmates, too. Violence among inmates is as common as
profanity. Rape, assault, fights over "punks" (inmates willing or hiring
out to be homosexually used), forcible collection of debts, attacks or
threats for blackmail purposes, fighting, racial or religious feuding, and
rioting—all occur frequently among inmates. "Anything can happen
here," a San Quentin inmate told Berry. "You might borrow a box of

cigarettes from one guy, tell him, 'Well, I'll pay you back next week.' Then if you won't pay him—it's a two-for-three thing, you know— borrow a box, you gotta give 15 packs back. So the money don't come in or 'mind if I pay you next week?' He'll say, 'well, it's gonna be two boxes next week.' And it could jack itself up like that. And by the time you know it, you're flyin' over the tier or you're walking around in the yard with a blade in your back or some maniac will come by, stick you in the back with a shiv or somethin'. One of my homeys, he was watchin' TV, and some dude come up to him and hit him right in the chest with a blade. For nothin'. He didn't even know him. He died about ten minutes later. Any number of things can happen."

There can never be enough guards to stop such violence. At the time of the 1971 uprising, Attica had 380 corrections officers, supervised by 17 men ranking as sergeants or higher. Only 57 percent were on duty at any given time, and less than that during the day when most of the 2250 inmates were out of their cells. This force could not possibly provide much security for inmates against other inmates, with the result that even in a "maximum security" institution most inmates had to protect themselves as best they could, usually with homemade blades—another sound reason why so many regarded "the law" as ineffective, biased, and contemptible. Blacks and Puerto Ricans regarded this lack of personal security as racial, and sometimes it was— just as there is some justice in city ghetto complaints that police do not think ghetto residents are important enough to protect. In any case, the lack of personal security for inmates is the main reason Bill Sands could write of his years in prison that "everywhere, every minute—like the air you breathe—there is the threat of violence beneath the surface . . . gray and swift and unpredictable as a shark. . . ."[22]

Still, the most serious, if not the most prevalent, form of prison violence is by guards and officers against the inmates—the most serious because corrections personnel are supposed to uphold the law, because the inmates have no real means of protecting themselves against official violence or gaining redress of grievances, and because guards have or should have at least *some* correctional function, if no more than to set a law-abiding example. In fact, most prison administrators and personnel take an entirely custodial view of their work, many fear and despise their charges, and the result is that force—instant and sometimes massive—is regarded as a necessary, even desirable, means of coping with their problems.

The Arkansas horror story has been detailed too often to require repetition and is certainly not typical nowadays, but official violence is nevertheless an American prison commonplace. Beatings, tear gassings, Macings, "sweatbox" or "icebox" solitary confinement, gaggings, chainings, various kinds of floggings, and other physical harassments—all have been documented in *recent* years in numerous prisons. It is not strange that Cell Block A at Attica believed automatically that Dewar and Lamorie were beaten the night before the 1971 riot erupted; that is the kind of thing that happens in prisons.

One reason is the inadequacy of so-called "corrections personnel." The prisoners call them "hacks" and "pigs," and no doubt, as some keepers of men have always been, some of them may be monsters of brutality, corrupted by the physical power inherent in their jobs, or inherently sadistic. In the main, however, prison workers are decent men and women who have little training for their heavy responsibilities and little understanding of their charges.

Dr. Bernard Finch, who served more than 12 years in San Quentin for murder, pointed out in a speech to the American Bar Association in August 1973 that under California civil service law a man could be running a gas station one week and conducting group therapy sessions in a California prison the next. Most—as at Attica in 1971—qualified for their jobs by passing a civil service exam and showing a high school diploma or its equivalent. They received less training for their posts than any city policeman or fireman. (Back in the 1930s, New York state did have a 90-day training course for guards, but it was discontinued after World War II for lack of funds.)[23]

The educational level among prison guards is not high because their pay scale is not high. New York corrections officers' salaries in 1971 began at $9,535 and reached $11,941 after 15 years.[24] The national average that year was only about $6,000. College men and women are not interested in that kind of money—nor often in the prison kind of life. So only one out of two guards is a high school graduate; one out of three has better than a high school education. Many are retired from the armed services.

Almost all guards are white, although prison populations today are heavily black and Spanish-speaking. Dr. Allen Berman of the University of Rhode Island, who studied 100 applicants for prison jobs in that state, found that they tended to "show emotional shallowness, alienation from social customs and relative inability to profit from social sanctions"—just like the inmates they wanted to be hired to keep.[25]

But that is not the only similarity between guards and inmates. Ultimately, both are "in the joint" together. "In my 21 years here," Captain L. E. Birchall of the Utah State Penitentiary told Wallace Turner, "you might say that I've done a seven-year stretch on eight-hour shifts." Locked in together, pitted in a nearly Darwinian struggle for survival, "pigs" and "cons" spend their terms in hate and fear of each other. If he were taken hostage in a riot, Guard Vern Clayson of the Utah prison told Turner laconically, "I expect I'd become dead wood." The life of many a prison guard is a life of nagging terror.[26]

"There's always ongoing searches for weapons," Sergeant Harold Brown of San Quentin told Berry. "Zip guns, stabbing instruments, those type of things. And quite a quantity is picked up each month. . . . They can be made from most anything, from a toothbrush handle ground down, which is a very effective stabbing instrument, to the more elaborate daggers or steel blades. Lately the zip guns we've been picking up are the muzzle-load type, made out of pipe; the explosive part would be made of matchheads, a projectile can be anything from broken glass to nails to little stones or pieces of concrete. Extremely dangerous and very, very deadly. And they shoot beautifully. These are the things the officers have to keep their eyes open for. If you don't know what you're looking at, you can get yourself killed. If you don't recognize sounds, you get yourself killed or hurt."

Little wonder, therefore, that most guards believe in a tough policy of physical restraint—"maximum security"—for prisoners. And since in most states guards form a well-organized bureaucracy with civil service protection, and in some, like New York, have an employees' union in addition, they generally are a powerful and vocal force against "prison reform"—just as policemen are opposed to many exercises of "constitutional rights" by criminal defendants and suspects. The guards' organization in Massachusetts was primarily responsible, for example, for the ouster of Corrections Commissioner John Boone after he began "phasing out" state prisons, an obvious threat to guards' job security as well as to their view of corrections necessities.

Nevertheless, inmates are substantially in the power of guards at most times, and since many guards *are* insensitive and overbearing, the prisoners, too, live in fear. Men who fear other men usually come to hate them, so in these vast and gloomy fortress prisons, where everything is largely hidden from the public, fear and hatred mount in an ever-tightening spiral. This hideous atmosphere can be felt in many prisons, almost as if it were tangible.

The master–slave relationship, moreover, can be corrupting for the master. To have absolute power over another human being can bring out the worst in a person—just as, in some cases, abject slaves have been known to rise to heights of character and nobility. When guards have constant fear for their own safety, when they are irritated and frustrated by the conditions in which they work, when they find a prisoner in their power, with no one to see, particularly if they dislike or distrust the inmate's race or origins—in such cases even good family men and churchgoers can be corrupted into physical brutality.

Even when they are not, there exists in prisons what might be called "psychological brutality." In fact, an Attica inmate said after the riot, "They can psychologically beat a man almost to death. For instance, if you approached a guard you had to call him 'sir.' When you asked for something the guard would never look at you. He would look at the ceiling or turn his back on you and say, 'Did you say something? What do you want, boy?' And you'd say, 'Well, sir, I've got this problem. . . .' And his answer would be something like: 'What in the hell do you want me to do? Get the hell back in that cell.' "[27] A federal court once found that in another prison, Martin Sostre had been put in solitary in a cell where a light was kept burning 24 hours a day, making it all but impossible for him to sleep. If he did doze off, it was not for long, as a guard came by every half-hour and ran a "nigger stick" noisily across the bars.[28]

Psychological brutality also includes prison's appalling lack of amenity—one shower and one clean pair of socks a week, one bar of soap and one roll of toilet paper per month at Attica, before the uprising; one razor blade per man per month and ten bars of soap a week for 130 men to wash themselves and their clothes at the infamous Arkansas state prison.

Meals—budgeted at 63 cents per day per man at Attica in 1971— were starchy, ill-prepared, monotonous, heavy on pork (to the distress of Black Muslims whose religion prohibits eating pork), and uncomfortable because of stiff security regulations. Supplements could be had from the commissary for those who could afford it. Heating appliances were not allowed in the cells (inmates were brought two quarts of hot water a day in cans), but homemade appliances flourished except when "hacks" decided to crack down. Limited numbers of food items could be sent by relatives and friends but were subject to inspection and confiscation, often for no clear reason.[29]

At Attica, books and magazines were scarce and restricted. Mail was censored and could only be sent to and received from a prison-approved list of persons. Before and after receiving visitors, inmates suffered a "skin search," including a rectal probe. They were separated from their visitors by a heavy mesh screen and observed during the visit by two officers. During his Attica term, at least one inmate refused to have his children visit him because, he said, "if they want to see an animal they can go to the zoo."[30]

What a person takes most for granted—his or her name—is for most purposes made a number behind the walls. He or she is subject to arbitrary search and peremptory discipline, and has little hope of appeal from either. If it is an inmate's word against a guard's, the inmate almost automatically loses.

"Prison was so psychologically damaging to me, I sometimes wondered if some guys wouldn't be better off dead," an ex-inmate, trying to make it as a journalist, reflected. "If a guy does over two years, he becomes so emotionally scarred he has a hard time coping with society. Maybe it'd be better to kill him. Of course, I'd be dead if you did."[31]

And always, day after day, several times a day, there is the most shattering psychological blow of all—the lock-up.

"Jars all through you when the door shuts," a man who had done 12 years told Berry. "You just feel all pent up like an animal."

There was very little "pent up" about Brother Herbert Blyden, who was holding his D-yard audience at a frenzied level, as he approached what Wicker took to be a peroration. There had to be an end, Herb proclaimed, to "the unmitigated oppression brought by the racist administrative network. . . . WE ARE MEN!"

This high-pitched refrain marked most of the oratory the observers heard from inmate speakers. Together with the insight he had had into the cruel reality of steel cages, this theme gave Wicker a new sense of the massed men shouting back at Brother Herb. He realized with shock the extent to which he, too, had acquiesced in the common attitude that thieves and rapists and murderers deserved anything they got. Logically, that depended on *what* they got; and anyway, a thief or a murderer or a rapist, however reprehensible, retained his tiny share of the human predicament. He did not cease to be human for having done something outrageous; quite the opposite.

That was the essential message from Brother Herb to Tom Wicker. But Herb's speech was not finished after all. It was not just the situation at Attica that had to be changed, Herb declared, not just better prisons they sought. They intended "to change forever the ruthless brutalization" the poor and the oppressed suffered throughout the United States. Borrowing from L. D. Barkley, Herb shouted again, "You hear but the sound before the fury of those who are oppressed!" And he added on his own, "When you are the anvil you bend—when you are the hammer you strike!" The brothers of Attica roared their approval.

Brother Herb then turned his attention to one of the five original demands, presented the day before to Herman Schwartz and Arthur Eve at the first negotiating session—"speedy and safe transportation out of confinement to non-imperialist countries." This was the least likely of all the inmate proposals to be realized—indeed, so lacking in practicality that Wicker was never able to take it seriously and doubted whether many inmates did. Nor did Brother Herb get the overwhelmingly favorable response he usually evoked. There was a mixed chorus of yesses and noes, indicating what Wicker thought was a general indifference to the matter.

Finally Herb brought his speech to an end by demanding complete amnesty, enforced by the federal judiciary against legal, mental, and physical reprisals. And furthermore, Brother Herb told the brothers, they wanted action and "no more fruitless rap." They sat him down with a thundering ovation.

In the glare of the television lights, Wicker realized that Brother Herb's relentless oratory had been filmed for the world, as well as heard by the brothers of D-yard. He was not optimistic about the reaction of that world, since most people, in his judgement, would not appreciate hearing themselves and their country denounced as racist oppressors. In that sense, inmate oratory could make it more difficult to meet inmate demands and work out a peaceful settlement. Herman Schwartz, reflecting on his experience of such oratory, decided it had a deliberate purpose:

"They don't come right to the point with detail. They attack. And then when you ask why, they give you more details. But the first approach is the blast of contempt and anger. . . . That initial blast throws you completely off balance, particularly if you're not expecting it and particularly when their negotiating tactics in general [are] continually changing demands and putting them in very general terms, continually interspersed with insults, so that you're constantly being forced to defend yourself."[32]

L. D. Barkley was next at the microphone—thin, intense, wearing the nearest thing the prison had allowed to an Afro haircut, his metal-rimmed glasses gleaming in the lights. In his reedy voice and with his precise manner, pointing with a long and emphatic finger, Barkley lashed out, as Herb had, at the racism and oppression of American society. But he also began to cite some details, and name some names—Judge John Conable of Wyoming County, for example, with whom litigious brothers had had much dealing, was described as "an old emaciated worthless person" who sometimes took 120 days merely "to reserve decision" on inmate petitions and appeals.

Brother L. D. told an impassioned tale of how the Black Muslim leader in Attica had been "held incommunicado" by the prison authorities merely for asking them for a place to worship. Most prison authorities were wary of Black Muslims although the Muslims had an outstanding record of rehabilitation, better than any corrections professional could show. Malcolm X, while in prison, had found religion, politics, and himself when he found the teachings and disciplines of the Honorable Elijah Muhammed. But the Muslims were *organized and disciplined* and that threatened the peace of the institution, as any administrator was likely to see it. Besides, for religious reasons, Muslims agitated against pork in the mess hall, and pork was cheap and filling, just the thing to feed inmates.

Barkley introduced one Brother Jones, with the comment that there should be a Grand Jury investigation of fraud in the commissary and metal shop ("the slave shop"). Brother Jones elaborated on the metal shop fraud in a rapid-fire address that Wicker could not follow. Jones rattled off figures to suggest that the metal shop turned a higher profit than reported because its workers' wages were held at slave level and that the unreported profits found their way into administration pockets and the town of Attica's shopping centers. The inmates seemed easily to understand this confusing account.[33] They cheered wildly for Brother Jones.

Wicker then had his first real look at Richard Clark in action. Brother Richard, given early by his parents to a series of foster homes in Manhattan and Queens, once a drug abuser and convicted of robbery and petty larceny, had been converted to the Nation of Islam at Auburn prison. There he also became a "revolutionary" leader, which got him transferred to Attica in 1970. He was slender compared to the burly Brother Herb, but just as intense—although, under his woolen cap, his face was impassive as he spoke. When he spoke, Brother Herb had been an orchestra leader, evoking Wagnerian melodies; by comparison, Brother Richard seemed cool, tough, nerveless, a Marine lieutenant briefing his troops before battle, with the crack of the lash in his voice. In fact, he was a Navy veteran—"tough, street-wise, and unlucky," said a school friend.[34] In September 1971, he was 25 years old. "He didn't have a lot of experience," Roger Champen said of him, but "not only was he quick to pick up the point, . . . he had a nice feeling for people, he could talk to people, relate to them . . . work out their problems."[35]

Richard Clark had his own blunt eloquence, too, less florid than Herb's, less conversational than Champen's. Clark was a phrasemaker. "We are all hostages here," he declared soberly, and Wicker thought of the guns, the troopers, the helicopters, all the firepower ringing D-yard, his own uneasy position; he decided Brother Richard had grasped the situation more accurately than Kunstler with his talk of political power.

But as for the guard–hostages, Clark went on, they were warm, safe, sleeping on mattresses if they wanted to, when some of the brothers had none. If the guard–hostages were uncomfortable, it was because "Mancusi is keeping them out in the cold." Quickly it became apparent that Wicker's fear was being realized; Brother Richard was pressing the demand that "Mancusi must go"—which seemed to Wicker even more hopeless than he thought the amnesty demand.

Mancusi was accused of withholding medicine and food, needed not only by the brothers, but by the hostages in the ring of benches. "Mancusi is a dog that has gone wild; we can't consider any kind of agreement unless Mancusi is out of here." That sounded less like a demand than a precondition, but Brother Richard wanted things in perspective—it was the guards and the troopers outside D-yard who had the guns, not the brothers. The brothers were not threatening to attack or harm anyone, if they were let alone. Mancusi and the pig, on the other hand, were beating and gassing the brothers in C-block and giving them no food and water (Wicker here encountered for the first but not the last time the question whether he should get up and tell the brothers the truth they did not want to hear and probably would not believe).

So "we are the only civilized men here," Clark said. D-yard was the only "neutral ground" in the prison. For the brothers, it was "a life and death situation." As for the observers, each of them had "the lives of about 10 men in your hands." Then Clark finished on a chilling note, addressed to the unseen ring of hostages beyond the television lights:

"How long do you think this [situation] will last? If we go, we got to take everything with us."

That was the key to it, that was the card Brother Richard and Brother Herb and Champ and the others had to play. That was what had brought the television cameras to D-yard, and the observer group in state planes and autos to the negotiating table, and the troopers with their guns to No Man's Land and the roof of A-block. The civilized men on their neutral grounds could kill the hostages if the troopers came over the walls, and the civilized men would hold the hostages either until the state met their demands, or until the troopers came, signalling death. That was the power the brothers had, and it had been effective so far, no doubt beyond their dreams; so effective that their demands were steadily accelerating as the brothers felt the tide running their way.

"Brothers!" Herbert Blyden had boomed. "We got This Man listnin'. Listnin' to you, Brothers!" The powerless had power at last.

But it was all wrong—not for the inmates to have power, perhaps not even for them to have taken it as they had. But Wicker believed deeply, hearing the lash in the voice of Brother Richard, that a threat to kill was not the right way—much less killing, in fact. He knew, too, how the inmates would answer, how perhaps Kunstler or Lew Steel would answer for them—that it was in fact the *only* way, that anything else would be playing games, white liberal games, or just white man's games. The pig only answered to the knife; The Man only yielded to the gun. That was what the brothers believed, what life had taught most of them.

If that were true, Wicker thought, he not only had no business in D-yard, with his white face and liberal mentality, he had no hope of accomplishing anything there that the threat to kill the hostages by itself could not achieve. He was trying to cling, as to a slippery rock in the roaring river, to a belief that good will and good sense and good nerves, just and responsive men, could prevail, or at least stalemate the guns and the knives—could make a difference between human beings thrown together, as they all were, and surrounded by the limitless indifference of chance.

Besides, as he had realized earlier, if the brothers actually had to exercise their power, it became no longer power worth having or power able to achieve useful ends. It became only the power to kill a few helpless men who were not the problem—men who were more nearly the class kin of the D-yard brothers than of the men and the institutions who *were* the problem, as far as "the problem" was definable. Wicker seriously doubted that the power to kill hostages could, by itself, gain the inmates the reforms they wanted.

Brother Juan was introduced next, a little fellow, an impassioned speaker with a heavy Spanish accent. The brothers, he said, were "treated like animals," hassled in every way, their mail tampered with and delayed. Guards and the authorities pitted race against race for their own purposes—"when they see any amity they lock us up and they brutally beat us and they accuse us of conspiracy." Spanish-speaking men had requested a library of Spanish books and the authorities responded with "comic books from Mexico." And "practically illiterate officers . . . want to treat us like cattle" for not speaking English properly. Dr. Williams had told a Puerto Rican brother at the infirmary one morning to "wait until you get out—learn English so when you come back we can understand you."[36]

"Are we to stop being treated like humans?" Brother Juan demanded of the observers, in conclusion. He was making no threats—just the opposite. "We need your help, this is no joke. . . . This could turn into another My Lai, right here."

It was a line that later rang piercingly in Wicker's head. At the moment, Brother Juan's plea was overwhelmed by the fierce, following oratory of Jerry Rosenberg, known in the prison as "Jerry the Jew." With his long hair and Brooklyn accent, his fierce, sharp, ferret face, his machine-gun delivery in his shrill voice, Rosenberg's manner seemed all but hysterical; he reminded Wicker vaguely of one of the Dead End Kids in long-ago movies.

The real hostages, Rosenberg declared, were in C-block and wanted to join the brothers in D. "We want 'em out tonight, now!" he screamed to roars of approval.

He had his own priorities, this jailhouse lawyer who had called Schwartz' injunction "garbage" and torn it up that morning. There could be "no negotiations" on the questions of full amnesty, federali-

zation of the state prison system, adequate water and clothing—
"We're not animals here!" These were nonnegotiable matters.

On the other hand, Rosenberg ranted, his voice rising to ever-shriller
tones, "If they want violence, we can give 'em plenty of violence. In
fact, I'm ready to die!" While the brothers cheered, Wicker reflected
that Jerry Rosenberg, reprieved to a life sentence after years on death
row, perhaps had standing to say that, if anybody did; he had seen
death up close. But Jerry Rosenberg did not strike Wicker as a man
anxious to die for a cause, even though he concluded his speech in a
blaze of brotherhood:

"We're all oppressed in this Attica Concentration Camp, whether
you're white, black, or Puerto Rican. But we are united!"

Most of these speakers had been scheduled and had been seated at
the negotiating table. But another sort of speaker then appeared,
making his way out of the crowd, through the security chain, to the
leaders' table. Brother Herb rose after a while, took the microphone,
and said, "This is a democracy here, anybody wants to can say his
piece, so we gonna hear now from Brother Phillip Shields."

Shields was a big, muscular black, wearing what looked to Wicker
like army fatigues. He had a mustache, huge hands, an ebony face that
glistened in the light. He braced one foot on a bench and leaned on his
knee as he spoke into the microphone someone had unfastened from its
stand and handed to him. His voice was rough, unmistakably Southern;
it carried Wicker back to many a Saturday on the streets of Hamlet,
many an hour in the company of yard men and washwomen and
laborers in the world of his youth.

"We gamblin' 'gainst the institution here," Shields said, haltingly but
with force. "We lose, somebody, lot of us gone get hurt, some gone
get killed. Now me, I stands on my own. I ain't speakin' for nobody
but Phillip Shields, I ain't even tryin' to speak for nobody else. But the
way I sees it, if amnesty can be had for all of us, and it's guaranteed
that we get it, I'm ready to do what we got to do behind that."
Amnesty was the thing, Shields said. Demands were something else.
Demands were all right, but not if they made you lose sight of
amnesty, which was the thing that mattered.

As for non-imperialist countries and free transportation, Shields said,
"The silent majority out here . . . ain't sayin' shit. . . . I stands on
my own, and I ain't concerned about Algeria, Africa, or anywhere
else."

This evoked considerable applause as Shields handed the microphone
back to a displeased Brother Herb. It took a Southerner, Wicker
thought, to get to the heart of the matter. He was tired of rhetoric,
tired of tirades, ready—as he had been for an hour—to pin down a

consensus of the brothers' demands, then to talk to Oswald about possibilities. He wanted executive efficiency, not political ranting. His nervousness had been overcome by boredom, and he needed sleep, a shave. Not far in the back of his mind, it bothered him that he had not yet written his Sunday article. He had a middle-class sense of obligations, and he wanted to be about them—not listening to endless speeches about things he could not change, could scarcely influence. Like Phillip Shields, he wanted only to stand for himself.

But Wicker's impatience vanished as Brother Flip took the microphone and began to speak, even though Flip's was the same message that had been spoken so often already—men in prison were still men entitled to be treated by other men like men, not as animals or numbers. But the conditions of prison life, of Attica, made it impossible for them to be treated as human beings. That was what the uprising was about, Flip said, that was what the world should understand.

The same message, but different. Wicker could feel, as could the other observers, its gathering power as Flip talked on almost conversationally. He was different from any of the speakers who had preceded him—soft-spoken where most of them had been ranting, persuasive as against their brute force, eloquent in a more learned and sophisticated way. Brother Flip seemed an educated man with a high sense of drama. Wicker speculated that he might have been an actor on the outside; where else could he have found the style to wrap himself in a blanket as if it were the toga of a Roman senator? He had a thin, sensitive face adorned with an elegantly trimmed mustache. His head was quite bald in the glaring lights. When he gestured, his long, expressive fingers underlined his relatively quiet words.

Flip moved toward a peroration as expertly as any politician Wicker had heard on the stump—better than most. D-yard was silent, listening; the bonfires flickered on the walkways. Beyond the linked men of the security chain, the mass of the brothers surrounding the dark circle of hostages were still upon the ground or in their makeshift tents.

"We no longer wish to be treated as statistics, as numbers," Flip cried, his voice rising in volume and intensity, but so controlled as to reinforce Wicker's belief that he was a professional actor. "We want to be treated as human beings." Then, sharp as the crack of a rifle: "We *will* be treated as human beings!"

The brothers were "not advocating violence," Flip said. "We are advocating communications and understanding." He mentioned Soledad, Kent State, Jackson State. Attica was not different; the brothers of Attica were calling only for what "oppressed people are advocating all over the world. . . . We do not want to rule, we only want to live." Then, the long arms, the sensitive fingers, swept wide to include the observers raptly listening at the table. "But if any of you gentlemen own dogs, . . ." the voice fell to a dramatic whisper, "you treating them better than we are treated here."

Scattered applause and yells broke the silence but quickly died, as if most of the brothers realized that Flip was about to reach for the highest, most demanding note.

"So we have come to the conclusion . . . after close study . . . after much suffering . . . after much consideration. . . ." In silence so deep that his voice rang back from the surrounding walls, Flip was marching to the inevitable point, taking his listeners with him so that they knew before the words came what they would have to say: "That if we cannot live as people, then we will at least try to die like men!"

The brothers erupted, long-held breaths burst forth in a shattering roar, a thunder of voices crying out at once—as much in joy, Wicker suspected, as in actual defiance, because he did not believe men cheered the thought of their own deaths, in whatever cause. He could well remember Lurleen Wallace explaining to him what she believed was the source of George Wallace's popularity in the South, and elsewhere. "He speaks out for the people. He's not afraid to say what they think. When he's on 'Meet the Press' they can listen to George and think, 'That's what I would say if I were up there.' "[37]

So it was with these men, who would not cheer more than any others for the idea of dying, but who would cheer getting it said, as Flip had said it, for all of them, for at least that one time—getting it said to the world that in the ultimate and unavoidable act of humanity, in the limitless brotherhood of dying, if in no other way, they would be men no less and no more than any others.

Flip stood motionless, as they cheered and fell silent. He was standing on one side of the table, the microphone in his hand, the toga flowing from his shoulders, when suddenly he leaned forward and across the table, the light gleaming from his bald, dark head.

"Brother Kunstler!" he cried, the microphone and his head thrust near that of the lawyer seated across from him. "What did they do with you in court?"

Kunstler was still for a moment, in the renewed, breath-drawn silence of the yard. Perhaps he was recalling the Chicago Seven, Judge Hoffman's courtroom, Bobby Seale in chains, the contempt sentence hanging over his own head. Then, like a woman surrendering to a lover, he rose, his glasses pushed up on his forehead into his long hair, and threw his arms around Flip. There was pain and rapture in Kunstler's face, in his voice, as he cried out, "The same thing they did with you, Brother!"

The two men embraced, and once again there were cheers. Then, releasing himself, Flip said quietly to the observers, "I want to thank all of you beautiful people for coming here. Stand with us now . . . walk with us . . . die with us, if necessary. . . ."

Die with us. With stunning impact, Wicker realized that the idea was implicit in all the emotionalism and brotherhood, even in Kunstler's symbolic embrace of Brother Flip. Suppose the observers were asked to move in, as it were, with their "brothers" in the yard? To become participants, shields perhaps, to remain in D-yard and guarantee with their presence—those of them at least who were white, influential, well known—that the state could not attack with deadly force? Suppose they were asked to become hostages, not so much to the brothers as to brotherhood?

Wicker had been moved by the men of D-yard and was profoundly affected by some of the things he had seen and heard at Attica. But he was not that strongly linked in brotherhood with the men around him. He was not that ready to sacrifice or to die. He wanted to help, not to give everything for a cause. Vaguely, he wished he did, but he knew himself too well. Besides, he was not at all sure that his and Badillo's and Dunne's and Jones' presence would stop the coming of the troopers—not for long. Would not the public be likely to conclude that they, like the criminals with whom they would be seen to have thrown in their lot, "deserved what they got?" Perhaps even more so for being traitors to their own kind and to law and order?

As Wicker mulled these unpleasant notions, the microphone was passed back to the observers, the brothers at the leadership table perhaps sensing that they could not top the emotional peak Brother Flip had reached. Robert Garcia had started to speak.

Kunstler, Garcia was saying, had made it clear in his earlier speech that "we are not here to negotiate with you." Instead, Garcia promised, the observers were "witnesses to what is happening." And their intention was "to make clear what *is* happening. . . ."

Suddenly, from the lighted windows of C-block in the distance, there were shouts, screams, the banging and clashing of metal against metal.

"Our brothers!" someone shouted. "They beatin' up our brothers!"

Other men in the yard began to shout. The commotion from C-block continued; and through these noises there was suddenly the sound of running feet on the elevated walkways above the passageways that met at Times Square. Wicker, shrinking in his chair, could see figures darting along the walkways toward the barricades.

"Red alert!" a voice shouted. "Red alert!"

"They comin' in!" someone else yelled. "They comin'!"

"Red alert! Red alert!"

To the top of the table in front of Wicker a man leaped as easily and as silently as a cat. Instantly, he assumed a rigid military posture, his legs spread, one arm behind his back, the other holding the butt of a tear-gas launcher against his hip. Vietnam, Wicker thought, he's been to Vietnam; but before he could make out the man's face, the lights went out in the yard.

September 11, 1971

6

Dying Jive

On one of those Southern summer nights breathless with heat and as still and deep as the black waters of a millpond, Tom Wicker—then about 14 years old—sat on the open porch of his father's house. His bare feet were braced against the wooden planter box of geraniums at the edge of the porch, and he was tipped back in a canebottom rocking chair, watching from under the green-striped awning that came down almost to meet the shrubbery occasional cars go past on Hamlet Avenue (which was also U.S. Route 74 from Wilmington to Charlotte). No doubt he had eaten too much for supper, or was tired from a day at Boyd's Lake. Otherwise, even in those days long before air conditioning he would have been reading inside by the light. But to have turned on a light on the unscreened porch would have been to invite the torture of clouds of insects that swarmed from the peach orchards and watermelon patches around the town. But the boy was not thinking about going in to read; he was listening. At least, he was trying to listen. He was not sure what he had heard was really a sound, lying weightless on the summer night.

But *something* piercing had touched his ear. Something ominous had trembled across the still surface of the evening, then was gone. It came again. The boy sat stiffly in his chair, not wanting to move, not knowing if he had heard or if there was only a strangeness in the night.

But then he knew he heard a sound. It was clear enough, although he could not be certain from which direction it came, or what caused it—a sort of shriek, with a thunderous undertone. Both were growing louder. The boy listened, a little frightened; such sounds were outside his familiar world of church bells and passing cars and calling voices and the faraway whistles of trains.

His mother came out on the porch. "What is it, Tom? Can you tell?"

His father was away; his father was often away, on the run to Cayce, Wilmington, or Richmond, or perhaps even Charleston. The boy cleared his throat bravely.

"Can't tell," he said. "Sounds like from that way." In the dim yellow light falling through the screen door from the living room, his mother came and stood by his chair. The shrieking was louder now—as if something inhuman were grinding and rending. They listened for a long time, sensing each other's unease, until the rumbling was loud, too, underlying the tortured shrieks. On the sidewalk in front of the house, a Negro man walking from town had stopped as still as they, looking back the way he had come.

"What is it, Uncle?" Esta Wicker called. "Can you tell what it is?"

The dark figure moved cautiously to the curb and peered along Hamlet Avenue. No car had passed for several minutes, not since the sound had first come like the tip of a knife on his eardrum. Now the grinding and rending was painful in his ears and the underlying thunder began to shake the porch on which he sat, so that he could not hear what the Negro said over his shoulder.

"He must see something," the boy said. Uncertainly, he stood up. "I better go see, too."

"Be careful," his mother said. "Don't get off the curb."

He went across the short stretch of lawn and the flagstone walk he and his father had embedded in the grass to the curb and stood closer to the Negro man than he might have at another time. The sound made his ears ache and his heart pound; it was nightmare noise, infernal, overpowering. He looked cautiously down the street, prepared for almost any unholy sight.

"Lawd God," the Negro was saying. "Lawd God Lawd God. . . ."

Even after he saw them it was a moment before the boy knew what they were. Like hideous beasts in search of prey, the tanks were rolling in a straight line up Hamlet Avenue. Their screeching tracks clawed indelible scars in its asphalt and underlying concrete, their pistons and valves and roaring exhausts snorted fire into the Southern night, their long cannon snouts thrust ahead as if to follow a spoor.

The boy was fascinated, awed. "Lawd God," the Negro said again, and the boy ran across the lawn to the porch. "Tanks!" He shouted to his mother. "Tanks from the maneuvers! They're coming right past!"

He ran back to the curb. His fingers in his ears, he watched them go by one by one for half an hour—squat creeping green monsters, each with its helmeted human head peering from its open turret. The tanks provided him his first glimpse of war and arms and murderous power. Seeing them, he also saw that the world, so far from being always the placid place of his agreeable days, could grind and kill and dismember—could, in fact, make industry of it.

In the dark and the hush that fell on D-yard, Wicker thought for a moment he heard the tanks again. Quite clearly, in mind's eye, he saw them again, moving past where he lived. Then he knew he heard something else, though perhaps with the same grim meaning. Coming from the direction of C-block, as best he could tell, it was an indescribable sound—there could have been in it the groans of men, the screeching of gigantic doors, the crunch of huge objects colliding, massive vehicles moving on ungreased axles, giant cracked bells with leaden clappers. Threatening, as unearthly as the first piercing whisper of the tanks had been, that sound from C-block was not then or ever explained to Wicker. Later, when he asked other observers and some of the inmates, all seemed to have heard *something*, none quite the same thing. No one knew exactly what he *had* heard. Wicker came to believe each might have been listening to his fears.

Whatever it was, the sound did not drown out the actual and identifiable din from C-block. Figures were still moving on the overhead walkways, the man with the launcher stood like stone above Wicker's head, and only the dim prison lights, high up on the wall of D-block, relieved the darkness. For a moment, Wicker expected to hear gunfire. He prepared to go under the table at the first shot. He noted to himself, surprised at his ability to see and record himself calmly, that he was not afraid, nor even as apprehensive as he was angry to think that Oswald, Rockefeller, or even Captain Williams could have ordered the troopers in while the observers were there.

Quickly, he realized how unlikely it was that they would have done so. Just then someone began moving along the leadership table, speaking softly, "All right, now, nothin' to be upset about. Let's get these brothers behind this table here till we gets the word what's goin' on. Right back here behind this table, brothers, nothin' to be afraid about. . . ."

It was Champ's easy voice. Wicker moved speedily behind the leadership table as directed. Then he realized he and the other observers were trapped between it and the brick wall and barred windows of D-block. If the inmate leaders believed the observers had played decoy while the troopers made ready to attack. . . . Wicker did not let himself finish the thought. He was not *exactly* afraid, but he was getting more apprehensive.

"What's going on?" The murmuring voice was Herman Badillo's, and its familiarity was a relief. Wicker peered now from *behind* the rigid, soldierly figure with the launcher toward the lighted windows of C-block.

"I don't think they're coming in," he said. "I don't believe they'd do that while we're in here."

Inmates from the leadership table were clambering up on them, forming a protective human shield for the observers huddled against the brick wall. It was a reassuring and moving sight—these desperate, driven men, denounced by the world as thieves and murderers, interposing their bodies between men like Tom Wicker and whatever threat they perceived. Through their legs, Wicker could see the arm-linked chain of security men pulled close to the other side of the table. No matter what grim acts might have brought them to Attica, they were honoring their commitment to the observers' safety, and Wicker could not help but think how relative were the judgements of men. Thieves and murderers compared to whom? Prisoners of society due to what accidents and perversions of the same society? Still, he wondered uneasily if the protective cordon meant the inmate leaders were afraid not so much that the troopers were coming in as of an uprising in the unseen mass of the inmates whom he would never know. He wondered, too, if such a ring of "security" was being thrown around the hostages—the *other* hostages, he suddenly thought.

Then quiet fell on D-yard, save for the diminishing sounds of yells and banging from C-block. Long minutes passed in the dim glow from the lights high above them. In the silence, the near-darkness, the tension, Wicker became fearful at last, rather than just nervous—as if it had taken a while for the dangers of the situation to make their way through the layers upon layers of his ordinary, everyday reliance upon the supposed certainties of an orderly world. When fear came, it struck him hard. He recited to himself, over and over, his illusory airplane takeoff refrain, *there's nothing I can do about it nothing I can do*. But fear was sour as vomit in his throat.

"I think they staged it," Badillo murmured in his ear. Wicker marveled more at the Congressman's calm then at his theory. "The leaders are showing us they're in control. Nobody's coming in here tonight."[1]

Almost as if to refute him, a scream rose sharply, just beyond the security chain. A man dashed into the dim light in the area between the chain and the huddled brothers in the yard. He was swinging a blade that seemed nearly as long as a sword and screaming words that Wicker heard as, "Everybody gonna die . . . gonna die!"

He ran along, rather than straight at, the security chain, his screams not really intelligible, and the more frightening for that. But after he had run a short way, vague shapes moved out of the security chain, closed in behind him, grappled with him, dragged him still screaming in the darkness. Then he stopped screaming.

"One of the brothers got a little nervous," someone said from the top of the table. "He be okay, we can look after him." It sounded like the ever-soothing Champ again.[2]

There was silence again for more long minutes. Then, gradually, the men atop the table began to relax, save for the stonelike figure with the launcher. Some of the men climbed off the table and began talking to a couple of the observers. Wicker, beginning to unwind, too, crowded closer. Arthur Eve and John Dunne were agreeing to make another inspection of C-block and to return as soon as possible so the "negotiations" could resume.

The two emissaries departed. The security chain remained in place; the man with the launcher on the table, the observers behind it, the lights out. But the sense of crisis had passed; even the din from C-block had subsided. The observers and the inmate negotiators were milling about between the long rank of tables and D-block wall. Wicker peered through a barred window into a littered cell. On a shelf rigged to one of its walls, he saw a tropical fish tank and, in the half-light from a corridor bulb beyond the cell, the little fish drifting about. This was the most incongruous sight Attica had afforded him—a man who lived in a cage keeping fish in a tank, a fish tank preserved amid the wreckage, a hobbyist's quiet pastime against the same fear that had so recently soured Wicker's throat.

Conversations sprang up. In the center of one was the animated figure of Brother Flip, talking to Kunstler but rapidly gathering an audience. His real name, he did not mind saying, was Crowley—Charles Horatio Crowley. He was not, it seemed, an actor as Wicker had supposed; he was an oft-convicted armed robber who had spent a good part of his adult life behind the walls. He had educated himself "in the joint" and now taught other inmates English. His own was all but impeccable, so that occasional ghetto and prison argot sounded strange on his lips.

Flip Crowley was revealing himself as a most peculiar political prisoner and revolutionary—too wise quite to consider himself the one, too cynical ever to be the other. He ranged at length over various subjects—the life of the streets, prison lore, racism, the causes and consequences of the uprising. A half dozen observers listened almost mutely to his intelligent monologue.

American prisons incarcerate numbers of men like Flip Crowley—men of intelligence, of potential, exactly the sort that a "corrections system" hopes to be able to "rehabilitate." But probably no American institution is a greater or more costly failure than the prison, and the measure of that failure is that so few Crowleys are turned from a life of crime or prevented from following it, while so many first offenders are made into hardened criminals—and at enormous cost to the law-abiding taxpayers.

The state of New York paid more than $8 million to operate the Attica Correctional Facility for the fiscal year 1971–1972. Most of that was budgeted for security and maintenance, with 62 percent going to corrections officers' salaries. Depending on the economy and the state budget, New York recently has been spending from $8,000 to $10,000 a year to keep just one inmate in a maximum security prison like Attica. At the beginning of 1971, there were 12,579 inmates in all New York prisons, and the state's correction budget exceeded $100 million.[3] Inflation may have driven the per capita figure to $12,000 or so since then, although little but custodial care is purchased by such an expenditure, which far exceeds the cost of keeping a student at the most expensive university.

New York's corrections costs are higher than those of many states, but prisons are expensive to operate anywhere. The collateral costs—welfare payments to the families of incarcerated men, for example—are impossible to calculate, but sizeable. The losses in tax base and productivity derived from keeping men in cages rather than having them in gainful employment are also high.

The outsize cost of the prison system might be justified, or at least considered acceptable, if persons dangerous to society were being separated from that society and kept separate, consequently reducing the threat of crime. Taxpayers might then be getting some value for their enormous investment. Even if most men and women who had done time returned to society repentant and productive, there would be little reason to complain of either the cost or the efficacy of the prison system. But the real situation falls far short of either of these goals.

Deterrence of crime might also justify the prison system. Some modern statistical studies have suggested that the threat of punishment does deter crime, although it is not clear whether the severity of the sentence or the certainty of the punishment is more important in producing this effect.[4] If the latter, the deterrence would really lie with the swift and efficient working of the entire criminal justice system rather than with prison sentences alone. If the former, how much more severe would prison sentences have to be to have a *substantial* deterrent effect, since crime rates have been rising despite the almost automatic recourse of courts to prison sentences for most convicted offenders?

Prisons undoubtedly do, to some extent, deter crime, particularly among middle-class persons. But that raises the questions whether the deterrent effect is sufficient to balance or overcome the monetary and social costs of the prison system and whether the effect is direct and constant; that is, whether substantially increasing the length of prison sentences, or the number of people in prison, would substantially decrease the incidence of crime.

It is certain, however, that prison does not really separate and segregate criminals from society—not for any great length of time. In 1970, for example, the national average prison term was 28 months, which implies that a good many sentences were shorter than that. This is scarcely locking the cell door and throwing away the key. Besides, this only takes into account offenders who are caught and convicted. Since most crimes go unreported and their perpetrators uncaught, the "protection" afforded society by prisons is much less than is supposed.

As for rehabilitation of those offenders who do serve time, the sad fact is that a high percentage of them, after release, go right back to crime and often right back to prison. The rate of recidivism—the committing of new crimes by persons convicted of earlier offenses—depends greatly on the terms of reference used in defining it, but by any measure it is high. Using new arrest figures, the FBI Uniform Crime Reports calculated recidivism at about 65 percent for 1972; but the Federal Bureau of Prisons puts it at 33 percent for its "graduates." Of all those admitted to California prisons in 1968, 28.7 percent had done "a stretch" before; of all inmates in the California prison system in the same year, 44 percent had been in prison before. The National Council of Crime and Delinquency found in 1974 that of all inmates *released* nationwide since 1968, 35 percent had been returned to prison; and of those released since 1970, 31 percent were back behind the walls. It is reasonably clear that at least a third of those who go to prison go there more than once; the actual percentage may be much higher.[5]

That is suggested by a comprehensive study conducted by the Hartford *Courant* of what had happened, by 1972, to 200 men released from Connecticut prisons in 1962 and 1967. Based on nationwide conviction records, the study showed that 60 percent of the 200 had been convicted of felonies after their release. Another 15 percent had been convicted of misdemeanors. Most of these 151 men had multiple convictions. *Sixty-eight percent* had been reimprisoned. Statisticians say these percentages could be applied to the total of 1041 men released from Connecticut prisons in the same two years with a margin of error of no more than 3 to 5 percent.[6]

Faced with these failures, American society conceivably could try to do a better job of catching criminals and could choose to lengthen prison terms, even drastically. Periodically it does so, as New York did for drug offenders in 1973. But unless life terms were decreed for every offender—remember, at $8,000 a year or more per offender—

doing that might only make the situation worse. And there is some evidence to suggest that the more people imprisoned, the more criminals are made; and that the longer the term, the likelier the inmate is to recidivate.

When the state of Florida, for instance, was forced to turn loose 1252 inmates in 1965 because they were found (as a result of the case of *Gideon* v. *Wainwright*) to have been unconstitutionally convicted, a study showed that the recidivism rate among them was only 13.6 percent nearly 30 months later—substantially lower than most recidivism estimates. Among another group of Florida convicts who served their sentences and were normally released, the recidivism rate was 25.4 percent, which led Florida's corrections chief, Louie L. Wainwright, to say, "This mass exodus from prison may prove that there are many inmates presently in prison who do not need to be there in order to protect society."[7] It also raises the question whether the *deterrent* effect of prison, whatever it may be, outweighs the number of criminals and criminal repeaters generated by prison life.

It cannot be statistically established that recidivism can be reduced by shorter terms, or even by "community treatment" of offenders outside prison walls. But most studies do strongly suggest that recidivism *is not increased* by programs that keep people out of prison or get them out sooner.[8] If that is so, immense sums of money are being wasted on prisons, and a great many Americans are being made to suffer the harsh and brutalizing experience of prison without the streets being made safer thereby.

Some figures from California are instructive. In 1970, for a prison population of about 53,000, the state spent $147 million, mostly in custodial and security services. For 221,000 on probation or parole—four times as many persons—California spent only $73 million.[9] If there is little statistical difference between the recidivism rate of probationers and parolees and that of inmates who serve their terms, a lot of money and emphasis has been put in the wrong place, and not just in California.

In fact, in 1965, state and local correctional services (exclusive of the federal prison system) cost $940 million, of which $754 million went to institutions like Attica, but only $186 million went to "community" treatment of offenders. And at that time, prison and jail construction underway or planned was estimated at $1.1 billion, if calculated at $10,000 per new bed.[10]

The obvious failure of prisons to "rehabilitate" leads some well-intentioned persons to advocate *more*, not less, spending on these institutions. They want more psychiatrists, better job training, intensive counselling, group therapy, improved educational services, a better institutional environment, "behavior modification"—that is, any tool or service that may finally reach the ancient, illusory goal of American corrections, the repentance and reformation of offenders. But while all such tools and services—save the many dubious aspects of "behavior modification"—may be worthwhile in themselves, there is no real evidence that any or all of them can sufficiently "rehabilitate" offenders. One authoritative study of the matter has been summarized this way: "With few and isolated exceptions, the rehabilitative efforts that have been reported so far have had no appreciable effect on recidivism."[11]

That is not the only consideration, of course. At Attica in 1971, for example, an inmate instructor and 15 typewriters were provided for a beginners' typing course—ludicrously inadequate for a prison population of 2250. For the prison printing course there were no linotype machines and 15 students had to be assigned to each of two presses that required only one operator apiece and had been obsolete since World War II. The auto mechanics class was not allowed to have gasoline, which the staff considered a security risk.[12]

Well-equipped and staffed job training programs might not directly reduce recidivism; but the farcical "vocational education" offered at Attica actually created resentment by its plain inadequacy. It was one more evidence to many an inmate that the state cared nothing for him—that its "correctional services" and commitment to "rehabilitation" were a joke. That kind of reaction causes contempt for law and those who administer it—and perhaps self-contempt for those to whom such sorry programs are offered.

Self-contempt, insofar as it is possible to say, seems to be important in the making of much criminal behavior. "I ain't shit . . . we ain't shit" is a common complaint among poorly educated, unskilled young inmates, particularly those belonging to racial and ethnic minorities. Self-contempt breeds the attitude that it is impossible to "make it" in a "straight" fashion, that is, to get a good job, keep a family together, and observe the laws. So, many an inmate returning to the street scarcely bothers to try, so sure is he or she that it is no use anyway. And all too often, "straight" society makes it so hard for an ex-inmate that, in actual fact, he or she has little chance to make a decent living outside of crime. That is particularly true, again, for the minority groups.

On the other hand, the awakening of self-respect seems to be indispensable to any real "rehabilitation" of an offender. That appears to be why, for instance, the Black Muslims have been so successful in redeeming inmates. The Nation of Islam concentrates on pride in being black and Muslim. The occasional spectacular reformation usually results from some accomplishment. An inmate may discover he or she is a good actor or painter or writer—Miguel Pinero, for example, wrote the successful Broadway play—"Short Eyes." If, in almost any fashion, an inmate can acquire a sense of self-worth, a feeling that he or she is as good as anyone else, he or she will at least *try* to make it in the "straight" world. But acquiring self-worth is not a process that prisons are designed to further—quite the opposite—and not even psychiatry can guarantee success in such a personal transformation.

Generally speaking, therefore, there is no known penological approach that achieves a significantly lower rate of recidivism. But prisons are the most costly and perhaps the least effective of all—draining taxpayers' money while failing to keep most criminals separated from society, probably not deterring crime to any great extent, and not achieving much "rehabilitation." The greater likelihood is that prison life, and what follows it for most ex-inmates, *increases* the incidence of crime and the danger of becoming a crime victim for every American.

How could it be otherwise, a Wisconsin study committee asked, with "an institution too large to provide individual services, too geographically remote to provide vital life contacts, and too regimented to foster self-esteem. . . . If you were required to live in a cell with few facilities, little privacy, limited contact with other persons significant to you, limited access to employment, and a high degree of authoritarian regimentation, how might you fare upon re-entry into the broader, more competitive society, there to be greeted by the stigma of having been 'away'?"[13] The committee's report recommended that Wisconsin's prisons be *abolished*.

"One thing I don't understand," Wicker said, breaking Flip Crowley's easy flow of conversation. "I see why you guys did what you did and the changes you want made. What I don't see is the logic of demanding complete amnesty for it. No matter what your justification, people were hurt and crimes were committed, weren't they?"

"Well, now as to that," Brother Flip said, "I'll put it this way for you, where we're coming from in here. You take my case. In for armed robbery. All right, I did it. My lawyer tells me that as these things go, I got a fair trial and a reasonable sentence. So here I am, teaching school in the Attica Correctional Facility."

His voice was calm, controlled, his words precise, with an unmistakable black tone and the flavor of the streets. But they lacked the pervasive profanity of the prison yard, and his sentence formation was oddly formal.

"So we're all even, right? I did it, I'm in here for doing it. Fair and square, no complaint. Paying my debt to The Man. But, brother, you got to understand that's just the way it *ought* to be, that's not the way it *is*. That Man is committing crimes against *me* every day I'm here. And nobody's saying shit about that."

He went on at length about these crimes, giving his listeners to understand that if all had not happened precisely to him, each had happened in the cell next door or on the tier just below. They happened all the time, too, could happen to him any day, could have happened last week or last month. Getting beaten, being robbed and ripped off, given swill to eat, cheated out of what were only slave wages in any case. Thrown in the box with no chance to argue or appeal. His mail censored, books he needed denied or taken away, that kind of chickenshit. Buggered without a finger raised to stop it. Or buggering somebody else. All kinds of spies and informers around. All kinds of dangers from other, more predatory inmates, and nobody to protect him or even to care. You borrowed a box of butts, you paid back two or the enforcers came and the hacks looked the other way. Throats got cut for less than two boxes of butts and nobody gave a damn.

"Now in the middle of all that kind of shit," Flip said, "in the course of the commission of all these crimes against *me*, brother, *I'm* up here paying my debt and squaring it out, if one of *them* gets hurt or held awhile, does that make it look different for me to demand amnesty? They holding *me* in the joint here for all these years, and we're holding these hacks a few days and treatin' 'em good, but they charge *us* with kidnapping. Does that put a different face on it for you, brother?"

It did, indeed, Wicker said politely, impressed but not convinced. He did not doubt Crowley's and the other inmates' tales of violence and oppression, and he believed them no more than slightly exaggerated. Nor did he argue with Flip's basic premise that doing his time ought to make him "all even" with the society whose rules he had broken; and that hence that society was itself criminal if it aided, abetted, or permitted crimes done to him—particularly if it committed them itself through its agents in the prison administration—while he was paying off his debt.

Wicker was persuaded that a human being had to be prepared to suffer the consequences of his actions. Justification had nothing to do with it, because every man could find justification for what he needed to justify. *Thou shalt not*—no ifs, ands, buts, or loopholes—was a necessary restraint without which no society of humans was possible, and to violate the commandments in whatever cause simply had to bear consequences; else the act could have no value no matter how powerful the cause. A violation was sometimes necessary and worthwhile; society, recognizing that necessity, might sometimes forgive, for what it considered good and sufficient reason. But the violator had to stand ready to accept the ordinary consequences of the violation. Only such readiness, not pleading for forgiveness, could give transgression value.

Besides, suffering the consequences of his acts was every man's *responsibility*, Wicker thought—in his positive white man's fashion forgetting to ask *to whom?*

". . . Ain't that shit?" another inmate was demanding in outraged tones. "Man, what the fuck they 'speck, The Man come round here fulla shit like that?"

"Talking about the guard with the busted head," one of the observers murmured to Wicker.

"Now what might of happened," the inmate said scornfully, "that motha fucka so fuckin' *scared* he had a *heart* attack."

"Yeah," another inmate said, as if providing a chorus. "Motha fucka had a heart attack and you know what them otha mothas done? *We* send 'im out the fuckin' gate, *they* try not to take 'im."

Black ghetto talk is full of such apparently mindless profanity. It rings with a fierce, desecrating exaggeration that has genuine roots in ghetto life. A people who can do little to change the actual circumstances of their grim existence, to whom acceptance of degredation and despair is a required daily adaptation to life itself, find release and relief in many ways—music, revolution, crime, athletics, the needle, not least the vengeful hyperbole, the threatening excesses of street language. In D-yard, the walls fairly trembled from these defiant blasts.

"Shit like that. . . ." The first inmate seized Wicker's arm and pointed up at the row upon row of barred windows marching along the face of D-block. "You tell *me* what the fuck, man? What kinda shit that Man say on the radio? We thow some fuckin' hack out the fuckin' *window?* In *this* joint?"

"Eva fuckin' window in the joint got them fuckin' bars," the other inmate said. "We gone push a fuckin' hack thew them *bars?*"

"Fuckin' *heart* attack what that motha fucka had, he so fuckin' scared, he seen the brothers runnin' loose."

The heart-attack version of William Quinn's broken head did not impress Wicker; the point about the barred windows did. Since there was another story that Quinn had been thrown down a stairwell, and still another that he had been hit with a pipe, it meant that the authorities did not yet have an eye-witness account, from a guard or an informer among the inmates, of the assault on Quinn. But at that time, Wicker did not fully understand what the authorities' window story, which they had heard on the radio, meant to the inmates, cynical as they were, and wise in the ways of the law.

When Eve and Dunne returned to D-yard, they brought with them David Rothenberg, Mel Rivers, and Ken Jackson of the Fortune Society, an organization of ex-inmates; Jim Ingram, a black reporter from Detroit who had been on the original list of invited observers, but who had just arrived; two members of the Young Lords Party from New York, José Paris and Juan Ortiz; and the strangest "observer" yet, one Jaybarr Kenyatta, a sullen-looking black who arrived in garish robes and turban, with a small rug draped over his arm. Oswald had mistaken him for Charles Kenyatta, a former associate of Malcolm X, a ludicrous but not unimportant error.

Eve reported that at least one C-block brother seemed to have been beaten by a guard, for what reason, if any, he did not know. While others were being harassed, no general assault had taken place or appeared to be in preparation. With that, the "red alert," which in fact had been relaxed half an hour earlier, was ended with none of the observers sure what it had been all about. The brilliant television lights came on, the man with the launcher disappeared, and the observers resumed their seats.

Kunstler had been keeping notes and reported that by his count the brothers had made 30 specific demands before the alert. As their lawyer, he needed to know where the brothers wished to talk, when, and with whom on the part of the state. But this effort to get down to cases was lost in oratory, as Jaybarr Kenyatta rose to introduce himself to the Attica brothers—one of whom, he said, he had just recently been.

Later, some doubt developed about that, as about Kenyatta's exact Muslim connections. But when he introduced himself in D-yard, many of the inmates seemed to welcome him as a friend. Tall but stooped, an incongruous figure with his robes and rug, speaking in the ranting dialect of the ghetto, Kenyatta was different even from the inmate speakers. A diatribe against the "motha fuckas" (white society, sometimes simply and scornfully called "This Man" or "the pig"), his speech was an undisguised appeal for rebellion against that society. It was a violent, revolutionary speech and, somewhat to Wicker's surprise, it evoked a huge response. Kenyatta was repeatedly interrupted by cheers and applause for such fiery lines as, "Freedom means dying to live like a human being rather than like a dog!"

Kenyatta made it clear, too, that he believed the revolution against This Man had been started at Attica and was going ahead in D-yard. Wicker was fascinated by Kenyatta's high-pitched eloquence. He was learning something about polemics, he thought; by comparison to ordinary political discourse he was hearing an authentic language, whether of revolution or hysteria it was hard to say. But either way, Kenyatta had fired up the brothers to the highest pitch of the evening; and Wicker saw no way that he or anyone could be negotiators between revolutionaries—if Kenyatta was in the true spirit of the

yard—and the society they aimed to overthrow. That was rather as
L. D. Barkley had earlier pictured the situation in D-yard: "We talkin'
about livin' or dyin'. They ain't no in-between."

But talk of dying had got on some of the brothers' nerves, as Clarence
Jones soon discovered. He returned to the microphone and surprised
Wicker with some fire of his own. In his well-cut clothes and his
educated voice, he ringingly declared that "if America has a soul, it's
right here." He pointed to the hard-packed dirt of D-yard. "Not out
there," outside the prison walls. In fact, Jones said, the real need was to
"rehabilitate what's out there." Moreover, he said, "some things in life
are non-negotiable—freedom, dignity, survival—those are non-
negotiable."

Herbert Blyden had heard one word too many. All that non-negotiable jive was fine, he rose to say, "but if you don't negotiate for your
survival, you gonna die right here." That was the first hint Wicker had
heard of any willingness to negotiate reasonably—reasonably from *his*
point of view.

Kunstler quickly seized the opportunity to return to practical
matters. Did the brothers insist, he asked, that there must be no
criminal reprisals, as well as no administrative reprisals?

No question about it, Brother Herb replied. That was the only
thing. What was more, nobody wanted to hurt the hacks they were
holding. The brothers wanted it recognized that they were not without power, but as for Herbert X. Blyden, he knew that "we're dealing
here with more than offing pigs. I don't touch the hog. We're dealing
with *our* lives here. . . . Some of you may want to die, but I want to
live. . . . Some of us ain't too smart but we not going for all this jive"
about dying.

Wicker could not tell to what extent Herb represented the general
view. But he was one of the leaders, and his realistic view, just expressed, was encouraging—particularly after the wild reception for
Kenyatta's call to revolution. There was no way to know which lead
might be followed in the end. Either way, there had been no "give" on
the amnesty question. But at some point short of dying, Herb, at least,
wanted to deal; and he did not want to "touch the hog." But, as the
meeting dragged on toward dawn, through more weary hours of
oratory, there was no more progress than that.

Jones tried again to pin down details. When would the brothers be
ready to negotiate? That question reflected the observers' failure to
recognize that these *were* the negotiations, so considered by the
inmates and the state. Jones evoked more speeches in response, from
which it developed that Rockefeller, Oswald, various federal judges,
the District Attorney, all these and more, ought to come to D-yard for
solemn conferences with the vanguard of a new society.

Every turn toward decision flashed away in such blazes of oratory. Whether cultivated as political theater for television—although Roland Barnes must long since have run out of film—or from an overenthusiastic sense that D-yard really might have the power to move the world, the brothers' manner was that of a liberating army nearing its final triumph.

Wicker calculated that the observers had entered D-yard just after 11 P.M.; his watch showed it well after 4 A.M.—five hours of fear, tension, calculation, anger, astonishment, physical fatigue, and boredom—when Richard Clark, blunt and staccato, made the closing speech and appealed for unity with his own kind of eloquence. "We started this thing together," Brother Richard told the yard. "Now we got the fist. Let's don't get divided into fingers."

With great relief, Wicker lined up with the other observers to be counted off and marched out of D-yard in the last dark minutes before dawn. The long night had taken more than a physical toll of him. His hopes for a rational and equitable solution had been all but destroyed. Every sign of realism had been overwhelmed with impassioned defiance. Every effort to develop a procedure—what was middle-class man without established procedure?—had been lost in rhetoric.

He was acutely conscious, too, that the hostages were not coming out with the observers, nor were the observers staying in with the inmates. The observers could pull out, go away, move at will, once out of D-yard—which only meant they had no real stake in the deadly game being played at Attica. The observers had no real base, no bargaining power of their own. How could they, in the final analysis, have an effect upon Richard Clark's fist *or* the troopers' guns?

But worse than all that was a thought that haunted him as he stumbled out of D-yard, through A, back toward No Man's Land and the hard, police faces above the clubs and the guns. Going into D-yard the first day of the uprising had left Herman Schwartz with a "sense of having touched, for the first time, the power of hatred when it gets a little power, deep hatred of the most bruising, scathing, scalding kind which obliterates everything else."[14] Coming out of D-yard in the gloomy darkness of Saturday morning, Wicker was thinking *I didn't really know*. Over and over, he thought it. *I didn't really know how much they hate us. I didn't really know. . . .*

The night was not over. The observers, probably 30 of them at that point, when the group was at its largest, filed wearily into the Stewards' Room. Some slumped on the floor; some perched on desks, some leaned against the walls. All were exhausted, none had had any sleep, but one in whom the juices of combat were flowing strong was

Alfredo Mathew, the fiery young school superintendent whom Herman Badillo had brought along from Manhattan to Attica. The group was no sooner gathered in the by then familiar room than Mathew fairly bounced to its center.

"Now *I'm* going to say something," he shouted. "Some of you guys didn't help a bit out there, all you did was make things worse. You, Kenyatta!"

Kenyatta, perched on a desk in his robes, his shoulders slumped, listened impassively, his eyes bloodshot and his mouth sullen, while Mathew shouted at him that his speech had been an incitement to riot and revolution. How could Kenyatta expect, if he urged the inmates on, that they would reach a conciliatory mood? He was inflaming the situation, not helping it.

Mathew was on ground nearly as firm when he next attacked Tom Soto and Kunstler. Soto had stayed behind in D-yard when the other observers came out, and an angry Oswald had sent for him to come out. Mathew shouted that Soto, too, in public statements and private conversations, was encouraging the inmates. As for Kunstler, he might be the inmates' lawyer, but in his opening speech he had come close to suggesting that if the D-yard brothers held out for truth and justice, they had the power to get it. This was playing with other people's lives, Mathew declared, and no one in the room had the right to do that.

Wicker generally concurred, and he was glad not only to hear this said but to hear it from the Puerto Rican, Mathew. He was becoming acutely conscious that he and the other WASP observers had to watch their steps lest they become identified with the prison authorities— such are the touchy realities of minority-group politics. That would do no more good than if the black and the Puerto Rican observers became identified with the inmates.

On the other hand, Mathew, despite the soundness of his argument, was overwrought—the long night had told on everyone—and lost force through overstatement. The counterargument could be made that Kunstler, at least, had won the inmates' solid confidence.

Kenyatta scarcely seemed to have listened. Kunstler appeared a little abashed, but with his natural force soon was leading a discussion that reminded Wicker of what he had heard of an "encounter group." At first, everyone tried to talk or shout at once. Order was restored by the "chairman," Arthur Eve, a forceful man in many ways. But Eve then adopted the principle that everyone had to be heard, in turn, at whatever length. The result was a disorganized, often irrelevant session with no continuity of subject matter, in which the exhaustion of the observers was no help. Some of the speeches seemed as impassioned as those of the inmates.

Gradually, however, two broad groupings became apparent to Wicker. One was dismayed by the vehemence of the inmates in the yard and fearful that settlement was not possible. The other regarded much of what they had heard as "bullshit" and believed that a deal was bound to be possible, primarily because both sides had so much hard interest at stake. Wicker was a shaky adherent of the latter group, but his attitude was more nearly the result of a lifelong way of seeing things than of any observed evidence in the yard.

Oswald and his aides apparently got accurate reports of what was going on in the Stewards' Room—probably from some of the state legislators who came and went. The commissioner took the floundering and lack of agreed purpose among the observers as a bad sign, suggesting that the observers might not be up to the heavy burden placed on them;[15] and he was right. David Rothenberg, for one, saw quickly that the observer group was far too big and diffuse to function effectively.

Rothenberg was a former Broadway press agent, an energetic and tough-minded man who had become sympathetic to the problems of inmates, not because he had ever been one, but through his share in the production of a drama, *Fortune and Men's Eyes*, about prison life. He had forsaken his well-paid Broadway life to organize the Fortune Society in aid of inmates and ex-inmates—which both his principal associates, Jackson and Rivers, were. The Fortune Society was one of the most effective of such groups, and Rothenberg had not made it so with Arthur Eve's tolerance of long unfocused speeches. What the observers needed, he said flatly, was an executive committee that could make decisions subject to ratification. He suggested five names, obviously with an eye to their public clout. Wicker's was one of them.

Tom Soto, retrieved from D-yard on Oswald's order, protested that Rothenberg's nominees did not sufficiently reflect the "third world." Wicker agreed with that; public clout was necessary but the observers' "ex-com," if there was to be one, needed the confidence of the inmates, too. He withdrew his name. By a hectic process of appointment, elimination, election, and assumption, an ex-com was finally chosen: Eve, Kunstler, Jones, Kenyatta, Dunne, and Badillo; three blacks, two whites, and a Puerto Rican; presumed public clout in Jones, Dunne, and Badillo, as well as inmate confidence in Eve, Kunstler, and Kenyatta. Unfortunately, the ex-com remained mostly a list of names rather than a useful tool.[16]

Discussion of the inmates' demands centered on amnesty and the removal of Mancusi. These were clearly the hardest issues to solve; most of the others involved conditions within the prison that Oswald could change, carry to those who could change them (Rockefeller, or the legislature, or both), or at least promise to consider. The latter group of issues, it was more or less decided, should be discussed by the ex-com and Oswald, as a first stop.

Wicker was intent on the amnesty question. The long night in D-yard had sharpened his conviction that amnesty was the key to the situation. He argued that the observers could not merely take the District Attorney's relayed "no" for a definite answer. Rockefeller and others would have to be consulted, but the first step was to find out if there was *any* "give" in Louis James' position. Perhaps if James knew the gravity of the situation, the danger of wholesale bloodshed— maybe if he were given a sanitized version of Flip Crowley's reasoning on amnesty—something that would mollify the inmates might yet be worked out with him. Wicker was under no illusion that a real amnesty was possible; he was not sure he favored it himself. True to his vicarious political experience, what he really hoped was that clever and determined men could devise an acceptable formula.

It was a successful argument—particularly since there obviously was nothing to lose. Wicker, Clarence Jones, and Julian Tepper—the latter two lawyers—were named by Eve to make the trip to Warsaw, 25 miles away. Too late, Wicker realized that his argument had postponed sleep.

CHAPTER

7

We and They

Tom Wicker could not help remembering the easy small-town life he once had known, as he and Jones and Tepper, all glum with fatigue, rode in Tepper's rented car over the rolling hills and farmland of Wyoming County. The countryside seemed isolated, cheerless, far more remote than his sunlit youth. In the early morning hours, the gaunt houses, the sad roadside stores and service stations, the emptiness, made him think of a moonscape, then of winter and of the great drifts of snow and the ceaseless winds he imagined coming down from the north across the frozen lakes, the barren hills.

But after they located Louis James' house in the outskirts of Warsaw, Wicker saw quickly that there was nothing bleak or forbidding or remote about the District Attorney, whatever his surroundings. Short, a little stout, with a round, florid face, he came hurriedly across the yard and greeted his visitors cordially as they climbed stiffly down from Tepper's car. Tepper had called from the prison to warn him that they were coming. If they'd been up all night, Louis James said, he knew how tired they must be. Come right in and Mrs. James would see about some breakfast.

Mrs. James, in fact, was at the door, with the same invitation. Small-town hospitality, Wicker was pleased to see, had not lost out to whatever might have happened since he had gone to the city. Small-town housewives still loved to feed their guests.

While Mrs. James hurried about breakfast preparations, the three visitors talked with the District Attorney in the living room. It was a comfortable room, not exactly decorated, but evidencing a restrained and orderly taste. Things seemed to match and to be each in its place. There was no clutter. The living room was not formal but suggested that there was a more relaxed place somewhere in the house—maybe a den in the basement.

Louis James proved to be a *listener*, a good deal to be said for any man. Clarence Jones talked first, lengthily and wearily describing the situation at Attica, coming around by inches toward the point of their mission. The District Attorney interrupted to express great interest. He regretted, he said, that in his brief term—he had been elected in 1970—he had not been inside the prison. He had no idea what conditions there were like. That was something he would have to remedy. To see the place under the circumstances in which his visitors had seen it must have been something of a shock to them.

Then Mrs. Jones summoned them to the table. Only as Wicker sat down did he realize that he was ravenous. He had eaten nothing but a dry prison sandwich since Franc Shor's admirable lamb chops at lunch the day before. Now, he and Jones and Tepper plunged with undisguised enthusiasm and fervent compliments to Mrs. James into a platter of bacon and scrambled eggs, with ample toast and coffee on the side. If not the best meal in Wicker's recollection, it was surely the most welcome. How strange was the world! His gourmet luncheon of 18 hours before followed by the lurid night of fear and exhaustion in D-yard, now this placid morning around a breakfast table out of Norman Rockwell's America.

Throughout breakfast, and as the four men relaxed over empty plates, Jones continued to lead the conversation toward the question of amnesty. They were all tired and less coherent than they might have been, and no one wanted to throw the matter straight into Louis James's teeth. Besides, Jones had an elliptical style, an approach thick in detail and rhetorical texture, but not one that moved quickly to the hard point. Wicker had seen this style before and had wondered if it was peculiar to middle-class blacks. Was it, perhaps, an echo of the biblical rhetoric of the black preachers who had first achieved education and set standards for the descendants of slaves? Or was it an instinctive effort on the part of men who had gained a foothold in a white-dominated society to speak with more eloquence and command of vocabulary than most in the white community ever felt the need to demonstrate—rather as Conrad and Nabokov, having acquired English instead of being born to it, had written English prose that plumbed vocabulary, syntax, and imagery to their depths, to an extent that writers native in the tongue seldom attempted.

Inevitably, the talk arrived at the question of amnesty. Yes, said Louis James, it was true; he had told Commissioner Oswald that he could "absolutely not" grant an amnesty. That was just the way it had to be. What his visitors were saying about Attica and the men in D-yard was interesting. He could understand that the inmates believed they had to have amnesty. But they were saying that they would kill the hostages if they did not get it—an exchange a prosecutor sworn to uphold the law could hardly accept. Even if, as Jones had been saying, the inmates were acting for reasons that were justifiable, or at least understandable, he saw nothing in the law that gave him discretion to grant an amnesty.

Why, Wicker wondered, had he thought there was even a chance that he would hear anything else from Louis James?

The day before, a busload of blacks from Buffalo had arrived before the gates of the Attica Correctional Facility. The occupants apparently hoped to be of some service, at least to maintain some kind of vigil outside the walls. There was nothing threatening about them. The proprietor of the nearby Tipperary Restaurant immediately locked her doors and put up a "closed" sign. The white customers inside went on buying and drinking beer. Elsewhere in Attica a guard's wife told a reporter, "The inmates aren't normal humans like you and I. We never committed murder."[1]

Perhaps it was natural enough, in the isolation of Wyoming County, to believe that "inmates" were different, persons set apart from the "normal"—by which was meant the housewife shopping in Attica's supermarkets or the service station operator on Warsaw's main street, in their rounds of work, home, children, school, civic clubs, Saturday nights, church on Sunday. That life was far removed from life in the explosive urban centers—New York, Buffalo, Rochester—where most of Attica's inmates had come from, where the busload of blacks had started their journey. So it was true that they were not "normal," as most of the good white folk of Wyoming County reckoned normality.

How could the people of the county sense, much less sympathize with, the anger and the desperation and the strange, elated pride of the dark men who had burst from the cages of Attica—of American underlife—and made their own fleeting place in D-yard? By turning down the television volume and standing a moment at their doors, the good people of Wyoming County could almost have heard the ranting voices of D-yard in their anguish and anger. But how many knew the meaning of those high walls rising in their midst—much less who was within them, even less than that *why* or to what end? What chance was there that the beer drinkers in the Tipperary could understand the other version of "normal" to be seen in the lives of the blacks on the bus, of Champ and Herb and Brother Richard Clark?

But the suggestion that the "normal" people of Attica town and Warsaw and Batavia and Hamlet, North Carolina—all those Main Streets stretching from sea to shining sea and back into the American past—"never committed murder" was as self-righteous as it was ignorant. As though no one had ever swung a beer bottle lethally in the roadside joints of America! As though no outraged "normal" housewife had ever plunged a kitchen knife into the heart of a lumpish husband or provoked him to murder by her adultery! Murder was primarily a crime of passion, most prevalent among family and friends and lovers, since passions waxed and waned most drastically among them. Murder could and did happen anywhere and to anyone.

But something else was implicit in the locked door of the Tipperary and in the woman's remark, something deeper than ignorance or self-righteousness or isolation. The ingrained American myth of violence rang in the words, the old Puritan notion that "we" don't commit crimes, only "they" do. Since their first effort to wrest the continent from the Indians, white Americans had seen only "the enemy" as violent, and themselves as peaceful, law-abiding, wanting only to be left alone to develop their civilization without hindrance.

But "they"—the Indians, the Tories of the Revolution, the Philippine insurrectionaries, the early labor agitators and "reds" and anarchists, the Germans in two wars, the Japanese and Koreans in a war apiece, the Viet Cong and the North Vietnamese, just to name a few—all have been seen as savagely destructive and violent, virtually inhuman, sometimes even "devils," capable of any act of treachery or brutality. So perceived, like wolves or mad dogs or savages, they could be destroyed without the taint of crime by justified people acting in defense of endangered civilization.

From the forests of colonial America to the campuses of Kent State and Jackson State, groups, particularly dark-skinned groups, who threatened or resisted existing authority or general notions of the progress of civilization have been viewed as irrational, uncontrolled, destructive, extreme (often in sexual proclivities as in violence), and usually treacherous and conspiratorial. Such people have been seen to deserve what they get from normal, peaceful, nonviolent, good Americans.

So American is this way of looking at violence that even those often victimized tend to share it. Black Muslims believe the white man is not just an enemy but the Devil. Urban rioters in the '60s burned and looted against an oppressor so evil that any violence was justified in fighting him. Youthful American terrorists of the antiwar movement bombed banks and government buildings in the certainty that they were acting justifiably against conspiratorial warmongers and capitalist exploiters.

When Mayor Daley ordered looters shot on sight in Chicago he was right in the American tradition. William Calley did not really regard the dead "wasted" at My Lai as having been humans. Ultimately, the North Vietnamese became unconscionable villains in American eyes for holding "our boys" as POWs when they were guilty of nothing but "re-taliatory strikes" on North Vietnamese cities in defense of an endangered "Free World" and a "tiny ally."

Francis Parkman, like the explorers and settlers he chronicled, saw the American Indian as a "murder-loving race," so incurably and irrationally violent that any measures against them were justified. Nowhere in his many volumes does he perceive a hint of a useful or healthy Indian culture, much less of racism, desire for land, brutality, or aggression in the advancing white forces. The latter are always peaceful but betrayed; attacked but resolute; often outnumbered by howling, conspiritorial demons but always superior morally —just as they were in Wild West magazines and cowboy movies, until recent years. In such a framework of good versus evil—we and they— Parkman and all too many other Americans have not had to bother with contemplation or analysis of the humanity of Indians or looters or gooks or Black Panthers, nor to face up to their own violence and aggression.

Puritan theology may be dead, but Puritanism lives in its tendency to divide everyone into two opposed camps, the saved and the damned, we and they, the forces of light and the forces of dark; and Puritanism shapes the myth of justified violence. To the early Puritans, the forest was the dark place of evil; its heathen inhabitants, the embodiment of that evil, were devils incarnate. Evil had to be stamped out, and anything done to exterminate it was justified. But evil was usually violent; so if violence had to be used to stamp out evil, that was justified violence. Today, the Pentagon calls it protective reaction.[2]

In the American myth of justified violence, burning Indian villages or napalming Vietnamese villages is not really violence at all because it is good versus evil, good triumphing over evil, moral values defending themselves against the demons. So it is, also, with the violent urban warfare of modern America. Police are not brutal or racist when they shoot to kill, or beat up or harass violent, subhuman beasts. They are protecting normal society. They had to get Fred Hampton before he got us. The head of the federal Drug Enforcement Administration was only stating a fact when he called "drug people" the "vermin of humanity."

So it is not surprising that it is not "we" but "they" who populate the Atticas of America—they, the violent, the lawless, the abnormal, the subhuman. Once it was the Irish, the Italians, the Eastern Europeans, whoever happened to be at the foul bottom of the American heap, unwanted, despised, feared, wherever possible arrested and jailed or even executed—Sacco and Vanzetti then, George Jackson now. The change was significant and represented an even greater change in the conditions of American life.

More than 30 years after Tom Wicker and his father had huddled by their old cabinet-model Philco radio in futile hope that some white bum-of-the-month might at least accidentally knock out the Brown Bomber, Wicker was well aware that not many white men regarded black life in America any longer as the kind of "play of shadows" Conrad's island adventurers could "walk through unaffected." Nor was that black life confined, as it so largely had been, to the towns and fields of the South and relatively affluent black settlements in Harlem and Washington.

There had been a tide flowing, out of the South, out of the Midwest, the Plains, toward New York and Washington and Chicago, Los Angeles and Kansas City and Houston, a tide drawing the people out of the countryside into the great population centers that lined the coasts and dotted the interior. Unnoticed, at first, in the tide flowing from the countryside had been the enormous migration of blacks out of the South to the cities of the North and West. The sociological and economic consequences of that migration dwarfed those of the more publicized "civil rights movement" that so changed black life in the South. The rights movement scarcely affected cities outside the South (at the end of the '60s, Boston's schools were more effectively segregated than they had been on John Kennedy's inauguration day). But the migration turned Newark and Washington black and brought huge black populations to every city, populations that were largely unlearned and unskilled and economically burdensome. The migration radically changed society, as blacks flooded the cities and whites fled to the suburbs.

In the new ghettos thus created there was an important difference from the old Irish, Italian, and Jewish ghettos of America. The new black population was not only essentially unprepared for modern, urban, industrial life, just as most of the earlier immigrants had been. The blacks not only found themselves discriminated against economically and socially, as all entrants on the bottom rung of American life have been. But they suffered an added handicap because, in the postwar years during which they came to the city, science, technology, and a changing economy were closing the traditional routes of upward mobility. The individual artisan, the small shopkeeper, and the unskilled laborer were in far less demand than in earlier decades. The construction trades were tightly controlled by exclusive, virtually all-white unions.

The new ghetto dwellers were *black*, too, with a history of tribal life and the degradations of slavery and segregation—the objects of a prevalent white view that they were barely human. The fear and hatred of whites for blacks was far more consuming than had been any

WASP disdain for ethnic origins or religious practices. Blackness was a greater handicap than any urban minority group in American history had suffered, and that handicap was superimposed on new economic and social conditions that had already made the road up from the ghetto more difficult than it had been for any of its previous residents.

Conditions in the black ghettos, where the black was more tightly trapped than any of his immigrant predecessors, rapidly deteriorated— past anything known by any other underclass. Crime, violence, and social instability of all sorts racked the urban black community. Family life was shaken. Unemployment, bad housing, ill health, and drug addiction were epidemic. Despair, hopelessness, and rage were the inevitable results and became visible for all to see in the great urban riots of 1965–1968.

In the far-off towns of the old America, meanwhile, the *real people* were already feeling their values threatened by strange new city products—hippies, radicals, drugs, criminals of all sorts. The Okie from Muskogee, who in Merle Haggard's lyrics clung to white lightnin' and pitchin' woo, was outraged, in the '60s, by pot, abortion, and dropping out—city ways all. But these were minor outrages compared to the nightly flame and violence suddenly appearing on the home screen, the black looters they could watch from their living rooms, as Watts, Rochester, Newark, Detroit, and even Washington were put to the torch.

As the *real people* saw it, the cities were black and the cities were exploding. The blacks were burning the cities. The violent, lawless, savage blacks, who were certainly not "normal human beings" by Wyoming County's lights, were taking over, making the cities into the kind of jungle their ancestors had come from.

Blacks were no longer laughable Stepin Fetchits, lovable Mammies comforting Clark Gable, musical Bojangles, unfairly oppressed although rightly kept in their place in the wicked South. Blacks, no longer harmless, no longer confined to the South, endlessly spawned by welfare mothers, suddenly were everywhere—or soon would be unless the *real people* took care.

Louis James looked to Wicker like one of the real people. He had his principles. He knew what was right. He could not grant an amnesty to criminals, and he could not see the men of D-yard as anything else. All he could do, he was saying, was his best to see that anyone who might be charged with a crime got a fair trial. That, the inmates could be sure, was the way Louis James operated.

Julian Tepper said he had no doubt of that. But the inmates were another matter. The inmates regarded the law as oppressive, unfair, full of booby traps for the unwary. The men of D-yard had reflected that attitude in their reaction to Herman Schwartz's injunction. Louis James' assurances would not be given much weight in D-yard—particularly if the young guard, Quinn, should die. That would bring the likelihood of capital charges against somebody; and in New York State, as the D.A. well knew, killing a prison guard was one of the few crimes that could bring the death penalty. Without something more than an unknown D.A.'s assurances of fair trial, a negotiated settlement in D-yard was going to be impossible.

Clarence Jones pointed out that if what Tepper said was true, it was safe to predict that the main casualties would not be just the inmates who might or might not have broken the law, and who therefore might or might not deserve what they got; he was not claiming everyone was innocent or deserving. The main casualties would be the hostages. The amnesty was not, therefore, as necessary for the inmates as for the husbands and brothers and fathers of the women and children of Attica, many of whom, no doubt, Louis James knew personally.

That was all very well, James said, and true enough. He regretted it as much as his visitors did. He would do anything he could to save the hostages. He wanted to do the right thing. But he had no power to grant amnesty even to save hostages' lives. He was just a county prosecutor, not a philosopher, but he doubted anyway that granting amnesty would be the right thing to do. How could society operate if people could coerce it into letting their criminal offences go unpunished? Besides, *he* knew he was not going to deprive anyone of his rights or punish him unfairly, no matter what the inmates might fear.

The District Attorney was being more understanding than Wicker had at first thought, but he was clearly not going to yield. On the other hand, James seemed not to be rejecting amnesty out of callousness or indifference or bureaucratic inflexibility. Wicker sensed a necessary condition for compromise—everyone *wanted* to agree. He moved in with an idea James' remarks had already suggested.

"Mister James, I think we all understand what you won't do, because you feel you can't. But suppose we turn it around. Would you be willing to give us a statement of what you *will* do?"

"I'm not sure I understand what that means," James said.

"Well, you gave us your guarantee that anybody charged would get a fair trial. That's a start. You take some of these inmates, they were at Auburn during the uprising there. They remember that afterwards some guys were charged with ridiculous things—like stealing a guard's keys. Just anything to get them charged with a crime so the state could pile extra time on them. At least that's what *they* believe. Maybe you could reassure these guys that this time it won't be like Auburn, if you give us some guarantees that we can stand behind."

James thought it over. He certainly had no intention of bringing any picayune charges just to be bringing charges, he said.

"Another thing." Clarence Jones quickly picked up the line of attack. "These men are worried that maybe everybody in D-yard will be prosecuted just for being in there." It might help a lot if the District Attorney could see his way clear to rejecting in advance any thought of "mass, indiscriminate prosecutions."

That went without saying, James said. "Prosecution can't be indiscriminate. You only charge a man with a specific crime when there is specific evidence to link him to it."

But he perhaps failed to grasp, the three observers took turns in pointing out, that while lawyers might understand that and the middle-class public might expect no less of its criminal justice apparatus, the men in D-yard saw things quite differently. Their experience—particularly the black and Puerto Rican experience—led them generally to expect that the law would be unfair, indiscriminate, and vindictive. Witness Auburn, with its grab bag of patently vengeful charges; witness the Tombs riots, as a result of which Herbert Blyden had had no less than 72 different counts leveled at him, although no one disputed the unspeakable conditions in the jail or the essential justice of the inmates' protest. In a more general sense, witness the Harlem Four, whom the state of New York was still trying to sentence for murder after six years and three trials—two mistrials and one overturned verdict. Those were only three examples out of an entire racial consciousness of dragnet arrests, trumped-up charges, manufactured or flimsy evidence, dubious identifications, legal technicalities, forced plea bargains, lack of decent or concerned counsel, delayed trials, vengeful prosecutions, excessive bail, stiff sentencing, and violations of civil rights and liberties—while all the time any ghetto black knew that *his* part of the city could count on less police protection for its decent citizens than any white neighborhood, affluent or otherwise. Such charges probably could not be brought against Louis James and the police officers of Wyoming County, but every ghetto black and Puerto Rican in the big cities was all too familiar with them, as the poor and powerless of all races usually had been.

Louis James could understand all that. It might seem a little overstated to him, but he was aware of much that went on in the cities. James conceded that the men of D-yard probably needed extra reassurance about the law in Wyoming County. If his visitors thought that that would help bring about a peaceful resolution of the crisis, he could not see how he could do anything else.

"I don't think you'll ever regret it," Tom Wicker said. "Maybe it won't do any good, but it can't do any harm. And you'll have the satisfaction of knowing you walked the last mile."

It was a corny remark, and calculated to be so. Wicker was not sure whether to be ashamed of playing on Louis James' desire to "do the right thing" or to be grateful that the three observers had been able to do so. In any case, they arose from the remains of Mrs. James' glorious breakfast with the District Attorney's agreement to write a statement of his intentions. There was no typewriter in the house, he said, so it would be better if they went to his office. With profuse thanks to Mrs. James, they left, again in Tepper's rented car.

The Wyoming D.A.'s office was on the second floor of an ordinary small-town office building. Whatever wild events might be taking place in nearby Attica, the office was closed for the weekend. James let them in and promptly retired to his inner office, produced a yellow legal pad, and began to write. It was not quite 9:30 A.M., and Wicker had a decision of his own to make.

On an ordinary Saturday, he had to have his Sunday article in *The Times'* New York office by noon. In any ordinary emergency, as the professional that twenty years' experience had made of him, he could have produced some kind of acceptable piece—four triple-spaced typewritten pages, 750 words—in an hour. Not good, but acceptable. Should he try it this time? The three observers had promised to be back at Attica by 10:30 or 11:00; so there was a bare hour in which Wicker could pound out a piece on James' secretary's typewriter.

On the other hand, he had nothing to write about, obviously, but the events at the prison. An Attica or Warsaw dateline on anything else would have been absurd. Whatever was happening at the prison was not conclusive but dynamic; so whatever he might write could be invalidated two hours later, or three, by an assault on D-yard, a new outbreak of violence within it, a statement by Rockefeller—any number of possibilities. Such a breaking-news story was a hazard of Wicker's trade; but in this particular case, he faced the additional risk that if events did outrun his copy, he might be so engaged as *an observer* that he would have no time—perhaps even no liberty—to function as *a columnist* and to make the necessary changes. Moreover, as *an observer*, Wicker was participant in the attempt to settle the uprising. He was personal witness to things being done and said not to the press or the public, but within the group. Had he the right to seize a journalist's opportunity out of his observer's experience? Perhaps later, it seemed to him, but not at the moment. Suppose his piece appeared on Sunday morning but the observers' tasks ran on another day or so, as was at least possible? If an observer, or Oswald, or an inmate were offended or put on guard by something he had written, he would have put one more burden on the observer group, one they surely did not need, as they worked for a solution.

It had already occurred to Wicker that perhaps he had no business among the observers. Over the years, he had developed a necessary aversion to any activity that tied, or even might tie, his professional journalist's hands. He believed, in the unique ethic of his kind, that it was his duty to learn, write, inform, publish, and be damned, if necessary. It was *not* his duty, or seldom so, to weigh the consequences of facts disclosed; nor was it his obligation to pursue causes *qua* causes. His commitment was to such truth as he could find, although the mere statement of the ideal was enough to suggest how often any descendant of Cain was likely to fall short of it.

He had, for instance, outraged some antiwar readers by refusing to put his signature to an ad urging citizens to withhold that portion of their federal income taxes that would otherwise go to the Pentagon. They argued that he was refusing to take direct action to support the ends he espoused in his articles. But he believed that it was not his part to take *action*, that his role was to discern truth and publish it, if he could. And he believed there was a certain difference, a difference vital to maintaining the confidence of his readers, between an unengaged journalist speaking in an independent (even if opinionated and wrong-headed) voice, and a committed activist pushing organized causes.

Believing all that, how had he got himself into Attica? In the first place, because he had not known what he was getting into or that it would develop so that he *had* to become more of a participant than he had expected. In the second place, because once having seen the hostages huddled in their ring and heard the impassioned plaints of the inmates, having seen the guns ready to settle the matter in blood, he was a human being first and a journalist second. In the third place, because—professionalism triumphant—however he might be tied up at the moment by his commitments to the inmates and to the hostages and to the other observers, his reporter's instinct still had led him into the most dramatic and interesting circumstance of his life. He was in the right place at the right time to add a few layers, however unpleasant or tragic, to his understanding of things. And that was his stock in trade.

There was another reason, too, but one that he would not fully understand until later. It had occurred to him within minutes of entering the prison, when he had thought that perhaps the time had arrived for his life to be put to the challenge. Later, examining that thought, reflecting on Attica, he discovered that he had arrived at an age and time—his divorce, the shattering of the stability he had come to depend upon, was a large part of it—when neither his profession nor his sense of self yielded him an essential feeling of worth. He liked and believed in his work; but its aloof, critical onlooker's ethic, valid professionally, could not sustain his life. His sense of self had finally required of him that he go into the pit. He did not believe unduly in his ability to do what others could not do. He did not have much confidence in the efficacy of enlightened action against the blind chance and indifference of the world. But he believed, finally, in the reserved places of his soul, that he was required, somewhere in his life, to set himself against fate—all the more so since he knew how slim was the possibility that he or anyone might prevail in the contest, and knew, too, that even if he did prevail, that also would be chance. Living itself was the essential guide; mere existence taught the essential lesson. Life had to be lived in the face of the certainty of death; and commitment had to be made even in the foreknowledge of failure. That was all the honor life offered.

So it seemed to Wicker, that morning, that the situation precluded his writing anything except possibly a descriptive article—a "color piece," in newspaper jargon. But he did not want to undertake even that in haste because he was vain about his descriptive writing. For the first time in his professional life, he decided to tell his office that he was not going to file. He had ample standing to do so. No one would penalize him for it. But it hurt him deeply, nonetheless—so much so that, the decision once made, he almost reneged on it. His own standards were the hardest to violate; his own expectations for himself the most painful to fail.

He felt vaguely that he should call the publisher to explain his momentous decision. But when his call went through, he did not even get the editorial department copy editor, who was not to come to work until later that Saturday morning. A nonchalant news clerk, as *The Times* insisted on calling copy boys, came on the line instead.

"Oh, yeah, Mister Wicker, sure."

"Tell Barzilay I'm not filing," Wicker said, as if announcing an armistice.

"Not filing. Gotcha."

"Just no time. I'm up here at the prison and I haven't had a minute even to think about a column. So tell Barzilay I'm not filing."

"At the prison. Gotcha."

"Tell him I hate it like hell."

"The prison?"

"No, not filing."

"Not filing. Gotcha, Mister Wicker."

Hanging up, Wicker reflected ruefully on the newspaperman's first and most basic truth: they could always get out the paper without him. Just then Louis James came out of his office, holding up a sheet of lined yellow paper.

"How's this?" he asked, and began to read. To Wicker, surreptitiously nodding at Jones and Tepper, the statement sounded generous, fair, persuasive. It was infinitely more than he had hoped for.

"That's great," Jones said, when the District Attorney finished reading. Wicker and Tepper agreed enthusiastically. A few minor changes were suggested, but the basic text that Wicker then rapidly copied off on the secretary's typewriter was Louis James' own:

> I have been asked by Messrs. Clarence Jones, Tom Wicker and Julian Tepper, representing the Committee of Observers at Attica Correctional Facility, to express my views as to the possible prosecutions that might arise from recent events at the Facility.
>
> First, I deem it to be my duty as a prosecuting attorney to prosecute without fear or favor ALL substantial crimes committed within this county, if sufficient evidence exists to warrant prosecution.
>
> Second, in prosecuting any crime, I do and would endeavor to prosecute fairly and impartially and for the sole purpose of attempting to see that justice is done.
>
> Third, under the circumstances of the present situation at Attica, I deem it to be my obligation to prosecute only when in my judgement there is substantial evidence to link a specific individual with the commission of a specific crime.
>
> Fourth, in this particular instance at Attica, I am unalterably opposed to the commencement of indiscriminate mass prosecutions of any and all persons who may have been present, and to prosecutions brought solely for the sake of vindictive reprisals.
>
> Fifth, in the prosecution of any crime, in this as in every other situation, I would endeavor to prosecute honorably, fairly and impartially, with full regard for the rights of the defendants.
>
> Finally, as a prosecuting attorney, I regard it as my paramount duty to attempt to assure justice, both in the trial itself, the outcome of the trial, and in the possible sentence.
>
> Louis R. James
> Wyoming County District Attorney[3]

The D.A. took the typed copy to a utility room and ran off copies on a small copying machine. It was all right with him, he said, if the observers wanted to distribute the letter among the inmates as widely as possible.

"Better still," Tepper said, "come with us and read it to them yourself."

James shook his head. "If I went there in person, they'd probably demand more of me, and I can't give any more than I have here."

"You've given plenty," Jones said.

Just then Tepper remembered his parking meter. "Don't worry," Louis James told him, grinning. "If you get a ticket, I can fix it."

Everyone laughed more than the joke warranted. Wicker was elated. He thought the formula they had been seeking might have been found. He thought his faith in the reconciliation of interests might have been justified. At least, the James letter gave the inmates something more than an inflexible "no" on amnesty. Surely, Wicker reasoned, the generous tone of the letter was bound to impress the inmates as considerably better than nothing. In particular, he thought the statements about "substantial evidence to link a specific individual with the commission of a specific crime" and opposing "indiscriminate mass prosecutions" would have weight in D-yard.

Wicker's view was backed by his memory of the rough-voiced Phillip Shields, coming out of the D-yard crowd to put down the revolutionary talk and to tell Brother Herbert Blyden that "the silent majority out here . . . ain't sayin' shit. . . . I stands on my own. . . ."

The three observers dropped Louis James in front of his house. Wicker got out with him.

"Mister James," he said, "if we can negotiate a decent settlement over there at the prison, it might be the beginning of something truly important. It could mean a new day for the criminal justice system in this country, and that could mean a new day in our whole society. If it turns out that way, you'll have had a lot to do with it. I think you just might have written a historic document this morning. And you may have helped save a lot of lives right away."

They shook hands. Wicker really believed what he had said. He believed it all the way to Attica.

8

The White and the Black

His boyhood in Hamlet had not seemed isolated to Tom Wicker. He knew his hometown was small and lacked the magnificence of great cities. But it did not seem out of the way. The trains came through incessantly, on their way to and from Florida, Atlanta, Birmingham, Richmond, even Washington and New York. The boys of the town could often turn a quarter or even 50 cents by hanging around the passenger station to run errands for the imposing people on the trains—a magazine from the newsstand, a candy bar or fruit from the Terminal Cafe. The rails stretching away north and south, east and west, the great locomotives (steam at first, diesel in later years), the crowded cars, the silent Pullmans with drawn blinds, seemed tangible links to the other exciting worlds Hamlet boys heard about on the radio or saw in the Paramount News or read about in the Charlotte *Observer* (then so anti-union that D. D. Wicker, a good Brotherhood man, used to become openly angry reading it at breakfast) or *Life* magazine or *The Saturday Evening Post*.

Early in the '30s, President Roosevelt's special train from Warm Springs had come through town (the President usually took the Atlantic Coast Line, not the Seaboard), and school had been turned out for the occasion. The Presidential train stopped for a few palpitating minutes with Secret Service men at every car entrance, but it was early in the morning and no one else made an appearance. Every window was shaded. Some said that just as the train pulled out, at the last moment, in the last window of the last car, the blind went up and a few lucky souls caught a glimpse of the famous smile and the uplifted chin. Although he was not one of those so fortunate, to Tom Wicker that day, it was as if the greatness of the world had embraced him and his town.

So he had not felt isolated in those days; and certainly not later, during the war, when the trains had doubled in number and passenger loads, when the flat cars would rumble, hour after hour, past the grade crossing on Hamlet Avenue, bearing their heavy green cargo of trucks, tanks, jeeps, armored cars, huge guns, and other military devices too exotic to define. The troop trains came through often, bringing jazzy times to the station when they stopped—all trains seemed to stop in Hamlet, whether for a reason or not—with the young soldiers or sailors hanging out the windows, jeering at the locals, flirting with the girls, passing out handsome tips for beer, Cokes, cigarettes, newspapers. D. D. Wicker was working harder and making more money than he had ever made in his life (so young Tom overheard his father confide to Esta Wicker). Hamlet was near important military areas—between Fort Bragg and Camp Mackall, the paratrooper base—and there was a well-authenticated rumor that if the Germans ever bombed the United States, Hamlet—"The Hub of the Seaboard," one of the most important rail centers in the Southeast—would be a major target. There was nothing isolated about *that*.

Like the other railroad boys, D. D. Wicker's son rated his own pass on the Seaboard and could travel free anywhere within the system. He was familiar in Charlotte and Raleigh—great cities, they seemed to him—and even, as a teenager, went occasionally to Atlanta to see Georgia Tech play football. He and his family could ride "trip passes" on other lines than the Seaboard. D. D. Wicker once took advantage of this to take the family to Washington on the Richmond, Fredericksburg and Potomac Railroad, just before Tom entered the fourth grade. The sharp edges of that experience never faded from his mind, so that 35 years later he could recall, as clearly as if it had been the day before, the vista across Union Station Plaza to the Capitol as it had appeared in its white magnificence to a boy from the South who did not know he was a provincial or that his ordinary world was out of the main stream of things.

But if he accepted his world without question, Tom Wicker was by no means always at ease within it. Sometimes he did not even feel a part of it, because he was not much like the other youngsters of Hamlet although he tried hard to be, throwing himself with painful desire into athletics, the rubber-gun wars of his long childhood summers, the bicycle and swimming races and wrestling matches, the tests of strength and sport through which his contemporaries earned respect and standing.

He was a big youth, tall and lean as a teenager, therefore expected to excel in the boyhood arts; but he seldom did. He was not physical, and neither his athletic skills nor his muscular strength anywhere near matched his robust appearance. Of all sports, he was avid only for leisurely baseball; and while he was always one of the last chosen for sandlot games and never achieved more than bare proficiency on the high school and American Legion Junior teams, he probably knew more arcane baseball lore, statistics, and strategy than any of his friends.

That was typical. In a society that exalted muscle and skill, he was essentially interested in books and in the long, wandering thoughts of summer days too hot for exertion, of winter nights beneath heavy quilts when his breath steamed in the darkness of his room and a quiet so profound would fall upon his world that it was as if all of nature and humanity were holding still for him to ponder. In a society, too, where sociableness was an absolute requirement, where to have real standing he had to be "popular" among his peers and considered "cute" by the peppy girls with whom he could never be at ease, he felt himself a loner, an introverted brooder who at one and the same time longed to be left alone and ached to be accepted—with the predictable result that he never quite achieved either. He deliberately coasted through the schools of Hamlet, recoiling from the distinction of superior grades. He drove himself to dances, parties, the fellowship of the church young people's groups that, in Hamlet as elsewhere, were mostly early-evening meeting places from which sprang later petting and beer parties. Always he held himself aloof in his heart, partially because he had no natural herd instinct, partially because his hidden interests were so little those of the (seemingly) nonchalant youngsters he had grown up with.

The truth was that he *considered* himself different, and quite consciously so. On occasion, the difference might appear primarily what his mother said was inherent in the character of his family. Some teachers suggested that the difference derived from an intellectual superiority with which they credited him. Sometimes he thought it was more nearly the lack of social and physical grace with which he taxed himself. Whatever, he wavered between thinking himself better and worse than his companions; but he always thought himself *different*.

This was probably due mostly to D. D. and Esta Wicker. For reasons never clear to their son, they sought—as in the expensive family trip to Washington—to put their two children on a different plane from the other young people of Hamlet. They largely succeeded, too; or perhaps only his mother did, while his father acquiesced.

From D. D. Wicker, his son gathered a powerful impression of excellence and rectitude. Gentle enough in personal relations, D. D. Wicker suggested, by example, a strength of character, integrity, moral purity, diversity of skills, and devotion to duty—a combination impressive to his son as the proper model of a man. This was only the more true because D. D. Wicker was often away from home, therefore less often on hand to display inevitable human weaknesses. D. D. Wicker seemed to his son scarcely to have any of the latter; to hear Esta Wicker tell it, he had none.

When Tom let slip the fact of having accomplished, for instance, the standard boyhood feat of sneaking into the local movie house without paying, D. D. Wicker sent him back to the box office to confess and pay, then disapproved of him long enough to bring the boy to gloomy reflection upon his own inherently criminal nature. Next time he at least knew enough to keep his mouth shut. Honesty was a passion in D. D. Wicker's house, and Tom learned from his father a lifelong aversion to personal debt, gambling, exploitation of others' misfortunes, and taking advantage of their generosity.

When, in the darkest depths of the Depression, weeks went by without Cary Hodges, the aging railroad callboy, summoning his father to work, D. D. Wicker did not merely mope about the house. One of Tom's most powerful childhood memories was of driving with his father to call on country stores in a largely fruitless effort to sell them cigars and candy under some commission arrangement his father had worked out. It was not a pleasant memory, for the boy thought of his father as a railroad man, stalking off to work with his brakestick over his shoulder, a lantern slung on the end of it—a romantic figure in a day when the railroads still had the power to evoke dreams of far places and extraordinary men.

D. D. Wicker could make and grow things with nimble hands. In the kitchen, his fried round steak with scorched water gravy was incomparable. From his railroad trips he brought back watermelons so consistently excellent in ripeness and flavor that others asked advice on his methods of selection. He cared for his automobiles—a square old Dodge for most of Tom's childhood—with such love and skill that he only needed and probably could only afford two from 1932 to 1946. His son had none of these abilities, nor the kind of muscles and athletic talents the town so esteemed, but D. D. quietly urged the boy to his own interests, to read and think and study—always, of course, to work. Even in death, his example was extraordinary; for at his funeral the minister announced what D. D. Wicker had never disclosed, that all his adult life he had tithed his meager income to the First Methodist Church.

But if to seem unworthy in the eyes of his father was something young Tom Wicker would have gone to any lengths to avoid, still it was Esta Wicker who was the most constant and insistent witness to his father's singular virtues. Observant, intelligent, talkative, she was not reluctant to point out the gross failings of others; nor, for that matter, was it hard for a watchful youngster to see these for himself. In his mother's view, like father, like son; if Tom encountered liars, cheats, and bullies among his companions, she was there to tell him that the example had certainly been set for them at home. But with such a father as his, *he* could never have that excuse. In fact, discreditable behavior on his part could only reflect badly and unfairly upon D. D. Wicker.

This insistence, Tom came to believe in later years, was a product of something subconscious that drove his mother, more than his father, to realize in her children things frustrated in her own life. In an era when no one questioned that woman's place was in the home, mostly the kitchen, Esta Wicker was a woman who quite likely had the ability not only to do far more than cook, clean, and attend the PTA, but probably to do almost *anything* better than most people around her.

In no way a feminist, at no point a person that her son ever discovered rebellious or overtly unhappy with her lot save for an occasional bitter remark about less deserving people with more means than she, Esta Wicker yet was probably a deeply frustrated woman, the more so for not being able in her time to identify the problem. Her intelligence, decisiveness, and vigor were of a high order. She was well read, politically interested, and the first "liberal" on race matters that her son encountered; and she had at times a personality of overwhelming vivacity and even brilliance, as well as an irrepressible wit. Yet, for all that, and for all the excellence of D. D. Wicker, circumstance had made them relatively poor working-class people in the small-town, Depression-ridden South.

So if his mother preached to her children the moral superiority to which she made them feel heir, and if she relentlessly egged them on to greater academic attainment and material achievement than she and their father could claim, making them feel that they owed it to such splendid parents as well as to themselves to excel (mediocrity would not do), it may well have been that Esta Wicker not only believed it, not only wanted the best for her children, but that she also was determined in her deepest heart that they should recognize in their parents the high qualities that lack of education and opportunity had limited— that these children should know the sources of their own excellence.

To a boy already more inclined to books than to backyard buddies, the high posture of his parents—not from blood or means, but from claims to character—made a striking difference in himself and those around him. Tom Wicker was left with a sense of moral obligation that he recognized as holding him to certain rigid standards not required of others, as well as firing him with an intellectual ambition that ironically contributed, or so it seemed to him in his small-town milieu, to a sort of physical and social inferiority. It was an ambivalence that he did not leave behind with his childhood, or Hamlet, North Carolina.

Most of the observers, after the early morning session in the Stewards' Room, had scattered to motels or anywhere they could snatch an hour or two of sleep. As they straggled back to the prison at the rendezvous hour of 11 A.M., the rebelling inmates were completing two full nights and days of "liberation" in D-yard.

"Compared to normal prison time," those 48 hours had been "euphoric," Roger Champen recalled. "They wasn't locked in the cells. . . . People functioned more on a normal level as opposed to prison level. And this was initially the feeling. Then . . . apprehension came in, but as it came in, it was still mixed with the euphoric feeling because you still were outside the cells.

"They realized there was some consequences to be paid for being outside that cell. And as I made my rounds—I called them rounds— each person I talked to felt differently. Some would be playing handball, some had set up showers and were taking showers. Some playing cards . . . and sitting down would be groups of guys who came from the same neighborhood and they'd visit about old times. And then you had guys sitting around and talking and cooking food and whatnot. This was the general feeling. This was mainly during the day. In the evening . . . when they gave you lights on the wall, that gave you some light, but there wasn't enough light to carry the whole yard so they had fires in the center of the yard. And it's chilly at night, in September, and the fire kept you a little warm.

"And they would tell stories, and it seemed like you were on vacation, you know, a picnic, so to speak. Because of the fact that no one was saying, 'okay, lock you in your cells.' That statement wasn't made to nobody and a person went to sleep when he felt like it, and if he felt like sleeping to mid-noon, he'd sleep. . . ."[1]

As the observers slowly gathered in the prison parking lot, trying to keep apart from the townspeople and reporters who thronged it, they found a phalanx of sheriff's deputies, armed to the teeth, barring the Gothic entrance to the prison itself.

Like those exemplary British guards in the bearskin hats, these worthies stared ahead, unblinking, when asked what was going on, who ordered them there, why they were barring entrance even to the duly appointed observers. Gradually, as the observers reassembled in the parking lot, it began to appear that they were being shut out deliberately and might not be readmitted. Most of them took the delay as a sign of a hardening official attitude. Some thought that the troopers were going into D-yard that sunny afternoon. No one knew.

Eventually, a few of the elected officials among the observers—Badillo, Dunne, Garcia—demanded admission to what was, after all, a state institution, and got it. Finally, appealing to Oswald, they also succeeded in getting the other observers past the obdurate deputies and the grudging corrections officers barring the entrance. This long delay, and the display of manpower–firepower at the gate, probably meant that the authorities were demonstrating in their own way that they still ran a maximum security prison—a "maxi"—observers or no observers. From that time on, at any rate, security restrictions became more stringent, and the good will of the state authorities appeared to decline—to the point, for example, that the observers had to get official permission to move anywhere outside the Stewards' Room, even to the toilet. Their welcome had swiftly been worn out.

By about 1 P.M., the observers were reassembled in their familiar headquarters, the Stewards' Room. Their ranks had been augmented by some newcomers, including State Senator Sidney Von Luther, a black from New York City whom Eve seemed to disdain; Minister Franklin Florence, a dynamic black community organizer from Rochester who immediately became one of the most forceful of the observers. Bobby Seale had not yet arrived; Kunstler reported him on the way.

The first order of business was a report from the group that had visited Louis James. Clarence Jones presented it, since Wicker and Tepper felt that his recommendation would be more persuasive to touchy black and Puerto Rican observers like Kenyatta and Soto.

Jones, the young lawyer-publisher, came out strongly in praise of the James letter. Before reading it, he conceded that it was not the complete amnesty demanded in D-yard, but neither, he said, was it an echo of the "absolutely not" that James had given Oswald the night before. The fact was, Jones said, that the observers, the authorities and—most of all—the men in D-yard were "approaching a moment of truth." The inmates would have to make their own decisions. Yet, it was "implicit in that repose of trust" they had put in the observers that the men in the Stewards' Room had a closer relationship to the inmates than to the authorities. That being so—Jones was laying out the strategy he and Wicker and Tepper had settled upon—the observers should try to put together "a package" of as many of the inmates' demands as Oswald would agree to, incorporate the James letter with Oswald's previous concessions on administrative amnesty, and present the package to the inmates. Such a package would not include everything they had demanded, but the observers could point out that "theirs is essentially a political struggle." In the give and take of politics, the package was "the best of all possible things which was capable of being achieved." That done honestly, the observers could do no more, Jones said. The inmates would have to decide for themselves whether to accept the package.

Then Jones read the James letter. It did not take long. The room was silent, with everyone attentive. As Jones finished reading, Wicker half expected the group to burst into applause. Instead, the James letter provoked the instant opposition of Kunstler, Lew Steel, and Herman Schwartz, who were among the observers most impressive to Wicker and most knowledgeable about the people with whom the observers had to deal. After a swift flash of anger that his handiwork should be so received, their response astonished, then depressed him—not least because he rather soon realized from their arguments that he had been euphoric. He and the others had not brought back from Warsaw a historic document but a weak substitute that the inmates were unlikely to accept in lieu of a pledge of amnesty.

In the first place, Kunstler pointed out, the James letter did little more than restate the law and the schoolbook ethic of any prosecutor. The jailhouse lawyers in D-yard would see that right away. Worse— Steel supported this point vehemently—if the letter became part of an official settlement, the state then could use it as support later on for a claim that *any* prosecution was neither "indiscriminate" nor "vindictive." Schwartz, still resentful of the short shrift the inmates had given the federal injunction he had travelled all Thursday night to get, pointed out tactfully that the James letter was neither as strong nor as tightly worded as the injunction had been. On its face, he said, the statement from the D.A. really meant very little and committed the state to practically nothing.[2] Schwartz nevertheless believed, as Wicker did, that there must be pressures in the yard to accept something less than a 100 percent guarantee on the amnesty issue.

At some point, as Schwartz saw it, "there are going to be among those twelve hundred [men in D-yard] a bunch of guys who are going to say, 'Jesus Christ, they're going to indict for murder, and murder of a prison guard is one of the few capital crimes left in New York. They're going to indict for murder, probably not me, they're probably going to indict 10 or 15. I don't want to die from all that firepower that's out there, and boy! That firepower is intense—helicopters, national guardsmen, and everything! I think I want to try to find out as quickly as possible what's going on. Turn on the radio, I think that's probably the best, right? I don't want to get one of those slugs in me for what the other guys did, because they'll never indict twelve hundred; and the D.A. said he wouldn't. They'll never indict even a hundred.' And sooner or later that's got to start operating. 'I don't want to die for what the other guys did.' Because there also have to be a lot of guys in there who are lukewarm about the whole business, but who joined in with the rest."[3]

Some other observers favored the letter. Most of them were of Wicker's moderate outlook—Dunne, Badillo, Wyatt Tee Walker. Von Luther sent Wicker a note praising the letter. Mathew, whose political views were milder than his temper, spoke strongly for it. Their point was primarily Wicker's and Jones'—that Louis James' letter was the nearest thing to a commitment the prisoners were likely to get.

That still seemed a reasonable point to Wicker, despite the new light in which Kunstler, Steel, and Schwartz made him see the letter. He took the floor and spoke rather passionately of the respect for Louis James that two hours of conversation had engendered. "I'd stake my life on that man's integrity," he declared. "If he said there'll be no vindictive or indiscriminate prosecutions, there won't be."

That wasn't the point, Bill Kunstler replied, politely but firmly. The point really was whether or not the letter would be convincing to the inmates, no matter what Tom Wicker might think of Louis James.

Besides, the acerbic Steel argued, with the cynical wisdom for which Wicker had developed considerable respect, how could they or the inmates be sure that Louis James would have anything to do with the prosecution a month or two months from then? In the final analysis, Attica was a political matter; Nelson Rockefeller would be the man who would set the tone of things, and he was not likely to leave anything that had become such a hot political matter to an up-country District Attorney.[4]

Yet, Wicker said, the opposition was not facing the matter squarely. Would the observers rather walk back into D-yard and face the inmates *with* the James letter, or with nothing but the flat and inflexible "no" on amnesty that was the only visible alternative? If nothing else, the letter was evidence of the observers' efforts and of the difficulty of the amnesty issue. Wasn't it better, as Jones had suggested, to give D-yard "the best of all possible things that was capable of being achieved" than to report abject failure to achieve anything?

With this view there was general agreement. Someone pointed out that maybe Bobby Seale, when he arrived, could persuade the inmates that no more could be done. Maybe they would trust him. Even Kunstler acquiesced, although Steel said nothing; he had argued earlier that the letter ought not to be shown to the inmates lest it discredit the good faith of observers who would even suggest that it might be acceptable. The general decision—again it more nearly evolved, rather than having been reached by orderly process—was that the letter ought to be presented without recommendation, but with the comment that it was the most the state would agree to. This was close to what Wicker, Jones, and Tepper had wanted, but the discussion left Wicker disabused of his high hopes that the letter represented a breakthrough, the "formula" they so desperately needed to solve the amnesty question.

The Saturday afternoon meeting in the Stewards' Room, moreover, had once again degenerated into such a free-for-all, with so little aim or control, that Wicker feared it would achieve no more than the encounter-group session they had held at dawn. He was bored by its repetitiousness and posturing and was anxious to get on with the job of working out the "package" Jones had talked about. So he moved, and there was general agreement, that the previously appointed executive committee begin winnowing down the inmates' demands to a coherent and reasonable list. Everyone else should leave the room, Wicker said, leading the way.

Outside the Stewards' Room, in the second-floor lobby, Wicker and Tepper discussed for awhile the dashing of the hopes with which they had returned from Warsaw. Gradually, it dawned on Wicker that only a few of the observers had left the Stewards' Room—in addition to himself and Tepper, only Tony Fitch, Tom Soto, José Paris (who was known as Brother Jay or "G.I."), and one or two others. All the rest had simply stayed put, as if there had been no executive committee appointed, no decision taken to let the committee act. Through the glass door of the Stewards' Room, moreover, those in the hall soon could see that Russell Oswald and Walter Dunbar had joined the group. The package was being worked out.

Tepper and Soto were outraged and demanded admission, but a guard at the door had his orders—nobody was to be let in. Some frantic arm signals finally brought out Juan Ortiz (inexplicably known as "Fi"), who rather lamely explained that the group inside, including Oswald, felt it was best to keep it small, as they were making progress.

Soto heatedly pointed out that most of those in the room—including Ortiz himself—had been supposed to leave. He, Soto, had as much right to be there as anyone who was not officially a member of the excom. And so he had; so had Wicker and Tepper; but with the guard on the door by Oswald's authority, there was little that could be done about it. Later, as Wicker suspected at the time, he learned that the exclusion was aimed mostly at Soto, whom Oswald and others felt would be disruptive in the Stewards' Room meeting. Later still, Soto was thus able to disclaim any connection with or support for the agreement Oswald and the observers reached that afternoon. Had he been part of the group, as he had tried so angrily to be, he could not fairly have dissociated himself from its product.

A long, dull afternoon ensued. Borrowing paper from one of the prison offices, Wicker desultorily worked on a possible column; but he had no heart for it and, by then, no deadline to make work necessary. Tony Fitch slept on a hard bench. Tepper and Soto stomped about, muttering and angry. Wicker was angry, too, but differently; he refused to show that he was hurt, or felt left out of the important discussions in the Stewards' Room. But he was, and he did—particularly since it had been he who had proposed that everyone leave but the ex-com. Then he had honorably led the supposed exodus, only to find that others had simply sat it out and usurped a place in the room. He half made up his mind to go back to Washington. If the meeting with Oswald produced a good package, there would be little more he or anyone could do. And the observer group was turning out to be one more society in which he felt set apart, superior or inferior to the others depending on the way one looked at it, but different either way.

How had he come to be there, anyway? Not just physically at Attica, but in the position to have been summoned by the brothers of D-yard? As the long afternoon crept by, Wicker sat unhappily on a hard bench in the second-floor lobby, brooding on his past, the winding journey that had brought him slowly—so slowly that in his mid-30s he had all but despaired of it—out of the South, out of the small town, out of all the influences that had shaped and deluded and persuaded him, to what, at 45, he had become. And what was that? Some called him a guilt-ridden "limousine liberal." Others looked upon him as a strong supporter of the weak and the disadvantaged. He had learned enough of life to know that probably both views were right and both wrong, since all but the basic truths about human beings were plural and depended heavily upon vantage point.

There he was, nevertheless, absurdly out of his depth—of anyone's depth—in a human situation that encompassed complexities and perversities with which men had been wrestling unsuccessfully from the beginnings of civilization. Amnesty, as against the needs of law and order, was not a quandary peculiar to D-yard. The violence implicit in the omnipresent guns, as in the pathetic ring of hostages, was not only "as American as apple pie"; it had been the ultimate recourse in all human history. By what arrogance did he expect to see it avoided here, where the stage was so conveniently set? The exploitation of humans by others, the cruelty, oppression, and inhumanity of men, wrong begetting wrong in the guise of right, the ultimate, desperate refusal of even the lowest order of men to be less than that even if death alone could establish their humanity—all these told nothing but the long, bloody, harrowing, mindlessly repeated story of mankind, irredeemable save for the unquenchable spark of man's insistence on his own humanity, guttering and flaring in D-yard as it had throughout history's savagery and indifference.

Certainly, the situation in D-yard could not be separated from the racial divisions and animosities of a society throughout whose history the black–white line had been as insurmountable as a Berlin Wall of the mind. Racism, its consequences, the modern attack on it both legal and intellectual, and its endurance in so many forms had been the central public concern of Tom Wicker's life—and one that, in his life's pattern, had set him apart from many of his contemporaries and peers.

He could not remember a time when blacks, however disregarded as persons, were not as much a part of his consciousness as music heard on the radio or the random passing of automobiles. There had been no moment in his adult, professional life when "the race question" had not been prominent in his mind and work. Its effect upon him and what he had written, he supposed, was responsible for his presence at Attica.

The first time he could remember shaking hands with a black, he had been 19 years old and a naval student at the University of North Carolina in the late stages of World War II. An assembly of student leaders was being held at the university, then an all-white institution; among the visitors were several blacks from other campuses. Wicker, still a loner, was in no sense a student leader, but he was introduced to one of the blacks by a friend, shook hands routinely, and only later realized it was a "first."

Routine or not, that belated handshake suggested the extent to which blacks and whites had grown up separately and lived as with a wall between them in the South of not too many years ago. True, there was a close physical proximity. Blacks were all about, they were as much a part of everyday life as the weather; and whites dealt with them constantly. But it was a Southern myth that therefore Southern whites knew "all about niggers." What they knew was more nearly what they let themselves believe, because they infrequently saw blacks, no matter how nearby or numerous, as *people*. Maybe an old family servant or a long-known gardener might register as a human being, hurting, sorrowing, striving, loving, living with the same fundamental problems of heart and soul that afflict all people of every color. But those few were exceptions. Otherwise, blacks were an unseen presence in the balcony.

White people who would never have dreamed of a personal discourtesy or an act of overt race discrimination against a black nevertheless found it impossible to conceive of his or her essential personality—which was why so many Southern whites could *insist* that blacks really liked their inferior status in the South, their seats in the balcony and the back of the bus. Individually separate, proud *people* could not have liked such status, on the face of it. Only niggers or colored people or even Negroes, not really being divided into individual personalities, could have liked it.

But the tendency to see blacks as a mass rather than as individuals was not, in Wicker's view, at the root of racism. At one time or another in America, virtually every group of lowly outsiders—Irish, Italians, Jews, Eastern Europeans—had been lumped together and treated as a herd, or a horde. While the discrimination against these groups had been real and had required heroic efforts to overcome, the attitude toward blacks among white people—*including* Irish, Italians, Jews, Eastern Europeans, and others who had themselves known discrimination—was markedly different.

No one had set up separate toilets and waiting rooms for white ethnics, however lowly, nor were many of the latter lynched for eyeing a white woman. Prolonged battles had not had to be fought in Congress so that Italians could order coffee at a drugstore counter, nor had any minority in America, save blacks, been legally in bondage sanctified by the Constitution itself and finally broken as part of the political maneuvering in one of the biggest, most vicious wars ever fought. It was never proposed in any part of the United States that there ought to be separate school systems and railway cars and water fountains for anyone but black people.

As for economic discrimination, ethnic immigrants, or at least their sons and grandsons, proved that that could be overcome eventually by hard work, talent, and an eye for the main chance. In the case of blacks, on the other hand, by the beginning of the 1970s, not only were low-skill jobs more difficult to find, but it was an accepted fact that the unemployment rate of the grandsons and the great-grandsons of slaves ran routinely at twice that of whites and ran even higher among young blacks, with the preponderance of all ages in low-paying, dead-end jobs. And there was ample evidence that not all of this was due to blacks' lack of skills and education (even if it were, what would that say about blacks' position in American life?), but that another major reason was the reluctance of American employers, including some of the biggest, to hire or promote blacks. Black enterprise, the siren song of the Nixon Administration in 1968 and 1969, proved a chimera. After a brief improvement in the '60s, the gap between median black income and median white income widened again in the early '70s.

At the heart of the matter, Wicker believed, was the idea of *blackness*. Black, in symbolism from the beginning of time, was the color of evil and death; blackness was to be feared and dreaded—whether as darkness of night, the color of the hangman's mask and the widow's cloth, that inevitable and unimaginable void of eternity that awaited all, or the unknown. Black was all of those things. Tom Wicker believed that the instinctive white man's reaction to the color black had set the nature of the white-black relationship.[5]

White fear had always been a part of that relationship and was still its overpowering ingredient. White fear was not just the fear of one person for another who might be dangerous, whether as a criminal, an addict, a bad influence in school, an economic competitor, a threat to property values, a sexual predator. White fear was deeper and more powerful for being indefinable—fear of the evil in man and nature, the blackness of life, the dark side of humanity, that dark side every human senses in himself, admit it or not. White fear was the fear of blackness, the fear of the worst in man and oneself.

White fear fixed itself upon the literal presence of black human beings. Black people, to whites, were the symbolic representation of the evil in man and thus were also the handy instruments by which white people could hold themselves symbolically innocent of that evil. To hold blacks in slavery, even, had been in a sense only to hold in check the evil in mankind; Southern slaveholders could preach the positive good of the "peculiar institution" with splendid fervor. Some great literature—*The Nigger of the Narcissus* or *Benito Cereno*—had reflected the deepest instincts of many white men in using blacks as symbols of evil.

To this ingrained white fear of blackness had been added many lesser levels of fear and complication, perhaps first among them the historic instinct of the bearers of the white man's burden that someday their irresponsible and subhuman charges would turn with cunning ingratitude upon them and exact with jungle ferocity the revenge of a savage nature no civilization could finally tame. The descendants of slave holders and slave traders never quite lost the fear of an uprising in the quarters or below decks, and what they saw in the 1960s seemed for many a nightmare come true.

Always there was the contempt of civilization for the savage's origin in the jungle; the need of society for a subservient underclass to scrub its floors and empty its bedpans; the psychological necessity of the poorest and meanest whites to have someone they could look down upon as they were themselves looked down upon by the affluent. To all these were added in the late twentieth century the unwelcome new insistence of blacks, whether by nonviolence or "black power," on a due share of jobs and affluence, and an equal opportunity or more in schools, unions, political parties, and the like. Opposing this was the determination of the just-risen ethnics not to lose to black aspirants the economic security and social status they had won by great effort.

And what weight can be assigned the more common and senseless slights and shudderings and ignorances of white fear—that blacks smell bad, speak English poorly, have kinky hair and thick lips, are prone to disease and theft and violence, have heads too hard to be broken and brains too slow to learn and penises too big to be tolerated, at least by white men fearful of white women's fidelity?

Blacks seem to fit perfectly, moreover, into the "we and they" syndrome of American violence—the insistence upon finding an inhuman devil or a savage demon as a threat to civilization, so that the violence of law-abiding American society, its police and its bombers today, its Indian fighters and lynch mobs yesterday, could be seen as justified, necessary, essentially not violent at all. It may not be a coincidence that when the last Indian warriors were slaughtered at Wounded Knee in 1890, the worst era of lynchings in the South was just beginning. One devil mostly exterminated, at least subdued, another had to be found.

As the black migration overwhelmed the northern cities after World War II, "we" and "they" collided on a national scale. More and more white Americans outside the South saw blacks as the enemy, savages at the gates, devils turned loose. The urban battle ground—crime in the streets—was the most pervasive and widespread case of "we" and "they" since the early settlers began pushing west over the Blue Ridge, sweeping the devilish Indians before them. Dragnet arrests, sidewalk shootouts, strongarm tactics of all kinds, punitive prison terms—all were justified in the righteous fight to protect civilization from the savage. And in his blackness, this particular urban demon of American life seemed perfectly to represent the rage, the hostility, the irrationality, the brutish force of an evil that had to be fought with any and every means at hand.

But when all of that was said, when a thousand other prejudices and misapprehensions and folk beliefs and inequities and hatreds and malices and plain stupidities had been added to the foul stew of American racism, the heart of the matter was the fear of blackness. Tom Wicker had shared some of that fear with the rest of white America, just as in one way or another, at one time or another, he had shared in most manifestations of his country's cancerous illness. He had not so much conquered or eliminated his racism as recognized it and compensated as best he could. But he was not sure that that was good enough, even for the circle in which he usually moved, let alone for the volatile, waiting world of D-yard.

Eventually, the long afternoon ended. The Stewards' Room was opened, Oswald emerged, the excluded observers entered, Wicker rather sheepishly, Soto and Tepper angrily—the latter so much so that his bitter words to Arthur Eve led Eve to take a swing at him. The two men were restrained and later made up their difference, but the near fight was evidence of short tempers, frayed nerves, too little sleep.

It was a sorry band of peacemakers, Wicker thought, who could not keep the peace among themselves.

Oswald later described the afternoon of negotiation, and his own reaction to it:

> All Saturday afternoon I conferred with the Citizens Observer Committee on the specifics of what now seemed to be our best if not our only mechanism for reaching agreement with the rebel leaders. These were the fifteen "practical proposals" of prison reform expanded during the all-night meeting in D-yard to almost twice their number. But I made it plain to the committee that the "immediate demands" for complete amnesty, transshipment to other countries, and removal of the superintendent were not negotiable.
>
> Then, together, we sat down as professionals, and we wrote, together, the twenty-eight points of prison reform at Attica.* It was the high tide of unity in the crisis. Assemblyman Emery was calling Mr. Kunstler "Bill," and Mr. Kunstler was calling Mr. Emery "Jim." I felt a tinge of optimism. If the rebel leaders were really interested in prison reform, then they might well accept the twenty-eight points. . . . I believed we might be able to obtain approval for all of them if the rebels released the hostages and honored their side of the agreement. When Governor Rockefeller telephoned his approval of the twenty-eight points, I was jubilant.[6]

Kunstler, the prime negotiator, regarded the 28-point package as probably the best deal the inmates could expect and hoped openly that Bobby Seale, upon arrival, might be able to "sell it" to D-yard. Steel had improved even the amnesty provisions, by wresting a pledge from Oswald that the Department of Corrections would file no criminal charges for property damage.[7] But Steel was not optimistic about the whole package.

Oswald thought the 28 points were "the most a modern prison administrator had ever offered rebellious inmates. . . . If the rebel inmates cared about prison reform they would accept the twenty-eight points."[8] But when he had cooled off from his fight with Eve, Tepper was not surprised that Oswald had agreed to the 28, "since most of them embodied measures which most penologists agree are basic and long overdue."[9]

But the inmates—as many of the observers knew, if Oswald did not—probably were past the point of merely "caring" about prison

---

* For the complete text of the 28 points, see Appendix Four.

reform. For them, the 28 points were likely to be important mostly because they did *not* solve the central question of amnesty. That Saturday, Norman Hurd and Michael Whiteman of Rockefeller's staff, alarmed that amnesty was even being discussed by the observers, reiterated to Rockefeller their legal view that "no member of the executive branch could offer complete amnesty since this was outside our constitutional limit"; nor could the governor bind a district attorney or a grand jury or any individual complainant.[10]

Besides, at 4:30 P.M. that Saturday, September 11, even as the 28-point package was being put together in the Stewards' Room, Corrections Officer William E. Quinn, aged 28, died in Rochester General Hospital of skull fractures received in the first attack on Times Square, nearly three days earlier. Now capital charges and the death penalty were hanging over D-yard. Amnesty was more than ever the only question that really mattered.

9

Waiting for Bobby

Nothing seemed to happen quickly at Attica. The 28-point package had been negotiated, but as yet the document only existed in Kunstler's handwriting. Tony Fitch, good-naturedly overlooking his long afternoon's exile, volunteered to type a clean copy with numerous carbons on an old machine crowning one of the Stewards' Room desks. The other observers milled around, apparently aimless. In fact, they were waiting for Bobby Seale.

During that Saturday afternoon, tireless Herman Schwartz had ventured off on yet another ferrying mission, this time to pick up Seale, the chairman of the Black Panther Party, at the Buffalo airport. Responding to Kunstler's phone call of the evening before, Seale had flown in from Oakland. To some of the observers, his prospective arrival began to appear as a possible turning point. This expectation was ample evidence of the gathering desperation in the Stewards' Room, 28 points or no 28 points.

Not many of the observers shared the optimism Oswald said he felt, although some of them probably did. Late that afternoon, Robert Douglass, Governor Rockefeller's secretary and one of his closest personal aides, arrived at the prison to assist Oswald at Rockefeller's instigation. Douglass, who was active politically, discussed the 28 points in the corridor outside the Stewards' Room with some of the observers he knew, Badillo, Garcia, and Dunne, and one he was meeting for the first time, Clarence Jones. Douglass found among these four "a very high degree of optimism that these items were significant, that there had been a long process of developing the exact points and [Oswald] was very hopeful at that time that this should do it."[1]

Douglass was talking to the more moderate observers, among whom Wicker was usually to be found. Others with a more highly developed sense of the atmosphere in D-yard, like Steel and Brother Jay, thought the 28 points were all too aptly labelled as "Proposals Acceptable to Commissioner Oswald." They were doubtful that the 28 points were going to be as acceptable to the inmates.

Wicker, at one level, agreed with the skeptics. Viscerally, he sensed that the situation was past the point of calm reckoning by which the inmates might persuade themselves that they had more to gain— "prison reform"—by accepting than by holding out. On a more intellectual plane, however, Wicker found himself, as have so many liberals and intellectuals in times of challenge to liberalism and reason, unable to concede the futility of sensible conciliation of interests. He thought it important to put the 28 points before the inmates at least in the terms he, Jones, and Tepper had recommended for the James letter— as the best that could be arranged. The inmates then could rationally decide whether or not to accept the package. It was an essential part of his life's rationale, his liberal credo, that the best decisions were reached through reason reinforced by knowledge. So believing, how could he concede without testing—though he sensed the bitter truth— that at Attica reason and knowledge would not be enough?

Some of the observers were reluctant even to present the 28 points to the inmates, lest the inmates turn in disillusionment on the hostages or even on the observers. But as the Stewards' Room talk progressed (if that is the word for such disjointed and often irrelevant proceedings), a consensus began to emerge that the package should be laid before the inmates as the best they could hope for, but without a recommendation that they should accept it. If this seems to make a distinction without a difference—surely reasonable men will, or ought to, accept the best they can hope for—it has to be remembered that few of the observers any longer thought the strange process in which they were caught was entirely rational. So much less did they think of the inmates as men who would calmly calculate their interests, as Oswald or Rockefeller or even the observers might see those interests.

Some observers, notably Franklin Florence and the Young Lords, Paris and Ortiz, insisted that the inmates form a political society capable of speaking and making decisions for themselves and that the observers must do nothing to commit the inmates to a position. According to this strongly stated view—Florence was a forceful speaker, Brother Jay a moving one by dint of an inarticulateness that reinforced his sincerity—it was not up to the observers to tell the inmates what to do or even what the observers thought best for them. The inmates had the right to judge that for themselves.

On the other hand, if the observers were unwilling or unable or ineligible to recommend acceptance of the 28 points, if they were willing only to certify them as the best to be had, for what reason could any of them expect that Bobby Seale would be willing to recommend acceptance? Seale would be no more likely than they to believe that the inmates would welcome the package with cheers. He had a militant reputation and a hypersensitive political constituency to consider. He was bound to be at first unsure of himself in a strange situation. For all these reasons he was most unlikely to recommend a course that many—in and out of D-yard—would see as surrender or selling out to The Man.

Yet, some of the observers did seem to develop the rather strange hope that perhaps Bobby Seale could and would persuade the inmates to accept the 28 points. Everyone assumed that Seale, upon his arrival, would be trusted, respected, and listened to in D-yard. As chairman of the Panthers and one of the famous Chicago defendants, his word, the observers told each other, would have more power in the predominantly black and militant society of D-yard than any other, even Kunstler's. If Seale *would* recommend the 28 points . . . but why *should* he do so?

The only explanation for any such expectation is hindsight and conjectural. Most of the observers believed, whether or not they admitted it to themselves, that if the 28-point package was not accepted, an attack on D-yard would follow with a great loss of life among hostages and inmates. They could only have been hoping that Seale would put the lives of his black brothers above his own politics and advise the men of D-yard to accept the package and save their skins. Unlike the observers, they reasoned, Seale could rely on his personal reputation and his great prestige to protect himself against charges of advising sellout or surrender.

This forlorn hope was enough to sustain some of the observers and to cause them to delay presenting the 28 points in D-yard until Seale should arrive. Emissaries were sent to No Man's Land to tell the inmates the observers were waiting for Bobby. Fitch went on with his typing; the other observers talked desultorily. At about 6:30 P.M., word reached the Stewards' Room that Schwartz had Seale at the gate.

The ride from Buffalo had been Schwartz's first encounter with the Panther leader, who impressed him as a man whose "dignity is very deep. . . . He's a major figure and he knows it."[2] But the men with Seale were "really scary looking guys. One is long and thin and reminded me in a funny kind of way—this may be unfair—of the thug in *Belle de Jour*. Not really, but there is a resemblance. Another guy, who was called Big Man, is *very* big, a huge black man, who was the chief bodyguard, who seems also . . . to be a fairly gracious person. . . . The scary guy's name is Van Taylor. Then there's another one named Mojo, who wore one of those floppy hats."[3]

No arrangements had been made for the entrance of this delegation into the prison, and the authorities, feeling, no doubt, that they had enough observers on hand and certainly did not need others who might be the most inflammatory of the lot, flatly refused Seale permission to come in. Douglass, for one, argued against admitting Seale on grounds that he might upset the possibility to end the uprising that Douglass thought the 28 points presented. Oswald was summoned to the Stewards' Room, where the observers pleaded that he relent.

In fact, Oswald had no real choice. The inmates had asked for a Panther representative; they knew Seale was on the way; press and television were already interviewing him at the prison gate. *Not* to admit him might more nearly jeopardize the acceptance of the 28 points. By then, Florence, supported by Kunstler, was arguing hotly that *only* Seale might be able to win acceptance of the 28 points. Having gone as far as he had, Oswald could hardly refuse Seale admittance in the face of these arguments. To do so might nullify the negotiations and thus leave Oswald in a position to be blamed if Seale's exclusion *did* upset the negotiations. About 7:15 P.M., assured by the observers, particularly Kunstler, that Seale would not be allowed to make inflammatory statements, Oswald reluctantly gave in.[4]

During this argument, Seale "sat in the car fuming for about an hour. Finally he said he wouldn't wait anymore and left."[5] There ensued what struck some of the observers as high comedy, no matter how near tragedy it appeared; perhaps their laughter verged on hysteria. Oswald dispatched a State Police car to bring back the famous Panther leader, who probably never before had been pursued by policemen whose purpose was to ask him politely to please come help the authorities restore the peace. So there was in the Stewards' Room much gallows humor; suppose, observers asked each other, Seale and his bodyguard chose to shoot it out when the police car tried to pull them over? How would Herman Schwartz perform as a getaway driver?

In fact, of course, this farcicial chase only caused more delay. Wicker took the opportunity to call his house in Washington in order to reassure his family of his safety. Turning his back on the other observers as he heard the faraway ringing, he felt vaguely guilty that he had waited so long to call. His 12-year-old son answered and they exchanged greetings.

"What're you doing?" Wicker asked.

"Watching TV."

"Oh. Well, I just wanted everybody to know I was okay."

"What are you doing up there, Dad?" Grey asked. "Where is Attica?"

"Upstate New York. I'm just trying to help settle things and not having much luck. I'll tell you all about it when I get home. Maybe tomorrow."

"Okay," Grey said, obviously anxious to get back to TV.

Wicker was glad that his young son, not really understanding the situation, did not seem upset by his presence at Attica. The less cause Grey had to worry, the better.

He ascertained that his daughter was also watching TV and that his estranged wife was out to dinner, said goodbye, and hung up. Everything was all right, everything was just as he should have expected. He loved his children and found great joy in their emerging personalities. Everyday that fall he fought down panic at his impending separation from them—not knowing how much they needed him, but acutely aware of his sense of obligation to them. He was not sure how to meet that obligation in the shaken circumstances of his life.

So he returned to the boredom of the Stewards' Room. Time seemed endless, shapeless; in its infinite passage, amid the mutter of aimless talk, more painfully than he could have believed possible, he realized how tired he was, how old, how inadequate, how disappointed in himself. He was a long way from his origins, all right, in more ways than he wanted to be. He was halfway down the slope, or further, with little accomplished, not much in prospect, and nothing better to do than to wait for Bobby.

In the hot, vanished summer of 1946, Tom Wicker—just turning twenty years old—was sent home from Seattle, Washington, for discharge from the U.S. Navy. He had been serving in the skeleton crew of a decommissioned aircraft carrier, the *Copahee*, one of those "baby flattops" with a flight deck jerry-built over the hull of a cargo ship, that was being laid up in mothballs in Tacoma. It was a thoroughly boring assignment, although free from the most picayune of Navy harassments. World War II was almost a year in the past. He had no taste whatever for military routine, much less for mindless work; and he welcomed discharge as a drowning man welcomes a rope.

But the day of his departure for the East was a glum one. The nearest discharge center to his home was at Little Creek, Virginia, outside Norfolk. He was being sent there by troop train—not in a relatively luxurious Pullman or even an ordinary day coach, but in what was known to servicemen of the time as a "cattle car." It was not much more than a box car with a sliding door in each sidewall, one toilet and 30 bunks arranged in 10 triple-decked tiers. The nightmare trip in prospect would take no one knew how long, but probably at least 10 days; troop trains, by the summer of '46, had less priority than chicken trains. In Wicker's car, bound for Little Creek and Southerners all, there were two other white boys and 27 blacks (segregation was the rule in the Navy, but it had to do with promotion and jobs, not cattle cars).

As if led by a string, the three white boys made a beeline for a tier of berths at one end of the car and appropriated all three. They did not do this by conspiracy but by Southern instinct. But Tom Wicker—his handshake with the black student at Chapel Hill a year or so in the past—had no racial hostility and not much overt race consciousness. In his Navy service, he had been thrown reasonably close to many black youths and he had been outside the South enough to count himself "liberated" from Southern attitudes. But he had imagined nothing like this—a week or more of using the same toilet and drinking fountain, sleeping elbow to elbow, eating together (there was one "chow car" for the whole train), in constant contact, having to *talk* to them. Even if he was to play bridge, which was then his favorite pastime, he would need a black fourth. They would all be living *alike*.

A burly white petty officer entered the car and shouted for silence. "I'm the honcho on this fuckin' train," he said. "No apeshit from you guys, no grabass, no gettin' out of the car for a fuckin' thing I don't say so. That clear?"

There were a few mumbled "aye ayes." The petty officer looked them over contemptuously.

"Good fuckin' riddance," he said. "Can't discharge you civilian assholes fast enough for me." He was all of three years older than Wicker. "Chow's three cars ahead, three times a fuckin' day when your turn comes, and don't expect a fuckin' thing but shit on a shingle. You, Red!"

Wicker had been keeping out of sight as best he could. He was by then something of a Navy veteran; he knew someone would have to honcho the car, that was the Navy way. Naturally, it would be one of the three whites. And he was the tallest of them and all too easily spotted.

"Yessir," he said, although he knew that he did not have to say "sir" to petty officers. D. D. Wicker, upon Tom's departure for the Navy, had advised him to be polite to all superiors, and Wicker had found it good advice, if often difficult to follow.

"You're master-at-arms for this car. Anything goes wrong, your fuckin' ass belongs to me. Muster every morning, post details, and send up a fuckin' mess cook every third day. You got sense enough to understand all that?"

"I got it," Wicker said unhappily.

"Okay," the petty officer said. "You guys keep it limp." He stalked out, walking tough, with his white hat down over one eye. The door had hardly closed behind him when a tall black sailor leaning against a tier of bunks at the other end of the car called out.

"Hey you, Red!"
Silence fell on the car like soot from a steam engine.
"Yeah," Wicker said.
"Suck my black dick."
Half the blacks laughed, a little uncertainly. Most of the others and the two other whites pretended not to notice. One or two blacks eyed Wicker stonily. He could not tell if he was being teased or challenged by the tall black, but as he stood with the other whites by the tier of bunks they had appropriated for themselves, he was astonished by the outburst—astonished in the perennial Southern manner that the tall black thought there was any reason to be hostile, even more astonished that a black man would dare to speak so to a white. He was not so liberated from his Southern background as he had thought, and he perceived that he would have to deal with this other youth as a Southern white man would deal with a colored person, whether nigger, nigruh, or Negro, and back it up; or else he would have to deal with him as one human with another, and live with the consequences.

He was young; his understanding of things was still limited, shaped largely by his family. His father, still living then, still Tom Wicker's model of a man, was a relatively poor working man, a devoted member of the Brotherhood of Railway Conductors, a New Deal Democrat who had fostered in his household a strong class atmosphere. The working people, the poor people, the downtrodden, the victims of the rich and the powerful were in D. D. Wicker's house much the same, just as there were few distinctions among Republicans, the wealthy, employers, bankers, big businessmen. There were two kinds of people, and Tom Wicker had understood early in his life that honor and heritage required of him that he stand for the underdog, that the place of a man was with the workers and the poor against the powerful and the greedy.

Blacks had never been specifically included on D. D. Wicker's side of this equation, but they had never been specifically excluded either; and he knew black working men who had sweated side by side with his father in the ancient brotherhood of toil. He had never known his parents to be contemptuous of blacks, or of anyone. He had never seen his mother or father humiliate or abuse another human being. He had been taught by them and by their lives to respect and consider others, not to walk over them or push them aside or pay them no heed.

He did not *think* at all about his response. Out of something stronger than mind, some instinct deeper than the Southern experience, from the core of what D. D. and Esta Wicker had made of him—by their lives and decency as much as by their overt shaping of his character—he set the face of his life away from the South.

"Why, your buddy there told me you didn't even have one." A fragment of an old joke had flickered in his memory. "Said a hog bit it off."

"Shee-it." The tall black sailor grinned. The other blacks laughed, all of them this time, some obviously in relief, some in derision of the tall boy as he thought up his reply. "You git home, man, you ask your girl friend, see if I ain't broke it off in her pussy." The blacks howled with laughter.

"After mine," Wicker said, hoping for the best, "I reckon she wouldn't even *feel* that little old biddy toothpick of yours."

There was more laughter and backslapping, and even the other white boys grinned, rather painfully.

"Hey, Red," another black called, amiably. "You the head man, when we gone chow down?"

Just then the train lurched off; there was a rush to the windows and doors, breaking up the exchange. One of the white boys lingered with Wicker.

"Ought to have bust his black ass," he said.

"We got to live on this thing," Wicker nodded at the crowded car. "A week, two weeks. We don't need fights and hard feelings."

"All the same, you got to . . ."

Wicker knew what was about to be said and broke in:

"We got to live with 'em, that's what we got to do." He walked away, deciding he would give the white sailor the first latrine detail, just on general principles and to balance the ticket a little. Maybe that would keep him in *his* place. Boldly, he punched the tall black sailor in the ribs. "Hey, Big Shot, where you from?"

"Where you from, to get that Southern accent?" Jim Ingram asked, lowering himself to the floor of the Stewards' Room beside Wicker. There were never chairs for all the observers. As the days and nights passed, some perched or lay on desks, some leaned against the wall, some moved about. Most sat on the floor.

"North Carolina." Wicker had chatted briefly with Ingram at noon, while the observers were waiting to re-enter. He thought the black reporter had made some sensible comments in the later discussion of the James letter.

"Me, too," Ingram said. "A long time ago. Whereabouts?"

"Little railroad town called Hamlet."

"The hell you say. That's *my* home town."

"Come on," Wicker said. "Hamlet?"

"Grew up on Charlotte Street."

"My God, I lived on Hamlet Avenue." Knowing where the Charlotte Street black section was, he realized that he and Ingram had lived at most a few blocks apart. But Ingram was much younger than he, so it had not been at the same time.

"Isn't that the goddamdest thing?" Ingram said. "Grow up in the same town, then meet at Attica."

"Reporters at that. I know somebody else from Hamlet."

"Who's that?"

"You know the great jazz saxophonist, John Coltrane?"

"Heard his records."

"Born on Charlotte Street," Wicker said triumphantly.

Ingram's brows knit. "Never heard of him there."

"His folks moved to High Point, he wasn't even a year old."

"But born in Hamlet?"

"Right there in Hamlet," Wicker said. "Same year I was. His grandfather used to be a dining car steward. He was still living on Charlotte Street a year or so ago. I went by to see him, the grandfather, I mean."

"What about that?" Ingram said. "John Coltrane and you and me."

And not a chance to get to know each other even if we'd all been the same age, Wicker was thinking. A corrections officer in uniform came in with a box of sandwiches. Amid welcoming sounds, he put it on a desk near Wicker, who realized how hungry he was, and stood up just as the corrections officer turned away. The officer peered at Wicker with contempt.

"I'da known this shit was for you guys, I'da never brung it," he said, and stalked out of the room.

Wicker stared after him. "Did you hear that?" he asked John Dunne.

Dunne nodded sadly. "And these are *our* people," he said. Wicker knew what he meant. The corrections officer wore a uniform, worked for the public, represented the law. He was white.

At 8:30 P.M., Bobby Seale finally appeared in the Stewards' Room.[6] Even before he got there, a nervous Walter Dunbar had warned him "not to inflame [the inmates]. You are going in there—do you understand this?—to try to make them understand that they must release these hostages and that we will bring about prison reform. . . . we will make meaningful changes."[7]

But it was not necessarily inflammation of the inmates that Dunbar and the other authorities should have been worried about. Like the townspeople of Attica, the waiting state troopers and deputies and especially the corrections officers were tired, tense, frustrated with the waiting, bitter at press and officials for seeming to be partial to the inmates, worried about friends, relatives, and colleagues held hostage and about their own fates in the impending assault. Into this atmosphere, in rapid succession late Saturday afternoon, news of the death of William Quinn was introduced, then news of the admission to the prison of Bobby Seale. Among townspeople, guards, and troopers, Quinn's death produced anger and grief and the sinking realization that the inmates had less to gain than ever by ending the revolt without an agreement. Seale's admission to the prison "appeared to troopers and corrections officers to be another concession to the same illogic that rewarded inmates with prison reform for taking over a prison and killing a corrections officer."[8] Seale had an impact almost opposite from that feared by Douglass and Dunbar. His appearance inflamed the troopers, deputies, and corrections officers with more resentment and bitterness than they already felt.

The Panther leader nevertheless agreed to Dunbar's strictures, although he had not yet heard or seen the 28 points. As a veteran of the racial wars, he must have been wryly amused by Dunbar's concession that "reform" was needed in the prison and that the state would provide it, but only because it wanted the hostages back, only because the state's hand had been forced by the inmates' direct action. That was an old story to every black activist from Martin Luther King to Rap Brown.

Wicker was as interested as the other observers in seeing the famous Bobby Seale, although he was much less optimistic than Florence that the Panther leader would urge acceptance of the 28-point package. Wicker found Seale thin, intense, disdainful, as if he smelled something bad in the room, a smaller man physically than Wicker had expected, not as impressive as Herman Schwartz considered him. "He's very thin, very reserved and dignified, moves very fast in a decisive way, and has an air of command about him. He walks with his shoulders slightly hunched, and his speaking attitude is with his head thrown back and a small goatee pointing out."[9]

It was a good description, but to Wicker in the Stewards' Room, Seale seemed worried, not sure what to do, not pleased to be there. Van Taylor, the smaller of his two bodyguards, seemed constantly to be whispering in Seale's ear.

Seale stared at one of Fitch's copies of the 28 points while Clarence Jones briefed him on the package. When Jones had finished, Kunstler rather deferentially said he hoped Bobby could support the 28 points in D-yard. A few other voices were added, then Seale and his bodyguards went to the end of the room where the telephone was; everyone else drew away respectfully. Van Taylor whispered interminably in Seale's ear.

Wicker resumed his seat on the floor, exhausted, inured by then to delay and boredom. He was grimy, unshaven, in the same clothes he had put on the morning before in Washington. He had not slept for nearly 40 hours. Yet, his brain seemed quick, alert, and sensitive after the long dull afternoon, as if he had gained a sort of second wind mentally, despite his lethargic body.

He watched Seale closely. When introduced to him, the Panther chairman had grunted and put out a limp and clammy hand—altogether a limp and clammy greeting for a newspaperman who thought he had championed the black cause. But Wicker had seen enough of the so-called black power leaders to know that they were different from the men of the old civil rights movement to which he had once attached so much hope. White reporters who had sought shelter from vengeful police in the black community of Birmingham had learned later that they could get their heads broken in Watts or Hough or Newark, not by police but by blacks. Things had changed irrevocably. Wicker did not resent—he rather understood—the change; but he was by no means convinced that Bobby Seale was an advance over Martin Luther King. Seale certainly was not a *symbolic* advance.

King, the apostle of nonviolence, if put in Seale's position, probably would have gone into D-yard, urged acceptance of the 28 points (perhaps having upgraded them a little by negotiation with Oswald or even Rockefeller), preached an end to violence, and advocated a return to peaceful methods of persuasion. The prisoners might or might not have accepted this advice. Seale did not look like—he did not have the reputation or the experience of—a man who would do that, much less expect to gain by doing it. At the precipice, Wicker believed, King had been human and Christian as well as, maybe more than, black and militant. But Bobby Seale had the hard edges and intense air of a revolutionary, one whose absorption in an abstract if genuine cause had dulled in him the sense of humanity that first had drawn him to that cause.

In the long afternoon dragging past, Wicker had remembered the interminable hours on the straggling troop train and the crowded cattle car that had brought him back to the South in 1946. After 10 days, during which the train had rattled from Seattle down to Kansas City, up to Chicago, then on to Norfolk, its 27 black and three white occupants had scattered to the four corners of Dixie. He had seen none of them again, could now remember none of their names and faces. But that 10 days had been the time of his discovery that black people were just that—people, individuals, human as he was, hurting, laughing, loving, worrying in much the same fashion about much the same things, whatever the inexcusable and ineradicable differences in their experience.

The blacks still were preoccupied, as he was, with families, jobs, schooling, girls. No two of them were much alike in temperament or personality. Some he liked, some he did not. One was better read than he; another was mentally deficient, or so it seemed; another had a flashing wit; still another organized a profitable black market for food and tobacco, out of whatever obscure sources of supply. Some gave Big Red, the master-at-arms of the cattle car, disciplinary problems, as both the white boys did. Others shared plans and memories as equals with young Tom Wicker. Since in 10 days all the men on the car got only one shower—at the St. Louis YMCA, to which they were marched from the city's magnificent old railroad station one blessed evening—it turned out that whites when dirty smelled as bad as blacks when dirty. In such close quarters, it became apparent that black penises were no bigger than white and no more thought about by their possessors, which was constantly. The only major difference, other than skin color, was that, with one or two exceptions, the blacks were not as well educated as the whites, although all had gone to school.

In later years, Wicker understood that the whole black experience made an even more profound difference than "separate but equal" schools. In 1946, he had made the great discovery that blacks were as human and individual as anyone. It was not much to learn, yet it was more than some people learn in a lifetime. A quarter century later, however, he could not help but wonder if his life had not led him too far from practical application of that knowledge. Did he not still act as if blacks were more nearly a class than individuals? In what way did he really recognize them as people?

It troubled him enough that he had moved so far from his more hereditary obligation—the notion ingrained in him from his father's life that a man's place was among those who worked and struggled, not with the wealthy and the powerful. Maybe it was part of the same long march of his life away from its bedrock, that he had too nearly ignored the lesson of the cattle car.

He lived in a largely white neighborhood, sent his children to private schools, employed a black woman for household work. He moved in powerful white circles. He knew personally blacks who were mostly educated, professional, middle-class civil rights and government workers. He feared some black areas of the city of Washington.

It was not clear even that his professional concern with the race question had been of useful consequence. Perhaps he *had* done more harm than good, as it had become fashionable to charge against white liberals. Wicker remembered painfully his confidence that the good people of North Carolina would not defeat the great Dr. Frank Graham for the U.S. Senate in the first racially influenced election of his personal experience, but they had.[10] He remembered his belief that a generous South would more or less readily accept the Supreme Court's ruling in 1954 that segregated schools were no longer permissible, but it hadn't.

Perhaps these early mistakes of foolish optimism about human nature had signalled a persisting but unwarranted assumption, on no historical or social evidence, that somehow the good in his fellow man would triumph over the bad. If so, had he kept pushing professionally for desegregated schools, public places and facilities, and unrestricted housing far past the point of any possible white acceptance, at least in his time and generation? Could it be true, for example, that having advocated pupil busing to achieve racial balance in the schools—no one opposed busing for any other purpose—he had only helped re-kindle white resistance even to the level of integration already achieved, not to mention a higher level? Had he made inevitable and even more pervasive the white resistance to "them"—the blacks, that faceless threatening, violent, insatiable breed that white Americans tended to see as a descending horde? Had he simply confirmed white fears?

Maybe he would have done better, he thought while waiting with the others for Bobby Seale to decide, maybe he would have done better somehow to recognize directly the unique humanity of at least one black person, and let the black cause take care of itself.

Seale ended his conference with his two aides and returned to the center of the Stewards' Room. It did not appear to him, he said, that there was much in the 28 points since there was no effective amnesty provision. In any case, he had to consult with the Black Panther Party central committee on the west coast, and that would take time.

"This was an appalling disappointment" to Russell Oswald, who was then in the Stewards' Room. "I realized with a sense of foreboding that Bobby Seale was not, in fact, going to support the 28 points at the decisive moment."[11] Even Oswald had gulled himself into believing that Seale's support was the key to a settlement. Seale probably realized, instead, that neither he nor anyone could then persuade the inmates to give up their hostages without amnesty, no matter how much "prison reform" they might win by so doing. Why should Seale urge them to do what they would not do, since in effect that was to side with Oswald and the state against the inmates' position?

The best he could do at the moment, Seale told the observers, was to tell the inmates that he was willing to support whatever they might decide. Since he recognized that that was not of much help to anyone, maybe there was no need for him to go into the yard at all. Maybe there was nothing useful he could do.

Kunstler, Florence, and others who had appeared to pin the most hope on Seale, and who were most deferential to him, almost immediately agreed. They argued that of course Bobby was right; Bobby could not, should not, try to tell the inmates what to do. It was understandable; Bobby had put his finger on the point; Bobby had got to the heart of the matter. Of course Bobby could not tell the inmates what to do.

Nevertheless, it was ventured, the inmates *were* expecting him. They would be disappointed if he did not appear. They looked up to Bobby. Maybe he could at least make an appearance, even if he could not possibly speak in favor of the 28 points. Seale finally agreed to this, and also to Clarence Jones' sensible stipulation that he not speak *against* the package. That cleared the way, at about 9 P.M., for the observers to return to D-yard.

While Wicker was waiting his turn to sign the list of those going in, he idly picked up a small, crumpled piece of paper from the floor and smoothed it in his hands.

"*Brother Bobby,*" the note read, in a wobbly script. "*Our lives are in your hands. Come! Attica prisoners.*"

Wicker stared at the note. One of the inmates must have smuggled it out of D-yard to Seale, probably via one of the observers sent as messengers to No Man's Land.

"Look at this," he said to Steel.

Steel read the note and handed it back.

"What do you think of that Seale?" Wicker said. "He gets that kind of a note from those poor dumb shits that believe in him, then he throws it on the floor like a piece of Kleenex."

Steel was not one of those who had fawned on Bobby. Lew Steel could not be imagined fawning on anyone. But he said, "What can Seale do? There's nothing he can do."

"He wasn't even going to go in if we hadn't talked him into it. He just threw the goddam note on the floor."

"He cares," Steel said. "Maybe he cares. I mean, the Panthers have been through a hell of a lot. They started out providing breakfasts for hungary kids, and look what's happened to them. Maybe they can't let themselves care too much about anybody in particular."

"I just don't see how a man could throw a note like that on the floor and walk away."

"It's not the same for us as it is for him," Steel insisted. "I've got a lot of respect for what the Panthers have done in this country. They've had to calculate what they're doing every step of the way."

Wicker stared at the pathetic piece of paper in his hands. He thought he had never seen anything that so graphically illustrated the difference in political objectives and human needs. Maybe Bobby Seale

did think he had no higher duty than to weigh the political consequences, the larger results, of every step he took, every word he
uttered; maybe he even saw no alternative. But if so, what about the
human beings in D-yard? What about humanity? What about the
human being who had to make such a choice, and live with it?

10

Package Deal

As the observers and Bobby Seale marched through the echoing corridors toward No Man's Land that Saturday night, Wicker sensed real hostility at last, just as he had seen it in the uniformed man who had unwillingly brought sandwiches to the Stewards' Room. Wicker wanted to be charitable—he knew the troopers were tired, away from home and family, unschooled in the subtleties of the situation, more comfortable in action than in negotiation, frustrated by the impasse, and in the nature of things unsympathetic to inmates. In some cases, they were genuinely concerned for the hostages; in others, they were fearful for their own safety. Wicker knew all that.

Still, these angry and frustrated men had an unbelievable number of guns, and they seemed to think the observers were part of the problem—instruments of protraction and delay for sure, subverters of law and order perhaps—rather than part of a possibly peaceful solution. Their hostility raised fears in Wicker's mind for his safety on the troopers'—not the inmates'—side of the gate. Besides, he thought rather bitterly, he and the other observers were unarmed and taking far more risks than any of the troopers. Police hostility to those who sought a solution without violence was, moreover, contrary to everything policemen *ought* to stand for. It brought one more unneeded pressure on Oswald and the observers to get their work done *quickly*, when what they needed most was time to work things out.

No one wanted another all-night session in D-yard. The observers' intent on Saturday night was only to reestablish personal contact with the inmates, mollify them if possible with Seale's presence, deliver the 28 points in documentary form for the leaders to study, and get out. Oswald, mindful that Tom Soto and others had attempted to stay in

D-yard the night before, had exacted a pledge from the group going in that all would come out together.

That suited Wicker. As the gates of No Man's Land clanked behind them and they emerged as before into A-yard to be counted off and marched on, his fatalistic mood vanished again. It was a clear evening, a little cool. Once again, bonfires flickered in the trash cans atop the walkways. Once again, idle inmates called down jovially to the observers. Once again, by twos, the observers went across the dark corridor into D-yard to face the human security chain and the faceless hundreds of men beyond it in the darkness. All seemed as before as the observers marched toward the leadership table in the white ring of light from the television arcs.

Yet, there was a difference Wicker could not fail to notice, although at first he thought it might be his own nerves. The observers had not been in the yard for 16 hours—16 hours during which tension among the inmates had mounted and much of the inmates' elation at "liberation" had worn off. The "euphoria" noticed by Roger Champen was dying fast. One of the hostages and Flip Crowley, the eloquent philosopher of amnesty, had had what were thought to be heart attacks and had been turned over by Tiny Swift to the state; this upset many of the inmates. The observers had been expected to return more quickly, too, and the impression began to get about in the yard that they and the authorities might be stalling.

"Without knowing what was happening during the day," Richard Clark recalled, "a lot of the brothers were becoming irritable." Besides, most inmates "had seen so much trickery going on within prisons from the officials and the administration that you became mistrustful of people, and anyone who has contact with the administration."[1]

Some of the brothers of Attica also had learned something truly disturbing—that William Quinn was dead. They had heard it in a radio broadcast, but no general announcement had been made, particularly since the broadcast included the obviously false story that Quinn had been thrown out a window. "The state has killed their own man and they're going to try to say we did it," Brother Richard thought.[2]

Dr. Warren H. Hansen of Warsaw, a physician who had courageously entered D-yard Thursday night to examine the hostages, had returned Saturday afternoon at the inmates' request. To him, the increased tension was apparent: "For one thing, arguments broke out readily, occasionally flaring into fights that had to be stopped by others. Then, too, many of the inmates who turned up for sick call required treatment for emotional reactions." Tension was not eased by a "big black man who wandered around the yard with a cross clasped in his hands, yelling, 'They're going to kill me,' and a lot of hysterical gibberish." Nor did it help anything that a band of inmates in what Dr.

Hansen thought "a bizarre array of costumes" had threatened the hostages' lives with homemade weapons, until Richard Clark, backed by the security guard, dispersed them.[3]

Dr. Hansen himself felt threatened; he was, in fact, subjected to verbal abuse and decided not to return to D-yard. That day, too, seven white inmates who had kept to themselves and out of any part in D-yard society were "sentenced" to dig a long trench, later used for security and partially as a latrine. This highly visible punishment for "traitors" undoubtedly helped increase the tension in the yard.

It may also have been on Saturday (the time is not clear) that three white D-yard inmates, Barry Schwartz, Kenneth Hess, and Michael Privitiera, were killed. It has not been established whether these murders were done deliberately for disciplinary purposes or, if so, who ordered them. Apparently, it was mostly a secret in D-yard that the three were dead. But many inmates did know they had been "detained" as "traitors" and troublemakers.[4] That was disturbing, too.

As the days in D-yard had worn on, moreover, "tempers naturally got soured because in the afternoons it was very hot. . . . Inside, the tents were not cool, it was hot in there. So . . . tempers flared, we had an argument or two, which was only normal in those conditions. . . . There was a fight or two going on . . . and someone might have taken someone's sheets when they came out of the tent . . . and consequently had to sleep on a mattress without sheets. And little arguments about this guy getting more food and so on." Roger Champen, putting down a plate of rice and beans while he talked to someone, was angered to have the food stolen from under his nose. Herbert Blyden then sent Champ off to a corner of the yard to eat a can of tuna fish in peace.[5]

But one possible cause for real trouble in the yard had not so far produced it. "You're *always* going to have a problem" with black–white relations, Champen believed. But in D-yard, "as days went by, food got scarce and the water began to be scarce, [blacks and whites] became more friendly. The issue about race became minimal. . . . As time goes on . . . race doesn't mean anything. Nothing means anything except the issue at hand." When he had made his first D-yard speech, Champ saw that "the whites had backed off and had a little, like, semi-circle off to the left." He told them the revolt was not a "racial thing," that they had "one common enemy, the wall. The wall surrounds us all. So if you don't like me, don't like me after, but in the meantime, let's work together." That advice had prevailed, and racial tension was not a problem in D-yard that Saturday evening.[6]

But there were plenty of other reasons why the inmates seemed angry and nervous, more hostile than before. "Where you guys been?" someone demanded loudly as they gathered at the leadership table.

There was no sign of the handsome, scowling black who had previously sat across the table from Wicker, but there were other familiar faces at the table—Champ, Brother Herb, Brother Richard, Jerry Rosenberg grinning, his long hair falling over his ears.

Arthur Eve spoke briefly. The committee, he said, was sorry to have been absent so long but had spent the day dickering with Oswald and the authorities. The best deal possible, as far as they could see, had been worked out. But before going into detail, he introduced "Brother Bobby Seale."

Most of the D-yard inmates "were relieved to see Bobby because of what Bobby stood for . . . a person who has gone through similar experiences, a person who has taken an outspoken view about certain types of treatment of people." Rather naively, some of the inmate leaders thought Seale was just the person through whose voice they could "touch the people," by which they meant "the poor working class people, the people who have sons and daughters and uncles and fathers and husbands and nephews in places like [Attica]. . . . Then, hopefully, they can reach those in political office to get some changes made."[7]

Surprisingly, however, Brother Bobby did not get much of a reception—nothing like the ovations the night before, first for John Dunne, then for Kunstler. "We wanted to see where Bobby was coming from," Richard Clark explained. "People have a tendency to praise a man for his rhetoric, but we wanted to know about his honesty and sincerity."[8]

Nor did Seale make much of his appearance. He perched on the leadership table, his feet on a bench, elbows on his knees, and spoke briefly, in a quiet voice. To Roger Champen, Seale appeared "agitated, apprehensive . . . perhaps he felt slightly intimidated."[9] Herman Badillo, too, speculated that "having spent several years in prison, [Seale] felt depressed at re-entering the gates."[10]

Seale began with an obligatory shout of "Power to the people!" But the rest of his speech was anything but revolutionary, or even inflammatory. He did observe that "it definitely looks like to me we gone get some kind of change—revolutionary change, you know." But this was said more of the general political situation than of the revolt in D-yard, and the inmates responded with none of the fervor with which, the night before, they had greeted the fiery speeches of Soto and Kenyatta.

Seale told the inmates he almost had been refused admittance to the prison and had been kept waiting outside. Then he spoke of the 28-point agreement. He said he understood the committee was giving them the package for their study, and that the committee then would leave. He, Bobby Seale, intended to consult with the Black Panther

Party Central Committee and with "The Servant," whom Wicker took
to be Defense Minister Huey Newton. The committee and Newton
were on the west coast, but Seale promised that he would "shoot back
an answer" on the 28 points within four hours and would return personally to the prison at 7 A.M. Then his speech—"very disappointing,"
Champen thought[11]—trailed into anticlimactic silence, followed by
little more than dutiful applause.

Clarence Jones announced that the observers were leaving with
inmate leaders "a package proposal that would meet your demands in
our judgement." Champen interposed that he could not understand
why the group was leaving so quickly when the inmates had been
waiting all day for them. Seale repeated that he would be back at 7
A.M. With his bodyguards, he started out of the yard.

A few feet away from Wicker, Badillo rose and started to follow
Seale. Bob Garcia followed Badillo, who paused beside Wicker.
"Aren't we going out with Seale the way we promised Oswald?" he
asked. "Wasn't that the arrangement, that we all go out at the same
time?"

That *was* the arrangement, and Wicker, too, followed along. Actually, Badillo had another motive. "Even if we had come back to the
yard with agreements on everything they asked for, the prisoners
would have insisted on hearing what Seale had to say Sunday morning.
I felt, therefore, that it was the worst possible time to reveal the
agreements. . . ."[12]

John Dunne had still another motive in leaving then. "When Seale
left, I left," he said later, "because frankly I saw him as my ticket to
getting out of there."[13] In view of the tension and hostility in the
yard, Wicker, too, was ready enough to go with Seale, Badillo, Dunne,
and the others who were following them.

Wicker thought, however, that *all* the observers were leaving, as
agreed. But behind him at the leadership table, the inmate leaders were
protesting angrily, "You haven't been here all day! You come in here
and you are going to stay here only five minutes? You mean there is
not going to be any negotiating? You're not going to give us any kind
of a report?"

On the spot, Eve, Jones and Lew Steel, alarmed at the inmates' show
of wrath and aware that none of the observers, including Seale, were as
yet out of D-yard, made the decision to present the 28 points personally. Tepper, Fitch, Kenyatta, Soto, the Young Lords, and perhaps
others also stayed. Wicker and most of the other observers followed
Seale out to No Man's Land.

They were met in the administration building by Oswald and
Dunbar. According to Oswald, he had the following exchange with
Bobby Seale:

"I asked, 'Why are you out this quickly? Did you tell them to end the rebellion at this point?' He said, 'No. I did not tell them that. I wasn't able to tell them anything they didn't want to do.' I said, 'That isn't the reason you went in there in the first place. We think you had an obligation to tell them that this rebellion should be ended and the hostages be returned.' "[14]

Badillo, who was there, recalled only that Oswald thanked Seale "on behalf of the state for coming."[15] Wicker could not later remember Oswald speaking so sharply to Seale; he did remember that Oswald shook Seale's hand almost fervently and that Seale repeated his promise to come back Sunday morning. Seale himself told Herman Schwartz as Schwartz drove him to the Holiday Inn in Buffalo that "when [Seale] walked out . . . some state trooper made some snotty remark of some kind. Oswald turned and just flashed on the guard."[16] Oswald also assigned a state police car to escort Seale to Buffalo.

To most of the leaders and many of the inmates, the departure of more than half the observers meant that the unity of the group must have "broken down"—that "the observer group had split among themselves, because some stayed in and some went out." Worse, "the remaining group that was in the yard was not as powerful as those who went out." Champen was particularly upset to see John Dunne leaving "very, very agitated . . . as if he was happy that the moment arrived and he could leave."[17] The tension was high, almost visibly at flash point, as Clarence Jones rose to present the 28 points.

Bill Kunstler, who had brought Bobby Seale to Attica, had left the yard with him and had walked with him to Schwartz's car, where he chatted briefly with Seale and Schwartz. Alfredo Mathew, trying to return to the yard to summon the observers still there to keep their agreement with Oswald, came back to report that Jones was, in fact, reading the inmates the 28 points. Kunstler went immediately back into D-yard to be with his "clients," if they needed him. This may have been the most courageous, as it was certainly one of the most important, personal decisions of the four days at Attica.

Kunstler arrived just as Clarence Jones finished his impromptu reading of the 28 points. In the angry atmosphere of the yard, this had been for the mild-mannered Jones a supreme effort of persuasion and eloquence, but nothing he could say could prevent what Oswald called "an emotional massacre."[18] According to another account:

> Jones began his speech with the statement that he was not a politician but a newspaper editor; that he did not ask to come to Attica but was invited, and that he assumed the inmates had asked for his presence because they believed he could be useful. He

noted that politics is the art of the possible, and that the greatest mistake a person can make is not to recognize who has the political power. He stated that the inmates had sent the observers' committee out to get a hundred things and they might be dis-appointed because the committee only returned with 98. But, he added, the inmates themselves had to decide whether they should reject the 98 simply because the observers were unable to get the 100.

Jones also told the inmates that he had been in and out of the prison and had observed things on the outside which the inmates had not. It was all very well to quote Chairman Mao about power coming out of the barrel of a gun, he stated, but men outside were the ones with the guns; they were carrying magnums and carbines—and he told them if the situation was not resolved by compromise, the "Kent State psychology" would take over. He added that the men outside were young, tense, and infected with racism, and would like nothing better than an excuse to blow the inmates' brains out. He concluded by saying he thought that the 28 points were the basis for a proper settlement and that, while this was ultimately for the inmates to decide, he believed that "from the bottom of his heart" this was the best they could expect to get. He then read the points.

The inmates listened quietly and intently until Jones reached the point on amnesty and read the District Attorney's letter. Observers noted that the reaction to that was bitter, derisive and spontaneous laughter. Jones made no comment on this reaction but went on to say, "Let's go through the whole thing" and read the rest of it.[19]

But from there on, the inmates laughed and jeered bitterly after each new point was read. Their anger became palpable. Ironically, Louis James' attempt to persuade them that only the guilty would be prose-cuted had backfired, because "who would determine who was guilty and who wasn't? As we viewed it, we were all guilty," Champen recalled. "At that point we all assumed responsibility for what hap-pened." The James letter, he thought, forced each inmate "to decide exactly what their role was and what were the possibilities of their suffering some consequences for what happened."[20]

But Jones went courageously on, despite catcalls, angry shouts, and the heavy tension in the yard. A lesser man might have given up well before the end. Lew Steel, sitting nearby, felt himself as the reading progressed in the greatest danger he had yet encountered; so did Tepper. Clearly the 28 points—weak on amnesty and with no mention either of the removal of Mancusi or of transportation to a "non-imperialist" country—were not acceptable in D-yard. If the package were labelled a sellout, as well, the inmates might turn on the remnant of observers left in their hands.

"We've got the body, but not the head!" one prisoner shouted at Jones.[21] Richard Clark, with his gift for the blunt phrase, told the observers, "You are now looking at a bunch of dead men. What amnesty means to us is what insurance means to a family."[22] It was at this point that Kunstler, the observer most trusted by the inmates, went to the microphone to make what Oswald later called "his most helpful contribution."[23] As Kunstler later said,

> I had all sorts of quandries as to what to say because the mood was so deep and intense and all of my white, middle-class fears and images about prisoners had come to the fore and I guess I was going to say that they were right in tearing them up, but when I got to the microphone, I said . . . that I thought they were the best they could get, that if they didn't accept them, people were going to die, but that the decision was their decision to make.[24]

Steel, Tepper, and Jones later told Wicker they had no doubt that at that frightening moment in D-yard Kunstler had saved all their lives with his statement that backed them and the 28 points. Kunstler had put all his prestige on the line at the one moment when it really mattered. It would have been easier for him to yield to his "middle-class fears and images" and urge the inmates on to defiance. That was what they wanted to hear; and he would have been for the moment a popular hero in D-yard, in contrast to the precarious position in which he would have placed Jones and the others. Kunstler's willingness to stand by the 28 points and the observers' stated position gave Jones the necessary backing and may well have staved off a violent reaction.

But the lawyer made another crucial and less fortunate statement. He realized, he said, that "the amnesty section is not acceptable to you now that a guard has died."[25] This was the first general notice to the D-yard brothers that William Quinn was dead, and it brought "a sort of loud gasp" from the assembled hundreds of inmates in the yard. Lieutenant Robert Curtiss, listening apprehensively from the circle of hostages, heard the "gasp" of the assembled inmates; then, to him, it seemed that "almost a silence fell over the yard and it was very solemn from then on . . . tense and moody."[26]

Kunstler's news of Quinn may have been a major reason why Brother Richard Clark ultimately leaped on the leadership table and, in full view of the D-yard brothers, ripped up the 28 points—just as, nearly two days earlier, Jerry Rosenberg had torn up Herman Schwartz's injunction.

However unreasonable these responses may seem, the parallel between Rosenberg's and Clark's actions is important. It illustrates how little trust the inmates had in anything promised by the law. In the one case, Rosenberg tore up a federal judge's order with the cry that it was "garbage"; in the other, Clark destroyed what was supposed to be the pledged word of the District Attorney of Wyoming County. In each instance, the spurned orders and promises purported to give the inmates at least some of what they had demanded. No doubt many motives and tactical notions went into each act. Nevertheless, both were wildly cheered, and nothing could more clearly show the mistrust amounting to contempt with which the men of D-yard regarded the law and the society it represented.

Despite their experience, the state officials most concerned never seemed quite to grasp the depth of this mistrust or the fact that it was as much a factor to be taken into account as any other involved at Attica. During his desperate Friday morning meeting with the inmates in D-yard, Oswald pleaded, "Sooner or later there is someone you are going to have to trust—you are going to have to trust me."[27] Seven months later, Rockefeller said that, in his view, Oswald "frankly felt that his personal presence and then going into the yard was going to bring about a settlement because he had evidenced his good faith. . . ."[28] But what Oswald considered "good faith" was fiercely suspect among the inmates.

That was not the least reason why the 28 points never had a chance in D-yard. These points represented what Oswald thought "the most a modern prison administration had ever offered rebellious prisoners."[29] They represented what Tom Wicker and most of the observers thought "the best deal possible." But the D-yard brothers did not trust the state or believe its promises.

Besides, the package itself is too glibly described as "28 concessions." The first three and the last of its 28 points, for example, are concerned exclusively with the immediate settlement of the uprising, and one of these promises nothing more startling than that the rebellious inmates could return to their cells "under their own power." Nine of the other 24 points are hedged and conditional—recommendations to the legislature, actions to be taken "where possible," and vague promises of broad general goals such as to "modernize the inmate education system."

Twelve of the remaining 15 points do represent "concessions"—but of things that a reasonable man might have believed a humane prison ought to have been doing or permitting all along. What is so revolutionary or progressive about permitting religious freedom to inmates? Why had they been deprived of it in the first place?

Nor could the state of New York be considered advanced in a humanitarian way for agreeing—only under duress—to allow inmates to telephone relatives at their own expense, to provide a Spanish-speaking doctor in an institution almost 10 percent of whose 2250 inmates were Puerto Rican, or to "institute a program for the employment" of black guards at a correctional facility where for years more than half the inmates had been black.

Looked at in that way, only three points represented real, practical steps toward a new corrections system rather than a tardy effort to reach a bare minimum standard of decency in the treatment of human beings temporarily confined. An ombudsman program for prisoners would have been started; political activity by inmates would have been permitted; and a regular inmate grievance procedure would have been established, with some inmate voice allowed in prison operations. (The latter point was just what the voluble inmate in C-block told Wicker had been resisted by Mancusi before the uprising; so why should any inmate who new *that* have had much confidence in that one of the 28 points?) It is fair to say, also, that Oswald's pledge, incorporated in the amnesty point, not to let participation in the uprising set back an inmate's parole prospects was an important and probably unprecedented departure from established practice.

But the inmates and their lawyers knew better than anyone that many of the demands on which concessions had been made had been before Oswald and Mancusi for months, without result. They knew the 28 concessions had been extorted from the state by the threat to the hostages. They knew that even if Oswald were to be trusted, he had no power to enforce some of what he had promised. They knew that bloated phrases like "institute realistic, effective rehabilitation programs" as well as specific promises like "remove visitation screens as soon as possible" *guaranteed* them nothing. Was this "prison reform" really worth giving up the hostages, the relative freedom of D-yard, and the limelight of national attention? Was it worth going back to their cells and the deadly prison routine and the dubious attentions of the "hacks"? Was it worth taking the risks of prosecution and reprisal?

Many of the men in D-yard probably did not believe the 28 points really represented the best deal they could make, either. They had the hostages; the state had not moved against them. If they could prize those 28 points out of the state, might they not yet get more—even amnesty? Still others probably were willing to accept the 28 points but were either unwilling or unable to speak up, or to risk harsh discipline from the leadership committee.[30]

Not every inmate in the yard felt *directly* concerned with amnesty—in a McKay Commission poll taken months later, about 68 percent of those who responded said they were personally willing to give up amnesty in order to get out of D-yard safely. But even some of these felt they had to support leaders who might be facing serious charges. Others were afraid of or prevented from dissenting. Many shared Richard Clark's view that the false story that William Quinn had been thrown out a window suggested a deliberate frame-up by the state—which in turned suggested vindictive prosecution. As an inmate announced to the yard, "Brothers, one of the pigs is dead. The pigs killed one of their own, and now they're going to blame us for it."[31] And it was believed by many in the yard that everyone there "could be charged with at least conspiracy of murder."[32]

Perhaps, too, the matter was just too elemental. After all, if the inmates accepted the 28 points, the state—Mancusi—would get back the institution *and* the inmates *and* the hostages. Once the hostages were out of the inmates' hands, by what means could the inmates make the state keep its word? In the closed world of American prisons, no inmate had to be told, due process was a joke and the state's word was what the guards with the clubs said it was.

Besides, "a confused and uncertain throng of inmates, easily swayed by the rhetoric of those on the inmates' committee, who were often in discord among themselves," had almost no way to conclude such a sophisticated arrangement.[33] After the initial emotional reaction of ripping up the document and denouncing the 28 points, there was not much chance that an open vote—even if there had been a mechanism to manage it—would have approved the package; nor would the leadership committee have permitted a secret ballot. Had the committee been willing to make the decision for the yard, it would scarcely have been a decision *for* acceptance, because these were the men who feared they had the most to lose if there were no amnesty, who probably had the best understanding of how weak the amnesty provision was, and who probably had the least trust in the promises of authority (Blyden, for example, with his 72 counts from the Tombs riot).[34]

In these circumstances, the first sharp reaction *was* the decision.

Senator Tom McGowan of Buffalo gave Wicker, Badillo, Garcia, and Mathew a ride to Batavia, where he had arranged for some rooms for the observers. The senator also loaned some shaving tackle to Wicker, who then was able to buy toothbrush and toothpaste at the Treadway Inn. He gratefully used these implements that night for the first time in more than 40 hours, since foolishly rushing off to Attica full of good wine but without a suitcase. At a late hour on Saturday night in Batavia there was no hope for acquiring a clean shirt or a change of underwear. Putting back on those he had been wearing, after a hot shower, was like burrowing head first into a basket full of prison laundry. While he was gingerly creeping back into his stiffened shirt, the phone rang in his room.

"This Wicker?" a gruff voice asked.

"Speaking."

"You guys in the press. Why'n't you get the names of every one of these no-good bastards over there't the prison?"

"What good would that do?"

"You know, print every goddam name in your goddam newspapers and right alongside it every goddam crime these bastards ever did. Let the public know the kind of thieves and murderers and rapists you got in there yelling all that shit."

"I'll see what I can do."

"The fuck you will, Wicker. You guys in the press, you ain't gonna do nothing but make heroes out of the bastards every chance you get."

"Sorry you feel that way."

"I asked for CBS first," the caller said. "You were the only one I could get."

A few minutes later, catching a welcome drink at the Treadway bar, Wicker found himself standing by Ernest Montanye, the corrections officer who had been listing the observers who went into D-yard. He repeated his caller's idea.

Montanye shook his head. "Couldn't do it," he said. "We don't know exactly who's in the yard."

"Can't you count up everybody you've got in custody and assume everybody else is in D-yard?"

"Well, when they recaptured the other blocks Thursday they just rammed guys in where they could." It was hard to know who was where, Montanye said, and with everybody preoccupied with the revolt and worried about the hostages there just hadn't been time for any kind of accurate headcount.

"It's not much of an idea anyway," Wicker said. "But to tell you the truth, with computers and all that, I'd have thought you'd have a trace on every man, know right where he is all the time."

"Computers?" Montanye said sarcastically. "You're talking about a prison, not IBM." Of course, prisons would have the lowest priority for such sophisticated, high-cost equipment. Still it seemed to Wicker that the corrections bureaucracy should have been able in nearly three days at least to find out which of its charges were in custody and which were in the yard. No wonder relatives of inmates were calling in from faraway cities, only to find that nobody knew whether their sons or brothers or husbands were in D-yard.

McGowan then appeared to deliver the four observers to a downtown bowling alley, which was appended to the most popular restaurant in Batavia. Horsemeat would have been tasty after the dry prison sandwiches, relieved in two days only by Mrs. James's sumptuous breakfast; but in fact the bowling alley–restaurant served them decent steaks. All were glad to be out of D-yard, out of the Stewards' Room, away from Attica; but it was by no means a cheerful gathering. Wicker sensed in each of his companions that their return to "civilization" seemed, as it did to him, vaguely unreal. They talked desultorily, watching cheerful Batavians enjoying themselves in the local hot spot. Yet each of the four was remembering that a few miles away, behind the walls, beyond the makeshift barricades, there was another life, another world.

Late Saturday night after the observers had all left, it began to rain. . . . The roof of my tent had a hole in it, and was leaking. I must have rolled off my mattress because I woke up . . . outside the tent on the grounds. . . .[35]

"What'll you do next, Herman?" Wicker said, trying to revert to political reporter. "Run for mayor again?"

Badillo nodded "It's a year and half off but I think so."

"Can you win?"

The congressman shrugged. He looked as tired as Wicker felt. "What's Lindsay gonna do? Tell me that, maybe I can tell you if I can win."

Both were political buffs but both knew they were only making conversation. Someone turned on the television set above the bar. Unreality drifted in the restaurant like cigarette smoke. Suddenly, there she was, Miss America. Miss America? Wicker watched the long lines of antiseptic beauties in their virginal gowns, the equine face of Bert Parks, the rictus smiles, the gleaming teeth, one of the ugliest halls in America transformed by cheap money and cheap talent into a bower of glitter and spectacle. It was indecent, he thought, these doll-like painted creatures being paraded in their sham world of pink and white.

"I'm for the tall blonde," a man said at the next table.

"I like Miss Missouri," his wife, or somebody, answered. "So ladylike. Miss Missouri's got it all over the rest."

"How 'bout the talent? I thought the blonde had the most talent."

"That's not the talent you been staring at," the wife said.

. . . your hands were tied part of the time. You had the blindfold on. And there isn't anything more miserable than having things

*happen around you and being blindfolded. They would yell
"security," and then back on our eyes would go the blindfold. We
would then sit there and you would hear a lot of shouting and a
lot of what we interpreted as fighting.*[36]

Miss America that year turned out to be Jo Anne Jones, Miss California, who played the mandolin. She wept and smiled, as Parks
quavered through the Miss America song, a performance which finally
drove the four observers back to the Treadway.

Lew Steel was trying vainly to book a room. Wicker offered to
share his. Steel told them about the reading of the 28 points in D-yard
and the fierce inmate reaction.

"Kunstler saved our lives," Steel said, and told that story, too.

Wicker was partially feeling like a shirker for having inadvertently
missed this tense session. Mostly, he was relieved not to have been
there. Badillo was angry that the 28 points had been presented in such
disadvantageous circumstances. Steel insisted that he and the others
had thought they had no choice.

"I'll tell you something else," Steel said. "I'm not going back in
there. Maybe some of the black guys can risk it, but I think we've had
it. The game is over."

If Steel, prisonwise and intelligent as he was, was not going back to
D-yard, Wicker thought, neither was Tom Wicker. He felt an immense relief to know that that part of the experience was over, that he
had survived it physically. But he knew he had accomplished very
little. The promise of the James letter had been illusory and he had
contributed nothing to the discussions in D-yard or to the negotiation
of the 28 points. He had had no good ideas, made no impassioned
speeches. What had been the use of it all?

Walking wearily down the corridor with Steel, he was depressed
and disappointed. Once again, as too often in his life, things had not
fallen together, he had not been able to use his gifts as he sensed that he
should have. In the final analysis, something had been lacking. If the
observers had needed pulling together, if there had been problems that
needed solving, he should have been able to do it. It was *expected* of
him that he should do what ought to be done—expected by Tom
Wicker, if by no one else.

Wicker was haunted, too, by the men in D-yard—by the hostages
huddled in their ring, by the strange, obstinate, disturbing men who
held them captive. He was in fear of the inmates but he felt a responsibility to them as well as to the hostages. The inmates had asked for
help, and he had not been able to give it. That was the hard fact, and
he had a strong Scotch notion that when he came to be judged—again,

if by no one but himself—there could be no excuse strong enough to justify the failure.

But a personal failure was one thing; the tragedy taking shape in D-yard was of a different magnitude altogether. "So what's going to happen?" he asked Steel, in darkness, as they lay in the sagging motel beds waiting for the sleep that should have come down quickly. "What happens now?"

"A hell of a lot of people are going to get killed," Steel said.

September 12, 1971

I I

The Woman in the Diner

There are few sounds more shocking than a hotel-room telephone ringing to awaken someone from a dead sleep in the grim hours before 8 A.M. When their call came, Wicker and Steel rose glumly, unspeaking, and moved zombielike about their room. When he could focus, Wicker contemplated his only shirt and the thought of returning to the prison with distaste. He remembered that he and Steel were resolved not to reenter D-yard, but even the prospect of another wrangling, fruitless day—that was what he feared it would be—in the Stewards' Room was unpleasant. Worse, it was likely, too, that this day would see the end of it. Surely the troopers with the guns would go into the yard before the sun set.

Steel was dressed first and wandered out into the corridor. He found William Kunstler a few doors away and returned to say that Kunstler had some important information for them. Wicker went down the hall with Steel to Kunstler's room; there he was introduced to Mrs. Kunstler, a pretty, quiet woman who immediately conveyed to Wicker, without anything being said, that she was intensely proud of her controversial husband.

Kunstler was still in his undershirt. "I just thought you fellows ought to know I've had a call from some of the New York Twenty-one," he said. The Twenty-one were a group of Panther leaders who had stood trial together, with Kunstler as defense counsel. Their message to him had been that they were in touch abroad and that there were, indeed, third-world non-imperialist countries ready to take the Attica inmates as exiles.[1]

This impressed Kunstler as an important development. Steel received it impassively, Wicker rather impatiently. Wicker still regarded Brother Herbert Blyden's talk of transportation to another country as the most wildly impractical of all the inmate demands. It was unlikely but not impossible that the state might remove Vincent Mancusi, and there was always the faint possibility of finding an acceptable formula amounting to amnesty. But there was no possibility at all that the state or federal government would wheel up a Boeing 707 to the gates of the Attica Correctional Facility, load aboard Brother Herb and his followers, and fly them off free and clear to Algeria or wherever. It did not make much difference whether some country was prepared to accept such an unlikely group of expatriates, or even to pick them up. The whole matter seemed irrelevant to Wicker, and he did not understand why Kunstler gave it such importance.

He was about to leave to find Badillo and Garcia, companions more to his own turn of mind, when Kunstler laughed and said, "You know, I was just telling Lotte. It would be the greatest irony in the world if Tom Wicker and I should die together in that prison yard."

Wicker laughed, too, although he was not sure he and Kunstler saw the same joke. Coming from their roughly equivalent middle-class backgrounds and respectable educations, where were he and Kunstler now, at roughly the same age? Orangeburg, the city riots, the Tet offensive, the Chicago convention, My Lai, Cambodia, Kent State, Augusta, Jackson State—these and numerous other shocks to his conventional understanding of things had carried Tom Wicker, by September 1971, a long way from the comfortable place in the mainstream of action and acceptance that he once had relished. He had suffered professional and social opprobrium for his developing view of a society gone seriously astray from proclaimed ideals; his "constituency" was made up substantially of alienated and protesting blacks, young people, the disadvantaged.

Still, he had not broken with conventional America. He was an editor of the establishment's proudest voice, an affluent, privileged member of society who had paid no real price for his political and social attitudes. He was a commentator, not an activist; he avoided marching, sitting-in, and going to jail. He clung to the faith that "the system" was out of kilter rather than wrong in itself, that things could yet be improved within the usual limits of political, legal, and economic moderation. As a critic, he believed in the theater though he disliked the play; as a humanist, he could not substitute ideology for humanity. He was a dissident, not a revolutionary.

Bill Kunstler, on the other hand, seemed to Wicker to have crossed the line—perhaps, as Herman Schwartz believed, during the scandalous trial of the Chicago Seven and Bobby Seale. At least as Wicker saw him, Kunstler *was* a revolutionary, who saw the system itself as having been so manipulated by predatory and conspiratorial interests that it was no longer possible to redeem it by political action within the system's own limits or by its laws. It was necessary, instead, to fight the ruling conspirators on their own terms, with power and guile and ruthlessness, and it was not the redemption of the system that was at issue, but the quest for justice whatever the system. To that end, Kunstler had been willing to abandon the system's structure of material and professional rewards—to throw his life and career into the struggle rather than to cheer on one side or the other from the sidelines.

Wicker did not believe in conspiracies. He believed human nature would prevail over any system, that justice would flag and power assert itself in any society of men; and that in all societies, the fight for justice and a limit to power would go on, indomitably, inevitably, the cycle dominating the generations, the struggle never ceasing, the victory never won. And the joke he saw was that the difference in Kunstler's view and his own—if the difference actually existed—would matter no more than a faded flag trampled in the dust if they "should die together in that prison yard."

Revolutionary or dissident, death would level the distinction. The forces that each to his different degree had sought to oppose and change would roll on unmoved, no doubt untouched, while those with whom Kunstler had aligned himself and whose plight Wicker at least hoped to see improved would be none the better off—perhaps worse! —for their actions.

But Wicker laughed too at the even more ironic notion that it would make no more difference if he and Kunstler lived. Revolutionaries and dissidents—did they change the world or cloak its face awhile? Dead in a littered prison yard or live on the soapbox, the printed page, the barricades? Wicker almost spoke the phrase that Kunstler's joke brought to his mind—"Well, there'll always be an Attica."

But he held his tongue. He did not want to be flippant about a faith so honorably held as Kunstler's.

Wicker, Mathew, and Garcia were able to commandeer a trooper driving a state police car to take them back to the prison. The trooper told them of a small motel and diner in the village of Alexander, a little over half the way to Attica, and they decided to stop for a quick breakfast rather than depend on the prison's uncertain coffee and sandwiches.

The motel was off the main route by a block or so, with the little diner next door. When the police car pulled up in front of it, several other cars were already there. As the sound of their motor died away, they could hear a woman's sharp voice exclaiming angrily from within the diner. Then there was a deeper male reply.

"Sounds like Arthur Eve," Garcia said.

They got out of the car, listening. A loud quarrel was going on within, but they could not make out the details. As they opened the door, the woman's voice rose again, almost to a scream. She was behind the counter of the diner moving about, scrambling eggs, making toast, pouring coffee, while she hurled words over her shoulder. Several people sat at the counter and at oilcloth-covered tables, looking down at their coffee cups, silent and embarrassed. Arthur Eve stood before the cash register.

"But it *can't* be for two nights," he was saying, forcefully but with more control than the woman behind the counter. "I just checked in yesterday morning and I paid you for one night in advance."

The woman was tall, thin, pinched-looking; she wore an open sweater over a nondescript dress. In her sharp, insistent voice, she poured a torrent of anger on Eve, who seemed amazed. No one tried to calm the woman; the other people in the diner would not even look at her. From the hard, high flow of her words, Wicker deduced that Eve had checked in on Saturday morning before Saturday's noon checkout time for Friday rentals. Now the woman was insisting that he therefore owed her a Friday rental as well as a Saturday rental, but had paid her only for Friday.

"But I spent one night here and I *paid* you for one night," Eve insisted, his voice also rising.

"Yes, and you brung that other one in with you, too!" The piercing voice came back at him instantly.

Wicker saw that she was almost hysterical, so the problem had to be more than the dispute over Eve's check-in time, or that he had shared his room Saturday night with Jim Ingram. Wicker sensed that he had seen this woman before—in front of Central High School at Little Rock, or in Albany, Georgia, or Selma, Alabama. She did not like blacks. She feared them unreasonably, hated having them "moving in." She did not want them in her respectable place.

From some shouted phrases about "murderers and thieves," he realized that the woman in the diner also was upset about the uprising in the nearby prison—blacks again. Perhaps she had a relative or a friend among the corrections officers or in their families. A hard, poor life was written on her face; its struggle, isolation, and disadvantage would scarcely have equipped her with tolerance for things and forces unknown, inexplicable by the lights of a drudge life in Alexander, New York. Her dispute with Arthur Eve—black, assertive, somehow linked to the unknown murderers and thieves running loose at the prison—had set loose in her hatreds the more hysterical because they actually were fears.

"All right, I'll pay for the other guy!" Eve yelled at her, scarcely interrupting her tirade. "But I won't pay for two nights. . . ."

"Then I don't want your damn money! Just get out of here!"

"Tell me how much it is." Eve did not move. "How much for the other guy?"

"I said get out of here, I don't want your stinking money, now you get out of here right . . ."

"Come on, Arthur," Garcia said, touching Eve's arm.

Eve shook him off. "Five dollars," he said. "You won't tell me, I'm leaving five dollars for the other guy." He had taken a bill from his wallet.

"You come in here two nights, you bring another one in, you ain't even asked or signed him in, you don't want to pay, I say you just get the devil out of here, you get out of my place *right now!* You hear me? Hear me?"

Eve put the five dollars on the counter and turned away. To no one in particular, he said, "My God, she's a crazy woman. I just come in, and she starts yelling like a crazy woman."

"Okay," Mathew said, "let's get out of here."

There was no question, by then, of their eating breakfast in the diner. As they moved toward the door, Bob Garcia said something to the woman; her voice went on unbroken, and he said sharply, "You ought to be ashamed of yourself acting like this!"

They were at the door, and the woman's voice did not even raise or break pitch. "They ought to kill all of you people!" she shouted. "Everyone of you!"

Then they were outside. Wicker was shaken by the implicit violence of the moment, though no blow had been struck. He felt himself trembling in nervous reaction, as if he had witnessed a vicious fistfight. He had seen raw racial fear at its evil work of generating unreasoning hatred, and he knew that even a black in a white world could seldom have suffered such a torrent of hysteria directly upon his own sensibility as Arthur Eve had. He could see in Eve's face and eyes that he was close to a state of shock. Wicker wanted to say something, but he did not know what to say; he doubted if there *was* anything to say.

"You heard that," Eve said. "They ought to kill all of us. You heard her say that?"

"We heard it," Wicker said. But neither he, Garcia, nor Mathew was sure *what* they had heard. Driving on to Attica, with Eve and Ingram following the police car in Eve's Volkswagen, as if for safety, they discussed what the woman had meant. The trooper sat silent at the wheel, obviously shocked, too, by the scene in the diner.

"It's the prison thing," Garcia said. "They're getting to hate all of us around here. They want to go in there and take that prison back and turn loose those hostages, no matter who gets killed. And we're the ones stopping them. So they lump us in with the inmates."

"But that doesn't make sense," Mathew said. "The hostages will be killed first. These people ought to be the last ones to want that."

"She may have meant that," Wicker said, "but I think she was mostly talking about the blacks. She meant they ought to kill all the blacks." He was aware of the trooper, shifting nervously in the front seat. This was, after all, his home country.

"No, she meant all of *us*," Garcia insisted. "They just want to go in there and end it, and they hate all of us that stand in the way."

Perhaps, Wicker thought, they were both right. The woman had been too out of control, in any case, to have had a considered intent or to have used precise words. He looked back at the Volkswagen following them. Even if Garcia was right, he thought, Arthur Eve would not believe it. Arthur Eve would have no doubt at all about who it was the woman in the diner wanted to kill.

Meanwhile that Sunday morning, action already had started at the prison. Some of the observers had remained overnight in the Stewards' Room; others returned early. They found the corrections officers at the gate and the troopers and deputies they encountered uniformly surly, some actively hostile. Two days of frustration and waiting and fear had worn out whatever tenuous welcome the observers had had. Some had to send inside the prison to the authorities for help in making it past the main entrance. Nevertheless, at least by 8:30 A.M., Bobby Seale had entered the prison with his two body guards and Herman Schwartz, who had driven them from Buffalo.*

Kunstler arrived somewhat later and briefed Seale on what had happened in D-yard after Seale had left the night before. There seemed to be two final demands, Kunstler said, on both of which the state said action was "out of the question." These demands were for the removal of Mancusi and complete amnesty for the D-yard rebels. Without state concessions on these, Kunstler told Seale, the 28 points accepted by the state probably did not much matter to the inmates.

Nevertheless, Seale said, he was ready to go to D-yard. Oswald, who was then in the Stewards' Room, said he was willing for Seale to talk to the brothers, but he underlined what Kunstler had said—Mancusi and amnesty were not negotiable. Oswald then added an ominous note. It was "absolutely urgent," he said, that the inmates accept the 28 points

---

* Accounts of Seale's movements and activities at the prison on Sunday morning are contradictory, as between testimony to McKay by Kunstler, Oswald, and others; and Tepper, Schwartz, Oswald, and Badillo. The account given here is reconstructed from all these sources and from the author's memories and interviews, in the belief that it is the most plausible summary of a disputed episode. Direct quotation is used only where the author is reasonably sure of the authenticity of the quoted statement.

and end their rebellion. If they did not, "matters will be very serious."

Some of the observers protested that if Seale was going into D-yard, they had a right to know what he was going to say, since they, too, might have to go in later. Wicker, impressed that Oswald's remarks clearly suggested an approaching attack on D-yard, said he wanted to be sure the commissioner's statement "was conveyed to the prisoners, that that's what's involved here, because we've got to tell them the absolute truth." Some of the black observers replied that Seale ought not to be accused of inflaming the brothers or of intending to do so. Seale himself had been listening impassively, a dignified figure who again had made himself the center of attention in the Stewards' Room.

"Okay," Seale said suddenly. "I'm going." He pointed to Kunstler, Schwartz, the two bodyguards. "Let's go." And he led them out of the room, the other observers watching.

A corrections officer standing guard at the door spoke to the departing group: "Just a minute. . . . I can't let you go out to the prisoners until I get permission." Schwartz, who did not wish to return to D-yard, took this as only a momentary reprieve. He thought the officer meant he had to get permission for the group to go past his checkpoint and on to D-yard—*not* that he had orders to stop them from going at all.

But Seale then announced that he was going "outside." Then he led his small retinue—Franklin Florence and Herman Badillo had joined it—out of the prison and to Schwartz' car in the parking lot. A major question exists as to what Seale thought his position then was. Some of the observers thought that Oswald had said Seale could go into D-yard and had attached no conditions as such. Oswald, writing later, conceded that "permission to reenter was denied," but said nothing about a conditional offer.[2] Herman Badillo, on the other hand, understood Oswald to have told Seale "that unless he promised to speak on behalf of the 28 points, he would not allow Seale to return to D-yard. Seale walked out."[3] Some of the observers certainly had conveyed the idea that, at the least, they did not want Seale to go into the yard and *attack* the 28 points. This could have amounted logically in Seale's mind to a demand by the observers and Oswald that he not go in unless he *supported* the 28; that is the view taken by the McKay Commission.[4] It also is possible that Seale had interpreted, or decided to use, the corrections officer's remark at the door of the Stewards' Room as a prohibition on his going into D-yard.

In any case, Kunstler, Franklin Florence, and Badillo soon reappeared in the Stewards' Room with the text of a statement Seale had made to television and radio reporters (after first making sure he was positioned against a prison background for the cameras):

This morning, the commissioner and his aides would not let me in, saying that if I was not going inside to encourage the prisoners to accept the so-called demands made by the committee, they did not want me. I'm not going to do that.

In addition, the commissioner said that full amnesty was non-negotiable and the removal of the warden at Attica prison was not negotiable. The Black Panther Party position is this: The prisoners have to make their own decision. I will not encourage them to compromise their position.

The Black Panther Party position is that all political prisoners who want to be released to go to non-imperialistic countries should be complied with by the New York state government.[5]

Florence, who had so eagerly welcomed the Panther chairman the night before, was doggedly loyal. He explained to the other observers, almost defiantly, that Brother Bobby's course of action had been dictated by the two "non-negotiable" points cited by Oswald. There was no reason for Brother Bobby to discuss the state's non-negotiable positions with the D-yard brothers, Florence insisted.

Whether Seale's broadcast statement about Oswald's position was accurate was never thrashed out in the Stewards' Room; black–white relationships there were perhaps too tenuous for that kind of discussion. But Wicker believed that Seale had simply ducked out of a hard case—perhaps justifiably—while putting the responsibility on Oswald. For Seale to have argued for compromise in D-yard would have belied his and his party's militant position and probably would not have swayed the brothers anyway. To have urged them to hold out would have risked his having to accept the blame for whatever violence might ensue.

As a black political leader wise in the ways of law and prison, Seale would have known that the latter course would risk his own indictment for aiding and abetting the rebellion. There was almost literally nothing Seale could do as a militant black leader except what, as Wicker believed, he did do—duck the issue entirely, except to endorse the proposed exodus to the third world, and put the blame on Oswald.

Whether Seale had planned it that way all along, or whether his tactics developed out of the situation, he had as a political leader extricated himself brilliantly from a difficult, if not impossible, position. But Wicker, perhaps ungenerously, wondered if at some point even a political leader's duty might not become simply that of a concerned human being. Oswald's statement that morning suggested how near the attack was—an attack that no one in the Stewards' Room doubted would snuff out many of the lives in D-yard. Could not Bobby Seale as a concerned human being have said to the inmates, "Look, you've gone as far as you can. You've made a political point to the whole world. You've made The Man listen. Now a lot of you are going to get killed if you push it further. I'm not telling you to compromise just to get whatever you get out of a compromise. I'm not telling you to give up because you're in the wrong. I'm telling you to stay alive, take your gains, and fight again another day."

Seale probably doubted his capacity to persuade men like Champ and Richard Clark and Herbert Blyden, whose necks were on the line, to take such a view without an amnesty. Unquestionably, Seale's political position was too important to be squandered on sentimentality and naïveté. Still, Wicker thought, all the talk of brotherhood would have something of a hollow ring after Bobby Seale's performance. He did not equate the skilled protection of a political position with an imposing human example. But then, he reflected wryly, he would not last long when the revolution came, nor would he much wish to. Which was, perhaps, only a way of saying that he had no real need of revolution.

With Seale out of the action,[6] the group in the Stewards' Room quickly relapsed into fine but fruitless oratorical form. No one had much remaining hope for the 28 points; all knew the attack could not be far off. Seale's absence seemed to symbolize the absence of any real power by which the observers could influence the course of things. All felt violence and bloodshed at hand; some felt responsible for failure; others identified themselves emotionally with the prospective victims in D-yard. Tense, tired, depressed, angry, confused, they struggled on—arguing, proposing, denouncing, as if talk itself might yet overwhelm violence.

Oswald had, in fact, left them more room for talk than maneuver, with his double-barreled message: one, that amnesty and Mancusi were "not negotiable" (blacks, antiwar demonstrators, student radicals, rebellious inmates, all had been criticized for the undemocratic practice of making "non-negotiable demands," yet here was the state of New York making a "non-negotiable response" to "non-negotiable demands"); and two, the implication that the rebellion had to be ended quickly to stop an armed attack. The first message seemed to Wicker to make the second futile. And the threat would not make it easier for the observers to work with the D-yard brothers if any of them again ventured into the yard. Bill Kunstler, predicting the inmates' reaction, conceded that he no more than the other observers wanted "to go in there and die."

Clarence Jones insisted, however, that the observers should "factually inform the prisoners of the situation that exists." After all, he observed sarcastically, whatever rights the inmates lacked, surely they did have "a right to choose the conditions under which they will live or die." To which caustic Lew Steel replied that whatever the observers said or did not say to the prisoners would make no difference. From the beginning, "one side had all the power," Steel said. At any point, that side—the state—"could have said there will not be bloodshed," but it hadn't and wouldn't. As a result of the state's failure to make such a guarantee, the D-yard brothers believed they had to hold out with their hostages until amnesty could be negotiated; but the state's silence actually meant an amnesty was not possible. Bloodshed was inevitable.

"Fi" Ortiz spoke up with forceful good sense. They appeared at the point, he said, when "it's the last time we'll be able to go downstairs" to D-yard. So G.I. (José Paris), who had been one of the brothers so recently, should explain the situation to them and warn them "the rap is gonna start." G.I. should remind them that they had seized the prison to let the world know about conditions inside it. Now it was up to them to decide if they had made that point and, if they had, whether to give up peacefully. The inmates had to decide for themselves if there had to be a "shootout" or if the message had been delivered without the shootout.

"G.I." Paris, in dark glasses and a porkpie hat, slight in form, with a husky, barely audible voice, had to that point been a relatively unobtrusive member of the group. Now he spoke with rough and moving authority. "The whole story," he said, "is the conditions." He had not much grammar, he groped for words, and there was a heavy trace of Spanish in his accent, but the other observers knew he had been there, had seen and felt "the conditions." They listened without moving, scarcely blinking or looking away.

"The story inside the institution is the treatment the people are put into." G.I. spoke of the steel bars, the hacks, the box, the lineup, keep-lock, the impersonality, boredom, loneliness—the utter waste of humanity. But the story outside the institution was also "the conditions"—on the block, in the tenements, in the uncaring schools, among the pushers and the junkies and the hustlers and the hard-eyed cops, in the crowded flats with jobless fathers and overworked mothers, the brothers and sisters hooked on dope, the hopelessness and the bitterness—the utter waste of humanity.

In or out, the story was "the conditions." And G.I. pled with them to understand what those conditions meant—"We didn't make ourselves; we were put into them." His voice was choking and there were tears behind the dark glasses as G.I. came to the end of his speech.

"The only thing I got to give is my life," G.I. said. "You unnerstan'?"

Wicker wanted to believe that he did. At least he sympathized, and that was something. But how could the gap between "the conditions" of G.I.'s life and his own—let alone those of the truly affluent—be really understood if it had not been lived? How could *he* fully know what "the conditions" did to men and women who were "put into them" rather than merely learning about them from the news and the scholarly studies and the accounts of inarticulate victims and the sudden deadly explosions of wrath and frustration that had shaken Newark, Detroit, Watts, Attica? He sensed the profound inadequacy of his understanding, greater than that of most whites as it might have been; but he knew he was not the man to give away his worldly goods, assume the lot of the poor, wash the dust from their feet, and come truly to know his fellowman. His understanding might be merely faulty, but his will and his charity were insufficient.

Tom Soto began in sharp contrast to G.I., and in his accustomed style of bombast and dogma. The observers had to make it clear that "the responsibility for violence" rested on prison officials, the governor, the corporations, the banks. "The victims are in the prisons and the real crimes are in the boardrooms. . . . The act of these prisoners is in the interests of all the working people and the oppressed people of the world, regardless of whether they get slaughtered. . . ."

Suddenly, and to Wicker's consternation, the assertive and unyielding Soto was weeping openly. Nothing could have more graphically demonstrated the level of emotion in the room; Wicker felt his own eyes damp, his throat tight. The utter waste of humanity was about to be continued, bloodily, unnecessarily. Outside their windows, the observers could see gas masks, ladders, arms, fire hoses being readied, troopers moving into formations and marching off, an unmarked white van filled with riot helmets.

"What these brothers have done," Soto mumbled brokenly, "will live on in the history of the story of all the oppressed peoples of the world." There was more emotion and human sentiment in him than his earlier demeanor had suggested—which should not have surprised Wicker as much as it had.

Jaybarr Kenyatta, incongruous as ever in robes and rug, but brooding rather than fierce, told them he had first gone to jail when he was 12 years old. He had learned never to trust the system and he knew the D-yard brothers "'cause the jailhouse is all I know." He and they knew "they ain't but two ways to fight That Man." One was force, but—looking at the whites—"none of you guys know the problem." So the observers had to go the other way. "We got to work together. We got to set aside our differences. If they can have unity [in D-yard], we got to have unity."

With sophistication that belied his odd garb, he said there were really two forces at work, politics and the media. Realizing that, he said, "I got the solution." The black brothers had "got to the point where we don't give a fuck. . . . We don't have but one education and that's to fight. . . . When The Man comes, we don't mind fighting." Such brothers ought to go in the prison and stay with the D-yard brothers to the end. The others had to pledge to carry the word to the public, to let the world know what had happened.

"We got to have a commitment," Kenyatta said, looking directly at Wicker, "that when you get out that door, you ain't going to forget."

Arthur Eve immediately called on Walkley, Emery, and the other legislators in the room to remember those words when social issues next arose in the legislature. Then he abruptly raised a new point. With high indignation, he told how a corrections officer, not knowing who Eve was, had called him "boy" to his face the day before. They all had that attitude toward blacks, Eve said. Most of the D-yard brothers were black; so after the insurrection was ended, there would be terrible retaliation on the brothers "unless all you guys are willing to come back here, be in here every day."

Wicker was quite sure that he was *not* willing to make such a commitment—indeed could not. But Eve said he was willing to live in the prison, if necessary; however, he didn't "want to die. . . . I want to exhaust every human possibility" before anyone died in D-yard.

Badillo and Mathew tried to cool down the emotions in the room. Ortiz's point had impressed him, Badillo said. He remembered a group of Young Lords who had occupied a church in New York City to dramatize a political point in their community. When they had made the point, they had voluntarily given up physical possession of the church. Maybe the observers could persuade D-yard that the inmates already had "proved their political point." Maybe it would help if the observers promised assistance in any prosecutions that might result.

To Mathew, it seemed that despite Oswald's statement, the Mancusi issue ought to be negotiable. Why could the state not manage that Mancusi be "suspended" or transferred, administratively avoiding any specific surrender to the demand for his removal? Bureaucrats could arrange anything if they wanted to. Why, at the least, could Mancusi not be removed from control of "reestablishing the institution" after the revolt was ended?

No one could answer. But Clarence Jones picked up Mathew's idea. What if a solution to the Mancusi problem could be found, but the state still refused amnesty? In wandering discussion, the consensus was reached that this would do little good; amnesty was far more important than Mancusi to the D-yard brothers.

Assemblyman Frank Walkley of nearby Castile, New York, who had been in and out of the observers' discussions, wanted to defend his constituency. He regretted what had happened to Eve. "But to expect a complete reversal of attitudes from everybody is more than we can seek at this time." He believed most people in the area "are concerned with the lives of the people who're in that compound," inmates as well as hostages. Only a small minority thought as did the woman in the diner (those who had been there had spread the story among the other observers).

But a "total amnesty," in Walkley's view, would cause too many problems. Oswald was a progressive man in the corrections system, and there was high public interest in his furlough plan for inmates and his other reform proposals. But the Attica revolt, if followed by amnesty for those who had carried it out, would "set back the cause we're all interested in. . . . We may go back a hundred years in this effort we're making." It was the classic protest of the mainstream—we must never go too far or move too fast.

That was not the kind of protest Bill Kunstler wanted to hear. In fact, he was wondering if he was "in Alice in Wonderland." He had heard all these fine speeches, he said, yet, "in my heart, I know we're facing a cosmic tragedy." What was happening out there in D-yard was "the end product of my society." Intercessions with Governor Rockefeller, negotiating conditions, references to future obligations, praise for Oswald "have no significance," Kunstler said. The truth was that "each one of us wants to avoid what we can't tolerate in our society," and he was no different from the others.

The D-yard brothers, Kunstler said, "must be told the absolute, utter truth as to what their situation is." As for the observers, "all that we can do is work for time." That was not much. In fact, Kunstler was "utterly sick at heart that these men will die and they'll die because of me." They would die because he, Kunstler, and those like him had "scrambled over their backs" in society. This did not seem melodramatic to Wicker since he was feeling much the same emotions. He did not shrink when Kunstler, somewhat roundly, took note of his own watery eyes and observed that "tears don't move monsters but they relieve the spirit."

But Wicker was less impressed when Kunstler declared that, all in all, "the Bobby Seale episode is irrelevant. . . . Whatever reason he gives to the public is immaterial." The lawyer, tearful or not, was defending his client, and Wicker was not persuaded at all, quite the opposite, when Kunstler went on to say that anyone who was thinking hard thoughts of Brother Bobby was hearing "just our intellectuality and maybe even our morality" speaking. Wicker rather liked to listen to both voices, when he could discern them.

Sensible Jim Ingram pointed out that the observer committee had a certain validity, both as a cross section of society and as a concept for the situation. If all else failed, it still was an apt instrument by which "to tell it to the people." Or was it not at least possible that the committee should "all go in and refuse to come out," thus interposing their actual selves between the guns and the inmates? Wicker was discomfitted to hear this notion again. In his heart of hearts, he had been wondering if it was not their moral duty to do just that. Yet, he knew he feared violence too much, had too little faith in either the moral or the political restraint of the state's armed agents—or of the inmates, for that matter—to risk such a course.

"And one thing's sure," Ingram said in his Southern accent, "if anybody's bullshittin', it's gonna come out on the floor here today."

That was another uncomfortable idea. The situation already was cutting too close to the bone, too far into what he was. No one wanted to face the whole truth about himself; in the final analysis no one wanted to be forced to know whether, or how much of, his life was bullshit—much less to be forced into the position where others knew, perhaps more quickly than he. But Ingram was right; they all were coming face to face with more knowledge of themselves than any could have wished.

As if sensing the same inevitability, Julian Tepper spoke up at greater length than he had done since his farcical swing-and-shove affray with Arthur Eve the evening before. "I'll be completely honest," he said, causing Lew Steel to raise his eyebrows, as if to ask if anyone could be. "I'm afraid to go back in" the yard. The prison administration had put the observers in an untenable position because it was clear that "there's going to be no resolution" of the deadlocked negotiations. Bobby Seale, too, had put the observers in an untenable position by leaving the impression he couldn't go in except to sell the brothers the 28-point package. So if the observers did go in again, the brothers would believe they could do so only on terms Bobby Seale had rejected. That was too dangerous.

It was a shrewd analysis. Tepper added that it seemed clear that there was "going to be force used." Therefore, and immediately, the observers had to use, at the least, whatever credibility they had with the D-yard brothers because, frankly, "we have always ducked the issue [of the force the state finally would use] when we're down there."

But, as usual, the Stewards' Room discourse slipped away from this essential point. Arthur Eve, shaking his head in warning, remarked that "if they come in there and kill people, Buffalo's gonna burn up. I mean burn up, man." What's more, he said, "if something happens here, it's gonna mirror in every community all over the country." Blacks, Wicker had noted, usually meant other blacks when they talked of "brothers" or "sisters"; similarly, when they spoke of "the community," they meant the black community.

Eve's remark seemed to be a final straw for the moderate John Dunne. There was no sense in the inmates holding out longer, he said; "their political point has been proven." They had made "more demonstrable progress toward penal reform in the last three days" than ever had been made before.

Without further ado, Dunne left the Stewards' Room. Was he going to see Oswald? Wicker wondered. To call the governor? Dunne carried political weight with both, although no New York Republican could dominate or instruct Nelson Rockefeller. But suddenly, as he watched John Dunne go down the second-floor corridor toward Oswald's office, it came to Tom Wicker that *someone* had to talk to Rockefeller. Someone had to go to The Man.

CHAPTER

12

The Man

Others were getting similar ideas. As Herman Badillo put it, after Bobby Seale left, the observers found themselves "with no place left to go. . . . It was necessary to come up with some alternative strategy."[1]

So, out of desperation as much as anything else, the idea evolved that Nelson Rockefeller should come to Attica to meet with the observers—*not* with the D-yard brothers. Some of the observers believed such a meeting would enhance the state's position in D-yard—"show them Rocky cares." Others thought the governor's presence—even his announced intention to come—might at least stop the impending attack, since Rockefeller probably would not wish to be present if it had to be undertaken.

The first real development of the Rockefeller strategy in the Stewards' Room came when someone mentioned Robert Douglass, one of the governor's closest personal and political associates. Douglass had come to Attica; Douglass had Rockefeller's ear; so the observers ought to talk to Douglass and get him to appeal to Rockefeller to come too. But when the call for Douglass went out, only Russell Oswald and Norman Hurd appeared. At 10:42 A.M. they came in, looking apprehensive and a little defiant.

Arthur Eve reacted strongly. The observers had asked to speak to Bob Douglass, he said. The observers knew Douglass had the most clout with the governor. The group, he said, could not "accept anything less" than a few minutes with Douglass.

"Mister Hurd," Oswald said pointedly, "is here as the governor's personal representative."

John Dunne had returned to the room. Acidly, he asked if Hurd had as much power with the governor as Bob Douglass did.

Everyone knew that was the point. Eve said that the fact that

Douglass had not responded to the observers' call, although he was known to be only a few feet down the corridor, showed that "no one really wants to give respect," either to the observers or to the inmates that the observers in some measure had to represent. In fact, Douglass' not coming was "a real insult to the efforts of all of us," even to Oswald, who had made strong efforts, Eve shrewdly pointed out, to get a peaceful settlement.

None of this could have been easy for the mild-mannered Hurd, who now said that *he* was the governor's personal representative at Attica; Bob Douglass was present only "to be of assistance" in any way he could.

Herman Badillo gave that short shrift. It was Bob Douglass personally who had prevailed on *him* to come to Attica, Badillo said; now it was vitally important that Douglass should hear personally what he and the other observers had to say.

Wicker strongly believed that Douglass should talk with the observers, more because of his belief that everyone should do everything he possibly could than out of any clear idea of what Douglass, in fact, *could* do. Wicker had no great concern about the observers' dignity or standing—to him, they seemed by Sunday morning to have little of either. But he saw no reason why Douglass should not meet with them, and he knew Rockefeller was more likely to do what was recommended by Robert Douglass than by Norman Hurd. As the morning had dragged along in more fruitless discussion, he had accepted, too, the notion that only Rockefeller coming personally to Attica—if that—could avoid the coming bloodbath. If Douglass was the man who could most nearly persuade Rockefeller to come, then Douglass was the man they needed to see.

Oswald departed and at 10:50 returned with a slight, handsome man of perhaps 40 years, looking Ivy League and wary. Robert Douglass, Dartmouth '53 and Cornell Law School, had worked for Nelson Rockefeller for nearly 10 years; he had been the governor's counsel until appointed his principal deputy earlier in 1971, and he was considered something of an authority on criminal justice and corrections.

"I'm Bobby Douglass," he said, "a friend of many of you here." He and Wicker had met once or twice, as news source and political reporter.

Wicker wondered why, if Douglass had come at all, he had not come at first. Probably because if he was the man who could most nearly persuade Rockefeller to come to Attica, he had sensed that that was what the observers wanted of him. That he had tried to avoid talking to them therefore suggested either that he had no intention of recommending that Rockefeller come, or that he knew Rockefeller would not come, or both.

But Arthur Eve told Douglass that the observers were "in unanimous agreement that the governor should come here." Rockefeller had to be made to see, Eve said, that if the troopers went in, "hundreds and possibly thousands will be killed." In that event, "every major city in this state" would see "rioting, killing, and really a form of civil revolution." The committee, knowing that, had worked hard to avoid bloodshed at Attica. Now, with the hour of decision obviously at hand, "We *must*—I repeat that a thousand times—we *must* . . . talk to the governor."

Wicker thought Eve had overstated the case, probably stiffening Douglass' resistance rather than persuading him. With some asperity, Clarence Jones—in no small way representing the political power of the New York black community—then told Douglass that the observers had "walked and gone the last mile." Could Rockefeller or the prison administrators say as much? Of course, Commissioner Oswald also had done all he could, Jones said (at which point there was a somewhat surprising interruption from Franklin Florence, who shouted, "That's right!"). There was "no lack of appreciation or lack of faith" in Oswald, Jones said, but it now was Governor Rockefeller's turn to go the last mile. Nothing less was going to make any difference.

Oswald, hearing himself thus praised, was less generous in return. It seemed clear to him "that members of the committee were afraid that if the governor did not come, the responsibility for any impending loss of life would fall on them."[2]

The observers had agreed to confront Douglass, an Establishment figure, with as much Establishment power of their own as they could muster. Douglass did not seem a man to be much moved by Soto or Kenyatta in full ideological or racial cry. So after Eve the legislator and Jones the black business leader, Wicker the political columnist took his turn. Beginning somewhat hesitantly, he first cited the Eve–Badillo view—persuasive to him—that an armed assault on the predominantly black and Puerto Rican stronghold in D-yard would produce rioting in the black and Puerto Rican communities throughout the state. If that was to be avoided, Wicker advised Douglass, it was important to "buy time." That the inmates were not willing to make an agreement on terms acceptable to the state on Saturday or Sunday did not necessarily mean that they would be as adamant on Wednesday or Thursday.

Inmate rhetoric, moreover, had suggested that D-yard clearly understood that Governor Rockefeller was The Man with the power. Obviously, they wanted him to treat them with some respect, as if they too were men worth negotiating with. But it was the observers who were asking Rockefeller to come to Attica, Wicker insisted, and it was only with the observers that the governor would be expected to deal. His presence, his mere intention to come, quickly would be well-known to the D-yard brothers. And that could even break the impasse because it would mean to the inmates that The Man cared what happened to them.

But if Rockefeller didn't come, Minister Florence again broke in to say, the brothers would just be confirmed in "what they know in their guts, that he *doesn't* care."

Wicker had a final point to make. Kenyatta had just exacted from them, he told Douglass, a pledge not to let the public forget what had happened at Attica. "Well, I won't forget," Wicker said. "I pledge you that, and I pledge it to the governor."

He watched Douglass' eyes narrow a little and was not surprised. Douglass knew a political threat when he heard one; and Tom Wicker thought with wonderment of what had happened to him in little over 48 hours at Attica. Never before had he deliberately threatened anyone with the latent political power of his well-displayed articles in *The New York Times*. He was ashamed of himself, but exhilarated, too, and angry. Listening to the others talk to Bob Douglass, hearing his own voice, he had become as convinced as he ever had been of anything that Nelson Rockefeller belonged in the Stewards' Room.

In New York, Rockefeller *was* The Man. Whoever held title, Rockefeller headed the state government, the state machinery, one of its major political parties; in fact, he headed the state "corrections" system. And that was just the political Rockefeller. The other Rockefeller—all the other Rockefellers of the world, the great owners and proprietors and investors and profit-makers—shaped, as nearly as any one human did or could, the society that had produced Attica and "the conditions" into which G.I. Paris and so many of the men of D-yard had been put. What right had the political or any of the other Rockefellers to send well-barbered aides like Douglass and Hurd to deal for them at arm's length and second remove when their own society, their own masterwork, began to rip at the seams? What right had Nelson Rockefeller to avert his face from the sores and abscesses of a society wrought as much in his name and faith as anyone's?

It did not even matter, finally, whether Rockefeller, political or other, could do anything to stop the shedding of blood at Attica. Maybe Steel was right that events were out of control, that by then nothing could stop the inevitable clash of forces that did not even fully understand themselves. But Wicker was not willing that the last effort, even if it proved only a hopeless gesture to decency and humanity, should not be made by one of the most powerful men in the world, representative of its proudest society. He was not willing for those with the most profound responsibility for what was happening to be allowed to pass by on the other side of the road.

And that, he said to himself more personally, was something worth using power for, to the extent that he had any. What would ever make power more nearly worth having? How else could power more properly be used than to force elementary humanity upon even greater power, if that should be possible? So, he told himself, he was going all the way, by God, for the first time in his carefully modulated life, and the chips could damn well fall where they might.

But Douglass, as might have been expected, considered the atmosphere in the Stewards' Room "very hostile." He noticed that while "they were directing their speeches at me . . . a gentleman was pacing around me and there was finger shaking and pointing. . . ."[3]

"Listen," Herman Badillo told him, "you send those troopers in there, you're not going to have enough National Guardsmen in Harlem and the South Bronx." Douglass and the governor might even need to alert President Nixon. But all that might well be avoided if the governor would only come to Attica and meet with the observers. "Please . . . can we say the governor is on his way?"

That would be "at least buying time and not lives," Kunstler put in. But if the governor didn't come, "he's condoning a massacre." Wicker thought that threat was a little more bald than his own, although it was not fundamentally different. But the bluntness of Kunstler's words offended his tactical sense; threats were better left unspoken but unmistakable. He feared that it was possible to push Rockefeller too far into a corner for anyone's good.

"I hear you. I understand," Douglass said rather patiently, but with the air of a man confronted with more argument than he wanted to absorb. As far as he could see, he went on, Oswald had made every effort possible for a peaceful settlement. The commissioner had done outstanding work in a terrible crisis. But he wanted to remind the observers that during the Tombs riots, Mayor Lindsay "finally reached the point where he had to . . . restore order in the city."

Wicker scarcely had time to reflect that it was a bad moment for the governor's representative to be measuring Rockefeller's course against that of his political rival, John Lindsay, when Badillo leaped to the counterattack.

"But Bobby," he said, "that's exactly the point. The mayor was *personally involved.*" Badillo had been at the Tombs, too, as Douglass well knew.

Quiet fell momentarily on the Stewards' Room, to be broken by Russell Oswald. It would be easier for him and "possibly even wiser to remain quiet," he said, but he couldn't do that. He recognized the problems that an attack might cause in the cities, but "I think it would be equally difficult if guards here died as a result of the actions of some. I suggest we have problems of that kind as well." He had been "besieged" by telegrams and other communications from corrections officers in New York and elsewhere, telling him that he already had "permitted one life to be taken. How much longer are you going to endanger corrections officers' lives?"

Since his arrival at the prison on Friday, Wicker's respect for Oswald had been steadily growing. Oswald obviously had been fighting a rearguard action against his own professional colleagues; and Wicker believed that Oswald's desire for a peaceful settlement was not only sincere but professionally courageous. It probably had been easier for Oswald to walk into D-yard on Thursday afternoon than for him to defy the pressures of the corrections bureaucracy and perhaps of his own political superiors, not to mention public opinion in Attica town, the growing displeasure of the troopers at what they saw as his inaction and lack of resolution, the buildup of sheer, impotent fury, machismo thinly bound, in the booted men with the guns. "Why don't you go home, you son of a bitch?" a trooper told Oswald to his face that afternoon.[4]

But surely the commissioner realized, Eve said, that since William Quinn had died, it was a "different ball game." Now, maybe as many as "forty of [the inmates] could get the electric chair."

On the other hand, Norman Hurd said, wasn't it true that the inmates had spurned the commissioner's offer of a 28-point package of prison reforms?

In fact, Eve replied, the dismissal of Mancusi and the amnesty plank were "the two hangups" that had made the package unacceptable. These were as much the state's "non-negotiable" positions as the inmates'.

Bill Gaiter, who had been silent for much of the morning, then spoke with passion. "I watched 'em tear up that damn list last night and I wanted to help 'em do it," he said. As the brothers saw it, they had "no squawk" for committing a crime, getting caught, being imprisoned. But as a result of their treatment in the cages of Attica, "they feel a crime has been committed against them." And who was being imprisoned for that? If somebody died while committing that crime against them, "on that rationale an amnesty makes sense."

Douglass listened patiently to this intense recital of a point of view Wicker had first heard expressed by Brother Flip Crowley during the all-night session in D-yard. Then Douglass pointedly returned to Eve's remarks. On those two particular points—Mancusi and amnesty—it appeared to him that "the observers are unable to resolve the impasse." Were the main issues, then, "Mancusi and total amnesty?"

"The issue is time," Kunstler insisted. Mancusi, for example, might be "negotiable" with the brothers by, say, Wednesday. G.I. Paris vehemently agreed.

"But I have to know what the issues are," Douglass said.

"The issue is fundamentally time," Clarence Jones said. Without time, any other possibility save an attack was foreclosed.

"And the governor needs time also," Badillo insisted, in pursuit of his theme that an attack at Attica would have riotous consequences elsewhere.

"Besides," Jones said, "the governor doesn't have to come committed to anything. We're just asking him to come here and talk with us."

"I know," Douglass said, inexorably, showing why he was so valued as assistant. "But the issues at this time are still Mancusi and amnesty. Isn't that right?"

Douglass left the room with that view of the situation obviously unchanged in his sharp brain. Before he had come in, there had been some talk among the observers of making a public statement on radio, before, as some of them were beginning to fear, the authorities turned off the telephone in the Stewards' Room. Wicker was less concerned about that than he was about the attack going in. Every glance out the window seemed to suggest the moment was nearly at hand—supplies were being stockpiled, troops lined up, weapons checked. Another helicopter had settled into the parking lot.

Clarence Jones had been working on a draft of the proposed public statement and he now read it to the group. It mentioned that "a massacre of prisoners is about to take place" and ended with an appeal to the governor to come to Attica so that the observers could "spend time instead of lives" working out a solution.

John Dunne objected immediately to the word "massacre." It was enough, he said, to point out that "force is about to be used." Whether with conscious humor or not, Tom Soto followed this archetypical moderate's remark with the announcement, "I got to take a bad leak." He slouched out, followed by the only laughter of a long day, and the tension in the room was at least momentarily broken.

But Dunne stuck to his point. Force had been used to quell the riot at the Queens House of Detention—Herman Badillo had been there and had seen it—but no death or injury had resulted. Why should the observers predict a "massacre" at Attica?

" 'Cause we know this Man gonna do what he gonna do," Kenyatta said. " 'Cause ain't nothin' out in that yard, far as he's concerned, but a bunch of ignorant, worthless nothin'." Moreover, Wicker thought, agreeing with Kenyatta, the situation was made infinitely worse than the Queens riot by the presence of so many hostages, by the hatreds that had gathered in the town, by the anger and frustration of the troopers, and—as they saw it—by Oswald's vacillation.

"But the minute that happens," Kenyatta went on, "that gives *us* the right to kill white folks. I got the same right to kill you out there" ("out there" apparently being the world beyond the prison) once the killing started at all.

"Listen," Jim Ingram said to Dunne, "these guards and troopers, they're no more than animals right now. They've been reduced to the lowest level of humanity by all this, and that's not rhetoric. They're straining at the leash. Once the restraint goes, I'm not sure anyone can assure even *our* safety." As for the inmates, "I suggest strongly that if one hostage is hurt, there *will* be a bloodbath. Confusion gonna reign when those beasts are turned loose on those people out there."

Ingram had established himself in the Stewards' Room as a sensible man; and he already had told some of the observers of his keen sense that guards and troopers were directing a sort of unconscious "hate stare" at his and others' black skins. The curiously stilted quality ("confusion gonna reign") of his remarks, taken with his obvious sincerity, had a considerable impact even on the moderates in the room. They knew Ingram was not given to bluster and revolutionary rhetoric.

Soto had returned. A statement had to go out, he said, "because of the obvious negative response that they [Douglass, Hurd, Oswald] made clear even before they left." There was no hope from the governor, only from the public. And "anyone who can relate to the prisoners should go down there and explain this development."

Argument developed, however, as to whether the observers had the "right" to issue a statement. Herman Badillo insisted that the inmates at least had to be informed of it. The Young Lords, Soto, and others believed even more strongly that the inmates had to *approve* the statement before it went out; otherwise, the observers would be "negotiating for them."

But Bill Gaiter contended that the committee of observers was "on the line" and had to "move on its own." The statement was not a negotiating move but a "political move." Unpredictable as always, the fiery Florence agreed. "We have to stop dealing in emotions and start doing some gut political reacting," he said. The "political realities" were that "we *are* negotiating for the prisoners, whether we like the responsibility we have been skillfully maneuvered into or not."

That debate ended in a decision to send a committee to No Man's Land to inform the inmates about the statement, although Wicker insisted that the committee avoid even the faintest suggestion that the governor might, in fact, be coming or that the observers had any evidence to suggest that he might.

The wording still had to be agreed upon. Frank Walkley thought "massacre" unwarranted by anything the observers knew. Dunne

wanted it made clear that the governor was being urged to meet with
the observers, not the inmates. Badillo proposed that a specific telegraph message be included so that "the people" would know what to
say to the governor. Debate led to a decision to say only that a massacre "may" take place. Wicker cleared up one sentence which could
have been read to exhort the people themselves to come to Attica
(which could really bring on a massacre, he thought). There was some
discussion whether to refer to "guards" as "hostages." Ingram inquired
drily, "Why don't we just say human beings?"

At about 11:45, the statement was completed:

> The committee of observers in Attica Prison is now convinced
> a massacre of prisoners and guards may take place in this institu-
> tion. For the sake of our common humanity, we call on every
> person who hears these words to implore the Governor of this
> state to come to Attica to consult with the observer committee,
> so we can spend time and not lives in an attempt to resolve the
> issues before us. Send the following telegram immediately to
> Governor Nelson Rockefeller in New York City: "Please go to
> Attica Prison to meet with the observers committee."[5]

John Dunne and Wicker were momentarily alone in a corner.
"Politically," Dunne said, "Rocky's not going to give an inch because
there are more of them out there," he gestured sweepingly beyond the
walls of Attica, "than there are in here." Wicker thought this a surprisingly cynical view of Rockefeller—that he was dealing with the
situation according to where he thought the votes were—to come
from a moderate Republican legislator.

"On this Quinn murder or whatever it was," Wicker took the
opportunity to ask, "why wouldn't it help get a settlement if Rocky at
least pledged clemency to anyone found guilty?"

Dunne shook his head. He and Kunstler were courtroom lawyers, he
said, and they agreed that if Rockefeller did that, it would be easy to
get a murder conviction on even the flimsiest evidence. Knowing no
death penalty would result, a jury would be eager to convict for a
guard's murder.

"What the hell are you doing?" someone shouted, and an uproar
suddenly rose at the end of the room where the telephone was. Tom
Soto had been discovered telephoning the text of the statement, before
the committee had informed the prisoners of it and before its public
release, to be recorded by his "organization" in New York. Even
Kenyatta, the revolutionary, was outraged.

"That's a breach," he shouted. "A breach!"

Eve and others were equally angered and Soto was forced to hang up. He managed to explain that he had meant no "breach"—that he had to have his organization's approval before he could give his own to the statement. It was the discipline of his group (apparently the Prisoner Solidarity Committee) that no one could take such an action individually.

"Well, I take the position," Eva said, "that if you can't speak for your organization, you ought not to be here."

"On some questions," Soto insisted doggedly, "I have to consult."

Wicker listened with a certain bitter amusement to this small tempest. The idea of revolution, he thought, was so much more attractive than revolution or revolutionaries. He hated the thought of collective decisions and disciplines. He supposed he believed more in equity than in equality, more in individualism than in solidarity.

Did that place him on the side of Rockefeller rather than at the side of Brother Herb and Richard Clark and the faceless masses of D-yard? How could his attitude be squared with the class sense he had absorbed from his father, the obligation to side with the underdog, the downtrodden, the poor and exploited? But D. D. Wicker had not been a revolutionary or even a radical; his sympathies were engaged, he had his views and instincts, but he had imposed no intellectual disciplines, no infallible dogma. Nor would his son. And was not the real fight against those who would make him choose, those who would have him believe in absolute right and absolute wrong, those who would insist that one portion of feeble humanity was better able to govern than another? He was not interested in an exchange of political power among a few or the loss of his intellectual freedom to any cause.

Others on the committee did not take Soto's "breach" so philosophically. "I'm the kind of nigger," Florence said menacingly, "that once a group agrees to something I take them at what they say until they prove otherwise." Ortiz and G.I. berated Soto for breaking the committee's "unity." Kenyatta was contemptuous. "One thing a revolution teaches you," he said, "you got to keep a united front." But Soto's phone call had showed Kenyatta that Soto was "not a revolutionary. You're a counterrevolutionary."

Soto stayed admirably calm, even at this unkindest cut of all. He had to consult, he said, for one reason because personally he didn't agree with every word of the statement. He believed "Rocky will ultimately massacre those guys, just from precedents that have been set everywhere." Nevertheless, he understood the observers had to work together to try to prevent the massacre, so he would "withdraw that okay" for the statement but would not "undermine" the committee's efforts. He personally was for "the governor coming because the inmates demanded that he come," not because the observers wanted him to come. And Soto didn't "look at the hostages as equal to the inmates."

"If you think you're more concerned about those guys than the rest of us," Eve said icily, "you're mistaken." Besides he knew Rocky; and everybody knew that the governor had been "sliding to the right." Rocky would just use a demand *from the inmates* as an excuse not to come.

Dunbar came in, unctuous and reassuring, his pipe his badge of respectability. Bob Douglass, he said, had taken time "to digest the matter that you presented to him and is presenting it to the governor and will get back to you." Douglass, this suggested, was at that moment on the line to Rockefeller and would soon return to the Stewards' Room. But he never did.

Shortly past noon a committee was dispatched to No Man's Land to inform the inmates of the planned public statement. The members were Eve, Kenyatta, G.I., Ortiz, Mathew, with Tom Soto, incongruously enough, to be the spokesman. Wicker seized the minutes of quiet that followed their departure to call his house in Washington again.

His wife answered, expressed proper concern for his safety, and he told her he was taking Lew Steel's advice—no more trips into D-yard. It was a hell of a situation, he told her; a lot of people were going to get killed. She was sure he had done all he could. She wanted him to take care of himself. The children were all right.

Soto and the committee returned in half an hour, not happily. The inmates had approved the proposed public statement, but there had been "critical developments," Soto reported portentously—although it seemed clear to Wicker that the only really critical developments were taking place outside D-yard. The inmates, "very uptight," wanted five observers, with one black and one Puerto Rican reporter, in D-yard within half an hour. That, they had said, was "an ultimatum." Soto and his committee seemed to take this seriously, but Wicker wondered wearily if the inmates really expected anyone else to believe they would kill their hostages—the only instruments of real power they had—if five observers and two reporters failed to show up in 30 minutes.

Soto explained that the inmates had been demoralized by the failure of the observers and Bobby Seale to return since Saturday night. Their threat, he thought, was "not a joke, not acting. There was clear desperation." Eve added that in addition to the five observers and the reporters, the inmates wanted another man to go in, one who could come back out and have "some credibility with the outside situation."

"Dunbar was standing out there," Soto said. "He heard the deadline."

But Wicker was not interested in the deadline; he was thinking with a tight feeling in his throat about who would have "some credibility with the outside situation."

The only persons in the observer group who met that criterion, Eve said, were John Dunne and Tom Wicker. Kunstler wouldn't do; he was too closely linked to "the liberals and the revolutionaries." Eve did not even have to say that he was thinking of "whites only," eliminating "credible" blacks like Jones and even respected Puerto Ricans like Badillo and Garcia. No one questioned his choices.

Dunne and Wicker looked at each other blankly while the report went on. The man with credibility was needed to attest to the good treatment the hostages had received. The hostages, in their turn, wanted to broadcast public appeals for their lives, which would bring additional pressures on the state to negotiate rather than attack.

"I can't make a commitment to go in there," John Dunne said straightforwardly, when he had a chance to speak. No one questioned that, either.

Eve turned to Wicker. "What about you, Tom?"

So he had come to the moment of self-definition. He respected Lew Steel's opinion that none of the observers could safely return to the yard, particularly the white ones. If the inmates were as apprehensive of a forthcoming attack on their stronghold as were the observers, why should they not eagerly seize custody of men like Wicker or Dunne, whose presence in D-yard they might think enough to hold off the state's attack for awhile? That could mean his life, either as an executed hostage or as an accidental victim of a general attack when the troopers finally did come over the wall. There was no moral or any other kind of law or situation that forced him to return to D-yard in such circumstances, particularly when it was not clear that anything would be achieved by it. He had faithfully done everything asked of him already; surely that was enough.

On the other hand . . . if much always had been expected of Tom Wicker, at least by himself, not all that much had been delivered. And he knew, that Sunday morning in the Stewards' Room with every eye upon him, that he must either finally meet his own expectations for himself or abandon them and his idea of who and what he was.

The brief conversation with his wife had had another effect. His children were old enough to have been decisively formed, his marriage had run its course, and that part of his life was over; there was not so much to risk as once there might have been.

He knew, perhaps ignobly, that he feared to be thought afraid. He did not want it said of him that he had played it safe in the end, and had failed to follow where his work and thought had led him. He was too vain to let anyone—himself most of all—think that physical fear had uncovered his pretensions and shown him at last to be, in Jim Ingram's phrase, just bullshitting.

Yet, he discovered to his surprise that none of these considerations mattered more than the fact that he wanted to do what he could. He wanted no one to die. He wanted no more bloody and shameful failures in the country that had bred him. He did not wish once again to be ashamed of his people and of himself, one of them, for their blindness, narrowness, and fears. He wanted to help men and things be better, for once, than they might have been. If he did not really believe that likely, he nevertheless hoped it could happen. And after all, he had been called upon.

"All right," Wicker said, "I'll go in, if . . . ." It had occurred to him vaguely that if it was all that important for him to go, he ought to set conditions, as any good bargainer would. But what conditions? "Oh, hell," he said, "I'll go in."

Clarence Jones, who by then had telephoned the "massacre" statement to two Harlem radio stations, spoke up immediately. He would go in, too, because "I can't let Tom take that risk alone." Wicker took that for what it was—a considerable gesture of courage and friendship. Jones, as a "respectable" middle-class black with an important political and business role in the state, would make a valuable hostage himself.

But in a moment, both his and Jones' decisions seemed moot. As if on cue, Russell Oswald appeared, his round, tired face mournful, his eyes red-rimmed and dull. None of the observers knew it, but once again Oswald had defied those around him, including Douglass and Hurd. Oswald, too, had recommended to Rockefeller that he come to Attica, although, unlike the observers, he did not believe there was a chance that that would break the negotiating impasse. Rather, he "was extremely concerned about the governor's great name as a humanitarian, and . . . felt it might be damaging for him in this context if he seemed in the public mind to be disengaged. . . . This, of course, was public relations advice."[6] It nevertheless took courage, not only to disagree with the powerful Douglass and all Oswald's own associates, but to suggest even tacitly to Rockefeller that it was not an attractive posture for the governor to seem "disengaged" with so many lives at stake—including the state's own men.

Oswald told the observers he had sent in a message to the inmates that no further visitors would be allowed in D-yard. *So the attack is going in,* Wicker thought, *anytime now.* His dominant feeling was relief that he would not have to go into the yard after all. He could have it both ways. He could genuinely say, even to himself, that he had been willing to go in; now Oswald had reversed that decision and relieved him of its risks, giving him no further choice.

Immediately, however, the other observers exploded in anger.

Oswald couldn't do that, they cried in their many voices. Dunbar had heard the inmates' ultimatum; Oswald's order was a direct contradiction. The inmates were expecting the observers. The state had no right to keep them out. The state was putting the observers in the position of having betrayed their commitments. Oswald had no right, no reason, no excuse. "What loss is there," Herman Badillo wanted to know, reasonably enough, "if we go in and talk to them one more time?"

Oswald wavered visibly. He was tired, whipsawed, disappointed, no doubt fearful; his career hung by a thread. Wicker guessed that every decision he made, as time narrowed his choices, was bitterly attacked by someone, just as the observers were attacking him now.

Oswald opened the door and spoke to the guard in the corridor. "Tell Dunbar to hold that thing," he said.

It was 1:11 P.M. Wicker would have to go into D-yard after all. He was committed.

To meet the inmates' request for representatives from the Puerto Rican and black press to accompany the man of credibility and the other observers into D-yard, the observers decided to recruit Dick Edwards, managing editor of Jones' *Amsterdam News*, and Rudy Garcia—Bob's brother—of the *New York Daily News*, both of whom they knew to be with the press outside the main gates. It would take time to have them admitted, and Oswald was still tracking down Dunbar and his ultimatum. Some of the Soto group went back to No Man's Land to tell the inmates their requests would be met as soon as possible. Once again, there was nothing for those remaining in the Stewards' Room to do but wait and talk.

"If Oswald was ready to lock us out," Wicker said to Badillo, "they're bound to be planning the attack this afternoon."

Outside the administration building, Clarence Jones said, it looked as if a war were about to start.

"I tell you we only got one chance," Badillo said. "We have to get Rocky to come here to give us some more time and some credit with those guys in there."

"If I had his number I'd call him," Wicker said. "How do we know Oswald and Douglass were giving him the whole story? They might not make it clear how bad the situation is. They might not understand themselves how much killing there's going to be once these guys are turned loose with those guns."

"I've got his number." John Dunne had moved into their small circle. He produced a pocket address book. "Rocky's at Pocantico Hills." Wicker was not sure where Pocantico Hills was, although he had a vague idea that it was a magnificent Rockefeller estate.

"If we call him," Wicker said, "it ought to be from all of us. Will you all speak to him?" Jones, Badillo, and Dunne agreed. Dunne gave him the number and Wicker—who usually hated telephoning, a severe handicap in his trade—went to the phone at the end of the room and dialed.

A secretary answered. Wicker gave his name and pointedly added "associate editor of *The New York Times*." Somewhat to his surprise, in about 30 seconds, he heard Nelson Rockefeller's familiar, hearty, rather nasal voice on the line calling him by his first name.

"Governor," Wicker said, "I'm up here at Attica, and I . . ."

"I know you are," Rockefeller broke in. "And I just want you to know how grateful I am and how much I really admire what you and the others are doing up there. I know you've all worked hard and taken great risks and I appreciate it, I really do. It's just great . . . just great."

It was unnerving to hear the enthusiasm in Rockefeller's voice, the fabled campaigner's manner coming across the long miles that separated Attica from Pocantico Hills. It was almost as if the governor were intimately squeezing his elbow, grinning the famous grin, winking the merry little wink, "working a crowd" as only he could. In four campaigns for the governorship and three for the presidency, Nelson Rockefeller had become as instinctively "political" as any Irish glad-hander. Wicker supposed that even in these grim circumstances it was almost reflexive for the governor to open with effusive praise of the observers, as if they were a delegation of Gold Star Mothers or 4-H Club leaders who might be persuaded to give him an endorsement in a future campaign. But he did not believe Rockefeller was calloused or obtuse. Instead, he was bolstered in his suspicion that, at a distance, the governor could not fully appreciate how threatening the situation was at Attica.

Wicker explained that Badillo, Jones, and Dunne were standing by. They had called, he said, because a desperate situation appeared to be coming to a head. They feared there was going to be much bloodshed and, as nearly as the observers could tell from what was going on outside their window, it might be coming any minute. There was a lot of tension among the troopers, who were angry and frustrated; when and if the violence came, it was going to be bad. All the observers were agreed on that.

"Our last card is for you to come up here and talk with us," Wicker said. He emphasized that the invitation was being issued by the observers and was for a meeting with them. They understood that the governor could not appear to be at the inmates' beck and call. But if he would meet *with the observers* at Attica, they thought there would be at least two useful consequences.

First, it would indicate to the inmates how much the governor—Wicker told Rockefeller the inmates sometimes referred to him as The Man—cared about their fate and that of all the hostages; this would "gain time" for and lend credence to the observers in their efforts to negotiate a peaceful settlement. Second, if after discussing the 28 points with the observers, the governor himself would be seen standing behind the package, it would be that much more persuasive to the inmates.

Wicker thought he could foresee another good result, but he did not know how to state it without offending Rockefeller. He already had told the governor that tensions and frustrations among the troopers and corrections officers would increase the violence of the attacks. He wanted the governor to come to Attica so that he could see and sense *for himself* the building mood of hatred, the eagerness to shoot. Wicker doubted that Oswald or Douglass had conveyed that atmosphere even in explicit phone calls; he doubted if anyone could have. It had to be felt, experienced, as he had felt it in every encounter with the armed men in their boots and uniforms, as it could be sensed in the hostility, even to the observers, of the corrections officers and troopers, and in the hysteria of townspeople in their vigil outside the gate.

The governor had to come to Attica to understand the threat of bloodshed in its full dimension. But it seemed to Wicker that to put this proposition straight to Rockefeller was not only to suggest that he was not doing his job but that his staff was not properly briefing him. On tactical grounds, Wicker left it unsaid, hoping the governor would become alarmed from his descriptions of the violence he thought impending and would be encouraged by the possibility of reassuring the inmates with his presence. The omission was probably a mistake.

Rockefeller listened patiently, occasionally interrupting to clear up details. His ebullient manner vanished, to be replaced by a crisply executive style. When Wicker had finished, the governor said that he had had many long talks with many competent people of differing views on the situation at Attica. He understood Wicker's position. He knew what the observers felt and had in mind. He admired the "superb job" of the negotiating team and he was well acquainted with the 28 points which of course he supported. There was no question but that everybody concerned was doing and saying what he thought was for the best.

Still, as Rockefeller understood it—showing how well he had been briefed by Douglass—the issues boiled down to Mancusi's dismissal and amnesty. Was that right?

This response was ominous, although Rockefeller had been courteous enough. It meant that Douglass' view of the situation was now

Rockefeller's; the governor was focussed on "the issues" and the dead-lock rather than on the possibilities, however faint, that Wicker and the other observers wanted him to explore. He would have to be dissuaded before he could be persuaded.

Wicker conceded that Mancusi and amnesty were the points on which agreement seemed least likely. But by Tuesday or Wednesday, he said, maybe something could be worked out, particularly if the governor came to Attica to help the observers gain time and credence.

Well, as to amnesty, Rockefeller said, still patient and courteous, he had had his legal people look into it, and they were convinced that he had no authority to issue an amnesty. That wasn't one of his consti-tutional powers. Besides, if he did have the power to grant amnesty, frankly, he wouldn't do it because he was convinced it would be wrong. It would "undermine the basic tenets of our society" for people to be forgiven their offenses just because they had momentary power over hostages. Holding hostages was the wrong way to get redress of grievances, and amnesty would violate the principle of the equal appli-cation of the laws.

Wicker had to stop himself from laughing—not with amusement—at this astounding irony. In a country where so many wealthy or well-represented lawbreakers could go free, where the killers at Kent State and Jackson State had not even been prosecuted, where minorities (blacks and Mexican Americans, for two good examples) suffered from openly prejudiced law in whole regions, where the poor and disadvantaged of all races usually felt the full weight of police, courts, and prisons—in that country, "the equal application of the laws" was to be upheld in the case of the Attica brothers! Many of them were in prison because of the *un*equal application of the laws; and no one gets less "equal appli-cation of the laws," than those who are in prison. But "the equal application of the laws" was being invoked to meet their protests—at that, by one of the most "equal" men in a nation where all too many are more equal than others.

But Wicker did not laugh. He interrupted the governor's confident flow to make sure Rockefeller understood that the amnesty demand was only for any offenses committed during the uprising, not for the offenses that had brought the D-yard brothers to prison in the first place. Rockefeller understood that perfectly well. He understood how the observers felt, too. After all, he said, they had been willing to risk their lives to get a settlement. But it was not as if the opportunity hadn't been provided through the 28-point package for the prisoners to make an agreement that would afford them some real gains. But since they had not been willing to accept that opportunity, he had no choice; so he had instructed Oswald to "reopen the institution."

This confirmed Wicker's worst fears—as to Rockefeller's attitude, the imminence of attack, and thus the scale of violence likely to result. The governor's tone was brisk, his argument carefully organized, as if his mind was made up and his doubts—if any—had been put behind. Wicker remembered once interviewing Nelson Rockefeller in the governor's campaign plane as it flew on an incomparably sunlit day over the magnificent mountain ranges of northern California and Oregon. Those are mountains to dwarf men's pretensions, but Rockefeller, then running for President, had talked expansively, confidently, of where leadership could take the country—of the responsibilities of those who could envision, plan, lead. In those days, in his campaign speeches, he had used the phrase "brotherhood of man, fatherhood of God" so frequently that Nick Thimmesch, one of the reporters trailing him, had coined the acronym "bomfog" as a derisive description of the candidate's speeches. But even then, Nelson Rockefeller was advocating the bombing of North Vietnam—a year before Lyndon Johnson finally started it. Rockefeller was not a man of many doubts. That year his rival, Barry Goldwater, had refused to campaign in the Oregon primary and Rockefeller's Oregon slogan had been: "He cared enough to come."

Doggedly, almost hopelessly, Wicker made his pitch once more, sensing its futility. The observers had deduced the governor's position, he said. That was why they were calling. They were not asking him to declare an amnesty. They only wanted the governor to give them more time, which they believed he could do by coming to Attica and meeting with them. What was non-negotiable today was not necessarily non-negotiable tomorrow. Who knew what could be worked out then? So far, the inmates had not harmed the hostages. There was no evidence to suggest that the hostages would be further endangered by another day or so of negotiations. But the inmates threatened, and had the power, to kill the hostages the moment an attack began. Why give them the reason for doing so?

For the first time, the governor sounded a bit edgy in his response. He understood, he said, that sometimes when people had worked hard, risked a lot, and felt strongly about something, it seemed to them that "any straw is worth grasping." He had to say, quite candidly, that it seemed to him that the idea of his coming to Attica was "just one of those straws." Mancusi was a major issue, but "the real issue is amnesty," on which all he could see was an impasse not likely to be broken by anything anyone could do.

What's more, he and his advisers were agreed that if he came to Attica, even to talk to the observers, the prisoners *would* be encouraged—so encouraged that they probably would escalate their demands. Probably, too, they would promptly demand that he talk to them personally, which he thought he should not do. Besides, it would just produce a duplicate of the present demands; if he came, they'd say if he'd only go in and talk to the prisoners, everybody could gain more time. Somewhere, he had to stand fast, Rockefeller said. Besides, he had to "stand with the position" of his people on the scene.

Wicker knew he could not overcome these arguments, which from Pocantico Hills, through Rockefeller–official eyes, must have had such validity. He could not guarantee results that would please the governor, if. the latter were to come to Attica. More than that, Rockefeller, Douglass, and their advisers probably would recoil from what Tom Wicker suddenly knew to be *his* deepest sense of things—that the "basic tenets of our society" or any other were not so easily known and fixed and beyond doubt or question as to warrant the calculated and accepted sacrifice of numerous human lives on their supposed behalf. Besides, were not *lives* the basic tenets of a humanity that transcended all societies? Was not any straw worth grasping at for the protection of those lives?

Wicker did not doubt Rockefeller's personal courage, if that was what it would take to bring him to Attica. Nor did he believe that Rockefeller was so calloused and careless of human life that he simply did not care who and how many might die at Attica. He wondered if the trouble was not, rather, that to the Rockefellers of the world, those institutions, processes, and arrangements by which humans had sought to order their affairs had become, finally, more·important than the people who had erected them and sought to live by them.

Perhaps that was why the state for all its good intentions and the system for all its idealistic trappings—democracy and representation and due process—so often produced injustice and myopia and indifference and rigidity. Perhaps that was why men like Tom Wicker could perceive the system as basically sound, the state as fundamentally well-meaning, the people as mostly decent—yet stumble time and again on the inequities and callousness and brutalities wrought in the name of society. Perhaps the fault lay not in any system but in men's profound instinct to establish and maintain, at all costs, an order of things.

Never mind, if so, the intrinsic value of Attica, the "institution" then in question, its palpable responsibility for the injustices and wastage happening within it. The state could sustain Attica, even call it a "correctional facility," because it was *an institution,* and official at that, a part of the order of things, serving that order against the frightening possibilities of unruly humanity, undisciplined conduct. Reopening it, restoring the order, was more important than that many lives might have to be sacrificed to do it. Captain "Starry" Vere could see no higher duty or obligation than maintenance of the King's established naval code. Indeed, he told his brother officers that "in receiving our commissions we in the most important regards ceased to be natural free agents." So it was not they who condemned Billy Budd to death, but only "martial law operating through us"—the order of things.

Similarly, neither Rockefeller nor any of his officials wanted to cause loss of life. But the order of things was operating through them. Institutions and processes required of them a way of doing and believing, a system of behavior, to which they gave allegiance, sometimes passionately, sometimes pragmatically, usually without question. "Tell me whether or not, occupying the position we do," Captain Vere demanded to know, "private conscience should not yield to that imperial one formulated in the code under which alone we officially proceed?" Rockefeller could have put the question to Wicker as dispassionately.

Institutions must not only function, whatever the end result; the order of things must be preserved. The powerful must not be at the beck and call of the powerless even when suddenly the powerless wield momentary power; for the powerful are obliged to meet great responsibilities to the order of things. That order gives them their power and must survive the moment. Governors must not deal as equals with law-breakers; that would endanger the order of things. Amnesty must not be granted to offenders; they must pay a debt to the order of things. If policemen and armies, being human, sometimes go too far, use unusual force, that is deplorable, but still they are the necessary enforcers of the order of things. For that matter, if lives sometimes have to be sacrificed to the order of things, what is the alternative? Only the unimaginable—that the order of things be sacrificed to life.

In Rockefeller's case, Wicker supposed, there might also be a class attitude. It was one thing to support civil rights bills but quite another to deal straightforwardly and equally with the lowest of the under-class—to see that it was a human obligation to do so. But Wicker believed the governor was moved primarily by his faith in the order of things. He was offended by the inmates' challenge to that order. And he was unwilling to set that order aside because he did not know—could not conceive—how to conduct himself except within it and by his perception of its "basic tenets."

Politely, Wicker thanked the governor for listening. Politely, the governor thanked him for "everything you're doing." And Herman Badillo took the phone to make his hard politician's argument that a massacre at Attica would set off rioting in every black and Puerto Rican ghetto across the state.

"You need the time as much as we do," Badillo insisted to Rockefeller. "So the best way, while you set this machinery in motion, is—you come and meet with us. At least you will have been able to get an opinion from the scene." Then Badillo put the political needle in deeply. "If you rush in now, Mayor Lindsay is probably going to tell you he'll need National Guardsmen in New York."[7]

Badillo was followed by Clarence Jones and John Dunne, who gave the governor their own versions of the "time" argument. Did the troopers and officials, Jones demanded to know, "want a settlement or a confrontation?" If a settlement was wanted, Rockefeller's presence might "provide us with that additional ingredient that could tip the scales toward the possibility of a peaceful solution."[8] And Dunne said that "time can be on our side"—except, he told Rockefeller, that he could already see the troopers outside getting ready for battle.

None of this much impressed the man at the other end of the line:

> They didn't see, any of them, how any of these last three demands [amnesty, flight, and the removal of Mancusi] could be acceded to. They thought we had given everything that we could give, but they didn't say it. I felt that they did not want to admit defeat in this and see this thing just go back to the Commissioner.
>
> So I said, "Well, what do you think would be accomplished by my presence?" And their answer was, "Well, we don't know, two things. One, something might happen, and two, we could buy time."
>
> "Well," I said, "who do you want to buy time from? Are you worried that the prisoners are going to move and kill the hostages or are you worried the state is going to move?" And they said, "No, we're worried about the state."
>
> "Well," I said, "if it's more time you want I can give you more time." "Well," they said, "your presence here would be a new element, and we admit you can't do any of the things, we know you can't go beyond the 28 points agreed to, but maybe if you just come."[9]

To Oswald, earlier that Sunday, Rockefeller expressed the fear that if he came to Attica, inmates at other state prisons would revolt and demand his presence. That, he said, could even set off a nationwide movement in all the prisons, with inmates demanding that all the governors come and negotiate with them. Besides, Rockefeller asked Oswald, if he came to Attica, might not the inmates then demand the presence of the President of the United States?[10]

Rockefeller also held, or developed, a more general political view:

> One of the most recent and widely used techniques of modern day revolutionaries has been the taking of political hostages and using the threat to kill them as blackmail to achieve unconditional demands and to gain wide public attention to further their revolutionary ends. I have followed these developments with great

interest and considered that, if tolerated, they pose a serious threat to the ability of free government to preserve order and to protect the security of the individual citizen.

Therefore, I firmly believe that a duly elected official sworn to defend the constitution and the laws of the state and the nation would be betraying his trust to the people he serves if he were to sanction or condone such criminal act by negotiating under any circumstance.[11]

Rockefeller saw a distinction between this general position and Oswald's negotiations with prisoners on the limited subject of prison reform. Besides, he said, Oswald as the responsible official on the scene had undertaken these negotiations on his own, obtaining Rockefeller's assent later. But the governor maintained his basic position that "if this business of taking hostages . . . whether it's in a prison or somewhere else and then threatening to kill them or killing them becomes an accepted method of accomplishing political objectives . . . this could lead to a very serious breakdown both of structure of government, the freedom of the individual, and the security of the individual. . . ."[12]

The general point is hardly arguable; but it presupposes a relatively flexible and responsible society in which just demands get a hearing and at least some effort is made to provide equity and redress of grievance. The weakness in Rockefeller's argument was that he failed to state the other side of the case. Perhaps he failed to see that people resort to radical action usually because governments fail to respond to their needs, fail to provide at least a rough measure of justice for all; witness the Boston Tea Party.

The state of New York had failed both to respond to needs and to provide justice in the case of its prison inmates. Nelson Rockefeller had been the state's governor since 1959, during which period the state had failed to do anything like what was needed to improve an antiquated and ineffective "corrections system" or to redress its gross inequities and hardships. Not until the D-yard brothers seized their hostages was even a credible promise, much less a performance, given to New York inmates. Until men like Rockefeller translate such promises into action, and do it *before* their hands are forced by radical movements, their indictments of radical action will ring more than a little hollow.

Rockefeller did not even understand any of the four observers who talked to him that Sunday to have expressed concern about the "mood and self-restraint" of the state troopers and corrections officers, or about racial tensions between them and the inmates. "Everything I got from what everybody was saying," he recalled, "the prisoners were getting more militant, they were making weapons, bombs, trenches, barricades. . . .".[13] Thus, he missed or disbelieved the observers' point that there was little reason to believe the inmates would harm the hostages unless the inmates were themselves attacked.

Nevertheless, having promised the observers that "I can give you more time," and perhaps mindful of Badillo's warnings, Rockefeller did tell Oswald to drop any plans for an attack on D-yard that Sunday afternoon. But he did not tell the observers he had done so.[14]

Wicker, listening nearby as Jones, Badillo, and Dunne stretched the call to Rockefeller to nearly an hour, could tell that the governor was listening politely but was yielding no more to the others than to him. None of them knew that Rockefeller already had told Bob Douglass and Oswald that he would not come to Attica and had set Douglass to work drafting a statement to that effect. But Wicker knew, as surely as if he had been told, that Rockefeller was not coming. And since he doubted the observers' planned visit to D-yard would soften the inmates' defiance, he saw no way, finally, to avoid the coming bloodshed. A violent clash was too nearly in the order of things.

CHAPTER

I3

A Time to Speak

At about 2 P.M., someone wandering outside the Stewards' Room learned that state officials had ordered the observers confined there, or in the corridor immediately outside. Most of the observers were too tired and disspirited to make much of a protest. At 2:10, word came that the inmates' ultimatum had been extended to 3 P.M. At 2:15, Oswald returned with a statement he had sent into D-yard. After setting forth all the efforts he had made to negotiate a settlement and win the inmates' confidence, the statement said:

> I urgently request you to release the hostages unharmed, now, and to accept *the recommendations of the committee of outside observers which recommendations were approved by me,** and join with me in restoring order to this institution.
>
> Only after these steps are taken am I willing to meet with a five-member committee chosen by you to discuss any grievances you may have and to create a mechanism by which you can be assured that the recommendations I have agreed to are implemented.[1]

Having so informed the inmates, Oswald said, he now had to inform the observers that he had "definitely decided that no one else in this institution will go into the yard." This was due to the "deteriorating situation."

What would happen at 3 P.M., Steel asked, when the observers had pledged to enter D-yard? And Kunstler said pointedly, "*We're* the only ones taking chances."

---

* Emphases added.

Oswald said he and the governor's staff wanted "to take no more chances" at all. But, he warned them, at some point, the state would have to go in and retake the institution.

Tom Soto had been closely scanning the Oswald statement. "This thing is a misstatement of the committee," he said angrily. He pointed out that it referred to the 28 points as having been *the recommendations of the committee of outside observers*, when in fact the committee had been careful *not* to "recommend" these points.

Oswald was puzzled. "I find myself completely at odds with you," he said. Hadn't he gone through all the 28 points with them just the day before?

Obviously, he did not understand the care with which the observers had tried to put the 28 points before the inmates *without urging them to accept;* or the distinction that had been made in labelling the package "the best that could be worked out" with the state rather than the observers' own recommendations; or the political problems involved at that point in the observers being made to appear to have "recommended" what Bobby Seale would not recommend and what the inmates already had said they would not accept. To describe the 28 points as the observers' "recommendations" was to picture them as urging the inmates to surrender, as the inmates would see it, and to end any possibility that the observers could retain the inmates' confidence. If they accepted Oswald's statement at face value, the inmates would have to believe that the observers had lied in D-yard on Saturday night when they had refrained from openly recommending acceptance of the package.

Arthur Eve understood these implications all too well, the moment Soto spotted the crucial sentence. "If you think those cats are jiving," he told Oswald, "and it comes out that we sold them down the river, then it doesn't matter whether I die in there or whether my house is bombed—you just jeopardized my life."

The inmates probably would think the observers had been stalling them with promises to return that morning while giving Oswald time to prepare his ultimatum. "Man," Eve told Oswald, his consternation and his voice rising, "you just signed my death warrant!"

How could Oswald explain such an ultimatum to the guards' families? Kunstler asked. The inmates had asked for someone to come in and vouch for the hostages' well-being; Wicker had agreed to do so. How could Oswald say he couldn't?

"I don't see how you can live with this," Kunstler added.

"You're jeopardizing peoples' lives," Eve insisted.

"We promised them someone and we picked this gent here," G.I. Paris said, indicating Wicker. "The only safety we have in there is our word. That's our bond. We gave it."

"So far as I know," Oswald conceded, "those hostages have been treated well. I do say that." He was weakening again. He asked how many would go in if he relented and was told.

"You done made us look like asses," Brother G.I. grumbled in the background

Oswald said he would talk to Douglass, perhaps even Rockefeller, and left, a sad and puzzled man. Wicker did not believe he was to be spared the visit to D-yard although it had been made more hazardous by Oswald's ultimatum. He believed the commissioner was going to yield once more.

But Arthur Eve had been shocked into a sort of despairing anger by Oswald's statement. "All right," he shouted, "anyone who is not pro-pro-PRO-prisoner, just leave now! Far's I'm concerned, I only want those here who are for the prisoners!"

This was a measure of Eve's emotions rather than a serious demand. Other observers protested instantly and Eve relented. Clarence Jones, although less emotionally than Eve, nevertheless stated flatly, as if to declare himself once and for all, "My commitment is to the prisoners."

"I smell gas!" someone shouted about them. This set off a quick panic. Within seconds, Wicker's eyes were smarting; the observers began milling about and shouting; some rushed to the windows. The prickly feel of the gas stung eyelids and nostrils.

"The attack's beginning!"

"That's why they got us up here," G.I. said. "It was a cross, man!"

Outside, however, nothing unusual appeared to be happening except that a few troopers had slipped on gas masks. Preparations appeared to be going forward, but there was no sign that the attack had been opened. After a minute or so of confusion and excitement, the observers also could tell that the gas level was not rising in the Stewards' Room; they had received a whiff, not a cloud. Later, they learned that a gas cannister had been accidentally opened outside, and an errant breeze had done the rest. But no one's nerves were the better for the experience.

Kenyatta reminded them that assurances had been given the inmates; the question was whether the observers intended to make good on them. "For myself," Kenyatta said, seeming to Wicker less strident than he had been, "I only got one position, because like Arthur said I got to walk the streets and I got a family to protect."

It was "time for more practical decision making," Bill Gaiter said. It had to be faced that if anyone went back to D-yard, they "may be there for good." This already had occurred to Tom Wicker, who was going.

Herman Badillo threw in the idea that a committee might meet the governor somewhere besides Attica. Assemblyman Clark Wemple of

Schenectady appeared to announce that Douglass was on the phone with Rockefeller, as if that were major news. Alfredo Mathew declared angrily that the observers were "trying to help them get over a problem here," yet were themselves being treated like prisoners. "Let's walk out of here," he demanded, unless there was more cooperation by the state. Jim Ingram, in his dry manner, suggested no one was to be allowed to go back to D-yard because "they've decided not to let the bloodbath be seen on TV."

But talk was getting them nowhere. Kunstler organized the seven observers, including himself, who were to go in if anyone did and marched them into the corridor where they were held up by a guard. Oswald soon appeared.

"Nobody wants anybody to go inside," he said. But he did not sound adamant.

Once again, Kunstler and Eve argued that the inmates had been promised a visit by the observers, including Wicker, and by black and Puerto Rican press representatives. G.I. and Tom Soto also wrangled with the commissioner. Wicker said nothing since he had a strong feeling that Oswald was going to yield. Finally, at 2:55 P.M., Oswald gave in—but not for any of the reasons put to him by the observers.

He already had defied Hurd and Douglass, who strongly opposed the Sunday afternoon observer mission to D-yard. When Douglass said Rockefeller also opposed it, Oswald "asked him whether he was telling me that Governor Rockefeller was replacing me. And he said no, he didn't mean that at all. I said, 'Well, I just wanted to be clear on that because I am letting them in.' "[2]

Oswald then staged what Tepper, who was watching, called a "desperate hallway meeting"[3] with the observers. This may have been for the benefit of watching corrections officers, to whom Oswald wished it to appear that he had strongly resisted another observer visit to D-yard. But he already had decided to let the group return, "simply to explore the possibility for a meeting on neutral ground," as he had proposed in the statement he had sent to the inmates. He "thought this was a risk worth taking."[4]

It was a risk, however, that the observer group, not Oswald, was taking. As if to dramatize that, Ernest Montanye—patiently maintaining station outside the Stewards' Room—produced waiver slips that the observers were to sign, by order of Governor Rockefeller. They said that even though "aware of the potential physical dangers to me personally," each observer going into D-yard "release[d] the State of New York and any official thereof from any and all liability." It was not a cheery document to read or sign, and it pinpointed the extent to which the state, having assembled the observer group, then left it to its own devices, not just for safety but as a negotiating team.

Montanye, carefully collecting the signed waivers, looked grave and disapproving. While he was waiting his turn, Wicker chatted briefly with Oswald who asked him to stress to the inmates the proposal that he and an inmate committee meet on neutral ground—perhaps Mess Hall A.

Downstairs, in the clanging steel and concrete corridor that led from the administration building through A-block to No Man's Land, there was a long delay while the group waited for Rudy Garcia, a huge, outspoken *New York Daily News* reporter, and Dick Edwards, the black managing editor of the *Amsterdam News*. The group was also to be accompanied into D-yard by Roland Barnes, the black cameraman for WGR-TV of Buffalo; Barnes probably had logged more time in D-yard during the revolt than any outsider. Garcia, Edwards, and Barnes all had to be located and cleared to enter the prison.

As the delay continued, the group milled about the narrow, chilly corridor. A corrections officer eyed them sourly. Then Dunbar came from No Man's Land to explain that the inmates would not send anyone out to conduct the observers into D-yard.

That, Eve and Kunstler declared bitterly, was what the commissioner had accomplished with his statement; he had discredited even the observers in D-yard. Wicker, listening, saw that once again reprieve was possible; but strangely, he no longer wanted it. He was bored and angry with the endless argument, sick to death of delay and vacillation and uncertainty, depressed by his conversation with Rockefeller and his perception of the governor's attitude. But he was clear in his own mind that even with the odds adverse and the miserable end in sight, everything conceivable still had to be done, any straw had to be grasped. Conviction surged in him. Let these others talk and talk and talk; but to hell with talk. The time had come for him to act.

"Kenyatta," he said, "these guys know you better than the rest of us. Come on, Dunbar, take us to the gate and let's get this thing moving."

No one argued. Briskly, the three men walked along the corridor toward No Man's Land. "Just tell them what happened," Wicker said to Kenyatta. "Tell them we didn't know anything about the damned statement until Oswald showed it to us."

Their steps and voices echoed in the narrow corridor. A gate slid open with a clang, and they went past it. They were in No Man's Land, and Dunbar went to the gate and summoned one of the inmate messengers stationed down the corridor at the entrance to A-yard.

"Ask some of your leaders to come out here," Dunbar said. "These committee members want to talk to them."

Wicker glanced around. The troopers and the guns were as overwhelming as before. The hard eyes, the unsmiling faces, the heavy boots, the steel and concrete—it was as if he were in a wartime bunker. But he paid little attention to the troopers or the guns this time. He felt no fear, no doubt. He was caught up in the euphoria of decision, leadership, action. He felt bigger, stronger, better than he ever had. He thought he could handle anything, and he was prepared to try. He felt true to himself.

Brother Richard Clark, his dark face impassive under a wool cap, appeared a few minutes later. When he was still halfway between the A-yard gate and No Man's Land, Kenyatta held up his hand and uttered some strange phrases. They apparently meant something to Clark, who then spoke in the same kind of phrases. Several such mysterious exchanges ensued. Wicker supposed that these were some kind of Black Muslim code words, but Kenyatta insisted that he and Brother Richard spoke Arabic. Their words, he said later, were, first, for recognition as Muslims, second, an assurance by Kenyatta that he came in the faith and was therefore to be trusted. Clark apparently accepted these religious assurances without dispute, although there was no sign of friendship on his face. His eyes, when he looked at Wicker, seemed blank.

Reverting to ghetto English, Kenyatta gave Clark a brief account of how the commissioner's message had been sprung on the observers after having been written and delivered without their knowledge. Richard's face did not change. Wicker repeated that no one had had any knowledge of the document. Richard's eyes flicked over to him and away.

"This brother's levellin'," Kenyatta said. "He volunteered to come in and interview the hostages, make sure they okay."

Clark did not even look at Wicker. "Some of the brothers would love to kill you guys," he said.

Kenyatta went through his assurances again, sounding a little desperate. Wicker added that the document was Oswald's own, as was the reference to "recommendations." The observers had had no part in drafting the statement.

"I can vouch for that," Dunbar said, pipe in hand.

"Why should we believe you?" Clark's voice was toneless.

"Because in 35 years in corrections work, I've never lied to an inmate."

"How 'bout to a man?"

Dunbar shrugged and stepped back, clutching his pipe. Once again, Kenyatta explained to Clark that there had been a misunderstanding; the observers were ready to make good their commitment. Once again, Clark listened without a flicker of expression. This time, when Kenyatta subsided, Brother Richard nodded abruptly.

"All right," he said.

But he remained impassive and uncommunicative as they waited for the other observers to march along the corridor to No Man's Land. Dunbar reminded Wicker that Oswald wanted his neutral-ground proposal stressed to the inmates. At 3:45 P.M. the gate was opened and the group—still without Edwards, Rudy. Garcia, and Barnes—passed through, once again into the hands of the rebelling inmates. They followed Clark along the ruined corridor and through the side door into A-yard. After a few steps, Richard swung around and stopped them; then he stood facing the group, his hands on his hips.

"Some of you guys can't look me in the eye? Why?"

There was an awkward silence. Wicker, having heard the exchange at the gate, was not much worried, although the thought did cross his mind that Clark might have lured them into the yard in order to take nine more hostages. The other observers, not knowing what already had transpired, were obviously frightened; some thought this the scariest moment of their experience at Attica.

As for Kunstler, "Again, my white middle-class fears came to the fore. I had never been in a position where I was completely under the control of another group of men to this extent. And a lot of fears, imaginary or otherwise, went through my mind. I think I was very frightened. I watched the other observers and I think they were equally frightened. . . ."[5]

He and others—notably Eve and G.I. Paris—went hastily through the same assurances Kenyatta and Wicker already had given Clark, who listened as if he had not heard them two or three times before. Wicker's euphoria had faded somewhat, and now that he was approaching D-yard again his depression and sense of unease were beginning to crowd down upon him; but he still was not much worried about his personal safety. For some reason, he had developed more confidence in Richard Clark than in most of the other inmates. He had thought the exchange at No Man's Land was genuine. It seemed to him that Clark, confronting the other observers, was only enjoying his power a little—savouring it, while he had it. He was making the observers sweat and worry, as no doubt the inmates had been doing all day.

Eventually, however, Clark again relented, again assured them that he understood what had happened and would explain all to the brothers. The march across A-yard was resumed and Wicker seized the moment to speak briefly to Clark and remind him of Oswald's hope for a meeting with an inmate committee on neutral grounds in Mess Hall A.

Brother Richard looked at him stolidly. "Ain't gone be no negotiation in Mess Hall A," he said. Wicker wondered how Richard could answer so confidently, on his own. In fact, the D-yard leaders had resolved long before that any negotiations with anybody were going to take place in full view of all the inmates in D-yard. That way, no inmates on a negotiating committee could secretly "sell out" the others; that way, too, no one dissenting from some agreement that might be reached could accuse anyone else of having secretly sold out. (This rationale has an interesting parallel in the reluctance of newspaper reporters to testify in secret to a grand jury. Since they can never prove what they did or did not say, they fear no one will thereafter be willing to talk to them in confidence or believe in their willingness to protect a confidence.)

As for neutral ground, the inmates reasoned that the state had all the guns. Hence D-yard, the only place where the state was not in control, was the only true neutral ground. This was not entirely a one-sided view. Oswald, for example, feared after Friday morning that if he went into D-yard again would be seized by the inmates. But the inmates trusted him no more than he trusted them; why should they not have feared that if their leaders ventured out of their D-yard stronghold, Oswald might seize *them* in an effort to pinch off the head of the rebellion? The inmates' record in safeguarding and safe-returning visitors was as good as the state's and remained so throughout the uprising (with the limited exception of the unofficial threats made against Oswald on Friday).

As Wicker made the familiar crossing of the passageway into D-yard, he felt more powerfully than ever the sense of impending violence and bloodshed. The knowledge that men whose faces and voices had become familiar might be dead by dark or by dawn cast an emotional spell of great intensity over him and, he thought, the other observers. From the moment of his entry into D-yard that Sunday afternoon, Wicker was less fearful for his physical safety than during any other of his four visits to the yard. Yet, he was more emotionally charged, felt himself less in rational control, sensed in himself the highest tensions of the entire experience. It was as if he were taking part with great excitement in some incredible adventure, knowing all the while that it could end only in defeat and disaster and death.

Rather surprisingly, there was no overt sense of hostility to the observers at the leadership table against D-block wall. Roger Champen was railing at the crowd of inmates, "Evrybody over here en massed! Evrybody over here but the guards on the gates!" Soto, Paris, Kenyatta—those of the observers who had acquaintances in the yard— were greeted cheerfully. At that point, apparently, few of the brothers knew anything about Oswald's statement or had grasped its implications.

Despite these appearances, tension had been greatly increased in the yard, even above the level of Saturday night. A major reason, one inmate said, was "waiting, waiting, waiting, waiting, wondering what the outcome would be." Food was scarce and unappetizing. Tempers were short and fights were breaking out more frequently. Homosexual acts and the use of drugs were threatening to get out of hand. There had been some stabbings and one multiple rape; the leaders had responded with harsh discipline, which itself increased tensions and anger. Optimism about a negotiated settlement had waned, and many in the yard shared the observers' feeling that an attempt to recapture D-yard might come at any moment.[6]

But there was much defiance, too, and the worst of the tensions and fears and hostilities in the mass of the brothers was not apparent to the observers at the leadership table. If anything, the expressions of and exhortations to unity seemed more passionate than ever, the responses from the crowd louder and more enthusiastic, the revolutionary spirit more ardent.

Richard Clark opened the proceedings by insisting that the observers had had nothing to do with the Oswald statement, which he read, and which was being circulated in the yard. The document itself, Clark said, was "full of contradictory statements." And he urged, "Look under the veneer of this thing, brothers!"

If Oswald said he had furnished food, clothing, water, and medical supplies, that was merely a threat—"be good or he's going to take all this back." Oswald boasted about a federal court order that, in fact, had been "no good, null, and void." And when Oswald said he would negotiate "only after these steps," he meant after the brothers had no more power.

So how did the brothers vote on such a proposal as that? There was a loud chorus of "No!" from the crowd.

"I can't hear you," Brother Richard shouted back.

"NO!"

He cupped his hand to his ear. "Still can't hear you!"

"HELL, NO!" came back the roar of the crowd, almost as if rehearsed.

Brother Richard was grinning broadly, like the master of ceremonies for the election of a homecoming queen. "Is this from everybody?" he yelled.

"YES!"

"Anybody disagree?"

"NO!"

" 'Cause I was wondering," Richard said conversationally, when the great shout had drifted into echo, "if maybe you'd changed your mind. We been here four days and Mister Big Stuff say he gone cut off your food. . . ."

"FUCK Mister Big Stuff!" somebody screamed.

". . . cut off your water, your medical supplies. . . ."

"Don't need it . . . fuck that!"

"That man talk out his ass!" a brother yelled from the front row.

Brother Richard laughed out loud. "We got a little jewel for them, too," he said. The brothers were playing host to reporters, he said, who were going to tell the world about the hostages. And the hostages knew by then that "Oswald talks out his ass." The hostages also knew that when and if an attack came, they'd be the first to go. Did the brothers realize that?

"YES!" The roar came in on cue.

"So these reporter brothers gone put out the *news*," Richard said, " 'cause *somebody* don't realize it."

That brought on another roar of approval. Clark was in the best oratorical form he had displayed. The brothers were *not* going to leave D-yard to negotiate, he said; they were *not* going to release the hostages "except under conditions we want." Already, the observers had talked to The Man and impressed him with the seriousness of the situation. They had put out a statement that would be heard worldwide, whereupon the world would learn that Attica—"even Attica is in the world!"

Clark read the observers' radio statement, emphasizing its prediction of a massacre. "I hope all the brothers in this yard understand the connotation of that word." The observers were not talking about General Custer. They were not talking about "some dude named Manson." They were talking about the D-yard brothers, who needed to remember "you can only die once." So how many times could they die when the massacre came?

Richard paused for effect. Then he drove home the point. "We can die fifteen hundred and thirty-nine times!" There was an immense cheer. Everyone in the yard was used to the figure "1500" being used to denote the number of inmates and to the figure 39 for their hostages.[7] Clark's meaning was unmistakable.

Champ took the microphone. "In order to do anything," he said coolly, "we got to do what?"

"Stand together!" It was like a catechism, Wicker thought.

"One body!" Champ called back. Then he directed attention to the hostages, somewhere off to his right.

"They look like they been beaten? They livin' a life they never led before. They sleepin' on mattresses but I ain't sleepin' on no mattress." The hacks had treated the brothers like animals in the old days, but the brothers had not treated these hacks in that way. So, Champ wanted to know, "does animals take care of people, or does people take care of animals?"

There had been considerable commotion off to the right of the leadership table as the observers looked out over D-yard toward C-block in the distance. The crowd parted and the security chain swung around; a long line of the hostages, each with his personal guard and clad in gray prison clothes, shambled into view. Some had bandages on their heads. All seemed to be walking and standing by their own strength.

"Look there," Champ said. "We know who that is at the head of the line, don't we? Sho' do know Cap'n Wald. And there's Lootent Curtiss, ain't it?" The crowd was laughing now, deriding the line of captives, following Champ's insistent sarcasm. "Our ol' friend, Sarg't Cunnin'ham. And look there if it ain't ol' Red Whalen, the big boss hisself, used to whale our ass." There was a roar from the crowd, half derisive laughter at Whalen's plight, half anger at the reference—all, Wicker thought, verging on the hysterical. Champ was playing with fire, but he skillfully began to "cool it."

"Well, now we bigger'n they are," he was saying. "We human. We gone be human to them. And the brothers gone let the world know that they was beastly to us, but we was human to them." He went on to explain that Wicker and the other "reporter brothers" would interview the hostages for the evening television shows, so that the world could see they were unharmed.

"And do you know one of these hacks say to me, 'Champ,' he say, 'why they doin' this to us?' Now that's unbelievable. That's unbelievable. They have so endowed their minds with the junk they been doin' to us they can't face reality any more. . . . They don't have nothin' to play with no more, no whips, no clubs, no toys." He gestured at the line of miserable hostages, most of whom were looking straight ahead with carefully expressionless faces. "Now there's an element over there that sees what is really hap'nin', that sees there's time for a change. But why didn't they see that before?"

Change was coming, Champ said. "This is the fifth incident like this I been in, but this is the only real one. We gone do this one right." The brothers had not stayed out of their cells for four days just to give up and get beaten.

By then, although he continued to evoke roars from his audience, Champ actually was stalling for time. Until Barnes was on hand with his television camera, with Edwards and Garcia to represent the black and Puerto Rican press, the leaders did not want Wicker going ahead with the planned interviews of the hostages. So they fell back on speech-making, while the hostages stood in line among the jeering inmates. With some apprehension, Wicker watched Jaybarr Kenyatta take the microphone. He had gained a new appreciation of the robed

Muslim at No Man's Land, yet he feared the effects of another revolutionary speech.

Kenyatta launched immediately into just such a speech. The situation at Attica was not new, he said. It had been repeated often because "when you don't give a damn, you don't have nothin' to give up but your life." Now, he went on passionately, there was a "holy war" coming. "Gone be a new song to sing and a dance to be seen!" Malcolm X had said "if you gone make a revolution you got to *believe!*" And Kenyatta *believed*. But not in a "Negro revolution" because "a Negro revolution consists of goin' to church on Sunday. My revolution is an M-16 in my hand!"

This got a predictably enthusiastic response, but just then Brother Herbert X. Blyden came to the microphone to interrupt Kenyatta and set off an incident Wicker did not fully understand. Proclaiming that an "impasse" was at hand, Brother Herb said he wanted the brothers to see "your first line of defense." At some signal, inmate security men suddenly were running along the walkways atop the brick corridors on two sides of D-yard toward the barricades that had been erected for defense.

Most of those watching applauded this demonstration. But from the leadership table, a thin, angry voice, that of L. D. Barkley, rose above the others:

"These people trying to cause you to become hysterical!"

Blyden swung toward him. "Don't *do* that, L. D.," he called in tones that could only be described as wounded. "Don't *do* that to me!"

Four or five inmates immediately gathered around him, as if to hold him back. But others were rushing for L. D. Barkley, and Blyden shouted at them, apparently fearful that they were about to attack the bespectacled young man. L. D. apparently feared attack, too.

"Tell him what I meant," he called out. "Tell him right now!"

The commotion quickly died, unexplained.[8] Blyden turned back to the microphone. He was, he lamented, "in the middle of so many factions. But let us be together! We got to forget these little differences and start remembering what time it is, man, 'cause the ball game's almost over, man. . . . Some of you gone panic, you might come at me, but I ain't committed no crime on you and you ain't committed no crime on me."

Herb finished his speech to great applause. Then, again in wounded tones, he said, "I don't sit down, I go out among the people." With a sure sense of theater, he wandered away from the leadership table into the crowd of inmates.

Kenyatta, by then an anticlimax, offered one more exhortation. "We gone overcome, one way or the other. We gone win. We gone win 'cause you gone win. We gone win one way or the other, 'cause that oppressor—he gotta go!"

Barnes, Garcia, and Edwards were just then arriving in D-yard, and Barnes was setting up his cumbersome equipment, but not in time to head Tom Soto off from the microphone. Now the observer committee had been "locked up" too, Soto declaimed, and members had to have "an armed guard to go to the bathroom." Soto appealed for unity, but did not neglect to add that "I, personally, was not for" the 28-point package that had been presented the night before. This was applauded.

"Okay," Champ muttered in Wicker's ear. "We ready to talk to the hacks."

Captain Frank Wald, wearing two shirts, blue trousers, shoes without socks, looked incredibly brave and serene as he was led roughly to a spot in Barnes' lights. Wicker, Garcia, and Edwards gathered around him, with Champ hovering over them. Feeling oddly like an actor on stage, Wicker asked Wald how he felt.

"Well, we've spent four days with these boys and we feel pretty good," Wald said calmly. "After the initial outbreak and after we were brought here we've had nothing but good treatment." The inmates, who could hear the exchange on the PA system, applauded wildly.

Under further questioning, Wald had "no complaints about the treatment at all." Someone asked about his family; he said he had two children and six grandchildren and hoped they knew he was all right.

Did he have anything to say to Rockefeller?

"Well, Governor," Wald said at once, "we are here in the yard with quite a group of people and anything that you can do I am heartily in favor of it. We lived for four days under the same conditions they are living in and we are 38 men with the best understanding of this problem . . . a nucleus crew of 38 men. It would seem a shame to waste a group of educated men like that."

This sent a delighted howl of laughter ringing through D-yard. Captain Wald smiled, too. Wicker admired his quiet self-possession, but he did not want to look at him. He feared Wald would be dead in a few hours and that there was nothing to be done about it. He did not know if he, Tom Wicker, was doing the right thing. Maybe he would be more useful outside the walls, calling Rockefeller again, writing an article. He did not know. He could only go on, grasping at straws.

"Ask him about amnesty," Champ muttered in his ear, crowding in among the three reporters. Suddenly Wicker was aware that Barnes' camera was on them all, its red light stark and unwavering. He said nothing about amnesty. When Frank Wald was led away, Wicker turned to Champ.

"Listen, Champ . . . don't prompt us like that right on camera. We're supposed to be interviewing these guys honestly, not playing a part for you. We got to go back to our world, too."

Champ stared at him. With a sickening clutch in his stomach, Wicker realized he was protecting his constituency as had so many others. Like Bobby Seale weighing the political considerations that dictated his departure, Tom Soto disclaiming the 28 points, Arthur Eve worrying that his house would be bombed if he "recommended" what Seale would not—like Kunstler anxious to put a good face on his client's departure, or Champ sitting silent while the brothers denounced the court order he had agreed to and helped write, or Oswald looking over his shoulder at the corrections bureaucracy—like Rockefeller and Bob Douglass calculating voter reaction (if that was what they were doing)—like all of them, he was trying to shield his own name and reputation.

While interviewing the hostages might be a respectable and useful thing to do and might even help save lives, in fact he *was* to some extent playing a part for Champ and the others. Either he ought to admit he was doing it and damn the consequences because it was worth doing, or he ought not to do it at all. But Wicker had asked Champ, to all intents and purposes, to help conceal the real nature of what he was doing and thus to help protect his reporter's constituency. The last of the euphoria in which he had foolishly entered the yard—that exalted sense of mastery derived from his decision to act—vanished in the knowledge.

Champ spoke coldly. "Brother, *we* ain't gone have no world to go back to."

It was not just that he had shown himself so little different from all the others, Wicker thought, squaring around to the next hostage. The very notion of action, the idea that he or anyone could seize the moment and control it, was contrary to the reality of D-yard and the forces of human nature in collision there. He watched glumly while the inmates brought forward Sergeant Edward Cunningham, a burly man with a heavy stubble, wearing overalls and street shoes.

Cunningham said he was speaking for all 38 men held hostage. They had been treated well and they had learned that the inmates "got certain demands and these demands gotta be met." He had eight children and two grandchildren and naturally he wanted out as did the other hostages.

> One more thing I would like to say to Mr. Oswald. I wish you would take any of the men that belong to us off the roof and any of the troopers out of here, because if you get these shaky guys

shooting off or getting up in a group or something, someone is going to get excited and then we are all going to pay.

This is not a joke. This is not some kind of a little tea party we have got here. You have read in the papers all these years of the My Lai massacre. That was only 170-odd men. We are going to end up with 1500 men here, if things don't go right, at least 1500.[9]

"And 39!" someone yelled.

"Well. . . ." Cunningham swallowed hard. "And 39."

He, too, was asked if he wanted to send a message to the governor.

I certainly would. One of the recommendations, if he says no, I'm dead. He must give them clemency. He must give them clemency from criminal prosecution. . . . Anything else other than this is just as good as dropping dead, because these things are what has got to be had and there is no tinkering or none of this stuff. I mean this is cut and dry. That's all there is to it.[10]

But Rockefeller was not going to grant amnesty. Wicker knew that. He wondered if he ought to tell Cunningham so. What was right for him to do? Destroy illusion, or permit hope when there were no grounds for hope? Who could answer such questions?

"Nobody's bothered me" since the takeover of the prison, Cunningham was saying. He had "no animosity." He wanted to thank the brothers for "this chance" to speak.

"And that," Champ said, over the applause, "is the toughest fuckin' sarg't on the job. He is the *brute*. Put more guys in keep-lock than any 40 hacks around. And you hear what *he* say now?"

Brother Herb Blyden, returning from his stroll among the people, was not impressed. He went to the microphone again, perhaps still annoyed by his exchange with Brother L. D., and put his view bluntly: "You niggers are fools!"

He was one of the Tombs Brothers Seven, Blyden reminded his hearers, an old hand who already had 72 counts on him—50 for kidnapping alone—from that earlier rebellion. And all those charges had been laid on him *after* Mayor Lindsay had promised clemency. So Blyden was not deceived by talk of Rockefeller coming to make concessions—"when y'all get them, see if you can get *me* a plane or a jet out of this country." What the D-yard brothers did not seem to understand was that "all these things are going to be done or said on TV—and you're still gonna die!"

Another hostage, later to be identified as Frank Strollo, a hefty corrections officer, had been led forward for an interview. But Blyden's reappearance at the microphone had touched off more speech-making—in D-yard, almost anything did. Minister Franklin Florence took the mike. He wanted, he said directly to Brother Richard Clark, with his voice amplified to the whole yard, "to pledge my life" to the inmates and "to address you as your brother in suffering."

Some were behind the walls and some were not, Florence said, "but all of us are prisoners." He was not, it seemed to Wicker, limiting this declaration to blacks like himself, or even to blacks and Puerto Ricans; rather, Florence seemed to be speaking more generally of the poor and oppressed of all races. Wicker thought again that there was little evidence of black–white antagonisms in D-yard in what the observers could see and hear. When black orators, like Florence spoke of unity in the yard but coupled this with blasts against "The Man" or "Whitey," white inmates seemed to be cheering with the rest. Similarly, Florence, Champ, Brother Herb, and Brother Richard all seemed to accept white inmates as legitimately a part of the oppressed class.[11]

Could he be seeing in D-yard, Wicker wondered, that class interest might overcome racial animosities? Was it possible that the dregs of the earth, in a citadel of the damned, somehow in the desperation of human need had cast aside all the ancient and encumbering trappings of racism to find in degradation the humanity they knew at last they shared?

Franklin Florence passionately denounced oppressive social conditions, including "an educational system that has done nothing but exploited us, and made everybody rich but made us poor, and made us the criminals, and themselves the victims." Again, no distinction was made between the white and black oppressed. Again, Florence blamed the situation on "This Man"—"oh, yes, he remembers Pearl Harbor, he remembers the Alamo, but we forget everything."

What the inmates had done was "something we couldn't do for ourselves. You have shown us unity." And that was important, because "we are all the same thing in the eyes of Oswald and his kind." This produced much cheering, white as well as black, and Florence concluded powerfully, "When I think about you not eating, and when I think about the way [Oswald] lied to you and lied to us, the only thing I can say, the only thing I can *pray*, is that we cannot afford to rest until his kind will be brought to an end."

Roger Champen obviously wanted to bring attention back to the hostage interviews. He seized the microphone from Florence before more oratory could be launched, speaking briefly himself while Frank Strollo was led forward again. "We *must* have Rockefeller," Champ said. "We got to have Rockefeller here to save our lives and those of his hostages. . . . I say *his* hostages because he created this situation."

Wicker thought rather ruefully that, in one respect, Rockefeller had been right. Nothing previously had been heard in the yard of the governor's coming to Attica, but since the subject had been broached, in Clark's reading of the observers' radio statement, it seemed to have pushed everything else to the background (save in Herbert Blyden's mind).

Wicker proceeded with questioning Strollo; this time, Champ kept his distance. Strollo's testimony was as much like that of Wald and Cunningham as if it had been rehearsed—as Wicker thought it probably had. The inmates had treated the hostages "100 percent." Yet Strollo knew they had real grievances "because I work with them." His message to Rockefeller was one all the hostages, he said, had agreed upon, "complete amnesty."

"I want him to come here now," Strollo said forcefully, "and straighten this mess out."

Wicker, the political reporter, wondered how much pressure, if any, the hostages were bringing on the governor with this kind of message to him and to the public, faithfully recorded on tape and by Roland Barnes's ubiquitous camera. Not much, he thought. There would be sympathy for the hostages but it would seem likely to most viewers, as it did to Wicker, that they either had been coerced by the inmates into delivering the right message to Rockefeller, or else had decided among themselves that this was the best means of saving their own lives. Not many would think, in the circumstances, that they were genuine in their praise of the inmates.[12] Nor, he thought sadly, would many question Rockefeller's position that at some point recapturing the prison and "reopening the institution" became more important than lives lost doing so. That was why it was so hard for him to look Strollo, Wald, Cunningham, and the other hostages in the eye. *He* knew, if they did not, that they were expendable.

That was a thought difficult to bear—and one that, viewed logically, signalled the end of the inmates' power, entirely dependent as it had been on the reluctance of the state to see the hostages killed. Once the hostages' lives were left out of account, the inmates had no power but that of physical resistance. This made it more likely than shrill Jerry Rosenberg probably realized that he soon would be called upon to make good his pledge, which he rose to repeat: "I'm ready to die for the cause!"

Arthur Eve followed Rosenberg, as another round of oratory opened irresistibly, and returned to Oswald's statement, about which Eve evidently was still nervous. "What Oswald did today is a typical indication of bad faith that we've all had to get used to." Actually, Eve insisted, Oswald had been trying to take advantage of "the diverse makeup of this committee" and split it into several factions. But the committee was more united than ever—"some of the brothers and some of the observers were saying 'I, I, I,' but as of today, only this morning, they were saying 'we' and that's what Oswald became frightened about." Wicker doubted that version of Oswald's motives, but it was true, he thought, that as the end came palpably nearer, the observers seemed more unified in their efforts to find a solution.

Eve told of his encounter that morning with the woman in the diner who had screamed at him, "They ought to kill all of you!" And he had come back and told the story to the observers, he said, "because we had to bring everyone together on what this struggle is." He could tell the brothers that "you have had a profound impact on the whole world" and that the observers were pledged to "get the story out and get the facts out."[13]

Eve had worked himself into a highly emotional, almost tearful state in the course of this speech, one that far surpassed any partial motivation of protecting himself against any conceivable charge that he might have collaborated in the Oswald statement. Eve was a profoundly shaken and disturbed man who more and more saw himself as one of the D-yard brothers, a prisoner as much as they, whose life experience therefore had pulled him steadily into their emotional orbit, and whose sense of what was going to happen had brought him to something like despair—the more so in that he clearly felt that, if he were even in spirit one of the brothers, what happened to them could not possibly leave him untouched. Wicker had great sympathy for Eve's involvement, the spiritual tangle in which this ordinarily mild and reasonable black man found himself, even for his more mundane need to protect his constituency. Yet, he feared that Eve might unintentionally have tempted some of the brothers to hope for more than was possible, particularly when he had said that "the request for amnesty is not unreasonable because of the hostility of the people who serve in these institutions with no training whatsoever in human dignity." It was not unreasonable, perhaps, but it was most unlikely to be granted.

Eve also had remarked that his office had bought airline tickets for the Young Lords and Bobby Seale to come to Attica. As he finished, someone asked how many tickets he was willing to buy for those who wanted to leave the country.

"As many as I can," Eve said.

Blyden, the evangel of this proposition, quickly called for another show of hands by those who wanted to leave. The result, Wicker thought—there was no formal count—was little more impressive than it had been on Friday night. But Blyden would not let the matter drop. Of Kunstler, standing nearby, he asked, "What's this I hear about foreign countries?"

Kunstler took the microphone and told the brothers, "There are four third-world and African country people across the street from this prison prepared to provide asylum for everyone that wants to leave this country from this prison."[14]

Kunstler then repeated Bobby Seale's version of why Seale had not returned to D-yard. "He walked out of this prison, although he wanted to see you, because he could not bring himself, as a black man, to come in here and tell you what The Man wanted you to do."[15]

Wicker, listening, was growing uncomfortable. If Eve had run the risk of raising the inmates' hopes for amnesty, here was Kunstler giving serious standing to the third-world flight proposition and putting forward as fact the questionable contention that Oswald had refused to let Bobby Seale return unless he would advocate acceptance of the 28 points. No one could calculate the net effect of these remarks, or that of the effusive praise Florence and others had heaped on the inmates, on the climate in D-yard. But all of this was the sort of thing, surely, the inmates *wanted* to hear. Was it what they *needed* to hear?

The observers had said publicly that a massacre was in prospect unless something—Rockefeller's intervention, for example—happened. But they knew no such intervention was likely. Was it not therefore altogether probable that a massacre *was* going to take place, that there would be no amnesty and certainly no flights to the third world—just bloodshed and death? The only visible alternative was for the inmates to end the revolt and accept the 28 points. The choice finally lay with them, if the state would not yield. Was that not what the observers should have been telling the brothers?

Kunstler knew there were no third-world representatives "across the street." His only knowledge was through the Panther phone call from New York.[16] He was certain that most of the inmates were "as good as dead" and believed that what he said "would make them feel better."[17] He made no real promises, held out no concrete hopes; perhaps he had concluded, as Wicker more than half believed, that nothing anyone said or did in D-yard could make much difference.[18]

But there was no way to avoid the question whether the inmates nevertheless should not be told unmistakably and forcefully that if the revolt continued the state intended to crush it, at whatever cost in lives, and sooner rather than later—perhaps that very day. But surely, Wicker told himself that afternoon, the inmates *knew* all that. What else but such knowledge could account for their solidarity in defiance? How could they have understood the Saturday night speeches of Jones and Kunstler any other way? Numerous inmates, both leaders and rank-and-file, had been able to see for themselves, or to hear about on radio, the armaments just beyond No Man's Land.

In those circumstances, surely the inmates expected shooting. As one

of them observed, "You read Kent State, Jackson State, go to Martin
Luther King, you know what they're going to do."[19] The observers,
moreover, *had* predicted a massacre and published that word to the
world. Brother Richard Clark had read that statement to D-yard and
pointed out that the word did not refer to General Custer or "some
dude named Manson" but to the D-yard brothers themselves. Sergeant
Cunningham had said within the hour that what would happen in D-
yard if the governor did not come would be far worse than My Lai,
with 1500 men—the brothers—dead. The rhetoric of D-yard, from
beginning to end—Jerry Rosenberg or Herbert Blyden, it made no
difference—the rhetoric of the yard was "live like dogs or die like
men."

If anything, the inmates' stated expectations of what the troopers
would do surpassed the direst predictions of the observers. "You are
looking at a bunch of dead men," Richard Clark had said when he
heard the amnesty letter from Louis James. And it was the inmates
who had first depicted D-yard as the scene of a potential holocaust by
their threats to kill the hostages if they were attacked in their
stronghold.

So it did not seem possible to Tom Wicker, that confused afternoon
in D-yard, that the inmates did not have a realistic view of what was
about to happen to them. Yet, as he had thought in talking to Rockefeller that any straw was worth grasping at to prevent a massacre, so it
still was true in the company of the D-yard brothers that any straw
was worth grasping at to prevent that same massacre. If the faintest
possibility existed that a blunt speech of warning might avoid calamity,
he ought to take the microphone and state the truth as plainly as he
could.

But what would happen, Wicker asked himself, if he in his Southern
accent and with his Establishment position went before the brothers
and said what Seale, Eve, and Kunstler had not said? Would he be
believed? Would he be seen as urging the inmates to surrender, or as
an agent of Oswald and Rockefeller, trying to impair or shatter the D-
yard brothers' unity? What if his speech did, in fact, divide them into
angry factions? Would that be for better or for worse, if his aim was
to save lives? Might not some faction turn immediately upon the
hostages, if Tom Wicker insisted to the brothers they had no hope of
winning, that the alternative was the troopers' guns? Might the inmates
not seize the observers, too?

Perhaps they might. Perhaps they might not. But the straw lay there
to be grasped at, that September afternoon in the fading light of D-
yard. Wicker saw it clearly. He did not doubt the imperative to speak
that had been placed upon him by the realization. Fear, not least for his
own safety, offered its insidious counsel, but he understood that the

possibilities were as unclear one way as the other, whether he spoke or did not. He knew what was expected of him, what he expected of himself. The moments passed. More hostages came forward to be interviewed. But he did not speak . . . it seems.

14

Midnight, Still Raining

Whatever the ultimate reason Wicker remained silent, he had once again made the mistake of assuming that the inmates thought and saw things more or less as he did. But in the consistent pattern of the Attica revolt, their experience and their situation caused them to see and understand the same events and circumstances quite differently.

For one thing, the guns probably were not quite real to many of them. They saw and knew about the guns, but as had happened to Champen on Thursday night when he had been taken to Oswald's office to help write the Schwartz injunction, their prison perception tended to be distorted. Having become used to guns that never were actually used in the prison, they, too, had come to think that "the gun is like part of the scenery." The guns did not have the fearful impact on the inmates that the mere sight of them had made on Wicker. As a result, said one inmate, "We didn't believe they'd come in with guns, just clubs and tear gas."[1]

Moreover, by Sunday afternoon the inmate leaders were vastly overrating the value of their hostages. "We felt that their lives meant something to the administration," Champen said. "How can you come in and kill the man you sat down with last week and drank a beer with or bowled with?" The presence of the hostages in the yard, he thought, "would prevent them from coming into the prison and killing people . . . [We thought] you couldn't come in like that, shooting fish in a barrel."[2] This calculation left completely out of the picture all the pressures from *outside the prison* that were converging on Oswald and Rockefeller, pushing them to "reopen the institution" at whatever cost and without further dealings with "murderers and thieves."

So the trump card had become the firepower of the state police, but the inmates continued to believe they held it, in the huddled circle of hostages. And in one other way, they seem to have been influenced by their prison experience. Because Oswald had taken the unusual course of negotiating with them, had for four days let D-yard and the hostages remain in their hands rather than immediately retaking them by force, the inmate leaders reasoned that when and if he did order an attack he would scarcely let it be a bloodbath.[3] This left out of the picture the mounting frustration and anger of the troopers—much of it created by what they saw as Oswald's "softness."

As for the rhetoric about "dying like men," it may have been the inmates who did not understand how the observers would hear and interpret such talk. Wicker, at least, had taken it almost literally. But Champen, conceding that "speeches were made about dying," explained that the speakers were really dramatizing how bad conditions were:

"Well, what have you got to live for? So you're ready to die because you're not really living . . . you're so appalled by the conditions that exist that, in essence, rather than continue existing, you'd rather die. But that doesn't mean I'm ready to die in the terms of . . . 'Look, I no longer wish to live.' "[4]

Later, it was argued that a strong warning to the inmates would have been risky. "If I had gotten on the PA system and said we're going to get attacked," one of the leaders said, "that would have created a panic and the hostages would have been in jeopardy." He thought that if one of the observers delivered such a warning, there would be "complete chaos."[5] Champen conceded that had the observer group or any of its members warned that shooting was going to begin unless the inmates changed their stand, "perhaps someone in the yard would have thought that you had sold them out. It's a possibility."[6]

Even so, there is little doubt that many of the D-yard brothers did not expect anything worse than tear gas and billy clubs, when and if the troopers finally came over the wall. A poll of inmates taken later showed that 46.8 percent of the respondents did not expect guns to be used; a bare majority said they did expect some shooting.[7]

Obviously, a clear understanding of the real alternatives facing them might have made a great difference in D-yard that Sunday afternoon. "Why didn't someone say, 'Listen . . . their position is that they will not move another inch and they're going to come in with guns and shoot you people to death'?"[8] Three years later, Roger Champen still was asking himself that question, and Tom Wicker could give no better answer than "You should have known." He knew that was hardly an answer at all.

The last two hostages to speak to the inmates and to Roland Barnes' camera on Sunday afternoon were Michael and Art Smith, not related, both young corrections officers who had been captured and beaten when the uprising erupted on September 9. They were outspoken.

"Get on the ball!" Art Smith advised the governor. And as for the troopers and other corrections officers, "Just get 'em off the roof." Like the other hostages, he was worried that state forces sometimes visible on the roof of A-block and elsewhere would alarm the inmates and turn them against the hostages.

What should Rockefeller do? Dick Edwards asked Mike Smith. "I'd suggest he get his ass here now," young Mike replied. Looking out at the inmates, he added, "We're not scared of any of you people. We know it's not you, it's the people outside." The unity in the yard, he said, "white brothers, black brothers, Puerto Ricans, shows that you've got yourself together. The mere fact that we haven't been hurt—you people have gone to extremes to take care of us."

The afternoon had passed rapidly; Barnes was running out of film and, in any case, after the Smiths, further interviews would not have been in time for the evening news programs. Slowly, the rough formality of the proceedings collapsed. The hostages were herded back to their sad circle of benches. Barnes's lights clicked off and late afternoon shadows fell across D-yard. More than in any of the observers' other visits, they mingled freely among the inmates, moving all the while toward their exit but without the usual counting off and lining up.

Richard Clark, grinning broadly, led a white inmate, young, lean, blond, with a towel around his neck, up to Wicker. "You got to interview this white brother," Clark said.

"Who're you?"

The blond man was grinning, too. "Blair McDonald."*

"Man, where you from?" Wicker's ears had immediately picked up McDonald's Southern accent. McDonald named a town in South Carolina."

"My God," Wicker said, "we used to drive through there on the way to Myrtle Beach. I'm from Hamlet, North Carolina."

"You sure did, then," McDonald said. "S'right on the way."

Rudy Garcia was holding a tape-recorder microphone between them, and Wicker spoke cautiously. "You a long way from home," he said; one Southern accent invariably thickens another.

In more ways than one, McDonald said. Here the white folks and the black folks were sticking together, helping each other. "But, man, you know there's people in here we treated like dogs down home . . .

---

* This is not the white inmate's real name, since his story is recounted to the best of the author's recollection but may not be accurate in every detail.

but I want everyone to know we gone stick together, we gone get what we want, or we gone die together."

McDonald had all the aspects of a particular breed of good ol' boy— the kind to be found hanging around gas stations, garages, pool halls, and drive-ins all over the South. They made the most dilapidated motors run, drove cars with straight exhausts at high speeds, bedded women in the back seat (or said they did), drank prodigious quantities of beer, exploded frequently into anger and violence, and despised niggers. So Wicker was not disposed to accept without questioning the apparent redemption that Blair McDonald was proclaiming.

"You learned about racism in *this* place?" he asked.

"Man, I learned so much that if I get out of this I want to ask that brother for a plane ticket out of this country."

Good ol' boys like McDonald were usually the kind of raving patriots who had the Marine Corps motto tattooed on one bicep and the Confederate flag on the other. Their lead-weighted cars glowed with fluorescent American flag decals. But Blair McDonald seemed deadly serious. Wicker led the blond Southerner away from Garcia's tape recorder.

"Man, what the hell you doin' way up here?"

"Well, shit . . . you know how it is, man. Couldn't make no money down home so I come North. Me'n this girl took up, but I couldn't do no good up there neither. So me'n this girl, we forged a check. Man, no shit, you know they caught us cashing it, the kind of luck I got? So me'n this girl, they put us in the back seat of the p'leece car on the way to the station and this cop, he's drivin', and he's got to stop 'cause this line of little kids is crossin' the street to school in front of us.

"So this cop he leans out the window and starts cussin' them little kids. Tellin' 'em to move their asses, stuff like that. Man, I ain't lettin' nobody talk to little kids like that, not in front of Blair McDonald. I tol'm to shut up talkin' that way to kids.

" 'Why, you Southern cocksucker,' he says, just like that.

" 'Fuck you, Jack,' I says, and he gets outten the car, leans in the back window and hits me with his goddam gun butt. Well, *man!* You can imagine what I done then."

Wicker could not imagine. "What's that?" he asked.

"Jumped outten the car and cut 'is goddam throat."

Wicker had tabbed Blair McDonald on the nose, he thought. It was a good ol' boy story, all right, a Southern story, of anger, violence, man-hood rites, that grotesquely warped chivalric streak that lingers in the South like the old battlefields. It made Wicker wonder even more about the racial views McDonald had just expressed.

"But I didn't kill the mother," McDonald said. "The son of a bitchin' judge gives me seven years anyway. And you know what that goddam cop that hit me got?" Wicker shook his head. "Disciplinary action, that's all. Shit, man, no wonder people in here just finally blew up. That judge looked at me and says, 'You Southern son of a bitch, you come up here to make money, didn't you?' And then he says, 'Unfortunately, I can only give you seven years.' And the fuckin' cop gets disciplinary action. Man, we ain't shit in here, white or black, don't make no fuckin' difference. We ain't shit."

An inmate Wicker did not recognize had seized the public-address microphone and was shouting, "To oppressed people all over the world! We got the solution! The solution is unity!"

Maybe it was, Wicker thought, wishing Blair McDonald good luck, as they were separated in the milling crowd. Unity would not save the brothers' or the hostages' lives; but maybe something else would be salvaged from the human wreckage that soon would litter D-yard more thickly than the debris of four days of revolt and "liberation." Maybe these murderers and thieves, these cutthroats and addicts and rapists—as society saw them—maybe these despised and despairing men of violence and anger had found something greater than survival in their realization that, to society at large and to all its institutions, "We ain't shit." Maybe it was not only in death that the least of men could find their humanity. Maybe the brothers of D-yard had found theirs in common degradation, in the common anger it gave them, in resistance the more inspiriting for being so nearly hopeless.

It was not an idea entirely congenial to Tom Wicker. He was an individualist, a loner who mistrusted the notion of the "greater good," just as he shrank from the impersonality of the many become one. He believed in the sanctity of human life, the worth of every man, not in great causes or class solidarity or the needs of society. Still, he had just that afternoon failed in his own way to meet his own ideal of behavior, while the men of D-yard, as far as he could see, were holding fast to theirs and might have found in their solidarity that sense of each other's worth and of their own that he professed most to value.

A slight, short black in inmate garb approached him.

"You Tom Wicker?" He had a quiet, rather high-pitched voice. He was young, smiling slightly.

"That's right."

"Jus' wanted to meet you," the youth said, putting out his hand. " 'Scuse my glove." He was wearing cotton work gloves, for no apparent reason. Wicker took the hand in the glove. "Brother," the black youth said, holding tightly to Wicker's hand, "we got to *win*."

Wicker had never seen him before, might well never see him again. He was acutely aware that this slight boy in his cotton gloves might soon be dead, yet had as much desire as anyone to live. In the prison yard, before the onslaught, for the first time in his life he sensed that nothing racial stood between him and a human being who happened to be black. He felt himself free, for once, of his prideful sense of individuality. He put his arms around the youth and held him fast, held him hard, believing he had overcome the deepest fears his life had given him. In that moment, for at least that moment, he knew himself to be at last an equal part of the great human brotherhood—no more, no less.

When he stepped back, Wicker put his hand on the youth's head, which came barely to his shoulder.

"We gonna win, brother," Wicker said. "We gonna win."

The boy smiled and nodded and Wicker walked on, thinking he was *free at last free at last.* . . .

The departing observer group stopped in A-yard and gathered around Richard Clark while the inmate "security force" milled about them. Almost formally, Clarence Jones put Oswald's question for the last time to Clark. Would the inmates send negotiators to meet with the commissioner on neutral ground outside D-yard?

Rudy Garcia held his tape recorder microphone to pick up Clark's answer. "The next move," Brother Richard said slowly and distinctly, "is entirely up to him. Anything that results will be the result of the commissioner moving—not us."

To all intents and purposes, the negotiations for a specific settlement were over. There was nothing else to be done or said to that end. But if the state for some reason delayed attack long enough, the situation in D-yard might change by its own internal dynamics. New leadership might come to power, or all leadership might collapse, leaving the individual brothers on their own. Even the present leaders might change their stand.

There was at least the chance, of course, that delay might increase the danger to the hostages. But four days had passed without harm coming to them; the inmates were bound to know that nothing would so quickly bring down fearful retribution on them as the deliberate execution of the hostages; and the odds seemed strong that any change of sentiment in the yard, as time passed, with food, water, and shelter in short supply—not to mention the awareness of guns beyond the walls—would be in the direction of ending the rebellion and freeing the hostages on easier terms.

The only *real* risk in delay, it seemed to Wicker, was that of some totally irrational act of violence toward the hostages, and there never had been any way to guard against that. It was unlikely to occur, if it had not already. On the other hand, the one certain way to get hostages killed seemed to be for the state to attack D-yard. Inmate rhetoric had left Wicker little doubt that the moment of attack would be the moment of execution.

Therefore, as he trudged out of A-yard into the corridor from Times Square to No Man's Land, it seemed clear that the strategy of the observers had to be shifted to persuading Rockefeller, Oswald, and the eager troopers to hold off any planned attack, to persuade them to accept the status quo a little longer on grounds that attack would *surely* cause many deaths, including those of hostages, while delay *might* mean no deaths at all.

And what harm would be done if the state tolerated the D-yard rebellion a while longer? The inmates were not going anywhere, third world or no third world. They had given no one real cause to believe that they would wantonly kill or injure the hostages. They might yet give up or compromise, however bombastic their rhetoric of the moment. The rebels were not paralyzing a great city or threatening some intolerable new act of violence or bringing the machinery of the state to a halt. Surely the state of New York could afford to wait at least a few days, if only to safeguard its own corrections officers' lives.

But Wicker knew, as all the observers and the few inmates who accompanied them to the barred gates seemed to know, that this was the last visit to D-yard. Oswald would not let them come back, even if they wanted to. They were coming out for the last time. For all any of them knew, the troopers might be going in within the next hour. No one could tell how many of the inmates, by tomorrow, would be living or dead. Each man could see the strains of that difficult moment reflected in the others' eyes. Each could hear it in his own choked voice. They shook hands all around, conventional words suddenly charged with great personal emotion. *Right on, brother! Keep it together, man! Power to the people!* Some of the observers and inmates embraced; several were weeping openly.

A burly black man—Frank Smith, by then known to Wicker as "Big Black"—seized Wicker's hand. His face was massive, contorted under a knitted wool cap.

"Good luck," Wicker said. "Good luck, brother."

Over Big Black's shoulder, in the dim light of the corridor and the failing day, Wicker saw the troopers beyond the steel gate. He saw the troopers staring at the white and black men embracing and weeping and shaking hands. He saw the troopers holding their guns. He felt Big Black's hand gripping his but saw past the knitted cap only the troopers staring at them. He was certain the troopers were about to shoot. They had waited long enough. They could bear no more. These embraces and farewells were too much, the final insult to their power, their faith, their whiteness. They were going to shoot. He wanted to

run. He wanted to throw himself on the concrete floor. He wanted to
keep Big Black between himself and the guns.

"Ah, fuck it, man," Big Black said. "I done had it all. It don't make
no difference."

At 6:17 P.M. they came through the open gateway and were back in
the charge of the state. Oswald was asked to come to No Man's Land
to hear the inmates' response to his request for a meeting on neutral
ground. But the inmates who were to deliver it apparently recoiled
from the sight of the armed troopers surrounding Oswald.

"Jones, you already have our answer, you give it to the commissioner," one of them called down the corridor.[9]

Clark's tape-recorded rejection of Oswald's offer then was played
for the commissioner, who listened closely. That afternoon, unknown
to the observers or to the inmates, Vincent Mancusi, knowing his own
removal was one of the inmate demands, had volunteered to resign if
that would help achieve a settlement. Oswald instantly, and on what he
considered principle, had refused.[10] Such decisions, flooding on him
thick and fast, obviously were taking their toll of Oswald, in body and
in spirit.

"I've given everything," Oswald said heavily, disappointment in
every line of his sagging face. "I've gotten nothing in return. It seems a
little one-sided to me."[11]

Nevertheless, some of the observers pressed him then to allow time
for other negotiations; since most knew negotiations at that point
could not succeed, they were asking Oswald, in effect, not to order an
attack. But he said flatly, "I can give you no more assurances."[12]

When he left the observers, Oswald ordered that no further admission to D-yard should be granted to anyone. Worried that "radicals" in
the observer group might be sending out messages from the inmates
and even that coded responses might be going back to D-yard from
sympathetic radio broadcasters, he also ordered the telephone discon-
nected in the Stewards' Room.[13]

After they came out of D-yard, Wicker, Rudy Garcia, and Dick
Edwards were allowed to go to the parking lot in front of the prison
where they were to brief reporters and television crewmen on the
condition of the hostages. It was growing dark and a drizzle was falling
by the time the press group had assembled. Scrambling atop an automobile with a variety of microphones thrust in front of them—some
live to radio audiences—the three newspapermen also were caught in a
blaze of television lights which made it almost impossible to see the
crowd in front of them. But a number of townspeople and other
spectators, obviously including some relatives of hostages, had

gathered to hear the report, too, and Wicker was uncomfortably aware of them. Almost immediately, some were shouting and catcalling, denouncing the reporters, demanding quick action. It was an eerie feeling, chill as the steadily falling rain, to hear this disembodied abuse coming from the darkness beyond the lights; an attacker could come out of that darkness as quickly, as impersonally, as a bullet. The three of them were targeted in the light, defenseless as blind men.

As the one specifically asked by the inmates to lend "credibility" to the report on the hostages, Wicker nerved himself to speak first. He reported the hostages' seemingly good physical condition and that "all five [of those interviewed], in summary, said they all requested strongly that full amnesty be granted the prisoners, that Governor Rockefeller come here." Someone yelled back, "Is there complete amnesty for murder?"[14]

Trying to be heard above such interruptions, Wicker testified strongly to what had seemed to him the remarkable evidences of "absolute solidarity"[15] among the inmates in the yard. Choosing his words as carefully as he could, he said,

> I want to add my further testimony to the unity that's shown in the yard. To the unanimous testimony of these men that they regard themselves as being aggrieved by the treatment that they say that they have received in the prison in past years. And they appear to be unwilling to give up the hostages—give up their situation in the prison for anything short of a complete amnesty.[16]

"Why don't you talk about the unity of the guards, you double-crossing bastard!" somebody shouted.[17]

Wicker added his voice to those of the inmates and hostages who had called for Rockefeller to come to Attica—carefully specifying that the governor should talk to the observers, not the inmates—and refused to speculate on the likelihood of what a reporter questioning him called "a violent solution."[18]

Then Wicker turned over the microphones to Edwards and Garcia and climbed out of the naked light, down into the darkness and the angry crowd he had not been able to see. As he became part of it, he half expected to be roughed up, but except for some close-range shouting—"niggerlover!" a woman screamed in his face—the attention of the crowd had shifted from him. Near the great wall towering over the parking lot, the television lights had picked out a bareheaded man in a poncho who was screaming through the drizzle, "What about my son? What about my son?"

Moving a little closer, Wicker could see that the man was wild-eyed, crying, almost out of control. Under the poncho, he had on a corrections officer's clothes; he was Steven Smith, the father of Mike Smith, whom Wicker had interviewed in D-yard an hour earlier.

Steven Smith was sick of hearing about the prisoners and the negotiations, he shouted into a battery of microphones that had closed around him. Didn't anybody care about the hostages? What about them?

"We have to go in and bring those people out," he cried. "Wet-nursing those convicts won't do it. We have to get our son back or just bomb the hell out of the place! That's all that's left."[19]

Around Wicker, not necessarily *at* him, townspeople were yelling their frustrations and anger into the darkness and the rain of the parking lot, garish with its great white spots of light from the television crews.

"Brutality!" shouted one man. "I don't give a good God damn."

"I'd like to show them a little brutality," screamed one woman.

"Is this being brutal to us or not?" a man yelled.

"Brutal? My husband brutal?" screamed the woman.

The shouts echoed.

"Rapers, murderers. Do you want 'em on the street? They're in there because they belong in there."

"The hell, it'll go on forever. It'll go on forever."

"Those troopers should have gone in for them."

"I don't want to see anyone die, but it's got to end sometime."[20]

Wicker began moving through the crowd toward the Gothic entrance. A reporter held a microphone near his face. "How do you feel about these people yelling at you like that?"

"I don't think they're really yelling at me," Wicker said. "They're upset, they're worried, they're scared. They've got to take it out some way, on somebody. I can't blame them for that."

Inside himself, however, he wondered. Distraught though he might be, how could a father cry out for bombing the hell out of any place when that would mean his son's death? Why not hold on, work and hope for a settlement without violence done to anyone? Calling someone a niggerlover might be an emotional release; but what was wrong with a peaceful settlement that would save a son's or a husband's life? He thought he knew what was wrong. As with the woman in the diner, he was watching and hearing fear become hatred, seeing both gone hysterical—a hysteria, moreover, with a nightmarish racial fever in it. "What kind of a white man are you?" someone had screamed, while he spoke. "Standing on a platform with a nigger . . . helping niggers against your own!"

Suddenly, Wicker was tired, physically exhausted—but more than that. He was sickeningly and hopelessly tired of the fear and hatred that had surrounded him all his life, poisoned his every year. He wanted to turn away from the prison, where fear and hatred, guards and inmates, blacks and whites, had circled each other so closely, so warily, for so long, that they could never disentangle themselves. He wanted to run as far as he could from that dark place where hate and fear had been made an institution, tax-supported, government-operated, sealed with the approval of society. He wanted never again to hear of niggers, pigs, The Man, oppression, resistance. He thought longingly of the fleeting moment when he had clasped a gentle youth in his arms and imagined himself *free at last free at last thank God thank God* . . . but, within minutes of that moment, he had wanted to hold Big Black between himself and the troopers' guns.

No American would ever be free, he thought in his exhaustion and despair. That was the inescapable truth of it, harsh as the story of Lucifer's fall. They who had sought to be masters would be forever slaves. Having loosed in the traffic of souls the darkness within themselves, they had loosed as well the black living image of that darkness; and the fear of darkness made flesh, darkness rising in savage triumph, not only had haunted their world and their children's world but would haunt the world of their children's children. Because what was feared so much had to be hated—relentlessly, implacably, ruinously hated. But hate only begot hate. The hating became the hated, and hated the more.

So he could not turn away from the prison, it seemed to Tom Wicker, in the chill drizzle of the night, under the loom of the walls. There was nowhere to turn. Inside or out, fear and hatred circled each other endlessly; inside or out, the guards could never turn their backs on the inmates. In that sense, Malcolm X had seen it clear—America was itself a prison whose occasional flaring D-yards could no more be tolerated than Attica's.

Wicker walked on toward the guarded entrance, conscious of the rain coming down, the damp clinging of his shirt.

"When you going in?" he heard someone say to a deputy in a uniform with gaudy patches on the sleeves.

"S'pozed to of been this afternoon. Sons of bitches called it off."

But atop the automobile where he was continuing the news conference, Rudy Garcia was telling the reporters with their tape recorders that he feared it would be "shotgun and tear gas time before seven in the morning."[21]

In the Stewards' Room, Wicker was handed a press release from Governor Rockefeller's office. After recounting and praising the efforts of Oswald, the observers, and "the State" to "establish order, hopefully by peaceful means," Rockefeller put his position bluntly:

The key issue at stake, however, is still the demand for total amnesty for any criminal acts which may have occurred.

I do not have the constitutional authority to grant such a demand and I would not even if I had the authority, because to do so would undermine the very essence of our free society—the fair and impartial application of the law.

In view of the fact that the key issue is total amnesty—in spite of the best efforts of the committee and in spite of Commissioner Oswald's major commitments to the inmates—I do not feel that my physical presence on the site can contribute to a peaceful settlement.[22]

This was a formal version of what Rockefeller had told Wicker on the phone. In typescript on the page, it seemed cold and final—and foreboding. Rockefeller closed with an "urgent appeal" to the inmates to release the hostages, restore order to "the institution," and "accept the commissioner's good-faith commitment to the 28 major proposals offered to the inmates."

Rockefeller might as well have asked for the moon. Yet his "urgent appeal" did not even include his own guarantee of the 28 points. There was only Russell Oswald's "good-faith commitment" to them and Rockefeller's implied support. In the practical considerations of the D-yard leaders, that would be a poor inducement for the surrender the governor was urging.

Oswald had agreed to meet with the observers at 9 P.M., so another long wait began. The time for oratory had passed, as all recognized; talk in the Stewards' Room was desultory, low-voiced. Another box of sandwiches arrived, carried reluctantly by another grim-faced corrections officer. Wicker settled down on the floor by Lew Steel and leaned wearily against the wall. The rain beat steadily on the window-pane above his head.

"Lew, are you a revolutionary?"

Steel said he thought American society was pretty rotten.

"I think it's pretty rotten, too. But I'm not a revolutionary, even though sometimes I think I ought to be." Wicker was rambling, groping. "I remember something old Congressman Manny Celler said once. He was talking about civil rights, but it stayed with me. 'You can't make a revolution with rosewater.'"

You certainly could not, Steel said, and Wicker talked on.

"I don't have the stomach to be a revolutionary. To do the things a revolution would require. And what bothers me most is when you get through with your revolution, won't what you've put in place of our rotten society turn out to be just as rotten?"

Not necessarily, Steel said. Wicker listened to him with respect, because he knew Steel had made real sacrifices, had paid an actual price, to act on his social and political views. No one could accuse Steel, as Wicker often was accused, of being a "limousine liberal." Steel had deliberately foresworn the big executive suite and the bigger corporate fees that lured so many in his profession. Steel believed American society was riddled with racism, capitalistic greed, and class exploitation. He pointed out with bitter anger that the law and the government were largely at the service of these forces rather than working in any conceptual way toward economic and political justice— such as the socialist ideal of public ownership of the means of production. Take Attica, for example. The system couldn't tolerate the inmates taking over, demanding change. If the inmates would not surrender to be punished for bucking the system, the state would have to go into D-yard and punish them anyway, even more severely.

Wicker did not doubt that. "But racism, greed, exploitation—all that's human nature," he said. "How does a revolution get rid of human nature? Did you hear what Florence said today?" During the flap over Soto's telephone call to his organization, Florence had taken the floor to denounce Soto's action as harmful to the observers' unity.

"He said something that put it all in a nutshell, although I don't think he'd necessarily agree. He said, 'We have to be realistic even if we are revolutionaries.' I think that's the whole goddam problem with revolution. At some point, you have to be realistic. Lenin had to establish order. Somebody has to exercise power. Somebody has to have power exercised over him, or he won't play ball. Isn't that the way it is in D-yard right this minute? Somebody has to decide which is which, who's who. Isn't that why every revolution sooner or later hardens into reaction? That's why Mao is the greatest social revolutionary in history. He knows the only revolution is permanent revolution— against the society revolution creates, as much as against the one it overthrows. But that's against human nature, that's not realistic. Human nature wants law and order, not permanent revolution. So Mao will fail eventually, or die, and so will his permanent revolution. But human nature won't. Not until the fire."

Oswald appeared at 9:26 P.M., haggard, spaniel-eyed, paunchy, and sagging. Wicker did not move from his place on the floor, against the wall. Most of the other observers seemed too tired even to acknowledge the commissioner's presence. If he looked as worn out as Oswald and the rest, Wicker thought, he must be a sorry sight.

The commissioner wasted no time. Because of the reaction of the inmates to his proposals, he said, "I no longer will attempt to negotiate in D-yard." Since the inmates would not leave the yard, that meant that the negotiations were formally as well as practically finished. Oswald went on:

"I have been racking my brain, and my brain apparently isn't too fertile anymore, trying to figure out some way to meet in a place other than that and to get some hostages released." But he knew nothing else to suggest, and the observers had seen Rockefeller's statement.

"Amnesty is what they need," Arthur Eve replied. But Oswald was right—Rockefeller's response to their plea had flatly turned down amnesty.

Oswald said rather mildly that even though it was true the hostages had not been hurt, "There's that one case [Quinn, the dead guard], and I don't know how to get rid of it." So there was not much use talking about amnesty, as he saw it.

Minister Florence sought to put the responsibility for negotiations back on the commissioner. The D-yard brothers had been angered and upset by his ultimatum that afternoon; they believed Oswald had tried to deceive them by misstating the observers' position. That was why they thought the next move was up to him, so that he could restore their belief in his good faith. Meanwhile, Florence said, "they would not think of" meeting him outside D-yard.

Oswald listened skeptically. "That makes a rather sad situation, doesn't it?" he said, his tired eyes wandering over the observers' faces.

Florence said he had to agree with the brothers. If they left D-yard, they'd never get back alive, because there were just too many "trembling trigger fingers."

"A pretty sad situation," Oswald repeated, "when I've spent three days with you and you wind up with this lack of faith and trust in me." He would be the first, he said, to charge murder if anyone got trigger-happy. In fact, he said, no one would need guns in a neutral place, if only the inmates would realize it.

But the "ultimate power," Bill Gaiter reminded him, "is with this institution." The inmates knew it was the institution and the troopers who had the helicopters and guns. D-yard was the only place the inmates had any power. Rather than submit themselves to the institution's power, which they'd be doing if they left the yard, "they're going to reserve one ounce of manhood and die like men." Gaiter was speaking with great power and emotion, and he added, apparently in reference to possible deaths among the inmates, "I don't think there's a problem in the world that's worth taking a father from his family."

This was said with so much sincerity that for the first time in the observers' long ordeal, applause broke out in the Stewards' Room. Sharing Gaiter's view, Wicker joined in but was not too moved to reflect that most of the hostages had children, too. But he was too weary and depressed to cope with such puzzlements of right and wrong; he could only applaud the sentiment.

Anyway, Arthur Eve said, even if acting in the best of faith, Commissioner Oswald could not oversee the behavior of every corrections officer and trooper everywhere on the prison grounds. State Senator Tom McGowan of Buffalo, who had entered with Oswald, reminded Eve sharply that on Thursday night Roger Champen had been invited out of D-yard and safely returned after having helped work out the abortive Schwartz injunction. At one point, McGowan said, Herbert Blyden had been allowed to inspect C-block. In both instances, there had been "nobody hurt and no clicking of the rifles."

McGowan once had been a Buffalo policeman, and apparently he was a little tired of the black rhetoric he had been hearing. All his constituents were not racists, he insisted. He regretted the incidents of racial feeling Eve and others had reported. But it had to be understood that people were under great strain and had been given considerable provocation. After all, the D-yard rebels *were* convicts—and they were all at Attica for the good reason that they had been found guilty of law-breaking.

Besides, McGowan went on, turning to Florence, "You're wrong when you say that everyone in this room is narrow-minded. There are some real gentlemen in this room. You may not know it but I do." Wicker had not even heard Florence make the charge; he wondered if in his exhaustion he had been dozing without realizing it.

Eve shifted the focus to Rockefeller. Citing Sergeant Cunningham's remarks that afternoon ("if he says no, I'm dead"), Eve asked Oswald to try to change Rockefeller's mind. "If he doesn't come," Eve said, "then I have to say he is irresponsible." The hostages, after all, were "38 men who are on his staff." If Rockefeller would not do all he could to come to their aid, "he's not fit to be governor of this state."

Oswald remained mild, subdued. His sad eyes, heavily bagged, roved slowly about the room. "I don't know this to be true," he said, "but I have the impression that if the issue were other than the issue of amnesty something might be done."

Herman Badillo was a man who moved always toward some practical point of procedure rather than debating abstract questions. Now Badillo put it directly to Oswald that the observers needed a "commitment" that the state would not try to take D-yard at least until the next day. Obviously, he said, the inmates were not going to harm the hostages at this late stage, and the observers needed more time to work out their own course of action.

Oswald seemed to brood on this through a long speech in which Kunstler skillfully set forth some international precedents for the "yielding of law in the face of emergency." These included, notably, the British release of a suspected Arab terrorist in return for the safety of the hostages aboard a British airliner that commandos had held in the Middle Eastern desert. Kunstler also suggested that maybe the governor could agree to commute the sentence of anyone convicted of a personal-injury crime at Attica.

> I thought that maybe we could work out a commutation, that the governor could agree, if he thought amnesty was illegal, that the governor certainly had the power to commute sentences in the state of New York and agreement that any sentence growing out of Attica for personal injury would be commuted to five, ten or fifteen years. I think I mentioned all three in the discussion, that might be satisfactory to the inmates and might obviate the need for a bloodbath.[23]

Oswald thought this "too slick a maneuver. . . . no governor would tolerate it, and neither, of course, would the courts."[24] He snapped at Kunstler, "This is dishonest. Either it's amnesty or it isn't amnesty."[25]

Besides, Wicker remembered, John Dunne had told him that morning that he and Kunstler believed that if the governor gave such a pledge of clemency in advance of trials, it would be easy to get convictions on even the flimsiest evidence since jurors would know that no death penalties or severe sentences could result. In any case, nothing Wicker had heard in D-yard suggested the inmates would accept or believe the clemency proposal any more than they had believed Louis James' letter.

Badillo's demand for a "commitment" against an attack that night seemed still to be on Oswald's mind. The faint anger he had shown in response to Kunstler flared a little higher as he complained that he did not see why all the compromising was expected from him and none from the inmates. "I have given everything and I have received nothing," he said, his hands rising and falling in exasperation.

Badillo demurred. The inmates had not harmed the hostages, had in fact taken good care of them. That was something—a lot.

And anyway, Gaiter put in, how much had Oswald really given? As Clarence Jones had read the 28 points the night before, Gaiter had realized that "there was nothing on that list that was worth anything . . . nothing definite."

Oswald strongly defended himself and the 28 points. The most important thing, he said, was "the training of corrections staff so that hopefully these people could be treated with some respect and dignity." What was needed was "a whole new climate," and "this is something I've dedicated myself to."

But didn't he realize, Florence asked, that when Brother Richard Clark had said the next move was up to Oswald, that also meant the inmates would precipitate no violence on the hostages or anyone else? "That to me suggests that these men are willing in some way to try to negotiate"—but not, he insisted, in "the trigger-happy atmosphere" they sensed outside D-yard.

Oswald's anger flared again. "There is no more sinister violence that I know of than holding hostages at ransom," he said.

Herman Badillo reminded Oswald that "the only reason they took the hostages was because it was the only way to get somebody to talk to them." All along, the inmates had wanted to talk. So why not give the observers another day before trying to take over D-yard with force? After they got some rest, maybe somebody could come up with something.

Oswald said that might be all right "if there were some avenue that you can explore that you haven't explored already" other than a "dead-end issue." He clearly thought amnesty was that "dead-end issue."

But Badillo was dogged. Red-eyed, his collar open, his lingering Spanish accent thickened a bit with fatigue, he said flatly that he thought the governor was getting bad legal advice. "The governor says amnesty is wrong. I want to talk to the governor. We say the issue is human lives." He thought Kunstler's point about clemency might be developed into an amnesty compromise—if the governor came to talk to the observers, and if the observers, above all, were given more time.

"We need the day," Badillo said; Oswald listened silently.

Florence cited President Kennedy and Premier Khrushchev in confrontation over the Soviet missiles in Cuba. Both had needed time, "and that's all we need, Commissioner." Wicker blearily thought of Kennedy in his armchair in the big, sunny parlor of his house in Palm Beach, a long way from Attica, conducting the annual year-end Presidential conversation with reporters. He had a hazy memory that Kennedy had expressed the view that powerful nations ought to be wary of inflicting major defeats on each other. Had the Soviets actually gotten an operational missile base into Cuba, which would have been a substantial American setback, Kennedy felt he would have had to react strongly. But that had not happened, and Kennedy thought he had made the ultimate Soviet defeat in Cuba not so harsh or extreme as to force Khrushchev into some strong retaliation. Wicker wondered if Rockefeller had such a historical and strategical view; the governor seemed more likely to believe in the crushing blow.

But the present flooded away the past. The talk went on. What was he to do? Oswald demanded to know, growing more animated. Did the observers think they were the only ones who cared what was happening? Just that evening, he had received three "hostage family" phone calls. And the callers had been all but "hysterical about the lenient and unproductive way we're dealing with this." And he *had* been lenient and understanding; he *had* tried to work things out. Yet, "has the situation deteriorated or improved? It hasn't improved, has it?"

Again Badillo, relentless as a bulldog, disagreed. The situation was down to one issue, he said, and that was an improvement. Oswald flared at him. "We haven't gotten off of D-yard as yet." Then, slowly, as if finally putting his frustration and disappointment on the line, his heavy body stiffening and his voice rising almost to a shout: "A committee as powerful as this ought to have been able to swing that group around to meeting with me on neutral grounds!"

Florence, a short but powerfully built man whose anger also appeared to be rising, pushed up close to Oswald. When the observers had come out of D-yard that afternoon, he said, the commissioner should have ordered his armed men back from the gate at No Man's Land. "Many people were frightened, scared to death that you're gonna drill them, your men are gonna kill them!" If *he* were in power, Florence said, he'd give time.

"And if I were you," Oswald said angrily, "I'd have talked those men into meeting with me out of D-yard."

Another reason it was important for Rockefeller to come, Eve told Oswald, was that "your credibility was very much damaged" in D-yard by the statement sent in that day.

"Well, that's too bad about that," Oswald said sarcastically. He felt that he had "agreed and signed and approved" 28 points that were the committee's recommendations to him. "If I hadn't believed it, I wouldn't have signed it."

Julian Tepper added his voice to those pleading for delay, and Clarence Jones, who had been silent and brooding throughout the discussion, said wearily to the commissioner that it seemed to him that there was "a relationship between time and humanity." Like the Paris peace negotiators talking about the shape of the table, they had a more serious point beyond the immediate demand for delay. They were too tired to make precise proposals, to devise new plans. They were too tired to think. But Jones believed "nothing is ever frozen forever." Amnesty was "non-negotiable only on a day-to-day basis." And all the observers could do was to "appeal to that thing that every man and woman has in them—compassion and love for life." So they were "pleading on behalf of those inmates that we have the time" to try again. And that was to ask for nothing more than the status quo.

Minister Raymond Scott, tall, thin, his face intense, said he had a feeling that all this was useless talk—that Oswald already knew "what you're going to do and when you're going to do it."

Oswald looked at him a long time, then shook his head slowly. "I'm going through the tortures of hell trying to make up my mind," he said.

There was a long silence. Then Alfredo Mathew reminded Oswald that the observers were not trying to cause trouble but to "save the situation from the bloodbath we know it would be"—indeed, that they had expected that afternoon.

"I changed my mind," Oswald said.

Wicker thought the commissioner was like a bear in a cage, with the observers surrounding him, thrusting at him—not to mention the corrections officers and their families, the troopers, the high officials in Albany and Pocantico Hills looking over his shoulder, the press of the world waiting in the floodlit parking lot. Slowly, Wicker got to his feet, aching in every bone. He knew his brain was working sluggishly, that he was near exhaustion, so he spoke cautiously to the observers and to the sagging little man at bay in the middle of the room.

He said that he did not agree with all of those in the Stewards' Room, certainly not with all the men in D-yard. He was not a revolutionary, not even a radical. He had hoped the inmates would accept the 28 points, end the revolt, and free the hostages. He wanted to see great improvement in the conditions the D-yard brothers complained of—even more, he wanted things done to change the social conditions he believed had sent many of them to Attica. He thought he understood at least some of the difficulties of Oswald's position. It was all very well for the observers to criticize the commissioner, urge him on, protest and denounce his actions. But in the end it was Russell Oswald who had to make the decisions. So it would be sensible, Wicker said, for the observers to remember that "few of us in this room will ever have to go through what Commissioner Oswald is going through."

Wicker spoke with genuine sympathy for Oswald and considerable respect for the restraint the commissioner had shown so far. But he saw no point, either, in badgering the very man they had to persuade. Quite deliberately, he had tried to get Oswald's good will with these remarks, sincere though they were. He believed that Russell Oswald, whatever the pressures on him, did not want men dead in D-yard if there was any way to avoid it.

So he went quickly through the litany of reasons for delay—the hostages were not being harmed, an amnesty plan might yet be devised, the inmates would not necessarily be as adamant on Wednesday or Thursday as they were on Sunday. Then he reminded Oswald of a biblical passage he could not quote precisely but which he remembered from Deuteronomy by virtue of the long years of Sunday School imposed upon him by Esta and D. D. Wicker:

I call heaven and earth to record this day against you that I have set before you life and death, blessing and cursing; therefore choose life, that both thou and thy seed may live.

"Commissioner," Wicker said, looking Oswald in the eye, "that's what giving us more time really means—choosing life. So I plead with you, in full understanding of all your problems—'therefore, choose life.' "

But he knew as he slumped back into his place on the floor, tired and disspirited, still watching Oswald's tired eyes, that he had merely added one more pressure to those buffeting the man. Maybe he had not even done that.

Kunstler pointed out that the commissioner could not "choose life" if he also ordered an attack on D-yard. "Everyone dies when they come through the fence."

Oswald was silent. No one else spoke. Most knew enough had been said. Around them, the night and the prison were silent, too, except for the rain scratching lightly at the window. Beyond the glass door of the Stewards' Room, Wicker could see the shoulders and head of a corrections officer standing guard outside. He could hear Jaybarr Kenyatta breathing heavily and Arthur Eve's heels barely tapping the side of a desk on which he was sitting.

"In this room," Oswald said finally, his voice slow and his face immeasurably sad, "in Mister Wicker's words, all of us choose life. Everyone in this room is partisan, and I like to think that I'm partisan in favor of life, too." But on the "other side of the fence" many people were finding his program for dealing with D-yard "too lax, too limited, too indecisive." For that reason, he said, "the pressures are tremendous" from hostage families and from corrections officers and their families. That made it difficult for "people such as you and, in large measure, me" who "hope that things can be worked out." So did "the intransigence of individuals with whom we've tried to talk" and the "innumerable butchery threats."

Trying to see it all clear, Oswald said, "I find a truly desperate situation and in that situation of course are desperate men." He paused. "I have a lot of soul-searching to do." He paused again, for a long time. "But I would say come in again tomorrow."

Something like a sigh of relief ran around the room. Oswald seemed to hear it clearly. "You better talk some more," he said. "I haven't made my mind up yet."

The rain showed no sign of letting up. Those who wanted to stay in the Stewards' Room overnight could do so, Oswald said. The others would be readmitted to the prison in the morning.

Tepper and Fitch were among those who stayed. They noted in their journal:

> *10:35 P.M. The meeting breaks up. A group of nine agree to stay all night in the prison, just in case. We are now confined to one room and a half-corridor.*[26]

The other observers dispersed, Wicker and Steel returning to their room at the Batavia Treadway. Oswald went down the hall to the office he was using, picked up the phone, and called Nelson Rockefeller:

> I suggested that it would seem that it might be appropriate for someone as warm and understanding as Governor Rockefeller to walk that last mile and come, although I went on to express the view that I didn't feel that it was going to be productive.

General A. C. O'Hara, the close Rockefeller associate who had once commanded the state's National Guard, also spoke to the governor and concurred—both that Rockefeller should come to Attica and that it would not be "productive." These appeals were unpersuasive; once again, Rockefeller said no.[27]

Midnight: Still raining.[28]

Oswald did not give up the search for an alternative to attack but had late conferences with his and the governor's aides and state police officers. Over the objection of John Dunne, who had joined the group of officials, Oswald decided to propose to Rockefeller that the inmates be told the governor would come to Attica after all and even meet with an inmate committee—but only *after* they had released the hostages. Dunne argued that this did not deal with the inmates' demands and would be rejected anyway, since it required them to give up their bargaining power, the hostages. Most of those conferring with Oswald agreed with Dunne's analysis; nevertheless, well after midnight, the commissioner phoned Rockefeller and put the plan to him.[29]

Rockefeller realized that Oswald, "the originator of this idea, felt that, well, that would put me in a better position, that I had offered to come to Attica but . . . I wasn't trying to posture myself in a good public relations position." In fact, Rockefeller believed that Oswald, like the observers, was "grasping at straws"; all of them having failed to work out a peaceful solution, he thought they were reluctant to face the responsibility for any loss of life.

In life, it's not easy to face a hard decision, particularly when human lives are involved. It isn't for me, either, but I think that we have to look at these things not only in terms of the immediate, but in terms of the larger implications of what we are doing in our society.[30]

The harder decision might well have been to stay the hand of society—to grasp at the straw of life rather than to send men with guns to D-yard. "In terms of the larger implications of what we are doing in our society," it might have been historic—in the best sense, even revolutionary—to have reversed those who argued that "the need to reassert the authority of the state over the rebels outweighed the risks of an assault."[31] To have rejected their advice certainly would have required "a hard decision."

Nelson Rockefeller did not make it. Oswald's last proposal was never put to the men in D-yard. In the commissioner's office, John Dunne sensed the reality. He had been told of an assault plan that called for a surprise attack, but he realized that this would probably increase inmate casualties without saving the hostages' lives, since the inmates still would have a few minutes before the hostages could be rescued. Dunne obtained an agreement that at 7 A.M. one last appeal would be made for the release of the hostages. The inmates would have an hour to respond.[32]

2:05 A.M. An absolute downpour.[33]

It rained all night. Not many of the D-yard brothers or hostages could sleep, as rain beat through their makeshift tents and shelters. One of the men in D-yard later wrote to Russell Oswald that God must have been crying.[34]

September 13, 1971

CHAPTER

15

A Time to Die

Morning came gray and misty. At 6:30 A.M., peering out of the windows of the Stewards' Room, the first observers awake saw through the slow drizzle the renewed preparations for an attack—men lining up, checking weapons, trying on gas masks. At 6:55, trying to find out what was happening, the observers learned that they were no longer allowed to see Commissioner Oswald.[1]*

Nor far away in D-yard, Brother Richard Clark also rose early, after a late night watching the 11 P.M. television news, which featured the Sunday afternoon interviews with the hostages. He shivered in the cold rain, drank some coffee, got a message that The Man wanted to see him, and went to No Man's Land.[2] Despite the rain, Clark was dressed neatly in prison fatigues; but Oswald thought his face and eyes reflected lack of sleep when he arrived just before 8 A.M. Oswald, Dunbar, and General O'Hara were waiting.[3]

Oswald told Clark that he understood the D-yard leaders refused to appoint a committee to meet him on neutral ground, that he nevertheless wished to continue the negotiations even though he doubted that a settlement could be reached "with a group as large as your whole body," and that he therefore hoped Brother Richard would give "most careful consideration" to a memorandum Oswald was handing him. Oswald did not call it an ultimatum.

> For four days I have been using every resource available to me to settle peacefully the tragic situation here at Attica.
>
> We have met with you; we have granted your requests for

---

* In this chapter, note references appearing at the end of a paragraph refer to the whole paragraph, unless another number appears within the paragraph.

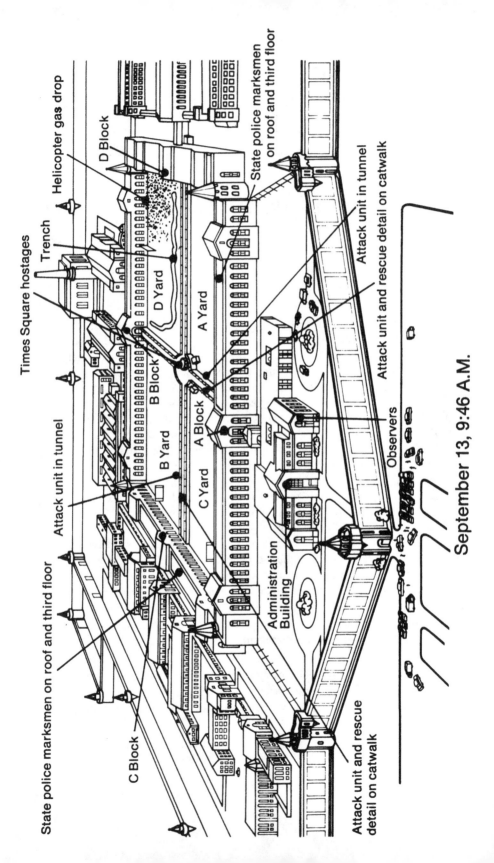

State police marksmen on roof and third floor

Times Square hostages

Trench

Helicopter gas drop

D Block

State police marksmen on roof and third floor

Attack unit in tunnel

Attack unit and rescue detail on catwalk

Attack unit in tunnel

C Block

B Block

B Yard

D Yard

A Yard

C Yard

A Block

Administration Building

Observers

Attack unit and rescue detail on catwalk

September 13, 9:46 A.M.

food, clothing, bedding, and water; for medical aid; for a Federal Court Order against administrative reprisals. We have worked with the special Citizens Committee which you requested. We have acceded to 28 major demands which you have made and which the Citizens Committee has recommended. In spite of these efforts you continue to hold hostages.

I am anxious to achieve a *peaceful* resolution of the situation which now prevails here.

I urgently request you to seriously reconsider my earlier appeal that:

1. All hostages be released immediately unharmed; and
2. You join with me in restoring order to the facility.

I must have your reply to this urgent appeal within the hour.

I hope and pray your answers will be affirmative.[4]

As he returned to Mancusi's office from the meeting with Clark, Oswald did not consider himself committed to an attack since General O'Hara and the state police commander on the scene, Major John Monahan, had assured him that none of the military preparations was as yet irreversible. There was yet time to work out a settlement, if the "People's Central Committee," to which Brother Richard had taken the "memorandum," wanted a settlement.[5]

In Batavia, Lew Steel and Tom Wicker had been the first breakfast customers in the Treadway dining room; then they and other observers were driven through the rain to Attica in state police cars. They were passed readily enough into the prison and up to the Stewards' Room, but they, too, noted the grim military preparations in the open space between the great wall and the prison buildings. Jim Ingram, coming in separately, was confronted by a corrections officer in a yellow rainsuit with a shock of hair falling across his forehead from under a rainhat. "Remember this, Buddy," he said, as raindrops streaked across Ingram's black face, "if anybody in there dies, you're it."[6]

Oswald might not have thought himself committed to attack; but at 7 A.M., in the prison mail room, Major Monahan had briefed the commissioner and other officials on an assault plan the major had worked on through the night. Monahan said the plan was based on the use of "minimal force" and concluded, "All supervisors must be advised that we do not wish to be placed in the position of being accused of turning this facility into a shooting gallery or, in slang terms, being accused of 'shooting fish in a barrel.' " Mancusi's deputy superintendent, Leon Vincent, then briefed correctional supervisors. He said corrections officers were to take charge of recaptured inmates, but he apparently did not pass along, if he knew, what Nelson Rockefeller, Russell Oswald, and state police officials had previously agreed upon—that corrections officers were not to take part in the assault itself since they were considered too emotionally involved to act with restraint.[7]

The observers who straggled back to the Stewards' Room early that wet morning heard another alarming report from one of their own. Domingo Rodriguez, a bearded young Puerto Rican from the Buffalo BUILD organization, who had joined the group with Bill Gaiter, had been told by a man in a gray uniform as he and Gaiter passed the prison gate, "We gone get you motherfuckers."[8]

Unknown to the men already in the Stewards' Room, Oswald soon ordered no more observers admitted. Those on hand did know that he had ordered them confined to the Stewards' Room, with a guard at the door. The hostile atmosphere caused some debate. Alfredo Mathew and John Dunne thought the observers should leave the prison before the attack that obviously was coming, but Ingram argued heatedly that the group should stay for whatever restraining effect their presence might have, even though he thought it possible that in an attack the troopers might shoot up the Stewards' Room, too. Dunne said sardonically that he personally was not worried about that: "I have legislative immunity."

This debate caused most of the observers in the room to sit on the floor out of line with the windows; at the time, it did not seem a ludicrous precaution. At about 8:30, Dunbar came in and gave the group a copy of Oswald's "memorandum." He also told them the administration building was being cleared, but he made no move actually to evict them and they made no move to leave, despite their nervousness. G.I. Paris, in his hoarse whisper, told Dunbar, "If people get hurt, it will be on your shoulders."[9] Dunbar, smoking his inevitable pipe, said nothing and left.

The Oswald "memorandum" meanwhile had been read aloud in the muddy, soggy atmosphere of D-yard. Either Brother Richard Clark or one of the other leaders went through the same routine Clark had used the day before. Did the brothers want to accept? "And all 1200 voices answered in unison, 'No!' 'I still didn't hear you. What did you say?' 'No!' "[10] A lone dissenter—a tall black man—spoke up and was threatened with attack until Roger Champen dissuaded the angered brothers and assigned two guards to the man.[11] A Puerto Rican member of the negotiating committee took the microphone and read the memorandum in Spanish, "and my brothers responded, 'If the blacks and whites are going to fight, we're going to fight.' Then I said, 'Let me tell you something. I have never in my entire life been so proud to be part of you like I am today.' I was on the verge of tears; I really wanted to cry."[12]

After Dunbar left the observers, he, Oswald, and O'Hara returned to No Man's Land for Brother Richard's response. Clark kept them waiting for 10 minutes or so but arrived before the hour deadline and dumbfounded the three officials by saying he did not know what the "demands" were that the commissioner had claimed in his "memorandum" to have approved. The amazed Oswald said he was referring, of course, to the 28 points Clarence Jones had read in D-yard on Saturday night. Clark stared at Oswald, then said calmly that to his knowledge Oswald had never approved those 28 points. Oswald, sputtering at this delaying tactic, asked Dunbar if he had a copy of the document. Dunbar pulled one out of his bureaucrat's pocket, and Oswald handed it to Clark, pointing to his signature beneath the word "approved." Impassively, Brother Richard said he would have to discuss the matter with "the people." He asked for half an hour more; Oswald gave him 20 minutes.[13]

Clark went to D-yard, Oswald to Mancusi's office to brief Rockefeller by telephone, and O'Hara to the third floor of A-block where he could overlook the attack he no doubt believed inevitable. Dunbar went to the Stewards' Room, arriving at 8:51, to tell the observers of the exchanges between Oswald and Clark, and that Brother Richard's reply would have to be in hand by 9 A.M. or shortly thereafter. The observers complained to Dunbar of the threats to Ingram and Rodriguez. Smiling, polite, Dunbar took his pipe out of his mouth and apologized for these remarks. Of course the observers understood, he said, that there was much tension among the corrections officers and the troopers.

"They got guns and tension," Jim Ingram said. "We just got tension."

On the roofs of A- and C-blocks, officers were quietly assembling state police teams of marksmen qualified with the service's standard .270 rifle—a big-game weapon that fired an unjacketed, soft-lead, expanding bullet with sufficient accuracy to hit a five-inch target at 800 to 1000 yards. Team members lay prone on the roofs to stay out of sight of D-yard. On the third floors of the same buildings, other rifle teams, similarly armed, were assembling with equal caution. These four sets of marksmen were instructed to provide covering fire, once the action began, for two attack units of 30 troopers each, all armed with pistols and Ithaca Model 37 five-shot, pump-action, 12-gauge shotguns. These attack units, then forming on the second floors of A- and C-blocks, were to move out on the open walkways atop the passageways that ran at right angles from the two cellblocks to meet at Times Square. They were to be followed along the walkways by 10-man squads of troopers equipped to remove barricades, then by 25-

man "rescue details" carrying ladders to descend into D-yard and also armed with Ithaca Model 37 shotguns—riot control weapons that fired cartridges containing nine to 12 pellets of #oo buckshot, each pellet a lethal missile approximately .33 inch in diameter. These pellets would spread, upon firing, in a fanlike pattern that would be two and a half feet wide at 50 yards from the muzzle. Some troopers carrying shotguns had loaded them, instead, with a 12-gauge rifled slug, a single lead projectile weighing one ounce and advertised by the manufacturer as for "antivehicle duty" or for "reducing a cement block wall to rubble." Two other contingents of 25 troopers each, similarly armed, were forming on the first floors of A- and C-blocks to move through the enclosed passageways toward Times Square. Some were to spill out and secure A-, B-, and C-yards; others were to pass Times Square into B and D tunnels. The entire attack force, with backup men, numbered 211 troopers. All wore gas masks.[14]

Far below and unaware of the rifle units prone on A- and C-block roofs, the inmate leaders in D-yard, granted a little more time by Richard Clark's poker-faced bluff at No Man's Land, decided on another maneuver. They still did not know that The Man and the state had decided that order would be restored and "the institution" retaken even if it cost the lives of some of their own. Thinking the authorities still wanted, above all, to spare the lives of the hostages, the leaders ordered eight hostages blindfolded, bound, and taken to the open walkway between A-block and Times Square. Each was made to face A- or C-block. Each was held by at least one inmate. Each was menaced with a knife or some form of "blade" at his throat or chest. All were in plain view of most of the assembling assault and covering forces.[15]

The plan of attack those forces were to follow did not contain provisions for orders to commence firing or for orders to cease firing. Each trooper *was* ordered to avoid hand-to-hand combat, so that force short of firepower was not available to him. The rooftop and third-floor marksmen were not to fire into D-yard itself unless explicitly ordered to do so, but only upon the exposed walkways. The other troopers were to use their own discretion in determining when, under what circumstances, at whom, and how often they were to fire.[16]

Seventeen observers had gathered that morning in the Stewards' Room;[17] but some of the most active and articulate of the group— Jones and Kunstler, in particular—had been shut out by Oswald's order to admit no more observers. Those on hand could tell by looking out the window, by the general atmosphere, and by Dunbar's news from No Man's Land that the attack was set to go in. Their talk was desultory, defeatist—no one thought the situation could be changed, a settlement worked out. It was decided—more or less, as everything in that volatile group had been—that once the guns could be heard it would make sense to pull a large cabinet across the Stewards' Room door, against any conceivable attack by anyone who linked the observers too closely to the inmates.

In that quiet room, Bill Gaiter spoke movingly, almost in wonder, about the "special relationship" that had developed among the observers—black, white, Puerto Rican, of vastly varied background and experience, most of them strangers four days before—in their common ordeal of frustration and failure. Still in his smelly shirt, Wicker remembered how naively he had come to Attica three days earlier, believing himself an observer of an agreement easily to be made, thinking he would not even need a change of clothes before he would be home, unaware until Attica's walls had closed around him of the fear and hatred rank in its air, of the violence and death they portended.

"I don't think we should ever relent," Gaiter was saying. The group should meet again, from time to time. The observers should "dedicate [them]selves to reforming the politics and the processes and the institutions of this sort not only in this state but all over this country." But what power did such a group have to do that? Wicker wondered. They had failed; that was the truth of it. Any minute they would hear the proof from D-yard.

Nevertheless, by acclamation, the observers—as if they were a kind of graduating class—chose Arthur Eve as permanent chairman. Seeming more in control of himself than he had been on Sunday, Eve echoed Gaiter. They had to build a constituency for prison reform, he said. They would have to come back to Attica itself, show as much concern later on as they had in the last few agonized days. "It's a hell of a thing when you're behind that wall to know there are people out here who care."

The room fell silent. "Yeah," Domingo Rodriguez finally said, unutterable bitterness in his voice. "After they're all dead." He put his bearded face in his hands and wept.

At 9:05 A.M., Walter Dunbar took station at No Man's Land for whatever response would come from Richard Clark. Then Dunbar was called to a window. From it, he could see the first two hostages being led blindfolded to the walkway near Times Square. He immediately reported this development by two-way radio to Oswald. The commissioner checked the report with General O'Hara, who was at his vantage point on the third floor of A-block. O'Hara confirmed it.[18]

In retrospect, at least one inmate leader conceded, taking the hostages to the open walkway was a mistake—"maybe it triggered the massacre." But Roger Champen insisted that the move had been "only

for the purpose of preventing the authorities from coming in there.
. . . [The leaders] assumed that the position of the state was a bluff
and this was a counterbluff." Had the inmates in fact planned to kill
the hostages, he explained, "there was time to kill . . . every hostage
in that yard. How long would it take? It wouldn't take long. . . . it
would have been impossible for them to get in there and save the
hostages if the point was that we wanted to kill them. . . ."[19]

But Oswald could not know that the hostages displayed on the
walkways were a "counterbluff," particularly since he was not really
bluffing himself. Instead, he was sure he had a final, defiant answer
from D-yard; and he wearily told Major Monahan to get set for attack.
Between 9:12 and 9:30, while the troopers made their last preparations,
Walter Dunbar, at No Man's Land, exchanged a few more shouted
words with inmates along the A-block passageway. Dunbar finally
called out, "Release the hostages now and Commissioner Oswald and
the citizens committee will meet you—with you!" Down the passageway, where the revolt had started four days earlier, came the last,
fitting words of the negotiations at Attica—"Negative—negative!"[20]

Among the silent observers, Alfredo Mathew was at one window,
Jose Paris at another. Rodriguez sat against a wall, his face still in his
hands. Kenyatta in his colorful robes had his hands over his eyes. Lew
Steel said quietly that there was one thing the group had worked into
the 28 points that they ought to try to insist on after the battle was
over. Oswald had pledged that an inmate's mere presence in D-yard
during the revolt would not be used to prevent a parole the inmate
otherwise would be due.

"That's important," Steel said, "but I guess . . . what I wanted to
say now was that we stop talking."

Major Monahan by then had confirmed the presence on the walkway near Times Square of eight bound and blindfolded hostages with
their guards. Seven were seated. Three faced A-block. Five faced C-
block. A total of 21 inmates were on the open walkways near the
bound hostages. Others were farther away, at the barricades. Reacting
swiftly, Monahan ordered the marksmen on the roofs and at third-
floor vantage points to attempt to protect the lives of the eight visible
hostages. They were to fire at the inmate "executioners" on the walkways at the first sign of an "overt, hostile act" toward the hostages. But
the riflemen were left to decide for themselves when to fire—when
such an "overt, hostile act" had occurred. They could distinctly hear
one of the hostages screaming repeatedly, "I don't want to die. . . . I
don't want to die!" The inmates on the walkways and in D-yard were
shouting, too—abuse at the troopers, threats to the hostages, defiance at

the world. Over the walkway from Times Square to D-block, a black liberation flag unfurled slowly in the misty morning air.[21]

"I can't stand this silence," Bob Garcia said suddenly in the Stewards' Room. "Let's talk!"

On the walkway at Times Square, one of the blindfolded hostages, Ronald Kozlowski, a civilian accounts clerk before the revolt, sat on a crate expecting to be killed, his back arched and his throat tight at the touch of something he could not quite identify. One of his captors asked if he was nervous. Kozlowski said he was. The inmate gave him a Tum and said it would all be over soon. Another inmate, standing behind the hostages, began to comb Kozlowski's hair. He said he wanted Kozlowski to "die pretty."

"But why me?" Kozlowski asked.

"Because you're white," an inmate said.[22]

Down in D-yard, in the remaining circle of hostages, Captain Pappy Wald thought he smelled gasoline. He knew he felt the point of a knife in his neck. The light drizzle was still falling, and Wald's Black Muslim guard, holding the knife to his neck, said, "As long as there is rain, it promotes life and growth and, also, it's a good day for death."[23]

About then, John Dunne was telling the other observers that they all had to expect to testify before his committee and other bodies later on; they had to be available to make the record. A corrections official entered and said that the inmates had made no response to Oswald but had taken hostages to the roof of Times Square, apparently for execution. The observers were ordered out of the institution by the commissioner—except for Dunne, who was asked to join Oswald and other state officials. Still, no one made a move to go, and the official left without saying more. Dunne followed him.

On the third floor of A-block, General O'Hara, ready to give the crucial signal, was discovering that his two-way radio would not work. This annoyance may have been one reason why he failed to notice 11 corrections officers in uniform, 10 of them with rifles and shotguns, the other holding a submachine gun, all ready to fire from the third-floor corridor. They had not been told that Rockefeller had ordered corrections officers not to take part in the assault. O'Hara finally borrowed a working radio from a trooper and ordered the helicopter gas drop that would set off the general attack.[24]

At 9:43:28 the sweep second hand of the big electric clock on the wall of the Stewards' Room stopped moving. Most of the observers noticed that at once, as if the clock had made a loud noise. The prison power circuit had been turned off.

"That's it," Alfredo Mathew said.

Then they heard the helicopter rise from the parking lot and pass overhead, toward D-yard.

Many of the inmates in the yard had worked themselves into something of a frenzy in anticipation of what some of their leaders were calling "war." There was much shouting and milling about. But suddenly the commotion in the yard "just died out." An inmate turned around and saw troopers standing up on the roofs of A- and C-blocks, "each one carrying a rifle with a telescope. I started walking back toward my people and then I saw a helicopter go up and begin to circle. . . ."[25]

It was 9:46 A.M. In his "command post," Russell Oswald heard a voice crackle on the police radio, "Jackpot One has made the drop." Captain Henry Williams's voice followed immediately, "Move in. Move in."[26]

A choking cloud of CS gas fell abruptly over D-yard. On the roofs of A- and C-blocks, the crouching riflemen were intently peering through their gas-mask eyeholes at the inmates on the catwalks; the riflemen were alert for any hint of "overt, hostile" action toward the hostages. As the gas came down, reaching the walkway quickly, both inmates and hostages instinctively moved downward. Several inmates dropped to the floor, pulling hostages down with them. These movements were taken by some of the tensely watching marksmen to be overt and hostile. A shot rang out from a rooftop post . . . a second . . . then a barrage, as the rifle units on the roofs and at the third-floor windows generally opened fire. (Roger Champen thought "it was a cannister exploding in the atmosphere, but they were shooting at us.") Almost at the moment the firing began, the assault units moved out on A- and C-walkways. They fired, too. In the enclosed A- and C-tunnels beneath them, the other two attacking forces advanced, laying down heavy fire. From the moment Jackpot One dropped the gas until all the attack units were firing, only a few seconds elapsed. "Suddenly the helicopter dipped and released the tear gas," an inmate said. "When I turned around to see where the helicopter was, the crossfire began."[27]

On the walkways during those first few seconds, four hostages suffered neck or throat wounds inflicted by inmates. Corrections Officer Frank Kline was cut severely enough to require 52 stitches. Ron Kozlowski also was seriously hurt. Neither wound was fatal. Both men heard the gunfire a split second *before* they felt the knives.

"Bullets were everywhere, chipping concrete," Kozlowski said. The other two hostages whose throats were injured—John D'Archangelo and John Monteleone—sustained only minor knife wounds but were killed by the rifle fire—one by a trooper's .270 and the other by a bullet from the personal rifle of one of the corrections officers who had not been seen by General O'Hara on the third floor of A-block. Nine inmates were killed on the walkway by the same burst of rifle fire; three of these also were hit by shotgun pellets from the advancing assault units. One inmate stood motionless at a corner of Times Square, five yards from the nearest hostage, until he was fatally struck by a .270 slug 40 seconds after the first shot was fired.* Everybody else near the hostages was down within 30 seconds. One hostage was critically wounded by a rifled slug, and 12 inmates were wounded by rifle or shotgun fire. The inmates had threatened to kill the hostages, so when the troopers and corrections officers loosed their barrage on what they believed to be the "executioners" on the walkway, "they were all mowed down like wheat on top of that crosswalk." When a trooper in one of the assault units got his first look at the area near Times Square, he saw that "the first volley cleared everybody off their feet."[28]

The firing could not be heard in the Stewards' Room after all. Except for the faraway roar of the circling helicopter, it was quiet there. For a few minutes after the power went off, few spoke. Then eyes began to smart and run; gas was coming in around the loose window frames. The observers began pulling out handkerchiefs, coughing, trying to get away from the gas. The guard outside, seeing through the glass panel of the door what was going on (they had not, after all, pulled the heavy cabinet across the door), came in and spoke politely.

He was sorry, but he'd been told there were not enough gas masks for the observers; he didn't have one himself. They should button their shirts to the throat, to avoid possible burns, sit on the floor against the walls, wet their handkerchiefs—he provided a pitcher of water—and hold them to their faces, being careful not to swallow any of the moisture. He did not know what was happening in D-yard.

"What is it?" Bob Garcia said through the handkerchief. "Pepper or tear gas?"

The assault units advancing along the open walkways from A- and C-blocks toward Times Square, unlike the protected riflemen above them, knew they were vulnerable to thrown objects, bombs, Molotov cocktails, and hand-to-hand attacks with knives and clubs. Beneath the

---

* As shown by a state police film record.

gas masks and yellow rain gear that made them look like men from Mars, these attackers were tense, nervous. Like the other troopers, they had seen the hostages at Times Square, the "executioners" with knives, the black flag of "liberation" billowing in the mist above D-walkway. They were in physical danger and anxious for the hostages. ("You better believe they were scared," Roger Champen said. "You could see it in their faces.") They were "fired up" at the black radicals and killers they believed they were attacking. So they came down the walkways behind a curtain of fire from their shotguns and sidearms. Some fired because they thought they saw inmates charging them or other troopers. Some said they saw inmates throwing or about to throw spears, Molotov cocktails, stones, and bricks. Others reported inmates waving swords and brandishing knives. A tear-gas projectile, Major Monahan reported, was launched from behind the barricade on the A-walkway. Even so, 65 percent of the walkway assault troopers did not fire at all. The state police made photographic and videotape records of the attack. These records fail to record most of the acts of resistance the troopers thought or said they saw on the walkways and at the barricades. High state police officials watching from A-block saw no such resistance except for the tear-gas missile Major Monahan thought he saw. The photographic records show that one inmate was shot as he retreated from the barricade on A-walkway and that none of the inmates behind that barricade when the firing started had offered any resistance. The films also show that several troopers fired on the barricade before they reached it. An inmate at Times Square was hit with three rounds of buckshot from less than 15 feet away. Another suffered wounds from two sidearms fired at close range, one from in front of and one from behind him. Both died. Altogether, five inmates died on the walkways from the fire of the assault parties. Three others, probably killed by rifle fire from the rooftops, were hit by shotgun pellets, too. Numerous other inmates were wounded on the walkways, some seriously. But the fire laid down on A- and C-walkways enabled the troopers to clear the barricades and move quickly on to Times Square where six hostages were still alive. Frank Kline, his throat cut and bleeding copiously, heard someone say, "This is an officer," and knew he was safe. A trooper found and rescued Ron Kozlowski just as "the gas got bad, real bad." The attackers pressed on. Three minutes after Jackpot One dropped the gas, troopers were looking down from B- and D- walkways into D-yard itself. The firing had been continuous.[29]

The gas was bad in the Stewards' Room, too, although after some minutes it began to diminish. It made Tom Wicker, sitting in a corner

Left to right, Tom Wicker, Dick Edwards, and Rudy Garcia, at news conference outside prison, Sunday, September 12.

(*NY Times / William E. Sauro*)

Commissioner Russell G. Oswald, Monday morning, September 13, after the assault. (*Wide World*)

Minutes before police assault, Monday, September 13. Inmates hold hostages blindfolded at knife-point on catwalks.

Minutes after the assault, dead and wounded lying on catwalk.

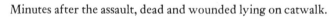

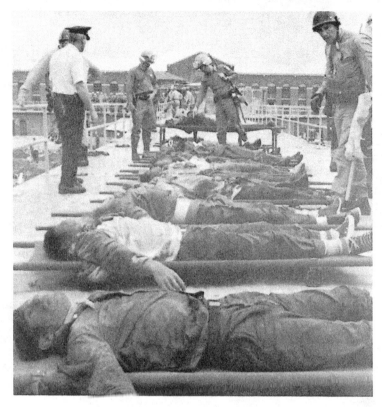

State police lining up dead for identification.

Hostage area in D-yard. Troopers have just arrived, and surviving hostages are identifying other hostages and inmates who protected them.

Troopers on catwalk lining up inmates by trench dug by inmates.

Police make inmates lie down before stripping and searching them.

Trooper and guard collecting weapons among debris of D-yard.
(Wide World)

Stripped inmates, in lines ready for running through tunnels back to their cells.

Personal property swept out by police before the prisoners were put back in their cells.

A row of Attica cells. Inmates are locked in from 5:00 P.M. until 7:00 A.M. every day.
(*Cornell Capa*)

away from the windows, his wet handkerchief pressed to his face, remember walking through smashed and looted stores in downtown Washington, along streets littered with glass and debris from the "Martin Luther King riots" that had followed King's assassination. The great urban riots of the '60s had mostly ended three years before, and no one had learned anything. No one had done anything. Or so Wicker thought that morning in the Stewards' Room, bitterly reflecting that society might even have gone backward since the heady days of the civil rights movement that King had symbolized—a movement that had been as badly mauled in the riots as any of the cities where they took place.

But it was not just that racial and economic injustice and black grievances lingered on or were worse. No one who could do anything about it seemed to have learned that shooting and killing, however effective at the moment, provided a solution to nothing. They did not answer the problems of Attica any more than they had answered the anger of the ghetto. Violent imposition of "law and order" did not end the threat to society inherent in its unjust and exploitative nature. How deep would the blood have to run in the streets before anything was done about what G.I. Paris had chokingly called "the conditions"? Or would the shooting just go on, as at Orangeburg and Detroit and Kent State and Augusta and Jackson State, intermittently, indiscriminately—as he imagined it to be going on at that moment in D-yard—until no one was left but men with guns?

He could hear no firing. He did not have to. He could hear Jaybarr Kenyatta weeping, his head down on his arms at one of the desks. Kenyatta might be a ludicrous figure in his robes and rug, a menace in his revolutionary views, but he could weep for his brothers, if not for the whole human race. Wicker could hear, too, the dim, deep bullhorn echo of a faraway voice beating through the sound of the helicopter: ". . . top of your heads . . . not be harmed . . . hands on top of your . . . not be harmed . . ." The bullhorn voice went on and on, like Kenyatta's sobs.

"Well . . ." Herman Badillo said. He was sitting on the floor next to Wicker and had momentarily removed the handkerchief from his lined and shadowed face. Badillo could cry, too. "We did all we could," Badillo said.

Wicker was not sure about that. He had not spoken in D-yard the afternoon before. But that was his to live with, not Badillo's. He had not found the amnesty formula, but at least that had not been for lack of trying. Badillo's statement seemed somehow self-serving, although Wicker knew it was not meant to be. No doubt they would all need a

lot of reassurance for a long time to come. Still holding his handkerchief to his face, he nodded at Badillo.

". . . hands on your heads . . . you will not be harmed. . . ."

Major Monahan, closely following his assault force along the
A-walkway, heard shooting off to his right from the third floor of
A-block, slightly behind and above him. These were not shots he could
"attribute to any detail" in his attack plan. They were from the eleven
corrections officers who had taken station there, although Monahan did
not know it. If he had known corrections officers were firing, in
addition to his trooper marksmen, he would not have ventured out on
the walkway, because he "was contemplating retirement." The unidentified shooting caused him to order all firing from the cellblocks to be
halted.[30]

The rooftop and third-floor riflemen had not been supposed to fire
into D-yard—only to protect the hostages on the walkways and to
provide covering fire for the walkway assault parties. But the riflemen
on C-block roof did not get the word, or did not heed it. They fired at
least 12 rounds of .270 slugs into the milling mass of men in D-yard,
mostly at inmates they thought were running in the direction of the
hostage circle. Riflemen on A-block roof—including three corrections
officers, one of whom had been accepted as a part of the state police
marksmen's unit—said they did not fire into D-yard at all. But more
rounds of rifle fire were poured into the yard than the C-block riflemen reported. That fire killed three hostages and at least three inmates.
It wounded another hostage. Nineteen inmates who were wounded
inside D-yard were hit during the first rounds of shooting, when only
the rooftop and third-floor riflemen were in position to have fired into
the yard. Two dead inmates were found so near the B-tunnel wall that
they could only have been hit by the A-roof riflemen (see prison
maps) who said they did not fire into D-yard. The third inmate killed
was Elliot "L. D." Barkley, aged 21, convicted once of a minor check
forgery, paroled, returned to Attica for driving without a license.
Barkley was hit in the back in the first minute of the attack by a
tumbling .270 slug, probably a ricochet, and died quickly, not far from
the spot where he had proclaimed to the world "the sound before the
fury of those who are oppressed."[31]

Tearful from the gas and incredulously aware that men were dying
violently a few hundred feet from where he huddled against the wall
of the Stewards' Room, Wicker remembered a nigger who had shot
and killed Chief John Fallaw of the Hamlet, North Carolina police
force many years before. The nigger had been thought to be a dope
fiend. He fled into the woods and many of the men of the town (not

including D. D. Wicker, who was away on a run to Cayce) formed an armed posse and went hunting. Early the next day, they surrounded the nigger and riddled his body with dozens of bullets. The body was thrown into the trunk of a police car and driven to town, passing along Hamlet Avenue. One arm trailed along the pavement. Avid with youth, young Tom Wicker had raced to the police station to view the dead nigger. The wounds and the blood on the body shocked and sickened him. As he turned away, the thought rose unbidden in his mind *like cherry on chocolate.*

He had later written a melodramatic novel about the manhunt and the dead nigger. But in the Stewards' Room, his handkerchief over his face against the gas, he realized that he had known nothing of blood and death. It was still like cherry on chocolate in his sheltered life.

Once the assault parties were past Times Square and commanded the walkways to B- and D-blocks, running along two sides of D-yard, the rescue details could put their ladders down among the inmates thrashing about in the gray cloud of gas. Aided by the damp weather, the gas lay close to the muddy ground. It was CS gas, which causes extreme eye-burning, a heavy flow of tears, choking and coughing, stinging, some dizziness, possibly nausea. CS gas can incapacitate most people within 60 seconds.[32]

Three to four minutes after it had been dropped into D-yard, by the time the troopers went down the ladders, most of the inmates in the yard were gagging and weeping, largely blinded and in poor shape to use whatever weapons they had. Many were trying to follow the surrender demands from the helicopter and had their hands on top of their heads. Lieutenant Joseph Christian, leading a rescue detail, was among the first down the ladders. He and the men coming down behind him dashed straight across the yard, leaping the trenches and "foxholes" the inmates had dug, toward the hostage area near the handball backboard. Christian saw an inmate who appeared to be assaulting a hostage, although it was difficult to tell similarly clad hostages and inmates apart in the rain and the gas cloud and the general melee, particularly with the gas masks inhibiting the troopers' vision. Christian nevertheless ran bravely ahead of his companions, aiming to stop the inmate he believed to be attacking the hostages. Tommy Hicks, an inmate, saw Christian coming alone and went after him with a club. The trooper went down from the blow, falling on top of his shotgun to keep it from being taken from him. More than a dozen other troopers, many of them on the walkways above D-yard, saw Christian fall. Several fired at Hicks and other inmates who appeared to be closing in on Christian. Hicks was fatally hit by five buckshot pellets, all fired from as far away as the walkways. Christian was hit by two pellets, in the arm and leg.[33]

There was more shooting from the walkways, in addition to the hail of fire over Christian into the vicinity of the hostage circle. At least 31 shotgun and pistol rounds were fired from the walkways down into the choking mass of men in D-yard—men to whom the firing troopers attributed various acts of resistance. The firing from the walkways continued over several minutes and resulted, as far as can be ascertained, in the deaths of five hostages who were in the circle where they had been held captive. Sergeant Edward Cunningham, who had warned of a "My Lai massacre" in his interview with Wicker the day before, was shot in the head and killed. Each of the five dead hostages was hit by three or fewer buckshot pellets, suggesting the shots had been fired from a distance. Other than Tommy Hicks, no inmate is known to have been killed by fire coming down from the walkways, but many, in every part of the yard, were wounded by that fire.[34]

Minister Raymond Scott, huddled with the observers, suddenly struck the wall of the Stewards' Room with his fist. The blow, suggesting the frustration of men who had tried to stop what they knew must be happening in D-yard, seemed to give the observers their voices again.

If only Rockefeller had come, Arthur Eve said sadly, slowly.

"Just to show he *cared* about what's going on up here," Wicker said. He had been thinking, as the long minutes dragged by, how little effort actually had been made to solve the central problem of amnesty. Oswald had made a phone call to Louis James, a small-town D.A. with no real power; three observers had visited James; Rockefeller's lawyers had looked up the state constitution; Oswald had promised no "administrative" reprisals. That was all. No urgent, high-level meetings; no expert committees with learned staff assigned to find a formula; not so much mediation and consultation as would have been devoted to a minor labor dispute.

If he had it to do over again, Wicker thought, before the state shut off the observers' telephone, he would get on the phone to Theodore Kheel, the lawyer–mediator in New York, or Edward Bennett Williams, the famous defense lawyer in Washington, or to Arthur Goldberg, another great mediator—no, Goldberg had been Rockefeller's last gubernatorial opponent and wouldn't do. But he would call someone, anyone, who could sit at a table with others in a quiet law office somewhere and work out a compromise arrangement, the kind of compromise arrangement that was worked out every day, every hour, in every kind of situation, when interests conflicted and men wanted compromise.

But Wicker did not have it to do over again; and anyway, why had it been up to him, or to Arthur Eve, or even Russell Oswald? Had the state and its governor no responsibility to find a way to avoid violence? Why was an amnesty solution at Attica not as important as a deal with some mayor on state aid to his municipality—a deal to which infinitely more time, thought, and effort would be given than had been given to the demands of the D-yard brothers?

"If he had come," Bill Gaiter said, "showed he cared—that could have made all the difference, couldn't it?"

Overhead, the helicopter roared by in its unceasing circle. At the desk, Kenyatta wept.

Gas fired into the tunnels toward Times Square made impossible any effective resistance in such close quarters; most inmates cleared out of the tunnels rapidly. When the attack began, at least six were in A-tunnel, along which so many fruitless negotiating missions had passed. They ran out of the same door the observers had used, into the wet gas cloud spilling over into A-yard, and were immediately spotted by troopers advancing along the walkway above them. These troopers variously said they saw Molotov cocktails, a spear, and an unidentified object about to be thrown; one said he saw inmates trying to climb from A-yard up to the A-walkway to get at the troopers. No one other than these troopers saw any of this hostile activity. The troopers on the walkway fired a number of times at the inmates running into A-yard from A-tunnel. One inmate was killed by buckshot and three were wounded.[35]

The attack parties in the tunnels soon flanked D-yard in B- and D-tunnels. An inmate saw them rushing out into D-yard to join the rescue parties who had descended the ladders—"about 35 altogether, with hand guns, shotguns, and a gas dispenser that looked like a flame thrower." By then, D-yard was full of masked, helmeted, and booted troopers in raingear; overhead, the helicopter boomed down its repetitious message (in English only), "Put your hands on top of your head . . . you will not be harmed." The troopers were taking no chances. They fired when they saw what appeared to be resistance. They fired at places where resistance might develop. They fired warning shots. They fired from considerable distances. They fired at close range. "A trooper would run up with a gun in his hand and rip aside the blanket covering a tent, and another trooper would saturate the entire tent with shotgun pellets." Two inmates were shot while they crouched in a trench; a single shotgun blast put one buckshot pellet in the heel of one of them, and eight buckshot into the inner thigh of the other, who bled to death. At least 39 rounds were fired within D-yard—not counting those from the walkways and from the roofs and upper floors of A- and C-blocks. At least 390 lethal buckshot pellets fanned out and crisscrossed in the mass of inmates, in the cloud of gas, in the slow drizzle, among the screaming men scrambling and grovelling in the mud.[36]

Herman Badillo took his wet handkerchief from his face and looked at Wicker, then past him at nothing. "There's always time to die," he said. "I don't know what the rush was."

About five minutes after the assault began, an investigator for the State Police Bureau of Criminal Investigation (BCI) reached Times Square from C-block. He was not part of the attacking force, but while observing the scene in D-yard he was handed a shotgun to keep for a trooper who had descended a ladder into the yard.

The BCI agent, holding the shotgun and overlooking the yard through the cloud of gas enveloping it, saw a man moving behind a crude bunker of fertilizer bags stacked against the wall of the passageway between Times Square and D-block. The agent lifted his gas mask long enough to shout at the man in the bunker to stand still. When the man moved again, the agent saw what he took to be a Molotov cocktail in his hand; the agent lifted the shotgun and put a single rifled slug into the man's chest. So died Sam Melville, whose skill at bombmaking had been so feared by the prison authorities. In the bunker with his body were several Molotov cocktails.[37]

Six minutes after Jackpot One dropped its load of CS gas over D-yard, the firing stopped. To most of the D-yard brothers it had seemed like hours. At the end, they lay in the mud of their stronghold, dead, wounded, bleeding, choking, and crying from gas, shock, pain, and fear. Most had offered no physical resistance. The vast majority had started surrendering as soon as the helicopter blared its message. D- and C-blocks were not completely cleared out until after 10:30 A.M.—without gunfire—and some peripheral buildings still had to be searched and cleared. But by 9:52 A.M., the battle was essentially over. Two hostages, Kline and Kozlowski, had been seriously injured by inmates; several other hostages had suffered minor injuries from inmates. Ten hostages were dead or dying, 29 inmates were dead or dying, three hostages, 85 inmates, and one trooper had been wounded—all by guns in the hands of state police and corrections officers.[38]

At 10:17, Norbert Woods, a corrections department official, came to the Stewards' Room to report that 22 hostages had been rescued but that some had had their throats cut. He could not say if any were dead. At 10:24, Wicker and Badillo saw corrections officers or troopers—it was hard to tell them apart in their raingear—begin to launch gas

cannisters from the inner walkway near the top of the great outer wall
of the prison toward a building near D-block. At 10:25, Tepper, at the
other window, saw Oswald cross the littered, crowded open space
between the administration building and the main entrance; he was
going to announce the victory to the press, although the observers did
not know that or even that the fighting was over.

By then, Tepper could see bodies being brought out on stretchers,
other men being helped along, still others with bloody clothes and
bandages—presumably rescued or wounded hostages. Woods came
back at 10:28 to say that 27 hostages were out and two were known to
be dead. Three minutes later, he was back again—the count had gone
to 30 safe and five dead. The five had been killed by the inmates, he
said. Woods had no figures on inmate casualties, but could say that
D-yard was "secured."

"We warned 'em," he said. "We *told* 'em."

By 10:10, less than half an hour after the first shot, the D-yard
brothers—those alive and able to walk or even crawl—were being
herded by the troopers toward the door leading through D-tunnel to
A-yard, the same door through which the observers had first been led
two by two nearly three days before. The brothers were required to
clasp their hands behind their necks, and they had to make their way
through the mud and the debris of the uprising and the attack, with
bodies lying all about and the remnants of the gas clinging in the damp
air. Most were still weeping and choking as they went up the steps,
across the tunnel, and down the four concrete steps into A-yard.
There, the corrections officers took over—in charge again, after four
days of frustration and anger. Numerous state troopers joined them in
the process of returning the inmates to the cells. The inmates were
pushed, kicked, or ordered to drop face down onto the muddy ground.
When the area around the steps began to pile up with prone, shivering
inmates, they were ordered to crawl—face down, hands still behind
the neck—farther into A-yard.

People were laying on the ground and as soon as you made any
movement to put your hands over your head, wham! I didn't
want to move until I was told to move. I waited for a trooper to
approach me with his automatic rifle and tell me, "Spic, get up!"
. . . Anybody who could stand, wounded or not, was made to
walk and led into another yard where about 50 troopers armed
with shotguns and rifles made us crawl on our bellies. The ground
was cold and wet, with a fine mist coming down. It was like
driving cattle. People were crawling over each other, and the

troopers were driving them with sticks, saying, "Crawl, you motherfuckers, crawl, crawl." We'd crawl this way and that, until all of us were in the yard.[39]

Dr. John C. Cudmore of the National Guard, entering A-yard at 10:25, observed corrections officers systematically clubbing inmates to the ground. Some were shoved or kicked down the steps as they came out of D-tunnel; one inmate suffered a broken leg as a result. "Start crawling, you white niggerlover," a guard or a trooper told one inmate. "Put your nose to the ground. If it comes up, your head comes off."[40]

The prone inmates farthest from the door were ordered, in small groups, to stand up and strip. Not just clothes, but religious medals, eyeglasses, and false teeth had to be removed in preparation for body searches. The corrections officers with their clubs had a special pre-occupation with the inmates' watches. Some they smashed on the inmates' wrists; some they tossed up in the air and hit like fungoes; some they threw on the ground and stomped. Dr. Cudmore saw one inmate selected from a line and severely beaten, for no reason the doctor could see. He had to stop another corrections officer from clubbing an inmate whose bleeding head the doctor was treating. A National Guardsman helping to carry out a wounded man was unable to stop several troopers from hitting the inmate with their clubs while he lay on a stretcher. The inmate screamed, and a trooper shouted, "Fuck you, nigger, you should have gotten it in the head!" Another trooper, however, attempted to stop corrections officers from beating inmates, and one of the corrections officers replied, "You don't understand what happened. Some of these men [hostages] were disembowelled, and they were abused sexually."[41]

A trooper who was in A-yard for an hour and a half after the attack ended saw not a single corrections supervisor in the yard during that period. The return of the inmates to their cells was left entirely to rank-and-file guards and to the troopers who joined them.[42]

At 10:35, Julian Tepper, looking out the window of the Stewards' Room toward the main entrance of the prison, said in a flat, tired voice, "I can see eight bodies on the ground dead." Wicker did not look.

A minute later, Tepper reported that a National Guard truck was being brought up for the removal of the bodies. By 10:40, four ambulances also were on hand outside the administration building.

"There's a black dead guy out there they didn't load," Tepper said. Then, after long silence, "My God. They picked up that dead guy.

About four feet. Then they dropped him. There's not even anything over his face."

Norbert Woods returned at 11 A.M. All 38 hostages were accounted for, he said. Twelve were dead. General O'Hara had said that all was secure in the institution.

"He's moving," Tepper said, still looking out the window. "The guy they dropped isn't even dead."

The recapture of the prison had scarcely been accomplished before the rumor spread among the corrections officers and troopers that one of the hostages had been castrated. As John Dunne heard it in Russell Oswald's command post—from a reporting officer, before 11 A.M.—the mutilated hostage had been found on the walkway with his testicles in his mouth. The mutilated bodies of two inmates, Schwartz and Privitiera,* were discovered at about 11:25, adding fuel to the rumors of atrocities committed by the inmates.[43]

The very real throat slashes suffered by Kline and Kozlowski, as well as the minor throat wounds sustained by two hostages killed by gunfire, had been observed by numerous guards and troopers. The inmates' rhetorical threats and their action in taking eight hostages to Times Square just before the attack began had conditioned everyone—even the most sympathetic of the observers—to the point of easy belief in the reports that the hostages' throats had been cut. In the prevailing atmosphere, even the atrocity stories seemed believable.

So the corrections officers, who had been officially deemed too emotionally involved to have a part in the recapture of the prison although nothing had been done to stop them from taking part, were excited, angry, shocked, and vengeful by the time they began taking charge of the inmates in A-yard. No corrections or other state official seems to have questioned whether they were also too emotionally involved for this responsibility. And since only the 540 cells in A-block were available or in condition to house the recaptured inmates,[44] they all had to be concentrated in one area, easy targets for physical reprisal.

A long snakelike line of naked inmates, many of them beaten, shocked, and still affected by the gas, was formed from A-yard to the door into the tunnel leading to A-block. From that door, to what had once been No Man's Land, numerous corrections officers stationed themselves on either side of the littered passageway. They all had clubs, banging them on brick walls and concrete floors and steel bars. As each inmate ran or stumbled by, with his hands behind his head, the corrections officers, public employes of the state of New York, agents

---

* See note 4, chapter 10, supra.

of law enforcement, hit him with their clubs. If he took his hands down, he was stopped and beaten in place. If he fell, they took turns hitting him while he was down. Shouts of "nigger" and "mother-fucker" rang through the echoing corridor. One guard chased one inmate all down the line, hitting him as he ran. John Dunne, being taken by Dunbar on a tour of the recaptured prison, came into the No Man's Land area at about 11 A.M. and saw naked inmates running the A-tunnel gauntlet.

"Walter, I see something I shouldn't be seeing," he said, "and it had better stop right away."

Dunbar ordered the gauntlet stopped, but inmates said it was resumed when the officials departed. Dunbar had no later memory, however, of having seen or stopped the gauntlet. No action was taken to discipline any officers by Oswald or Mancusi, neither of whom observed the rehousing of the inmates and both of whom spent most of Monday in Mancusi's office. Deputy Superintendents Vincent and Karl Pfeil observed some of the rehousing, but said they saw no reprisals.[45]

Oswald conceded that there had been beatings, but considered the A-tunnel gauntlet "more in the manner of an old fraternity hazing" which he "could . . . understand."[46]

At 11:29, Woods came to the Stewards' Room to say that only nine hostages were dead, after all. At least nine inmates were dead, too, and there had been many wounded.

There was not much talk in the room after that. Eighteen dead, Wicker thought. At least 18. It really had been a massacre. The observers really had been right. But what good did that do anyone?

Kenyatta had long since stopped weeping and sat motionless at the desk, his red-rimmed eyes staring at the floor. "You ain't seen nothin'," Wicker thought he heard him mumble. "Not yet."

Arthur Eve talked again of the necessity for outsiders to keep coming back to the prison, particularly those who lived nearby. Wicker agreed with the principle, but he never wanted to set foot in Attica again if he could help it.

"I was amazed at Kent State," Bill Gaiter said, to no one in particular, his voice calm but ringing in the silence of the room. "Shocked by Jackson State. But this . . . to see a decision being formulated that leads to so many deaths . . . I don't believe I'll ever forget this."

When inmates emerged from the A-tunnel gauntlet, they found more corrections officers, joined by some troopers, waiting for them on the stairs and cell tiers of A-block. The beatings were resumed as the men were shoved, dragged, and in some cases thrown into cells. One inmate saw another, scared and crying, who refused to come into a cell tier. "Come on, nigger, your day ain't over yet!" a trooper yelled, taking the sobbing inmate by the hair and lifting him off his feet. He threw the inmate to the floor, kicked him in the stomach, and dragged him into a cell. A corrections officer saw another trooper in A-block pick up a guitar from a pile of inmates' belongings. An inmate ran past and the trooper broke the guitar over his head, driving the inmate to his knees, to much laughter from the other agents of the law on that tier. When National Guardsmen brought an inmate wounded in the legs into A-block on a stetcher, a corrections officer showed him a Phillips screwdriver and said to the wounded man, "If you don't get moving—if you don't get up on your feet you are going to get this right up your ass." But the wounded man could not get up. Before the Guardsmen could stop him, the correctional officer "did stick this man in the anal area five or six times," until the wounded inmate managed to crawl away toward a cell.[47]

These cells had been prepared for new tenants. All personal gear—pictures, books, hobby equipment, musical instruments, clothes—of former occupants had been removed from them and piled in the corridors. Then it was taken to the prison dump and buried.[48] Roger Champen's meager law library was discovered and destroyed.[49]

Frank Smith, Big Black, had been identified during the strip search in A-yard as one of the inmate leaders. In the mysterious way of rumors, he soon was "identified" also as the man who had castrated a hostage. Smith was marked on the back with a chalked "X," as were other suspected leaders. He was made to lie on his back across a recreational table, and a football was placed under his chin. He was told that if the football fell he would be killed. That was between 10 and 11 A.M. At about 2 P.M., legislators being given an official tour of the institution by Walter Dunbar saw Smith still lying on the table with the football under his chin. Dunbar told the legislators Smith had castrated a hostage.[50]

Later in the day, Smith was taken to Housing Block Z, "the box," with other X-rated inmates suspected of having been leaders of the uprising. There, a National Guardsman, inadvertently opening a door, saw Smith lying naked on the floor while five or six corrections officers beat him with clubs.[51] Other inmates taken to HBZ ran still a third gauntlet of officers with clubs outside and inside the building and on the stairs to the third-floor cells. Since the men taken to HBZ were suspected leaders—although in many cases they had not been leaders at all—the beatings they sustained appear to have been frequent and severe.[52]

"They went crazy in that place," Champen recalled. "There were three of us in one cell . . . but that wasn't enough to them. They came by and stuck guns through the bars and said 'this is a correction officer.' I do recall a state trooper came by and told them to get away from the door because they were hysterical. . . . But they stuck the guns through the bars and in some cases a guy was putting empty shotgun shells through, saying, 'I shot at you, I don't know how I missed you.' "[53]

Smoking his pipe as usual, Walter Dunbar came to the Stewards' Room at 12:16 P.M. The observers should know, he said, that "Operation Go to recover the institution" had been launched, according to his watch, at 9:48 A.M. He had been on the walkways until the gas became too bad; then he had observed the action from enclosed corridors. Although there was still some minor resistance—some inmates were still to be cleared from D-block and the schoolhouse—he could say that the institution had been secured. As a former naval officer, he also could say that Operation Go had been carried out "with precision and excellent coordination" between state police, local sheriff's departments, and fire departments. The National Guard had been used mostly for medical care. A chopper had circled over the prison, promising no harm to those who surrendered. The state police and the corrections officers had handled the surrendering inmates "with excellent discipline and without brutality," even though the observers would understand that the emotional tension was great. The inmates, of course, had been made to sit or lie with their hands behind their heads, and had been grouped in A-yard for return to A-block.

The large majority of the inmates had not been wounded or killed, Dunbar said, puffing his pipe. A preliminary coroner's report showed that about seven to 12 hostages were dead, and maybe 23 to 28 inmates. Some hostages and more inmates had been wounded.

No, he was sorry, it was not yet possible for the observers to go into the yards or cellblocks.

Dr. Selden Williams, Jr., the senior but part-time prison physician, had arrived at the institution at 7:30 A.M. Someone—he is not sure who it was—instructed him to set up a first-aid station. He was not told there would be an armed attack, or what to do if there should be one, or how many casualties to expect, or what type of medication and equipment would be needed—even what arms might be used. He did not know that no procedure to evacuate the wounded had been arranged. Although he also did not know that the National Guard was coming with medical units, he did not set up an evacuation procedure.[54]

He learned soon enough that "they were going in," but Dr. Williams did nothing beyond the preparation of the first-aid station. "How could I know how many would be hurt?" he explained. "I had no way of knowing what would happen. Maybe the prisoners would give up at the last minute. Maybe there would be no injuries. So I thought it would be a waste of physician time to have a lot of doctors on hand."[55]

When Jackpot One's drop signalled the attack, Dr. Williams, his assistant, Dr. Paul G. Sternberg, two male nurses, an X-ray technician, two local veterinarians who had deserted the Lions' Club food station in the prison to volunteer their services, and three hospital orderlies and ambulance drivers from Batavia constituted the available medical force. There were no surgeons, no anesthesiologists, no litter bearers, no field hospital, no preparations in the 50-bed prison infirmary (which already was 80 percent filled), no preparations in its one operating room, no reserves of blood, plasma, or general anesthetics, no laboratory or technician to check blood types, and no realization of any of these deficiencies. The authorities knew the attack would be made with buckshot, rifled slugs, and .270 soft-lead bullets. They feared the inmates had bombs and zip guns and that they would cut the throats of the hostages. They claimed after the attack that it had resulted in fewer casualties than they had expected. They had the foresight to order additional leg irons for the recaptured inmates. But they made no preparations for medical care for anyone, including their own. Dr. James Bradley, the Corrections Department's chief of medical services, normally stationed at Dannemora, was told he was not needed at Attica, and never came. An Erie County Health Department official, at the prison only on a civil defense mission, not one of the state police or state corrections or state civil officials, told Dr. Williams to get all the hostages out of D-yard before moving any wounded inmates.[56]

New York National Guard units had been ordered to Attica, and the statewide Guard commander, General John C. Baker, had arrived at the prison on Sunday afternoon. He was not given a specific assignment, although General O'Hara had asked him if medical units would be available. General Baker said yes, but was given no idea of what would be needed. So an air ambulance unit in Buffalo was never called in, field hospitals were not set up in advance, and when Jackpot One dropped its choking gas, C Company of the 50th Medical Battalion, 27th Brigade, at the head of a convoy of 600 guardsmen en route from Buffalo, still was a quarter mile from the prison entrance. When they heard the shooting, C Company knew for the first time that its medics would have gunshot wounds to treat. By 10 A.M., the unit was inside the walls.[57]

The three Batavia hospital orderlies, entering the yard right after the attack began, had given crude first aid to wounded hostages and to Lieutenant Christian, all of whom had quickly been evacuated from the yard by troopers pressed into service as emergency stretcher bearers. Before the guardsmen arrived, and within 15 minutes of the last shot, every wounded or sick hostage was in an ambulance headed for Warsaw or Batavia. Drs. Williams and Sternberg, with the male nurses, the X-ray technician, and one of the veterinarians, also had entered D-yard briefly. None had supplies with which to treat the wounded, and the two doctors soon went to the prison infirmary to get it ready for treating casualties—a quarter hour after the shooting had ended. On reaching the infirmary, Dr. Williams put in the first call for help, to Dr. Worthington Schenk, chief of surgery at Meyer Memorial Hospital in Buffalo, an hour away.[58]

Dr. Cudmore, a Guard major but ordinarily a staff surgeon at Buffalo General Hospital, made his own way—without help from police or prison officials—to the "awesome sight" in D-yard where the inmate dead and wounded lay in the mud, some of them dying. He got a chain of Guard stretcher-bearers moving through A-yard and into D-yard for the evacuation of casualties there, treated several wounded inmates who had been herded with the rest into A-yard, and discovered eight to 12 severely wounded inmates who had been given first aid, moved to C-yard, and left unattended for over an hour. C Company's trained medics were sent to the prison hospital, and ordinary guardsmen were pressed into service as first-aid men and stretcher-bearers.[59]

> They were confronted by a scene of mass confusion. Dead and wounded lay everywhere, and many of the guardsmen had no instructions regarding which men to evacuate first. Their vision restricted and their breathing labored through the gas masks, they made their way through the rubble and placed the wounded on litters. . . . Each man had to be physically picked up off the ground, placed carefully on a stretcher and carried a distance of more than 300 yards to the prison hospital. Gaping gunshot wounds were something few of the guardsmen had seen before. Although fresh litter teams were deployed as long as the manpower lasted, some guardsmen returned to D-yard only minutes after recovering from fits of nausea induced by revulsion or exhaustion.[60]

At 1 P.M., after what seemed to him "a relative eternity," roughly three hours after the last shot, Dr. Cudmore made a complete check and found that all the wounded men had been evacuated from the yards and walkways. At about the same time, Dr. Schenk, with surgical teams and equipment from Buffalo, was setting up for business in the prison hospital and in the nearby E-block. The first surgery on wounded inmates could not be performed for another hour.[61]

The observers sat quietly in the Stewards' Room, in which faint traces of gas still lingered. They did not talk much. They could see frantic confusion in front of the administration building; the helicopters roared around; but the observers were no longer a part of things, if they ever really had been.

John Dunne came in at 1:05 P.M. He was close to weeping and clearly had been. Red-eyed, his voice weak and shaking, he leaned against the wall. He had toured as much of the prison as he could, he said. It was "completely under control," the inmate wounded had been taken out of the yards, the wounded hostages had been driven to local hospitals, and the recovered inmates were being locked up two to a cell in A-block and HBZ. Dunne stopped, gulped, looked at the floor.

There were 35 dead, he said. Eight hostages were dead. Twenty-seven inmates had been killed. Many others were in serious condition. The death toll could go higher.

Thirty-five dead. Standing alone, the words were shocking enough. Still, it was only a number. Wicker tried for a moment to think of 35 bodies. Then 35 faces. He tried to think of 35 lives. But he had no idea who had lived or perished in the D-yard carnage, or how. He did not know if the youth in the cotton gloves was dead. He did not know if Brother Phillip Shields had come through alive, or Blair McDonald, or Michael and Art Smith, or Pappy Wald, or Champ, or Big Black, or any of the faceless men who had been out there beyond the arm-linked security chain or in the hostage circle. There was no way to tell whether any of the people he had known in D-yard were living or dead.[62] There was only one flat and searing fact. Thirty-five dead.

Three days earlier, Tom Wicker had said to himself, looking at the hostages in D-yard, "Nobody gets killed." That had been his aim. That had been his promise to himself, never spoken to anyone else. That was what he had set out to achieve, with his gifts and his standing and the trust men placed in him. He looked at John Dunne's grief-lined face and at Arthur Eve's lowered head and at Kenyatta motionless behind the desk. At the window, Tepper maintained his vigil over the confusion outside. At Wicker's side, Herman Badillo slumped in exhaustion.

They had all failed. Thirty-five dead was evidence enough. Lew Steel, grimly hunched in a corner, could think what he would about inevitable class and racial forces colliding in D-yard. Obviously, there was much truth in that nightmare vision. But Wicker believed he had witnessed, had been part of, a profound human failure, too—a failure of understanding, of courage, of intelligence, above all a failure of the human spirit. He did not know how much of that failure was rightfully his alone to bear. But it was enough, he knew, enough for anyone.

In addition to the National Guard surgeons and those from Meyer Memorial Hospital in Buffalo, six doctors and several nurses from local hospitals, responding to a call from a public health official, went voluntarily to the prison early Monday afternoon. Some were shocked by what they found.

"There were inmates lying out there for hours without any kind of care," said Dr. Robert S. Jenks of Batavia. "There wasn't a pint of blood anywhere. It was inexcusable; they just didn't ask for it, because I know plenty was available. There are several blood banks around here and they could have gotten all they needed beforehand."[63] Dr. Murray Anderson from Meyer Memorial began keeping records on wounded inmates and their treatment. Nobody asked him to. Nobody asked for the records for seven months.[64]

By midafternoon, a reasonably effective hospital operation was going forward, despite the "chaotic circumstances" the arriving doctors had found and despite the corrections officers' unwillingness to help with the wounded and their hostility to some of the doctors. "While I was treating prisoners, one guard told me, 'Why do it? They're not people, they're animals,' " Dr. Jenks said.[65]

Only three operations could be undertaken at any one time, however, and many inmates in need of surgery did not get it until Tuesday. According to prison regulations, those requiring transfers to better facilities could only be taken to Meyer Memorial, an hour away. No one made an effort to suspend those regulations for the emergency. Other red-tape rules slowed to a crawl the sending of badly wounded inmates even to Meyer Memorial. The first ambulances did not leave Attica until after 4 P.M. or arrive at the hospital until about 5:30 P.M., more than seven hours after the shooting stopped. Only eight inmates were received at Meyer Memorial on September 13; in the next two days, 11 more were moved there. Dr. Anderson's records showed that 83 inmates were treated in one fashion or another for gunshot wounds, of which 20 to 25 were major wounds.[66] None of this medical care had been planned for, arranged, or supervised by the corrections, police, and civil officials who ordered the attack on D-yard. Nor was it for any deed or care of theirs that no inmate is known to have died because of delayed and inadequate medical care.[67]

After making his brief report to the observers, John Dunne had taken Badillo, Eve, and Garcia to Oswald's command post in Mancusi's office. At 1:14 P.M., the four came back to the Stewards' Room. No one else was to be admitted to the prison, they said. They, as elected officials, were to be given a guided tour of the institution and would be able to report their findings. Everyone else in the Stewards' Room had been "requested" to leave the prison—and this time, Oswald meant it. The state police would provide transportation to the Buffalo airport.

So the observers pulled themselves up from the floor and out of the few chairs, gathered together their jackets, notes, and other belongings, and stumbled out of the room where they had come together nearly three days before, where they had wrangled and wept and fought and talked and waited and hoped and failed. Wicker did not look back at the Stewards' Room. He did not look back at the prison, either, as he came out of the Gothic entrance for the last time, under the overhanging wall that shut out an unknowing world. No prison or state official saw them off. Corrections officers and troopers paid them no mind. The observers were no longer in the way.

Reporters, however, crowded around them as they made their way across the parking lot to the waiting police cars. Clarence Jones, who had stood all that morning in the rain and heard the six minutes of firing from faraway D-yard, fell in with them. He and Wicker clasped hands briefly. They got into the same police car, but before Wicker could close the door, the familiar figure of Gabe Pressman, the New York television reporter, blocked it. Pressman held a microphone near Wicker's face and asked for his reaction to what had happened. It was a fair question, the usual question. In other circumstances, Wicker had asked it himself of dozens of shocked or dazed or bewildered people. It wrenched him from the prison world into the ordinary cruelties of life. The one reality began to fade, as reality does, into the next. He tried to order his words professionally:

> As an individual, speaking for myself . . . I suppose many other people . . . I think any event in which 35 people are dead is. . . .[68]

Several voices from the crowd of reporters around Pressman informed him that there were 37 dead.

> Is it 37? Whatever the figures are . . . any event of that kind can only be termed . . . can only be termed a tragedy . . . ah . . . any event of that kind, one is certain . . . you just feel that somehow all of us who were involved should have avoided it. Some way we should have found some way not . . . not to have 37 people dead.

The chorus of voices wanted to know, in simultaneous questions, if Rockefeller could have avoided it.

> I'm not going to comment on that at this point, not either as an individual or as a member, because we're all in the grip of emotions, we're all tired. I'm not going to make anything . . . I'm not going to say anything.

Pressman got the next question in ahead of the reporters around him: "I gather you feel that this was unnecessary?"

> I think any event of this kind when 37 people are killed is unnecessary . . . but I'm not saying it's unnecessary by somebody's . . . dereliction. I just don't know. . . . I'm expressing regret, not making an accusation.

So he was a moderate to the end. He could not be sure where the fault lay, how much in men, how much in systems. He did not know what might have been done. But he could not see himself, or Oswald, or Nelson Rockefeller, the dead hostages, the brothers cut down in the mud of D-yard, as the helpless pawns of relentless forces.

As the police car pulled out of the parking lot and wound down the hill, past Mancusi's white Georgian house and the booted and armed men at the road block, through the town of Attica, and on to the bleak road to Buffalo, he was not even angry. He was just tired, but not too tired to be professional again. He calculated that if he could catch a midafternoon plane to LaGuardia, he could make his first edition deadline.

But he knew there would have to be a time for anger.

Afterwards

The death toll at Attica finally reached 43. Corrections officer William Quinn died on September 11, of injuries received during the uprising on September 9. Dates of the deaths of Inmates Hess, Privitiera, and Schwartz have not been established.* Nine hostages and 26 inmates were killed by gunfire on September 13. One hostage and three inmates died between September 15 and October 9 of gunshot wounds suffered in D-yard on September 13.

The family of Corrections Officer Carl W. Valone, 44, one of the hostages killed on September 13, was told by corrections authorities that day that he had died with his throat cut by an inmate executioner. That same day, an autopsy was performed on Carl Valone's body at the Genesee Memorial Hospital. Still later on September 13, the family learned from the hospital that the cause of death was a bullet in Valone's side. Incredulous, a relative rushed to view the body.

"There was no slashing," he said later, "[Carl] was not even touched." Valone, he concluded bitterly, had been killed by "a bullet that had the name Rockefeller on it."[1]

That Monday, the families of the other dead hostages—all of whose bodies were taken to the Monroe County Medical Examiner's office in Rochester—were told with the rest of the world that the dead men had had their throats cut by inmate "blades." Walter Dunbar announced to reporters keeping vigil at Attica that two hostages had been killed "before today" and that one had been emasculated. Dunbar also stated that Sam Melville had been killed while running with four bombs

---

* See Chapter Ten, Note 4.

toward a fuel tank. Gerald Houlihan, an aide to Russell Oswald, informed reporters that the dead hostages' throats had been cut.[2]

Herman Badillo, calling Tom Wicker in New York City by pre-arrangement, told Wicker the authorities had said all the hostages had died with their throats slashed. No reporter was given the opportunity to examine the bodies. No doctor was asked to report to the press. Newspapers and television—in most cases making too little effort to check the apparent facts—carried the throat-cutting story to the nation. Some reported it as a literal fact, without even attributing it to prison spokesmen.

On September 14, Dr. John Edland, the Monroe County Medical Examiner, found the bodies of eight hostages and 19 inmates awaiting his examination. True to prison custom, the dead guards were tagged with their names, but the dead inmates were tagged "P-1," "P-2," and so on. That afternoon, Dr. Edland—after what he later called "the worst day of my life"—made public his findings. Not a single hostage had been killed by knife wounds. None had been castrated or mutilated. All had died on Monday morning, September 13. All had been killed by bullets or buckshot—some hit as many as "five, ten, twelve times."[3]

When queried, Corrections Department officials said that no firearms had been found among the "hundreds" of weapons taken from the inmates when D-yard was recaptured. Walter Dunbar, pursued by reporters in the parking lot at Attica, "shook visibly and said, 'It deserves to be investigated.'" Russell Oswald was at pains to inform the press that he had never said the hostages' throats had been cut.[4]

On September 15, the Department of Corrections asked two other medical examiners to review Dr. Edland's findings—not "to contradict them" but to "make sure an independent report is made," said Deputy Commissioner Wim van Eckeren. Houlihan explained to reporters that the throat-cutting reports on September 13 had not been "meant to be a factual account as to the cause of death."[5]

Dr. Edland had already shown himself to be unflappable. State troopers had watched as he performed the autopsies, he said. "I think they kept waiting for the next case to show up. Finally we ran out of hostages. I'm used to not finding what people tell me I will find." And he added, "I am my own man and I call things as I see them. All I know is I have 27 bodies in my office, which is more than I ever want to see again in one day."[6]

When he heard a double-check would be imposed on his grim work, Dr. Edland invited Corrections Department officials themselves to come to his office and view the bodies. "It doesn't take a medical degree to tell if someone's genitals are lacerated," he said.[7]

On September 19, the two pathologists summoned by the Department of Corrections confirmed Dr. Edland's findings that the hostages had died of gunshot wounds. One of them, Dr. Michael Baden, deputy chief medical examiner for New York City, said that of the 27 inmates killed by gunfire, some had been shot in the back.[8]

Many in Attica town continued to believe that the inmates had killed the hostages, but Nelson Rockefeller accepted Dr. Edland's findings readily enough, as proof that the hostages could only have been shot by the state police—although, on September 13, he had issued a statement flatly attributing the hostages' deaths to inmates who had "carried out cold-blooded killings they had threatened from the start." Asked at a news conference in New York on September 15 if the attack on D-yard had "come out" better than he had expected, he said "Frankly, yes . . . I think [the attackers] did a superb job."[9]

But what did "the fact that so many [hostages] did emerge unharmed" tell him about the inmates? he was asked.

"I think what it tells is that the use of this gas is a fantastic instrument in a situation of this kind," Rockefeller replied.[10]

This was not an isolated reflection. During the four desperate days of the Attica revolt, Governor Rockefeller had given some thought to other technological means of avoiding bloodshed in recapturing the prison. As he later testified:

> I raised [the question] . . . as to whether it wouldn't be possible, in trying to get a solution of this, to use tranquilizers as a means of quieting everything down. I thought it was an interesting idea. Practically it just wasn't possible and obviously if anyone felt it was being done it would have incited rather than quieted. So there was no way of doing it anyway.[11]

Rockefeller is a forceful and decisive man, and by his own testimony kept in close, virtually controlling touch with events at Attica during the revolt. In fact, he called off the planned Sunday afternoon attack, and he said later that although Oswald made the decisions, he—Rockefeller—could have overruled them or suspended the commissioner.[12] His unpursued question about the use of tranquilizers suggests, as later testimony confirmed, that he had a different attitude toward the state police:

MR. LIMAN:* Did they review the assault plans of the State Police with you?

---

* On September 16, 1971, Governor Rockefeller and the majority and minority leaders of the New York legislature asked Chief Judge Stanley H. Fuld of the Court of Appeals and the four presiding justices of the state's Appellate Division to appoint a fact-finding commission, without authority to prosecute, to determine what had happened at Attica. Judge Fuld and his colleagues named a nine-man

GOVERNOR ROCKEFELLER: No. I'm not a military man or a police official. These are professional judgments. . . . I do not feel I have the competence to make the judgments and I think there's nothing more dangerous than a civilian messing in military activities and trying to impose, superimpose, his judgment over those of the professionals.

MR. LIMAN: Did they ever tell you what types of ammunition they intended to use in going into that yard?

GOVERNOR ROCKEFELLER: No, nor what type of equipment. I just assumed they would use what in their opinion was the safest and least dangerous but would satisfy the requirements.

MR. LIMAN: I can tell you, Governor, from having interviewed State Police officials that the opinion and explanation that we get is that they used the ammunition and equipment that they have. . . .

GOVERNOR ROCKEFELLER: You are making an implication there that I'm not aware of or, with the knowledge I have, can I accept, I just want to say for the record. I don't know how much of a military expert you are but I just raise that point.

MR. LIMAN: All right. Did you ask General O'Hara to review the plans of the State Police?

GOVERNOR ROCKEFELLER: No. General O'Hara was not in charge. . . . I think that you would have to agree that the retaking of the first three cell[blocks] with the use of no ammunition, no weapons except tear gas and sticks, was a perfect evidence of the kind of restraint and control that they used. I am satisfied that these men in their best judgment used what they thought was necessary to minimize lives—to minimize the loss of lives and to save to the maximum degree possible the security and well-being of the hostages and the prisoners.

MR. LIMAN: What do you base that on, Governor?

GOVERNOR ROCKEFELLER: My experience of 14 years with these men and what they have done. . . . I would just like to go on record that to second guess is awfully easy.

MR. LIMAN: You mentioned in the Rochester difficulties the State Police had moved in without the use of arms.

GOVERNOR ROCKEFELLER: That's correct. That is perfect evidence of why I have such confidence in them.

MR. LIMAN: And was there any consideration given to attempting

"New York State Special Commission on Attica" on September 30, with Dean Robert B. McKay of the New York University Law School as chairman, and Arthur Liman, a New York city trial lawyer, as general counsel. The commission had specific authority to look into the governor's actions, as well as those of all others involved at Attica.

to retake [D-] yard without armed force?

GOVERNOR ROCKEFELLER: Oh, I'm sure there was.

MR. LIMAN: Was that discussed with you?

GOVERNOR ROCKEFELLER: No. I have got to reaffirm that I think—I don't know how much responsibility you have had in administration or in government or in military affairs, but my experience is that the best thing a well-intentioned civilian political personality can do is not try and impose his judgment on professional matters but to pick good people and back them up and, as I say and as I repeat, these men were all there, had been there 14 years and served with me and everything that had happened to this time had demonstrated their dedication and capacity.[13]

It was not only the details of the attack that Rockefeller left to his commanders on the scene. He did not appear to realize, even months later, the implications of two cardinal facts—that the attack force was all white and that the rebelling inmates were heavily black and Puerto Rican:

MR. LIMAN: Was there ever any discussion with you during this period about the possibility of trying to use some integrated forces to take the prison?

GOVERNOR ROCKEFELLER: What do you mean "integrated?"

MR. LIMAN: Well, for example having even one black trooper participate in the assault.

GOVERNOR ROCKEFELLER: No, I leave these questions—I have done a great deal to encourage the recruitment and membership of the police to reflect the broader base of our community make-up but when it comes to the deployment of personnel, this is a matter of responsibility of the people who are in charge. But I think to just give you an evidence of the distance to which it seems to me you are reaching in your question, remember these people were all going in with gas masks so what purpose does your thought serve?

MR. LIMAN: I'm not quite sure I understand the question.

GOVERNOR ROCKEFELLER: An integrated force with a black member, you say. How do you identify him with a gas mask?

MR. LIMAN: I think the question really was whether you gave any consideration to the possibility that racial attitudes might affect the capacity of . . .

GOVERNOR ROCKEFELLER: If you will excuse me, I don't think the question is pertinent because I don't think that it's relevant to the action that was taken.[14]

But as if sensing that there was a relevance that had eluded him, Rockefeller returned to the matter a few moments later:

> . . . I would like to say, seeing you have raised this question, I don't think there is anyone who is more conscious or concerned about the problem of equality of opportunity, of representation of government at all levels and in all activities and that I take second place to no one on the record in our government in this field.[15]

The governor was also asked if he had given any thought to having someone from his "immediate staff" in the prison yard after the battle to "protect the inmates against hostile reaction." He had trusted Oswald and Dunbar for that, Rockefeller said, and

> . . . I've got to say to you that I think that under the trials and tribulations that everybody had been through, the prisoners and hostages and guards alike, that there was in broad terms, there was a reasonably restrained showing if you go backwards in history.[16]

Rockefeller saw little to criticize in the handling and suppression of the rebellion at Attica by his police and civil officials. He said in a statement issued the day of the attack on D-yard that the uprising had resulted from "the revolutionary tactics of militants," and that "outside forces would appear to have played" a role in bringing it on. And he congratulated the attacking forces on their "skill and courage" in rescuing 29 hostages and for their "restraint [that] held down casualties among prisoners as well."[17]

He seemed to see no conflict between these views and his later concession, in a speech on September 24, 1971, that "we can no longer delay in making radical reforms in our whole system of criminal justice [including] protecting alike the rights and dignity of both prison inmates and correction officers." Preventing future Atticas, he said then, would require "fundamental changes in the attitudes and human relations in our institutions." The time to start such reforms, he continued, was "yesterday. It's overdue."[18]

For that failure, he finally accepted a broad responsibility:

> MR. HENIX:* In life I've done some things badly and some I've done very well. There are very few things I would do the same way in hindsight. I'm just curious, is there anything

---

* Amos Henix, a member of the New York State Special Commission on Attica.

which you could see that took place on those days [at Attica]
if you had it to do again, you would have done differently?

GOVERNOR ROCKEFELLER: Primarily what we are now working on,
namely the rebuilding of the prisons, a whole different approach to the concept of prisons as such, rehabilitation instead of custodial care, both physical and in terms of program
. . . if I could go back 14 years instead of six months . . . I
would have to say to you that one of the things I regret most
is my own lack of perception of the tremendous need which
existed in this area, which our society—I'm not blaming anything on society—I say this is a big area that I did not fully
understand and perceive and that had I done then 12 years
ago, 14 years ago, what I was doing now, I'm sure this
wouldn't have happened.[19]

In August 1972, a year after the State Police recaptured D-yard, a
few improvements could be noticed at Attica. The screens in the
visiting room and the sick-call room had been removed, although Dr.
Selden Williams was still the prison physician. Inmates were being
permitted two showers a week and given fresh fruit daily. Restrictions on correspondence and literature had been somewhat relaxed.
Guards were pleased with new gun towers rising at the corners of the
recreation yards. Vincent Mancusi, though only 57 years old, had retired on January 27 and had been replaced by Ernest Montanye. The
new superintendent had instituted an "evening recreation" program that
allowed each inmate to be in the yard until dark, one night in four.
The prison population was down to 1308, and there were 19 new black
and Spanish-speaking guards.[20]

But in June 1973, nearly two years after the uprising, the impetus to
reform seemed to have run its course. A special state committee reported that New York's prisons had made "some progress" but that
"change which has a fundamental impact on the day-to-day existence
of the inmate population remains elusive."[21]

The committee, appointed by Governor Rockefeller in late 1971
said that the New York prison system generally continued to be plagued
by lack of money, legislative indifference, poor morale, and persistent
violence. Education programs, so far from having been improved as
abortively promised in the 28 points, had been restricted, and the
number of functionally illiterate inmates in reading programs had been
cut. Most efforts to get the inmates out of their cells more often had
failed for lack of money to pay guards the overtime that would have
been required.

On the other hand, work-release programs had been expanded somewhat; the 1972 legislature provided funds to add such programs for

135 inmates at three institutions, for a total of 210 persons at six prisons. Elected liaison committees of inmates had been authorized to consult with prison administrators. More black and Spanish-speaking guards had been recruited, partially due to federal grant money. The prison system had changed "to a nutritional rather than economic food standard."

That was all. Even the Correctional Association of New York, a 127-year-old private organization of prominent bankers, lawyers, and businessmen, had fallen victim to the failure of reform. In the association's original charter from the state, it had been granted the "power" and charged with the "duty" to visit the state's prisons and to report on conditions there, in pursuit of one of its major objectives—"the amelioration of the condition of prisoners."

The Correctional Association had not used these unusual powers since 1924. After Attica, its officers raised with Russell Oswald and Nelson Rockefeller the idea of vigorously resuming its ombudsman role. Receiving no answer from the governor, the association announced its plan publicly. On the same day, the governor's office submitted a bill to the legislature to remove the association's "power and duty" to visit prisons. The bill was passed, barring any possibility of an ombudsman not controlled by state officials or a part of the corrections bureaucracy.[22]

By June 1973, Russell Oswald had been eased out as Commissioner of Corrections and shifted to a less visible post, taking a salary reduction to become a member of the Crime Victims Compensation Board. Walter Dunbar had been promoted to be State Probation Director at a salary of $39,825 a year. Most prison inmates were still being paid less than 50 cents a day.

Reflecting on Attica as the months and years passed, Tom Wicker realized that the involvement of Nelson Rockefeller had been extraordinary. For once, the hand of established power in America had been seen directly at work. Usually, the headlines traced deaths and destruction to no higher sources than obscure Southern governors or big city police chiefs or pompous generals in their rows of ribbons; and the forces beyond them could be but dimly glimpsed, and impersonally at that—the "military-industrial complex," "the imperialists," "the money men." But at Attica one of the richest men in the world, possessing as much of the power of wealth as anyone could, had been seen in direct command also of the political and military powers of the state. At Attica, there had been a rare and chilling glimpse of the real thing at work—power itself, as well as the agents of power.

Wicker also returned, again and again, to one essential contradiction. All the state officials, all the observers—so far as he knew—had believed explicitly that the inmates would kill the hostages if D-yard was attacked. But the inmates *had not done it.*

Some of the black and Puerto Rican observers might have expected the inmates to kill the hostages only because they believed the inmates to be desperate enough to do anything. But Wicker, trying to analyze his own attitudes, playing back scenes from Attica until they formed a nightmare movie in his mind, saw finally that from the start his had been a classic case of "we" and "they." Inmates were vengeful blacks, the embittered poor. Inmates were from the underside of life, the criminal side. So inmates would kill. "They" were that kind of people. Whatever his sympathies, however he had rationalized, his conditioned instinct, too, had been that the Attica brothers were killers, outlaws, different—something less than "we" are.

Why should he have supposed, then, that the state police, the corrections officers, the state officials, Nelson Rockefeller would not feel the same? Why should he have thought the state would tolerate dealing with lesser men as equals, binding itself with them in a contract? In the long run, the power of the state had not believed it possible that the men of D-yard could behave with decency and humanity.

But in D-yard, behind their futile trenches and barricades, in their vivid flights of defiance, even in the suspicion and distrust of their hard experience, many of these despised inmates finally had not believed that the state—society, The Man—would shoot them down. The hard truth was that the Attica brothers had had more faith in the state than the state had had in them. Both had been wrong.

On the third anniversary of the attack on D-yard—September 13, 1974—61 of the Attica brothers stood indicted for crimes ranging from murder to sodomy. Over 1400 counts of criminal actions had been cited in the indictments. At least 40 separate trials were in prospect, although none had been started, and a maze of defense appeals, courtroom motions, and procedural disputes made it impossible to predict when, if ever, any of the trials could begin. When they did, defense attorneys predicted, four years might be required to complete them.

Among those indicted were Roger Champen and Richard Clark, each on 34 kidnap counts; William Ortiz, on 14 kidnap and 4 assault counts; and Frank Smith (Big Black), on 34 kidnap counts, 2 coercion counts, and 2 counts of unlawful imprisonment. For the death of Corrections Officer William Quinn, two inmates, John Hill and Charles Pernasilice, were indicted for murder. Although two other inmates were accused of the actual killings, Champen, Big Black, and Herbert Blyden were indicted for murder during the commission of a felony—

kidnapping—in the killings of two inmates, Barry Schwartz and Kenneth Hess, who allegedly died during the uprising and before the attack on September 13.

All these indictments were returned by a Wyoming County Grand Jury that was still sitting on September 13, 1974. The Grand Jury had worked, first, with Assistant Attorney General Robert Fischer, then with Special Assistant Attorney General Anthony G. Simonetti, and an investigating staff that at one time included 14 lawyers and 25 detectives. The Attica Brothers Legal Defense estimated that state prosecution costs had reached at least $4 million by mid-summer of 1974.[23]

The Grand Jury had been empanelled in Warsaw on November 1, 1971. Simonetti called it the "longest-sitting Grand Jury in history" but it indicted no one for the killing of any of the hostages—Corrections Officer Harrison J. "Red" Whalen died on October 9, 1971, of gunshot wounds received in D-yard on September 13, to bring the total to 10 hostages dead. The Grand Jury indicted no one for the killing of the 29 inmates fatally shot in the recapture of the prison. The Grand Jury indicted no state official, state trooper, corrections officer, or anyone else for indiscriminate firing or carelessness or manslaughter or any other possible offense committed during the recapture of the prison and the reprisals that followed. No one was indicted for failing to take proper steps to provide medical care or to prevent reprisals. Inmates alone were indicted.

On April 5, 1974, a second Grand Jury was empanelled at Simonetti's request. It was reported that the first Grand Jury had refused to indict a state trooper against whom evidence had been presented. Patrick Carroll, president of the State Police Benevolent Association, said that forming a second Grand Jury was "beating a dead horse, attempting to get a conviction [sic] when [Simonetti] failed during the original investigation. . . . There can be no other reason for seeking a new jury."[24]

In September 1974, three years after the attack on D-yard, Nelson Rockefeller was nominated by Gerald R. Ford to be Vice President of the United States. During his confirmation hearings, he was asked what lessons had been learned from the experience at Attica. Rockefeller said he thought "that if this would happen again I would think that . . . the proper way to proceed" would be "to go ahead . . . without weapons."[25]

But by then, not even the second Grand Jury had indicted anyone who had proceeded with weapons or who had ordered or allowed weapons to be used on the morning of September 13, 1971. That seemed not to be in the order of things.

Afterword

Long after *A Time to Die* was published in 1975, Governor Hugh Carey of New York pardoned everyone who had been concerned in any way with the Attica revolt and the attack that ended it. That had the effect of cancelling the indictments of sixty-one inmates who had been charged with everything from murder to sodomy. But Governor Carey's action also meant that no state policeman, corrections officer, or any state official would be charged with anything that had contributed to the deaths of twenty-nine inmates and ten hostages in the deadly, six-minute fusillade fired into D-yard on Sept. 13. Nor would anyone be indicted or tried for the failure to provide adequate medical care for the wounded after the firing stopped, or for the repeated torturing and beating of inmates when the revolt had been crushed, or for prison officials' failure to put a stop to these reprisals.

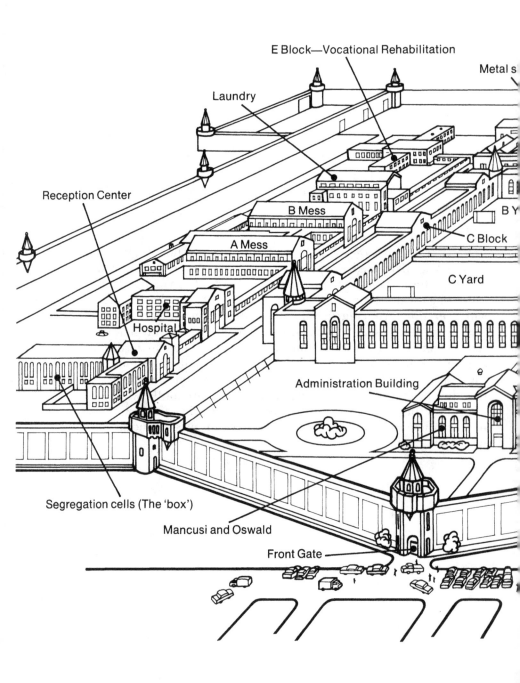

E Block—Vocational Rehabilitation

Metal s

Laundry

Reception Center

B Mess

B Y

A Mess

C Block

C Yard

Hospital

Administration Building

Segregation cells (The 'box')

Mancusi and Oswald

Front Gate

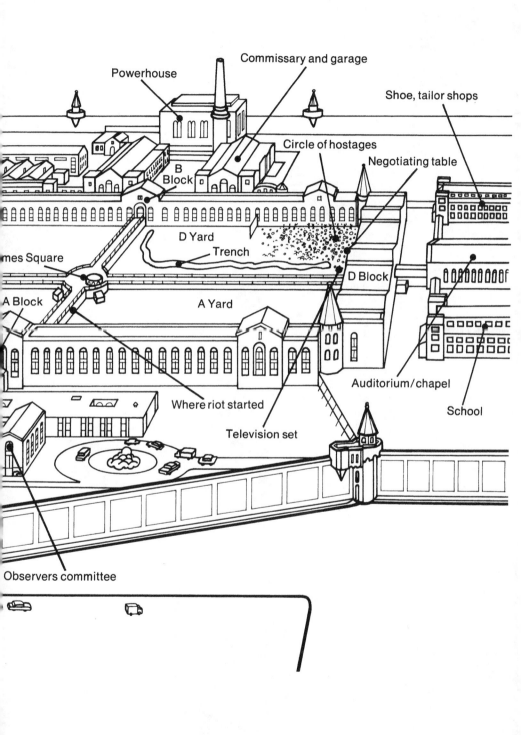

Powerhouse

Commissary and garage

Shoe, tailor shops

Circle of hostages

Negotiating table

B Block

D Yard

Trench

mes Square

D Block

A Block

A Yard

Where riot started

Television set

Auditorium/chapel

School

Observers committee

Chronology of Events

July, 1971   Commissioner Oswald receives petition from Attica Liberation Faction.

Sat., Aug. 21   George Jackson dies, supposedly shot while attempting escape from San Quentin prison.

Sun., Aug. 22   Attica inmates fast and hold a silent protest at breakfast.

Thurs., Sept. 2   Oswald confers with Attica Superintendent Mancusi and prisoner representative Lott over July petition. In a tape-recorded message to the inmates, Oswald promises that changes will be made eventually.

Wed., Sept. 8

3:45 P.M.   Inmates Dewer and Lamorie defy Corrections Officer Maroney and are ordered to solitary confinement in Housing Block Z.

AFTER DINNER   When Dewer and Lamorie are taken to HBZ Corrections Officer Boyle is hit in the face with a soup can reputedly thrown by William Ortiz.

Thurs., Sept. 9

6:30 A.M.   Ortiz is liberated from his cell by other inmates to go to breakfast.

During breakfast, authorities discover that Ortiz is absent from his cell. Five Company is ordered back to its cells.

8:55 A.M.   Lt. Curtiss approaches Five Company in A-tunnel to effect this. Curtiss is knocked unconscious and other guards are beaten, their keys taken. The intraprison phone is ripped from the wall.

9:05 A.M.   A defective bolt in the gate at Times Square gives way under the pressure of a group of inmates and the rebellion spreads through the prison. Quinn, the guard on duty there, sustains serious skull fractures. Fifty hostages are taken.

MIDMORNING   Hostages are protected, in particular by Black Muslims. Roger Champen begins to organize inmates in D-yard.

EARLY AFTERNOON   Authorities regain control of part of the prison. Mancusi alienates inmates in a negotiation attempt at No Man's Land.

Inmates appoint lookouts and guards for hostages, ration captured food, organize clean-up details, and nominate a negotiating team.

2:00 P.M.   Commissioner Oswald arrives at Attica.

3:00 P.M.   Schwartz and New York State Assemblyman Eve arrive in D-yard and are presented with the Five Demands and a list of persons to be invited as observers of the negotiations.

4:45–5:15 P.M.   Oswald, Schwartz, and Eve confer with inmates in D-yard.

Oswald is advised by state police that sufficient force is present to retake the institution.

5:45–6:44 P.M.   Oswald returns to D-yard with *New York Times*, Buffalo newspaper, radio, and TV reporters. Inmates present the Fifteen Practical Proposals.

7:30 P.M.   Assistant Commissioner Dunbar, Assemblyman Emery, Eve, and Schwartz enter D-yard and are asked for a federal court injunction against administrative and physical reprisals.

Champen, Oswald, and Schwartz draft the injunction outside of D-yard.

11:30 P.M.   Schwartz leaves to obtain injunction.

Fri., Sept. 10

8:30 A.M.   Schwartz returns with the injunction from Federal Judge Curtin. It is rejected by inmates.

11:25 A.M.   Oswald enters D-yard. The injunction is torn up by Rosenberg. Oswald decides that he will no longer negotiate directly with the rebelling inmates.

LATE AFTERNOON   Observers contact D.A. James but fail to obtain amnesty guarantee.

EVENING   Observers enter D-yard and inspect hostages.

At inmates' request, some observers inspect C-block.

Kunstler arrives in the Stewards' Room and telephones Bobby Seale of the Black Panther Party.

11:30 P.M.   Observers again enter D-yard. Inmates add demands that Mancusi and Dr. Williams be expelled from the Attica staff.

LATER   Unexplained noise from C-block prompts fear of attack and "red alert" in D-yard. Eve and Dunne ascertain that no reprisals are taking place and return to D-yard with members of the Fortune Society, Ingram, and Kenyatta.

Sat., Sept. 11

4:30 A.M.   Observers leave D-yard.

The observers choose an executive committee from among their number.

Wicker, Jones, and Tepper visit D.A. James in Warsaw in an attempt to obtain something similar to amnesty for the inmates.

10:00 A.M.   James gives them a statement that there will be no prosecutions or vindictive reprisals.

11:00 A.M.   Observers who have left the prison have difficulty being readmitted.

1:00 P.M.   Observers meet again. James' letter is not well received. Wicker proposes that the executive committee should attempt to winnow down the inmates' demands and that all others leave. Only six others leave, and they are locked out.

4:30 P.M.   Corrections Officer Quinn dies.

Observers finish 28-point package and decide to wait for Seale before presenting it to the inmates.

6:30 P.M.   Seale sits in a car outside the prison for an hour and then leaves, while Oswald and observers discuss his admittance. State police are sent after him to request his presence.

8:30 P.M.   Seale enters the Stewards' Room and refuses to endorse the 28 points. Observers enter D-yard to present the 28 points. Some observers leave upon presenting the sheet of paper, but others, upon seeing the inmates' anger, make the decision to present the points orally.

The 28 points are ripped up. Remaining observers leave.

Sun., Sept. 12

MORNING   Woman managing a diner becomes hysterical over the presence of Arthur Eve.

8:30 A.M.   Seale arrives at Attica. Observers group again in Stewards' Room. Seale walks out.

10:50 A.M.   The observers try to influence Governor Rockefeller's representatives to advise him to come to Attica.

11:45 A.M.   The observers draft and complete a statement to the public.

1:11 P.M.   Oswald agrees that observers may enter D-yard at 3:00.

Observers telephone Rockefeller themselves, trying without success to persuade him to come to meet with them.

3:45 P.M.   A small group of observers enters D-yard, followed later by black and Puerto Rican media representatives. Hostages are interviewed.

Inmates officially reject the 28 points. They leave the next move up to the commissioner.

6:17 P.M.   Observers leave D-yard for the last time.

Rockefeller states publicly that he will not come to Attica.

9:26 P.M.   Oswald meets with the observers, who plead for more time.

10:35 P.M.   The meeting breaks up. Nine observers agree to spend the night in the Stewards' Room.

MIDNIGHT   Oswald phones Rockefeller in a last attempt to persuade him to come.

Mon., Sept. 13

6:55 A.M.   Observers learn that Oswald has broken contact with them.

8:00 A.M.   Oswald presents inmate Clark with a final statement of his position.

8:30 A.M.   Observers read a copy of Oswald's memorandum to Clark.

Inmates stall for time.

State police marksmen assemble unseen on the roofs and third floors of A- and C-blocks.

Attack units assemble on first and second floors of A- and C-blocks.

9:05 A.M.   Hostages are seen being led blindfolded to a walkway near Times Square, knives at their throats.

9:30 A.M.   Inmates' response to 28 points is negative.

Eleven corrections officers with weapons gather, ignorant of orders, in a third-floor corridor.

9:43 A.M.   The prison's power circuit is turned off. A helicopter drops CS gas on D-yard. Marksmen fire and attack begins.

9:52 A.M.   Firing stops.

10:30 A.M.   D- and C-blocks are cleared.

1:40 P.M.   Badillo, Eve, and Garcia are told by Oswald that, as elected officials, they will be given a tour of the institution. All other observers are requested to leave.

Afterwards   The results of the carnage are tabulated and it becomes known that two hostages were seriously injured by the inmates, whereas 10 hostages and 29 inmates were killed by corrections officers and state troopers. Three hostages, 85 inmates, and one trooper were wounded.

The Five Demands

To the people of America

The incident that has erupted here at Attica is not a result of the dastardly bushwacking of the two prisoners Sept. 8, 1971 but of the unmitigated oppression wrought by the racist administration network of the prison, throughout the year.

WE are MEN! We are not beasts and do not intend to be beaten or driven as such. The entire prison populace has set forth to change forever the ruthless brutalization and disregard for the lives of the prisoners here and throughout the United States. What has happened here is but the sound before the fury of those who are oppressed.

We will not compromise on any terms except those that are agreeable to us. We call upon all the conscientious citizens of America to assist us in putting an end to this situation that threatens the lives of not only us, but each and everyone of us as well.

We have set forth demands that will bring closer to reality the demise of these prisons institutions that serve no useful purpose to the People of America, but to those who would enslave and exploit the people of America.

OUR DEMANDS ARE SUCH:

1. We want complete amnesty, meaning freedom from any physical, mental and legal reprisals.

2. We want now, speedy and safe transportation out of confinement, to a non-imperialistic country.

3. We demand that the FEDERAL GOVERNMENT intervene, so that we will be under direct FEDERAL JURISDICTION.

4. We demand the reconstruction of ATTICA PRISON to be done by inmates and/or inmate supervision.

5. We urgently demand immediate negotiation thru Wm. M. Kunstler, Attorney-at-Law, 588 Ninth Ave., NYC, Assemblyman Arthur O. Eve, of Buffalo, the Solidarity Committee, Minister Farrakhan of MUHAMMAD SPEAKS, Palante, The Young Lord's Party Paper, the Black Panther Party, Clarence Jones of the Amsterdam News, Tom Wicker of NY Times, Richard Roth of the Courier Express, the Fortune Society, David Anderson of the Urban League of Rochester, Blond-Eva Bond of NICAP, and Jim Ingram of Democrat Chronicle of Detroit, Mich. We guarantee the safe passage of all people to and from this institution. We invite *all the people* to come here and witness this degradation, so that they can better know how to bring this degradation to an end.

THE INMATES OF ATTICA PRISON

APPENDIX TWO

The Fifteen Practical Proposals

PRACTICAL PROPOSALS

1. Apply the New York State minimum wage law to all state institutions. STOP SLAVE LABOR.

2. Allow all New York State prisoners to be politically active, without intimidation of reprisals.

3. Give us true religious freedom.

4. End all censorship of newspapers, magazines, letters and other publications coming from the publisher.

5. Allow all inmates, at their own expense, to communicate with anyone they please.

6. When an inmate reaches conditional release date, give him a full release without parole.

7. Cease administrative resentencing of inmates returned for parole violations.

8. Institute realistic rehabilitation programs for all inmates according to their offense and personal needs.

9. Educate all correctional officers to the needs of the inmates, i.e., understanding rather than punishment.

10. Give us a healthy diet, stop feeding us so much pork, and give us some fresh fruit daily.

11. Modernize the inmate education system.

12. Give us a doctor that will examine and treat all inmates that request treatment.

13. Have an institutional delegation comprised of one inmate from each company authorized to speak to the institution administration concerning grievances (QUARTERLY).

14. Give us less cell time and more recreation with better recreational equipment and facilities.

15. Remove inside walls, making one open yard, and no more segregation or punishment.

APPENDIX THREE

Comprehensive List of Observers Committee at Attica Correction Facility—September 9–13, 1971

David Anderson,* Rochester Urban League.
U.S. Rep. Herman Badillo of New York.
Alberto Cappas, Office of Minority Student Affairs, State University of New York at Buffalo.
Rev. Marvin Chandler, Rochester minister.
State Senator John Dunne of Nassau County, New York.
Assemblyman James L. Emery of 136th District, New York.
Assemblyman Arthur O. Eve* of 143rd District, New York.
Tony Fitch, Washington lawyer.
Minister Franklin Florence, former President, FIGHT, a Rochester community organization.
William Gaiter, BUILD, a Buffalo community organization.
State Senator Robert Garcia of the Bronx, New York.
James Ingram,* reporter, *The Michigan Chronicle*, Detroit.
Kenneth Jackson,* officer of Fortune Society, New York.
Clarence Jones,* publisher of the *Amsterdam News*, New York.
Jaybarr Kenyatta, Black Muslim, a former inmate at Attica.
William Kunstler,* Center for Constitutional Rights, New York.
State Senator Thomas McGowan of 58th District, New York.
Alfredo Mathew, school superintendent, New York City.
Juan "Fi" Ortiz,* member of Young Lords party, New York.
Jose "G.I." Paris,* member of Young Lords party, New York.
Al Poder, State University of New York at Buffalo.
Mel Rivers,* officer of Fortune Society, New York.

* These members of the Observers Committee were invited to Attica by the rebelling inmates, either personally or as representatives of their organizations.

Domingo Rodriguez, member of BUILD, a Buffalo community organization.

Richard Roth,* reporter for Buffalo *Courier-Express*.

David Rothenberg,* founder of the Fortune Society, New York.

Herman Schwartz, law faculty, State University of New York at Buffalo.

Minister Raymond Scott, director of FIGHT, a Rochester community organization.

Bobby Seale,* chairman of the Black Panther Party.

Dan Skoler, Washington lawyer.

Thomas Soto,* member of the Prisoner Solidarity Committee, New York.

Lewis Steel, vice president, National Lawyers Guild, New York.

Julian Tepper, Washington lawyer.

State Senator Sidney von Luther, New York County, New York.

Rev. Wyatt Tee Walker, Urban Affairs advisor to Governor Rockefeller, New York.

Assemblyman Frank Walkley of Castile, New York.

Assemblyman Clark Wemple of 107th District, New York.

Tom Wicker,* Associate Editor of *The New York Times*.

APPENDIX FOUR

The Twenty-eight Points

Following are the proposals that State Correction Commissioner Russell G. Oswald has said he will accept:

1. Provide adequate food, water and shelter for all inmates.
2. Inmates shall be permitted to return to their cells or to other suitable accommodations or shelter under their power. The observer committee shall monitor the implementation of this operation.
3. Grant complete administrative amnesty to all persons associated with this matter. By administrative amnesty the state agrees:
   A. Not to take any adverse parole actions, administrative proceedings, physical punishment or other type of harassment, such as holding inmates incommunicado, segregating inmates, or keep them in isolation or in 24-hour lockup.
   B. The state will grant legal amnesty in regard to all civil actions that could arise from this matter.
   C. It is agreed that the State of New York and all its departments, divisions and subdivisions, including the State Department of Corrections and the Attica Correctional Facility and its employes and agents, shall not file or initiate any criminal complaint or act as complainant in any criminal action of any kind or nature relating to property damage or property-related crimes arising out of the incidents at the Attica Correctional Facility during Sept. 9, 10 and 11, 1971.
4. Recommend the application of the New York State Minimum Wage Law standards to all work done by inmates. Every effort will be made to make the records of payments available to inmates.
5. Establish by Oct. 1 a permanent ombudsman service for the facility, staffed by appropriate persons from the neighboring communities.
6. Allow all New York State prisoners to be politically active without intimidation or reprisal.
7. Allow true religious freedom.

8. End all censorship of newspaper, magazines and other publications from publishers, unless it is determined by qualified authority, which includes the ombudsman, that the literature in question presents a clear and present danger to the safety and security of the institution. Institution spot-censoring only of letters.

9. Allow all inmates at their own expense to communicate with anyone they please.

10. Institute realistic, effective rehabilitation programs for all inmates according to their offense and personal needs.

11. Modernize the inmate education system, including the establishment of a [Spanish-language] library.

12. Provide an effective narcotics treatment program for all prisoners requesting such treatment.

13. Provide or allow adequate legal assistance to all inmates requesting it, or permit them to use inmate legal assistance of their choice in any proceeding whatsoever. In all such proceedings inmates shall be entitled to appropriate due process of law.

14. Reduce cell time, increase recreation time and provide better recreation facilities and equipment, hopefully by Nov. 1, 1971.

15. Provide a healthy diet, reduce the number of pork dishes, increase fresh fruit daily.

16. Provide adequate medical treatment for every inmate. Engage either a Spanish-speaking doctor or interpreters who will accompany Spanish-speaking inmates to medical interviews.

17. Institute a program for the recruitment and employment of a significant number of black and Spanish-speaking officers.

18. Establish an inmate grievance commission, comprised of one elected inmate from each company, which is authorized to speak to the administration concerning grievances and develop other procedures for inmate participation in the operation and decision-making processes of the institution.

19. Investigate the alleged expropriation of inmate funds and the use of profits from the metal and other shops.

20. The State Commissioner of Correctional Services will recommend that the penal law be changed to cease administrative re-sentencing of inmates returned for parole violation.

21. Recommend that Menenchino hearings be held promptly and fairly. [This concerns the right of prisoners to be represented legally on parole-violation changes.]

22. Recommend necessary legislation and more adequate funds to expand work relief programs.

23. End approved lists for correspondents and visitors.

24. Remove visitation screens as soon as possible.

25. Institute a 30-day maximum for segregation arising out of any one offense. Every effort should be geared toward restoring the individual to regular housing as soon as possible, consistent with safety regulations.

26. Paroled inmates shall not be charged with parole violations for moving traffic violations or driving without a license unconnected with any other crimes.

27. Permit access to outside dentists and doctors at the inmates' own expense within the institution where possible and consistent with scheduling problems, medical diagnosis and health needs.

28. It is expressly understood that members of the observer committee will be permitted into the institution on a reasonable basis to determine whether all of the above provisions are being effectively carried out. If questions of adequacy are raised, the matter will be brought to the attention of the Commissioner of Correctional Services for clearance.

Notes

Chapter One

1. *The New York Times* (hereafter referred to as NYT), September 23, 1971, p. 67. Julio Carlos appears to have been the first inmate who took part in the Attica rebellion to have been released afterwards (he had served his time). His recollections 10 days after the revolt are of some significance. This and subsequent quotations attributed to him are from *The Times'* story by Eric Pace.
2. Governor Nelson A. Rockefeller to the New York State Special Commission on Attica, April 5, 1972, p. 10.
3. NYT, September 19, 1971, p. 60.
4. *Five Days at Attica* (hereafter referred to as Five Days), a pamphlet of reprints from the Rochester, N.Y. *Democrat and Chronicle*, issues of September 10–14, p. 4.
5. *The Official Report of the New York State Special Commission on Attica*, official edition, pp. 28–29. The chairman was Dean Robert B. McKay of the New York University Law School. The commission and its report are referred to hereafter as McKay.
6. Five Days, pp. 5–6.
7. *Letters from Attica*, by Samuel Melville (Wm. Morrow and Co., New York), pp. 168–169.
8. Five Days, p. 4.
9. McKay, pp. 139–140.
10. Five Days, p. 5.
11. McKay, p. 140.
12. *The Brothers of Attica*, by Richard X. Clark, edited by Leonard Levitt (Links Books, New York), pp. 12–13 (hereafter referred to as Brothers).
13. McKay, p. 137.
14. Five Days, p. 3.
15. NYT, September 6, 1971, p. 23.
16. McKay, p. 138; Brothers, p. 70.
17. McKay, p. 141.
18. NYT, October 4, 1971, p. 44.
19. The account of the beginnings of the Attica uprising on September 8, 1971 is derived primarily from McKay, but also from Five Days; NYT, particularly for October 4, 1971, p. 44; Brothers; and *Attica—*

My Story, by Russell G. Oswald (Doubleday & Co., New York) (hereafter referred to as Oswald). Where these accounts are in conflict, the author has followed the "official" version in McKay.

20. The completion of the account of how the rebellion at Attica began, on September 9, 1971, is taken from the sources cited in n. 19 supra; from an article in the *Boston Globe*, December 13, 1973, by Mike Barnicle; and from an interview taped by the author with Roger Champen, transcribed into a manuscript in the author's possession, and hereafter referred to as Champen.

Chapter Two

1. NYT, June 18, 1970, Editorial page, "In the Nation: Due Process for Prisoners."
2. NYT, August 24, 1971, Op-Ed page, "In the Nation: Death of a Brother"; NYT, September 9, 1971, Op-Ed page, "In the Nation: Surface and Core."
3. Robert T. Barnard is now editorial-page editor of the Louisville *Courier-Journal*.
4. Oswald, p. 76.
5. Brothers, p. 67.
6. In the several days following the Attica rebellion and the recapture of the prison, Herman Schwartz made a tape recording of his memories and impressions. Transcribed, these make a double-spaced manuscript of 52 pages, which, though not in literary form, is of rare interest and sensitivity. Professor Schwartz has kindly provided the author a copy. The "petty grievances" episode is recalled at p. 20. The unpublished memoir is hereafter referred to as Schwartz.
7. McKay, pp. 193–206.
8. Ibid., pp. 217–218.
9. Schwartz, pp. 15, 23.
10. Brothers, pp. 51–52. Of this encounter, Mancusi gave McKay (p. 215) a different account that makes the same point: "I had a conversation with about six individuals. Everybody was trying to talk at once. I told them to shut up and let one man tell the story, and this was like waving a red flag before a bull and they would have nothing to do with me from that time on. They informed me that they would only speak to the commissioner or the Governor. And left."
11. Oswald, p. 85; NYT, October 4, 1971, p. 44.
12. Oswald, pp. 85–88; McKay, pp. 220–221.
13. Oswald, p. 81.
14. Ibid., pp. 88–89.
15. Schwartz, p. 23.
16. McKay, pp. 181–182; NYT, September 21, 1971, p. 46.
17. Champen, p. 52.
18. Oswald, p. 90.
19. McKay, pp. 221–222.
20. Oswald, p. 92.

21. Champen, pp. 10–11.
22. Oswald, pp. 98–99.
23. McKay, p. 225.
24. Oswald, p. 94; McKay, pp. 225–226.
25. McKay, p. 226.
26. Interview with an unnamed Attica inmate by Robert Harsh, *Christianity and Crisis*, May 29, 1972, p. 129 (hereafter referred to as Harsh).

Chapter Three

1. Schwartz, pp. 15–16.
2. Champen, p. 46.
3. This account of the fate of the injunction and of the important Friday morning negotiating session is taken from McKay, pp. 226–232, from Oswald, pp. 100–108, and from Schwartz, pp. 30–31. These accounts agree substantially, except that Oswald leaves the impression that most of the inmates wanted to hold him hostage and that only Blyden's insistence caused them to let him go. The Rosenberg quote is from McKay, p. 230; McKay does not identify Rosenberg, but Oswald and Schwartz do. The remark about the hanging is quoted from Oswald, p. 107. The demand to take Oswald hostage is quoted from Schwartz, pp. 30–31, as is the Blyden quote, p. 31. Oswald, at p. 107, and Schwartz, at p. 31, agree substantially on the Clark quote, except that Oswald attributes it to Blyden.
4. McKay, p. 232. Here Oswald no doubt was referring to the hostages, but this and other remarks of his about the bloodshed that would be required to retake D-yard suggest that authorities never gave thought to means of reducing the rebel stronghold in D-yard *without* violence.
5. McKay, pp. 235–236.
6. Montanye later was named superintendent of Attica, succeeding Mancusi.
7. *A Bill of No Rights: Attica and the American Prison System*, by Herman Badillo and Milton Hayes (Outerbridge and Lazard, Inc., New York), p. 58 (hereafter referred to as Badillo).
8. Herbert Blyden sent the author a handwritten autobiography, from which these biographical notes and quotations are taken.
9. Champen, pp. 42–44; McKay, pp. 198–200, 201–202.
10. Champen, pp. 49–51.

Chapter Four

1. New York State Department of Correction, *Sing Sing Prison: Its History, Purpose, Makeup and Program* (1968).
2. *American Notes*, Charles Dickens.
3. *Adult Correctional Institutions in the United States*, by Austin McCormick.
4. *After Conviction: A Review of the American Correction System*, by

Ronald L. Goldfarb and Linda R. Singer (Simon and Schuster, New York, 1973), p. 39.
5. Schwartz, p. 27.
6. McKay, pp. 243–244.
7. "Attica Chronicle," by Julian Tepper and Tony Fitch, *Washington Post*, September 19, 1971, p. A18, col. 1. Tepper and Fitch wrote this account in the first person plural, but it is hereafter referred to as Tepper.
8. As the author described it, not unaffectionately, in NYT, September 14, 1971, p. 29, col. 1.
9. Schwartz, p. 29; Oswald, p. 99.

Chapter Five

1. This is an edited excerpt from the author's article in NYT, September 14, 1971, Op-Ed page.
2. Tepper, p. A18, col. 1.
3. Oswald, p. 113. The commissioner writes that Melville slipped this note to one of the observers to take outside.
4. Schwartz, p. 14.
5. Champen, p. 27.
6. *Medical World News*, October 1, 1971, p. 17, "What the Doctors Saw and Their Conflicting Reports from Inside Attica." Hereafter referred to as Doctors.
7. McKay, pp. 63–71.
8. On July 8, 1970, the state of New York renamed all its maximum security prisons "correctional facilities" and retitled all its guards "corrections officers" and all its wardens "superintendents." But no jobs, functions, duties, responsibilities, training, or attitudes were changed. McKay, pp. 18–19.
9. *Washington Post*, September 19, 1971, p. D1.
10. Harsh, pp. 128–129.
11. McKay, pp. 36–40; 49–50.
12. Ibid., pp. 43–44.
13. Op. cit., n. 9 supra.
14. NYT, January 24, 1970, p. 30.
15. Hearings before Subcommittee on National Penitentiaries of the Senate Committee on the Judiciary, 88th Congress, 2d Session (1964), pp. 6, 7, 26.
16. NYT, August 6, 1973, p. 14, article by Martin Waldron.
17. *Prison*, interviews by Leonard V. Berry, edited by Jamie Shalleck (Subsistence Press, New York, 1972), p. 218. All other quotations attributed to Berry's interviews also are from this book. Page citations, in order, are 245, 249, 250, 238, 132.
18. McKay, p. 288.
19. "Sex in Prison," by Gene Kassebaum, Ph.D., *Psychology Today*, January, 1972, p. 39.
20. NYT, April 25, 1971, p. 40.

21. Op. cit., n. 9 supra.
22. McKay, pp. 26, 78–79. *My Shadow Ran Fast*, by Bill Sands (Prentice Hall, Englewood Cliffs, N.J., 1964), p. 54.
23. McKay, p. 27.
24. Ibid., p. 26.
25. NYT, September 26, 1971, p. 1, cont. p. 74, article by Wallace Turner.
26. Ibid.
27. Harsh, p. 130.
28. *Sostre* v. *Rockefeller*, 309 F. Supp. 611 (S.D.N.Y. 1969).
29. McKay, pp. 47–49; 51–52.
30. Ibid., pp. 55–62.
31. Roger Brusewitz, a University of Wisconsin journalism student, in a conversation with the author, July 28, 1974.
32. Schwartz, pp. 15–16.
33. New York prison industry revenues were pooled and used to pay supervisors and inmates and to buy raw materials and new equipment. Inmate earnings averaged 30 to 50 cents per day in 1971. Prison industry profits were about $150,000 that year. McKay, pp. 38–39.
34. NYT, September 15, 1971, p. 33.
35. Champen, pp. 50–51.
36. NYT, September 12, 1971, p. 72, col. 6, article by Fred Ferretti, cont. from p. 1.
37. NYT, December 1, 1966, Editorial page, "In the Nation: Waiting for Lurleen."

Chapter Six

1. Badillo was at least partially right. According to Roger Champen, the inmates were changing their security guard, both to relieve those who had been on duty and to impress the observers. They turned out the lights to prevent the state troopers from taking advantage of the several minutes required to change the guard. The observers were asked to stand behind the table as a precaution against any possible attack from any of the inmates massed in D-yard. Champen, pp. 36–38.
2. The screaming man was angry, not crazed. He had just made his way out of detention that had been imposed on him by some other inmates, during which he had been given nothing to eat. He was shouting threats at inmate leaders for letting this happen—not at the observers. At the time, the distinction was hard for them to make. Champen, p. 38.
3. McKay, pp. 16, 24.
4. "Does Punishment Deter Crime?" by Gordon Tullock, *The Public Interest*, Summer 1974, p. 103.
5. Statistics provided by the National Council on Crime and Delinquency.
6. The Hartford *Courant*, p. 1, article by Stan Simon and William Cockerham, February 24, 1974. Available from the *Courant* in a reprint pamphlet.
7. Op. cit., n. 5 supra. The Wainwright quotation was provided by the same source.

8. For example, "What Works–Questions and Answers About Prison Reform," by Robert Martinson, *The Public Interest*, Spring 1974, p. 25.
9. Statistics provided by Robert E. Keldgord, director of a study of the California prison system.
10. *Correction in the United States*, a survey by the National Council on Crime and Delinquency, 1966, pp. 230, 236.
11. N. 7 supra.
12. McKay, pp. 42–43.
13. Wisconsin Council on Criminal Justice, Final Report to the Governor of the Citizens' Study Committee on Offender Rehabilitation, 1972.
14. Schwartz, p. 16.
15. McKay, p. 247.
16. Rothenberg apparently sensed this would be the case. He, Jackson, and Rivers went back to New York City after this dawn session and did not return—a considerable loss to the observers.

Chapter Seven

1. NYT, September 11, 1971, p. 31, story by Francis X. Clines.
2. For many of these ideas about violence the author is indebted to "Parkman's Indians and American Violence," by Robert Shulman, University of Minnesota Dept. of English, an article in *The Massachusetts Review*, Spring 1971. See also the author's "Gooks, Slopes, and Vermin" in NYT, May 4, 1973, Op-Ed page.
3. This text appears in McKay, pp. 248–249. Louis James' handwritten draft is in the author's possession.

Chapter Eight

1. Champen, pp. 47–48.
2. Schwartz, p. 32.
3. Ibid., p. 4.
4. Steel was right. Rockefeller almost immediately assigned the Attica prosecution to Deputy Attorney General Robert Fisher of the State of New York. Louis James never participated in it.
5. Writing in another age, Herman Melville thought that despite its association with the "sweet, and honorable, and sublime," the "elusive quality" of whiteness was actually to "heighten . . . terror to the furthest bounds." He thought it was "the marble pallor" that evoked the worst fears of "inhuman solitudes"; he saw "all the prospect around him" wrapped in a "monumental white shroud." White or black, for the author as for Melville, "somewhere those things must exist. Though in many of its aspects this visible world seems formed in love, the invisible spheres were formed in fright." See the chapter on "The Whiteness of the Whale" in *Moby Dick*.
6. Oswald, pp. 117–118.
7. McKay, pp. 251, 257.
8. Oswald, pp. 118, 122.

9. Tepper, p. A18, col. 2.
10. Oswald, p. 117.

Chapter Nine

1. McKay, p. 258.
2. Schwartz, p. 1.
3. Ibid., p. 6.
4. Oswald, at p. 233, writes that he "was trying almost everything to win back the hostages safe and well."
5. Schwartz, p. 33.
6. Robert Douglass imposed on Dunne, Garcia, and Badillo to make a public statement that Seale was admitted only at the request of the observer committee. McKay, p. 259.
7. Oswald, p. 233.
8. McKay, p. 309.
9. Schwartz, p. 9.
10. In the Democratic primary of 1950, Dr. Graham, serving by appointment, was defeated by Willis Smith in a runoff that still influences North Carolina politics.
11. Oswald, p. 224.

Chapter Ten

1. Brothers, p. 78; Champen, p. 3.
2. Brothers, p. 77.
3. *The New York Times Magazine*, October 31, 1971, at p. 82, in an article by Warren H. Hansen entitled "Attica: The Hostages' Story." It begins at p. 18 and is hereafter referred to as Hansen.
4. McKay, pp. 281–286. Schwartz and Hess had been talking to a reporter on Friday afternoon and were accused of treason. Privitiera, who may have been a mental case, had threatened the hostages and assaulted two other D-yard inmates. The three bodies were not discovered until after D-yard had been retaken, and none of the observers had any knowledge that the murders had taken place.
5. Champen, pp. 48–49, 44–45.
6. Ibid., pp. 21–22.
7. Ibid., pp. 1–2.
8. Brothers, p. 79.
9. Champen, p. 1.
10. Badillo, p. 70.
11. Champen, p. 1.
12. Badillo, p. 71.
13. Oswald, pp. 224–225.
14. Ibid., p. 225.
15. Badillo, p. 71.
16. Schwartz, p. 6.
17. Champen, pp. 4–6.

18. Oswald, p. 226.
19. McKay, pp. 262–263. Various sources, including an inmate who took shorthand, contributed to this account.
20. Champen, p. 5.
21. McKay, p. 263.
22. Oswald, p. 226.
23. Ibid.
24. McKay, p. 263.
25. Oswald, p. 226.
26. McKay, pp. 263–264, 266.
27. Oswald, p. 107.
28. Rockefeller to McKay, p. 15.
29. Oswald, p. 118.
30. McKay, p. 265.
31. Hansen, p. 85.
32. McKay, p. 266.
33. Champen's account of how the inmate leadership committee made decisions is as follows: "Before we made a decision we talked about it among ourselves. Like say for instance, I would talk to Herb and Herb would talk to me and we would talk to Sam [Melville] and we would talk to Richie [Clark] and we would come to a general consensus among ourselves as to what we were talking about and how could we best approach it. Then, for the most part, I would raise it with the general population. And then we had a Latin brother who would then go and speak to the Latin brothers and interpret it right. And then we . . . would say, 'Well, what do you feel about it? Yes or no?' . . . There were times when something came up that had to be handled abruptly—then we took it upon ourselves. . . . But for the most part, if there was time, we would put things to a voice vote." Champen, pp. 39–40.
34. McKay, p. 264.
35. Brothers, pp. 80–81.
36. Captain Frank "Pappy" Wald, one of the hostages, to McKay, p. 283.

Chapter Eleven

1. Kunstler had been called that morning by Afeni Shakur, one of the 21, and told that North Vietnam, North Korea, Algeria, and Congo Brazzaville were willing to accept the inmates and send a plane to Kennedy Airport to pick them up. NYT, September 23, 1971, Op-Ed page, an article by Afeni Shakur.
2. Oswald, p. 228.
3. Badillo, p. 76.
4. McKay, pp. 268–269.
5. Oswald, p. 228.
6. Seale made one more effort, although it is not clear what he hoped to accomplish. He returned to California, picked up Charles Garry, the Black Panthers' attorney, then left at about midnight, PST, for

Buffalo. Arriving at approximately 8:30 A.M., he heard on the way from Buffalo to Attica that the attack on D-yard was talking place. He never completed the journey.

Chapter Twelve

1. Badillo, p. 76.
2. Oswald, pp. 231–232.
3. McKay, p. 273.
4. Ibid., p. 312.
5. Ibid., p. 271.
6. Oswald, pp. 232–233.
7. Badillo, p. 82.
8. McKay, p. 275.
9. Rockefeller to McKay, p. 28.
10. Oswald, p. 234.
11. Rockefeller to McKay, pp. 7–8.
12. Ibid., pp. 38, 40, 81–82.
13. Ibid., pp. 49, 52, 56.
14. Ibid., pp. 80–81.

Chapter Thirteen

1. McKay, p. 277.
2. Ibid., p. 279.
3. Tepper, p. A18, col. 4.
4. Oswald, p. 238.
5. McKay, p. 280.
6. Ibid., pp. 287–288.
7. In fact, 1281 inmates and 40 hostages were originally in D-yard, and these numbers did not vary much from September 9 to September 13. McKay, p. 109.
8. Champen told the author that Barkley felt that Blyden held the microphone too much and talked too often about the wrong issues.
9. McKay, p. 293.
10. Ibid.
11. Yet, both Blyden and Clark were Black Muslims, who professed to believe, as their faith taught, that the white man is the Devil.
12. Most of the hostages later told McKay that these spokesmen had accurately portrayed the feelings of the hostages as a group. McKay, p. 293.
13. Eve's remarks here are from the author's notes but partially also from McKay, p. 289, and Oswald, pp. 240–241. Both had access to tapes made in D-yard on September 12.
14. The controversial Kunstler quotation is taken for accuracy from McKay, p. 290. The identification of Blyden is from the author's recollection.
15. Oswald, p. 242. The author has the quotation similarly in his notes

except that they have the sentence ending "come in here and try to make you do something you didn't want to do."

16. McKay, pp. 290–291.
17. *Newsweek*, September 27, 1971, p. 37, col. 3.
18. Reflecting on that Sunday afternoon months later, the author concluded, "Things were said, I think, throughout that period that perhaps might better have been unsaid had wise men had long, quiet hours in which to deliberate what to do. Not every moment of a circumstance like that can be carried out in the cool pursuit of some rational strategy. I think we all did what we thought was best at the given time. I am not aware of any speech that was made that in my judgment ever gave the prisoners any reason whatever to think they were going to win their struggle. I know of no speech that was made at any time that ever gave them any cause to believe that if they would just hang on a little bit longer, they were going to get amnesty and go home free. I know certainly of no speech of any kind that made the suggestion that they were indeed likely to be flown off to any third-world country." McKay, p. 291.
19. McKay, p. 298.

Chapter Fourteen

1. Harsh, pp. 134–135; Champen, pp. 7, 15.
2. Champen, pp. 7–8.
3. Ibid., p. 11.
4. Ibid., pp. 11–12.
5. Harsh, pp. 134–135.
6. Champen, p. 8.
7. McKay, p. 297.
8. Champen, p. 7.
9. McKay, p. 314.
10. Ibid., pp. 314–315.
11. Oswald, p. 246; McKay, p. 314.
12. McKay, p. 314.
13. Oswald, pp. 246–247.
14. Ibid., p. 243.
15. NYT, September 13, 1971, p. 71, col. 4, story by Fred Ferretti.
16. A television documentary film, "Conflict of Interest," produced by WNET-TV (Channel 13) in New York and broadcast January 31, 1974, included a film clip of the author making these remarks.
17. Badillo, quoting Dick Edwards, at p. 88.
18. Op. cit., n. 16 supra.
19. Five Days, p. 22.
20. Ibid.
21. Op. cit., n. 15 supra.
22. Oswald prints the full text of the governor's statement at p. 237.
23. McKay, p. 316.
24. Oswald, p. 248.

25. McKay, p. 317.
26. Tepper, p. A18, col. 6.
27. McKay, p. 322.
28. Op. cit., n. 26 supra.
29. Oswald, pp. 250–251.
30. McKay, pp. 322–323.
31. Ibid., p. 329.
32. Oswald, p. 252; McKay, p. 349.
33. Op. cit., n. 26 supra.
34. Oswald, p. 250.

Chapter Fifteen

1. Tepper, p. A18, cols. 6–7.
2. Brothers, p. 83.
3. Oswald, p. 254.
4. Ibid., pp. 254–255.
5. Ibid., p. 256.
6. Ingram to the observer group, September 13, 1971.
7. Oswald, pp. 260–262; McKay, p. 398. Oswald says at p. 287 that Mancusi signed written orders for corrections officers to stay out of the battle.
8. Rodriguez and Gaiter to the observer group, September 13, 1971.
9. Oswald, pp. 256–257.
10. Harsh, p. 135.
11. Champen, p. 40; McKay, p. 367. Yet, a poll taken months later by McKay disclosed that over 50 percent of those in D-yard had favored accepting the 28 points rather than holding out for amnesty. Much of this sentiment no doubt was hindsight.
12. Harsh, p. 135.
13. Oswald, pp. 257–258.
14. McKay, pp. 350–351, 353–356, 370.
15. Ibid., p. 368.
16. Ibid., pp. 351, 360, 362.
17. Wicker, Eve, Ingram, Steel, Badillo, Dunne, Kenyatta, Paris, Rodriguez, Gaiter, Mathew, Tepper, Fitch, Chandler, Robert Garcia, Scott, and Ortiz.
18. Oswald, pp. 267–268.
19. Champen, pp. 28–29.
20. Oswald, p. 268; McKay, pp. 369–370.
21. McKay, pp. 351, 371–372.
22. McKay, p. 369; Oswald, pp. 266–267.
23. Oswald, p. 267.
24. McKay, p. 372. Oswald, at p. 287, says O'Hara saw the corrections officers and asked them to pull their guns back from the windows.
25. Harsh, p. 135.
26. Oswald, p. 273.
27. McKay, pp. 373, 377–378; Champen, p. 41; Harsh, p. 135.

28. Oswald, p. 275; McKay, pp. 377–378, 380–381 and Appendices E and F.
29. McKay, p. 73, pp. 381–388; Oswald, p. 278; Champen, p. 30.
30. McKay, pp. 399–400.
31. Ibid., pp. 390–391, 396.
32. Ibid., pp. 347–348.
33. Ibid., pp. 391–392, 396–397; Oswald, p. 280.
34. McKay, pp. 392–394.
35. Oswald, p. 277; McKay, pp. 388–389.
36. McKay, pp. 394–395. The quotations are from Harsh, p. 135.
37. McKay, p. 397. Oswald, at p. 279, repeats the baseless story that Mel-
    ville was killed while running toward a 50-gallon tank of inflammable
    liquid with four Molotov cocktails. Melville, Elliot Barkley, and
    Tommy Hicks all became the subjects of an inmate belief that they
    had been executed *after* D-yard was subdued; but McKay established
    to the author's satisfaction that their deaths occurred as recounted here.
38. Oswald, p. 288; McKay, pp. 373–374.
39. Harsh, p. 136; McKay, p. 428.
40. McKay, p. 429.
41. Ibid., pp. 430, 433.
42. Ibid., p. 432.
43. Ibid., pp. 427–428.
44. Ibid., p. 430.
45. This account of the A-passageway gauntlet is taken from McKay,
    pp. 433–435.
46. Oswald, pp. 289–290.
47. McKay, pp. 435–437.
48. Ibid., p. 430.
49. Champen, p. 26.
50. McKay, p. 431. McKay does not identify Smith, but the author
    established identification to his own satisfaction.
51. Ibid., p. 438.
52. Ibid., pp. 437–440.
53. Champen, pp. 15–16.
54. McKay, p. 407.
55. Doctors, p. 17.
56. McKay, pp. 403–404, 406–408, 422, 424; Doctors, p. 16.
57. McKay, pp. 409–410, 423.
58. Ibid., pp. 406, 408–409.
59. Ibid., pp. 411–413.
60. Ibid., p. 413.
61. Ibid., pp. 414–416.
62. Of those named, none was killed.
63. Doctors, p. 17. Blood and plasma did arrive in the equipment from
    Meyer Memorial Hospital.
64. McKay, p. 416.
65. Doctors, p. 17.
66. McKay, pp. 415–418.

67. Ibid., p. 420.
68. WNBC-TV, New York, provided the author with a tape recording of the interview with Gabe Pressman.

Afterwards
1. NYT, September 15, 1971, p. 1, story by Joseph Lelyveld.
2. NYT, September 14, 1971, p. 29, story by Michael Kaufman; p. 1, cont. p. 28, story by Fred Ferretti.
3. NYT, September 15, 1971, p. 32, story by Lawrence Van Gelder; p. 1, cont. p. 32, story by Fred Ferretti.
4. Ibid., p. 1, cont. p. 32, story by Fred Ferretti.
5. NYT, September 16, 1971, p. 1, cont. p. 48, story by Fred Ferretti.
6. N. 4 supra.
7. N. 5 supra.
8. NYT, Sept. 20, 1971, p. 1, cont. p. 29, story by David Shipler. Two other inmates died later.
9. NYT, September 14, 1971, p. 1, cont. p. 30, story by William Farrell.
10. NYT, October 4, 1971, p. 1, cont. pp. 44–45, story by a team of reporters.
11. Rockefeller to McKay, p. 23.
12. Ibid., p. 54.
13. Ibid., pp. 44–48.
14. Ibid., pp. 49–50.
15. Ibid., p. 52.
16. Ibid., pp. 70–72.
17. NYT, September 14, 1971, p. 1, cont. p. 30, story by William Farrell.
18. NYT, September 24, 1971, p. 1, cont. p. 16, story by William Farrell.
19. Rockefeller to McKay, pp. 78–79.
20. McKay, pp. 466–469.
21. NYT, June 12, 1973, p. 26, story by Fred Ferretti.
22. NYT, March 25, 1973, p. 47, story by James Markham; May 28, 1973, p. 32, legislative roundup by Alfonso Narvaez.
23. NYT, June 10, 1974, p. 61, story by Fred Ferretti.
24. Ibid.
25. Rockefeller to the Senate Rules Committee, transcript pps. 199–200, September 24, 1974.

Index

CPSIA information can be obtained
at www.ICGtesting.com
Printed in the USA
JSHW051300160122
22035JS00002B/3